*Lincoln's Rail-Splitter*

Lincoln's Rail-Splitter

*Plummer*

2001 — Urbana

# oln's Rail-Splitter:
## Richard J. Oglesby

ARK A. PLUMMER

*University of Illinois Press*

URBANA AND CHICAGO

Library of Congress Cataloging-in-Publication Data
Plummer, Mark A., 1929–
Lincoln's rail-splitter : Governor Richard J. Oglesby / Mark A. Plummer.
p.   cm.
Includes bibliographical references and index.
ISBN 0-252-02649-7 (alk. paper)
1. Oglesby, Richard J. (Richard James), 1824–1899.
2. Governors—Illinois—Biography.
3. Lincoln, Abraham, 1809–1865—Friends and associates.
4. Illinois—Politics and government—1865–1950.
I. Title.
F546.O44P58      2001
977.3'03'092—dc21      00-011864

For Betty,
Chelsea, and Joshua

# Contents

# Preface

I WAS SURVEYING the eight-foot-tall bronze statue of Gov. Richard James Oglesby that stands at the highest point of spacious Lincoln Park in Chicago when a passerby queried, "Who is that anyway?" The inscription had long since been vandalized, but Leonard Crunelle's sculpture still stands resolute. I quickly recited what the missing inscription would have told the questioner: Oglesby was the man who introduced the rail-splitter slogan into Abraham Lincoln's successful presidential campaign of 1860, a major general who had been critically wounded in the Civil War, and three-time governor of Illinois. But there was much more to tell.

Richard James Oglesby, born July 25, 1824, was among a coterie of Illinois politicians who promoted Abraham Lincoln's political career. He worked for Lincoln's election to the U.S. Senate in 1854–55 and 1858 and to the presidency in 1860 and 1864. Oglesby's major contribution was as the originator of the rail-splitter image in 1860. The rail-splitter symbol was apparently initiated without Lincoln's participation. He probably preferred to be known for his talents rather than as a "common man," but he soon embraced the symbolism that helped propel him into the presidency.

By the accidents of time and geography, Lincoln and Oglesby had experienced similar environments. Both were born in Kentucky and had lost their mothers (Oglesby lost both parents at age eight). Both spent some of their youth in Indiana before migrating to frontier Illinois. They lived most of their lives in central Illinois. Each apprenticed as lawyers in Springfield. Both were Henry Clay Whigs who were superior speakers. Each stood for election to the Illinois legislature, to the Congress, and to the U.S. Senate.

Oglesby was a participant in the seminal events in the critical "middle period" of American history. He played a role in the Mexican War, the California gold rush, the rise of the Republican Party, the election of Lincoln, the Civil War, and the Reconstruction Era, and he experienced the tensions of the Gilded Age.

He seemed to have a knack for being where the action was. He first experienced war in the battles of Cerro Gordo and Vera Cruz during the Mexican War. He made a small fortune in the gold rush of 1849. He took the grand tour of Europe and the Holy Land in 1856–57 but returned to Illinois in time to run unsuccessfully for Congress in a campaign that featured the Lincoln-Douglas debates of 1858. In 1860 he was elected to the Illinois senate as Lincoln was being elected president. When the Civil War came, Oglesby resigned his seat to lead a regiment into the Union army. He was prominent in the victory at Fort Donelson before being critically wounded at Corinth, Mississippi. Promoted to major general, he was assigned to court-martial duty in Washington, D.C., until he resigned his commission to successfully run for governor of Illinois in 1864. The new governor returned to Washington on the fateful Friday, April 14, 1865, and was at Lincoln's deathbed before accompanying the funeral train home to Springfield. Oglesby served as the only president of the association that built the Lincoln tomb, and he delivered the major oration when it was dedicated.

In the postwar years, Oglesby's popularity, buttressed by his association with the martyred Lincoln and his extraordinary stump-speaking skills, rescued the Illinois Republican Party in time of political crisis. The party named him as candidate for governor during the Liberal Republican challenge of 1872. After serving as governor for a few days, he resigned to accepted a seat in the U.S. Senate, where he served a single term. In 1884 he was elected as governor of Illinois a third time. Anticipating a quiet tenure, he was buffeted by massive labor unrest and was required to act upon the appeals for pardon that were made on behalf of the "Haymarket Anarchists." He retired to his home, "Oglehurst," in Elkhart, Illinois, where he died in 1899. In 1919 the statue was unveiled in Lincoln Park.

# Acknowledgments

As a small child, I sat on the floor by Grandfather Mark Plummer's rocking chair and listened to his recollection of Lincoln's "rail-splitter" election of 1860. Although he would have been only six years old at the time, my ninety-plus-year-old grandfather vividly recalled seeing a Lincoln campaign wagon on which men were splitting rails. When I arrived in the "Land of Lincoln," I was surprised that no one had written a biography of the man who introduced the rail-splitter slogan. Perhaps potential biographers had been discouraged by the assumption that the Oglesby house fire in 1891 had destroyed his papers. Actually, only the trophies were destroyed and the papers were saved. The materials, enough to fill a large steamer trunk, were retrieved by James Hickey for the Illinois State Historical Library. There, Paul D. Spence helped organize and catalog the collection.

Among persons who were especially helpful through the years at the Illinois State Historical Library in Springfield were Spence, Hickey, Roger Bridges, Janice Petterchak, Cheryl Schnirring, and Mark Johnson. The Lincoln Legal Papers Project, housed above the library in the Old State Capitol, was represented by Cullom Davis, William Beard, and others. From the Illinois State Archives, Wayne Temple, Mark W. Sorensen, Karl Moore, and Roy Turnbaugh offered expertise in locating the governor's official papers. At the Oglesby Mansion Foundation in Decatur, Martha Montgomery, Amelia Mulrooney, and Linley Hurtt were helpful, as were their latter-day successors Bruce Leonard, Joanne Forrest, and Roy Schilling. Among the Oglesby descendants, Carolyn Ogen shared some of her documents with me. At the Illinois State University library, bibliographer Garold L. Cole energetically facilitated my research, as did his successor, Vanette Schwartz.

Other sources came from the Library of Congress, the National Archives, the Huntington Library, and the Bancroft Library at the University of California, Berkeley. The Chicago Historical Society and the Decatur Public Library offered useful documents.

Colleagues at Illinois State University who read the manuscript and offered constructive suggestions included L. Moody Simms, Mark Wyman, and William Linneman. Other generous scholars who read the manuscript included John Hoffmann at the University of Illinois at Urbana-Champaign, Rodney Davis at Knox College, and John Y. Simon at Southern Illinois University–Carbondale. Each saved me from making embarrassing mistakes, but those that remain are clearly mine. I owe a debt of gratitude to my department, dean, and the graduate school for offering various research grants. The secretarial staff of the Department of History at Illinois State University, including Julie Ruby, Sharon Foiles, Sharon Garee, and Cherie Valentine, were extremely helpful, as were various student secretaries and student assistants. Richard L. Wentworth and Mary Giles of the University of Illinois Press graciously facilitated and improved my rough-hewn text.

Two master's theses have explored Oglesby's life through his first term as governor. Henry Lee Payne ("Richard J. Oglesby: Politician and Soldier to 1865," University of Illinois, 1961), graciously offered his helpful research notes, which included extensive use of printed materials, especially contemporary newspapers. Dean M. Folkes ("Governor Richard J. Oglesby: First Term," Illinois State University, 1966) was probably the first graduate student to use the Oglesby Papers for a master's thesis. Other Illinois State University graduate students who also contributed to my education about Oglesby and his time through their masters' theses include: Warren H. Johnson, *"Illinois State Register:* Influences and Attitudes, 1860–1863" (1966); Donald Cavallini, "The Copperheads in the Old Northwest" (1967); Paul Gleason, "John Dean Gillett: Elkhart Hill's 'Cattle King of America,'" (1970); Marilyn Ames, "John Hanks: Lincoln's Rail Splitter Cousin" (1974); James Goben, "William Ward Orme of Bloomington, Illinois" (1975); Scott W. Rager, "General John McNulta: Illinois Soldier and Statesman" (1981); Michael A. Mattingly, "Lincoln's Confidant: Leonard Swett" (1984); Randy L. Nichols, "Role of Illinois Adjutant General during the American Civil War" (1989); Camilla A. Quinn, "Lincoln's Hometown: Springfield, Illinois in the Civil War" (1990); and Michael Starasta, "The Democratic Party in Illinois, 1862–1864" (1993).

# Abbreviations

| | |
|---|---|
| Bancroft | "Stenographic Report of Interview with Governor R. J. Oglesby Held July 17, 1890." Interview by Washington Davis. Bancroft Library, University of California, Berkeley. |
| Banton | O. T. Banton, ed., *History of Macon County 1976* (Decatur: Macon County Historical Society, 1976). |
| *Browning Diary* | Theodore Calvin Pease and James G. Randall, eds. *The Diary of Orville Hickman Browning,* 2 vols. (Springfield: Trustees of the Illinois State Historical Library, 1925–33). |
| Church | Charles A. Church, *History of the Republican Party in Illinois, 1854–1912* (Rockford: Wilson Brothers, 1912). |
| *Collected Works* | Roy P. Basler, ed., Marion Dolores Pratt and Lloyd A. Dunlap, assistant eds., *The Collected Works of Abraham Lincoln,* 8 vols. plus index (New Brunswick: Rutgers University Press, 1953–55). |
| *Lincoln Day by Day* | Earl Schenck Miers, ed. *Lincoln Day by Day: A Chronology, 1809–1865,* 3 vols. (Washington: Lincoln Sesquicentennial Commission, 1960). |
| *Grant Papers* | John Y. Simon, ed., *The Papers of Ulysses S. Grant* (Carbondale: Southern Illinois University Press, 1967–  ). |
| *IHJ* | *Illinois Historical Journal.* |
| ISA | Illinois State Archives, Springfield. |
| ISHL | Illinois State Historical Library, Springfield. |
| *Journal* | *Illinois State Journal* (Springfield). |
| *JISHS* | *Journal of the Illinois State Historical Society* |
| LC | Library of Congress. |

| | |
|---|---|
| Lusk | D. W. Lusk, *Eighty Years of Illinois Politics and Politicians* (Springfield: H. W. Rokker, 1889). |
| Moses | John Moses, *Illinois Historical and Statistical, Comprising the Essential Facts of Its Planting and Growth as a Province, Territory, and State,* 2 vols. (Chicago: Fergus Printing, 1892). |
| *Official Records* | *The War of the Rebellion: A Compilation of the Official Records of the Union and Confederate Armies, Published under the Direction of the Secretary of War,* 70 vols. in 128 (Washington: Government Printing Office, 1880–1901). |
| Oglesby MSS | Oglesby Family Collection, Illinois State Historical Library, Springfield. |
| *Register* | *Illinois State Register,* Springfield. |
| Richmond | Mabel E. Richmond, comp., *Centennial History of Decatur and Macon County* (Decatur: The Decatur Review, 1930). |
| RJO | Richard J. Oglesby. |
| Wilkie | Franc B. Wilkie, *A Sketch of Richard J. Oglesby* (Chicago: Tribune Company, 1884). |

*Lincoln's Rail-Splitter*

# 1. An Orphan Boy

EARLY IN 1884, a self-styled "pilgrim" stepped off the Chicago train in Lincoln, Illinois, during a snow storm. His mission was to interview former governor Richard J. Oglesby and produce a campaign biography that would help Oglesby lead the Illinois Republican ticket to another victory. Oglesby had been elected governor in 1864 and again in 1872. Perhaps the popular "Uncle Dick" could be elected governor yet another time in a last hurrah for the Civil War veterans who had dominated the political arena for two decades. The would-be biographer was Franc B. Wilkie, who had gained fame as a Civil War correspondent. Wilkie had been sent by a *Chicago Tribune* editor. Twenty-four years earlier, a *Tribune* editor had sent another reporter to Springfield to write a campaign biography for Abraham Lincoln. After a long life whose varied parts often coincided with that of the assassinated president, Richard Oglesby's connection was direct yet again—he was living in a city named for Lincoln.[1]

Wilkie found that the sixty-year-old Oglesby was five feet, ten inches tall but fifty pounds lighter than the two-hundred-twenty-pound general he had known during the Civil War. "The face is cleanly shaven, the complexion fresh, the expression on the whole virile—a youthful face beneath a crown of snowy hair" Wilkie noted. "Geniality and thorough good nature are predominant traits."[2]

Richard James Oglesby had been born on St. James Day, July 25, 1824, in Oldham County, Kentucky, near Louisville. He was named for his grandfathers, Richard Oglesby and James Watson of Virginia. The Oglesbys were of Scotch descent and the Watsons of English descent. Richard J. Oglesby's father, Jacob, had been born in Virginia on September 27, 1791. Governor Oglesby believed that his paternal uncles were named Washington, Jesse, Richard, and Willis. His father's sisters were Suzanne, Rachel, and a third whose name had escaped his memory. All sisters married persons named Head: James, Zachary, and John, respectively. The oral tradition was that grandfather Richard had migrated to Kentucky and given each son a slave. On April 1, 1815, Jacob married Isabella Watson (born November 1, 1792, in Virginia) in Oldham County, Kentucky. Jacob was a schoolteacher, distiller, "common merchant and hotel keeper," and cooper, a skill he learned from his slave. Court records indicate that Jacob was appointed deputy sheriff by his brother, Sheriff Richard Oglesby, in March 1826. He became a member of the Kentucky legislature in 1829 and a colonel in the militia.[3]

The future governor of Illinois was the fifth of eight children born to Jacob and Isabella Oglesby. He had three sisters, an older brother, and a brother and two sisters younger. The family was tragically dismembered by the cholera epidemic in the summer of 1833. Within weeks, Oglesby, then eight, lost his mother, who died on June 26, 1833; his father on June 30; a younger sister, Mary, on July 6; and the older brother, Jefferson Woodford, on July 12. There was nothing to do but to sell Jacob's modest estate and divide the remaining children among relatives. The tragedy also extended to the family's only slave, who became a part of the estate.[4]

Wilkie the interviewer inquired how it was "that you, a Kentuckian, became such a confirmed abolitionist." "Well, for many reasons, but one of the principal ones was a negro man called Uncle Tim [Tilman]," Oglesby confided. According to Oglesby's story, told repeatedly in his later years, Uncle Tim was to be sold to settle the modest estate after the death of his parents. Oglesby attended the sale and was grieved "deeply and intensely" as "the tears ran out of his eyes, poor fellow, as he stood there and asked my uncle to buy him." But his uncle could not buy him, and young Richard was "very indignant" and told Uncle Tim that he would go to work and buy him and set him free. The black man picked him up in his arms and said, "You are a poor orphan and won't never be rich enough to buy Uncle Tim." Tilman sold for about $400 to Katharine Rice Bradshaw. As he grew up, Oglesby saw Tilman occasionally and renewed his promise whenever Uncle Tim complained of his treatment at the hands of Mrs. Bradshaw. Finally, in 1851, Oglesby returned from the California gold rush with some money. He learned from his brother-in-law, Col. James F. Wilson of Kentucky, that Tilman was being sold at an estate sale. Oglesby authorized Wilson to purchase him, and he did so, although unfriendly Kentuckians bid up the price to $267, considerably more than the going market price for a sixty-five-year-old slave. Wilson had Tilman to do light work and later, when Oglesby visited Kentucky, he freed

"Uncle Tim." As Oglesby remembered it, the graying Tilman greeted him by exclaiming, "My God! My God! Has the little orphan boy lived to buy and set me free!?" He then "turned his face toward the sky" and shouted, "Hallelujah! Hallelujah! I'se Free."[5]

Uncle Willis Oglesby accepted the orphan Richard into his household in Brownsboro, Kentucky. There, Richard attended school for about nine months and learned to read and write. In 1836 Willis decided to move to Decatur, Illinois, following a migration pattern similar to that of the Lincolns. Uncle Willis brought young Richard, his older sisters Amanda and Ophelia, and a younger sister, Sarah Eleanor, who died in Decatur soon after their arrival. They lived in a log cabin and tried to survive by farming as the Lincolns had done six years earlier on a site southwest of Decatur. The Oglesbys were apparently attracted to Decatur because Uncle Richard Oglesby had already settled there with his wife Judy. Aunt Judy Oglesby and his older sisters provided the Decatur family connection to which young Richard returned repeatedly during his teenaged years. Oglesby later referred to Aunt Judy's Christian Church (the Disciples of Christ) as "the church of my youth," although he, like Lincoln, apparently was never a formal member of any church.[6]

Uncle Willis and young Richard returned to Oldham County in 1837, and Richard was apprenticed to a carpenter and then farmed for a few months before returning to Decatur. Uncle Willis next took Richard to Terre Haute, Indiana, but decided to move again. The future governor remembered nearly drowning when he went swimming without permission during the journey from Terre Haute. Willis Oglesby gave Richard "his benediction and a dollar" and started him on the hundred-mile walk back to Decatur. At one point on the road, Richard was attracted to a traveling troupe of actors, the Jeffersons. Mr. Jefferson, who traveled with his three daughters, contemplated asking the willing Richard to join them but declined after discussing the matter with an acquaintance of Willis Oglesby. Richard continued his journey back to Decatur. Once there, the sixteen-year-old worked in a hotel and looked for excitement.[7]

Excitement came during the log-cabin campaign of William Henry Harrison in 1840. With Wilkie's prompting, Oglesby remembered joining a group that journeyed to Springfield for a Young Men's Whig convention. There he first heard Lincoln speak. He "was fascinated with the simplicity of his character, his droll anecdotes, and fund of sayings" and by "the charming manner in which he discussed politics on the stump." Lincoln was active in the 1840 campaign as a successful candidate for reelection to the Illinois House and as an unsuccessful candidate as a Harrison presidential elector. Although little survives concerning Lincoln's speech at the Whig rally, numerous memoirs attest to his participation. Oglesby was correct in remembering the great Whig rally of June 2–4, 1840. Both his attraction to Lincoln and the log-cabin campaign may have contributed to Oglesby's ingenuous presentation of Lincoln as the "rail-splitter" at the Illinois State Republican Convention of 1860 in Decatur.[8]

In 1840 Oglesby returned to Kentucky to learn a trade and live with his eldest sister. He learned carpentry and returned to Decatur in 1842. Jobs were scarce in the winter, so he continued his elementary education by attending the school of Lemuel Allen for three months. But Oglesby admitted that, as a youth, he never read a book and was "fond of fishing, hunting, birding and horse racing. I was a wild, healthy, untrained, harum-scarum young man." Upon entering the U.S. Senate in 1873, Oglesby recalled to Ben: Perley Poore, that he had "received less than a common school education." He did, however, learn to play the fiddle well enough to play at informal dances. Oglesby and Allen later jointly rented forty acres of land and tried their hand at growing oats, corn, and hemp. They used the hemp to bind a flatboat that they launched on the Sangamon River at Decatur, as Lincoln had done a dozen years earlier. When they sold the boat they netted $6.50.[9]

At age eighteen, Oglesby made his first Fourth of July speech. Lincoln had made his first political speech at age twenty-one, also in Decatur. By the time he was twenty, Oglesby had seen enough of manual labor and had begun to recognize his powers of persuasion. Henry Prather, who had married Oglesby's sister Amanda, agreed to support his study of law at the office of Judge Silas W. Robbins in Springfield. The first book he "read through" was Blackstone's *Commentaries.* In the autumn of 1845, Oglesby was admitted to the bar and began practice in Sullivan, Illinois. He announced in a notice in Springfield's *Sangamo Journal* dated Christmas 1845 that "Richard J. Oglesby. Attorney and Councilor at law—Sullivan, Moultrie County, Illinois—will attend to all business entrusted to him in the eighth judicial district." He conducted some cases in the 1846 spring term and then returned to Decatur. Both Sullivan and Decatur were regular stops for Lincoln and the entourage of lawyers who traveled the Eighth Judicial Circuit.[10]

Oglesby always spoke modestly about his law career. In response to a request from John M. Palmer, also a former governor, who was preparing a book entitled *The Bench and Bar of Illinois,* Oglesby wrote that he was "never much of a lawyer, hardly enough to get in your book, still I was a lawyer, and practiced on and off for fifteen years." For a year in 1846 and 1847 he would be "off" his legal career and in the army in Mexico.[11]

Congressman Lincoln and the National Whigs were hostile to President

James K. Polk and his expansive policy toward Mexico, in part for fear that new slave states might be annexed. But to most Illinoisans, Democrat and Whig, the president's call to arms in 1846 was consistent with their patriotism and their belief in the "Manifest Destiny" of the country. In the case of the twenty-two-year-old Oglesby, it provided an opportunity for adventure, leadership training, and making some money. Illinois was initially authorized to raise three regiments, but four were raised, more than any other state. Secretary of War William L. Marcy and Illinois Congressman O. B. Ficklin successfully pressed for the muster of the Fourth Illinois Regiment to be placed under the command of Edward D. Baker. Oglesby and many of his Decatur friends joined Company C, and Oglesby was elected as first lieutenant under Capt. Isaac C. Pugh, a veteran of the Black Hawk War. But Oglesby found that he must literally win a foot race against a challenger to keep the position, which paid $40 a month. For years thereafter, he was fond of telling how he won the contest by six inches and thus kept the position and the respect of his comrades.[12]

As Blackstone's *Commentaries* had served Oglesby the lawyer, Hardie's *Tactics* served the young lieutenant. He established a reputation as the best drillmaster of the company. He also knew when to treat "all the boys to as much [rum] as they could drink." As popular as he was with "the boys," he perceived that he was liked by his superiors as well. As his company moved from Decatur to Jefferson Barracks in St. Louis in June 1846, to New Orleans in July, and on to the Rio Grande River, his confidence grew. In a letter to his sisters and brothers-in-law, he confided that he could "beat any man or officer in our company, three to one for captain." From Matamoros, Mexico, Oglesby noted that he had "interviewed" Gen. Zachary Taylor, their commander. He also wrote of accompanying Gen. James Shields and his regimental commander, Colonel Baker, on a boat ride up the Rio Grande River, a trip that far exceeded "in real pleasure and novelty" any he had ever taken. He observed Mexican women with "exceedingly luscious" bosoms "all exposed to full view." He described one from a discreet distance as "one of the loveliest, richest and most god-like looking ladies that my eyes ever beheld." She was "everything you can imagine in the way of beauty, coal-shining black hair, finer than silk, that swung down in such rich folds as to excite every emotion of the foulest woman-hater," he teased. He began to contemplate a military career.[13]

Lieutenant Oglesby's first battle was not against Mexicans but with an unruly company of Irish volunteers. On August 31, 1846, a riot occurred on board a Rio Grande river steamer carrying two Georgia volunteer companies. Col. Edward Baker was ordered to intervene, and Oglesby and some men of Company C were directed to join Baker in storming the deck and restoring order. Three men were killed, and several were wounded. A dispatch to the *Sangamo Journal* concerning the incident included: "We learned that Lt. Oglesby of the Decatur company was severely, and we fear mortally, wounded, in the riot." By the time of his letter from Camargo on November 16, Oglesby could laugh about reports of his death. "I regret exceedingly the news you received of my death," he joked. "No doubt my valuable life was much lamented." He did admit being in danger as he attempted to parry a bayonet aimed at Colonel Baker only to have his sword knocked from his hands. Lt. Anderson Froman, in turn, knocked off "three bayonets and actually thought he saw one enter my body and hollered I was killed." But, Oglesby explained, he had "only raked a slight punch from the hand or musket of some damned Irish-man."[14]

In December 1846, Oglesby and the Illinois Third and Fourth Regiments were among the troops based in Matamoros under the command of Maj. Gen. Robert Patterson. The plan was to capture Victoria, 150 miles to the southwest, and continue to the southeast until they broke out at the newly captured port city of Tampico. Oglesby expected a serious fight from the troops of Gen. Antonio López de Santa Anna. "One thing is now reduced to a certainty, that the Mexicans will fight, and that too d—n hard," he wrote to Henry Prather. The march to Tampico, "four hundred miles under the most inauspicious circumstances," would test his leadership of the company, relinquished to him by "old [Capt. Isaac] Pugh." To his sisters he confided that his "body might be found lying on some battlefield between here and Tampico" but that he was determined to do his duty. He asked them to give his foster mother, "old Aunt Judy," "my best love and [to] tell her I shall remember her as long as life lasts."[15]

Oglesby was spared a fight because General Taylor had sent Gen. John A. Quitman to occupy Victoria ahead of Patterson's march. Gen. Winfield Scott had been put in charge of the Vera Cruz expedition in Central Mexico. The armies of Maj. Gen. Robert Patterson and Maj. Gen. David E. Twiggs were transferred to Scott and sent marching on to Tampico for trans-shipment to Vera Cruz.[16]

On February 1, 1847, Oglesby was able to report to his sisters that he was in Tampico and in good health after a march of 450 miles from Matamoros via Victoria at the head of his company. "I walked every step of the way in twenty days," he wrote. "Tis true that my feet often wore into blood blisters, and the skin came off in pieces as large as half-dollars, but I had to go it. I knew well that it would not do to despair whilst there were so many of the men looking on anxiously for my example." A month later, under specific orders to sail to Vera Cruz for an attack on the city, Oglesby expressed fear about "the hazardous enterprise" and sent instructions as to disposal of his money and property in case of his death. "Tell sisters Amanda and Ophelia they need have no fear of my safety, but I must do as I do" he told his brother-in-law. He added that he would trust his good luck and his "sentimental religious views" to protect him on all occasions.[17]

"You know the wonderful city of Vera Cruz is ours," Oglesby wrote to Decatur friends on April 8, 1847. "You also know that the more marvelous labyrinth of San Juan de Ulua is ours, both by the most skillful generalship ever known." Scott's forces had landed below Vera Cruz on March 9, with almost no resistance. The army, which included the volunteers under Patterson, quickly drove the Mexican forces into the city and laid siege to it. Oglesby reported being in the company of General Shields and Colonel Baker when he observed the bombardment begin and a few days later when Mexicans raised a white flag. "So you see," he bragged, "that I have actually been in one fight which lasted three days with our brave little company." The formal surrender came on March 29, and it included the relinquishment of the island fortress San Juan de Ulua, which Oglesby, upon inspection from the inside, pronounced "the most impregnable fortifications under the sun, Gibraltar only excepted." In his exuberance, Oglesby unfurled the eight-by-twelve-foot flag that the ladies of Decatur had presented to him for Company C upon the occasion of their enlistment.[18]

Scott was pressed to move toward Mexico City quickly by an impatient president, the impending expiration of the one-year volunteer term of service, and the need to leave the "disastrous black vomit in Vera Cruz" (the yellow fever zone) for the higher ground of the interior. Meanwhile, Santa Anna seized control of the government in Mexico City and rushed eastward along the national road to block Scott's path to the capital. Santa Anna chose to defend the pass at Cerro Gordo, located fifty-four miles upland from Vera Cruz. Although his position was well fortified, Capt. Robert E. Lee of Scott's staff discovered a route around the Mexican left that allowed envelopment of the Mexican forces.[19]

On April 18, 1847, Shields's brigade followed the path Lee had discovered for about two miles and emerged on the left flank of a Mexican five-gun battery and camp near Cerro Gordo. Three guns were turned on Shields and his three hundred raw volunteers who had no cannon. "Shields fell and his men recoiled," but the brigade regrouped and charged the battery at the same time another Yankee unit was attacking from the center. The surprised Mexicans withdrew in great disorder. Oglesby later claimed in his pension application that "Gen. Shields was almost fatally wounded at the head of Col. Baker's regiment, at the head of which regiment was company C and at the head of which company was your humble servant, commanding." During the pursuit of the fleeing Mexican army, the men of the Fourth captured Santa Anna's carriage, which contained $20,000 in gold and the general's cork leg. Company C was honored by being ordered to provide the escort for the wounded General Shields. Oglesby reported that his company had suffered ten casualties out of a company of forty-one engaged in the battle. Overall, the Americans lost thirty officers and 387 men compared to about a thousand men of Santa Anna's army.[20]

General Scott decided that it was prudent to send the one-year men home in advance of the yellow fever season. Thus seven regiments, including the troops from Illinois, were shipped home. Only one in ten felt obliged to reenlist. Although Oglesby had considered a military career, he thought his politics were wrong for advancement. "I expect if it were not for my strong Whig notions, I might have an opportunity afforded me to stay here till the war is over, but such being my fix, I can hardly expect such a favor" he had written in February 1847. He and his comrades arrived in Decatur via New Orleans and St. Louis on June 1, 1847, bearing the flag the women of Decatur had presented to the regiment. By December 22, 1847, when Congressman Lincoln introduced his "spot resolutions" demanding that President Polk identify the location where Polk said American blood had been shed on American soil, Oglesby and his men were safely at home, although two more Illinois regiments had been recruited to serve to the end of the war.[21]

Oglesby may have disagreed with Lincoln's assessment of the war as being "unnecessarily and unconstitutionally commenced" by Democrat President Polk, but both Whigs quickly recognized the efficacy of nominating a Mexican War hero, Gen. Zachary Taylor, for president even though it meant abandoning Henry Clay. Lincoln explained that Taylor was the only Whig who could be elected and brushed off arguments that he had abandoned Clay and principle by noting that the Whig Party was not the only party to put "old horses out to root." On behalf of General Taylor's candidacy, Lincoln wrote letters, participated in the Whig nominating convention in Philadelphia, made speeches in Congress and on a New England tour, and encouraged his law partner William H. Herndon to form "Rough and Ready" clubs among Springfield's young men to support Taylor.[22]

Oglesby, who admired General Taylor, plunged into politics and political speech-making during the campaign of 1848. The twenty-four-year-old veteran soon received favorable notice in the state's Whig organ, the *Illinois Journal,* for his involvement in Macon County, in his Illinois senatorial district convention in Waynesville, and for his speech at Herndon's Rough and Ready Club in Springfield. The *Illinois State Journal* reported, "Lt. Oglesby, of Decatur also made a spirited address, and gave most encouraging information of the progress of old Zack's army in Central Illinois."[23]

Neither Lincoln nor Oglesby was rewarded for their support of Taylor in 1848, however. Lincoln reluctantly returned to the law from his two-year stint in Congress, and Oglesby returned to the law from his one-year adventure in the Mexican-American War. Lincoln was content, for the time, to practice in the Eighth Judicial Circuit, while the younger Oglesby sought to better prepare himself by attending law school in Louisville, Kentucky, during the winter of 1848–49.[24]

Oglesby's destiny was intertwined with the nation's "Manifest Destiny." When he returned to Decatur early in 1849, he was swept up in the excitement of the California gold rush. California was among the prizes acquired by the United States as a result of the war, and Oglesby saw the possibility of gaining his own reward. Henry Prather encouraged him to join the eight other members of the central Illinois "Independent Company" being formed to go to California to the extent of lending Oglesby the necessary $250 stake in the enterprise. It was money well-lent. The young Oglesby offered organizational skill, physical endurance, adaptability, and an entrepreneurial spirit.[25]

Oglesby and the company were among the winners in the 1,950-mile race to the Sacramento goldfields because of foresight and organization. Between St. Joseph, Missouri, where the race began on May 8, 1849, and Sutter's Fort, California, on August 10, they were able to drive their three wagons and eighteen mules past some 1,600 wagons because they had the forethought to bring a supply of mule shoes. Oglesby and another company member had taken lessons in shoeing in St. Louis, and the treasured animals arrived in California with good feet and full stomachs because they made the trip early enough to enjoy good grazing along much of the route. Their speed was also increased by the company's vote to accept Oglesby's suggestion, made early in the trip after much confusion and indecision, that the members should rotate as "emperor of the day." For twenty-four hours an emperor would designate the starting, lunch, and stopping times, the speed, and the assignment of night guards. According to Oglesby, "never a cross word or a single dispute" resulted, and the company arrived in Sacramento City in ninety-five days, ahead of all but 109 wagons.[26]

The Independent Company drove their three wagons about twenty-five miles a day following the traditional Oregon Trail up the Little Blue, North Platte, and South Platte rivers, arriving at Fort Laramie on June 5. Oglesby found the Indians unthreatening and the grass sufficient for the hundred thousand immigrants he expected to traverse the route in 1849. The company passed Independence Rock well ahead of schedule, traversed the South Pass of the Rocky Mountains, and arrived at Fort Hall in the newly acquired Oregon Territory on July 2. Oglesby complained about the "exorbitant and unchristian" prices at Fort Hall and the control exerted by the "foreign" Hudson Bay Company at the fort. Always patriotic, he and his Decatur friend William Rea had concealed a two-gallon jug of the finest quality brandy for a "Jolly Time" on the Fourth of July. The Illinoisans left the Oregon Trail some sixty miles southwest of Fort Hall and followed the Humboldt-Carson route, arriving at their destination on August 10.[27]

In Sacramento, Oglesby quickly discovered that he had a talent for sales-manship, "Christian or not." The Independent Company, eager to race to the goldfields, became more independent than any other company by voting to sell the "property of our company to ourselves." Oglesby successfully bid $250 for the smallest of the three wagons and "a span of mules." He then proceeded to drive the team around Sacramento under a "for sale" sign. He expected to sell it for $250, but he shrewdly coaxed $450 from a prospective miner. The future governor quickly observed that he could make more selling than min-ing. Oglesby and Henry Prather then bought one of the larger wagons and six mules for $800 from the company and sold it for $1,700. By the evening of the third day in the mining city, Oglesby had paid off his $250 stake and his expenses and had $570 in gold. Prather and Oglesby joined Jacob Hum-mell, another member of the former company, and opened a successful mine on the Mokelumne River at Dry Town about forty-five miles from Sacramen-to City.[28]

Desperate for mail from home, Oglesby's partners contracted with him to go to San Francisco at his own expense and agreed to pay him $5 for each letter and $1 for each newspaper received for them at the San Francisco post office. Oglesby recruited another dozen subscribers to his mail service, walked to Sacramento City, and took a steamer to San Francisco. There he found a long line of men waiting at the post office. Always resourceful, he arranged with a postal clerk he met at dinner to retrieve his mail at night for $1 a let-ter and a quarter a newspaper. Oglesby was able to make the trip in ten days, retrieve his own mail, and make a tidy profit for delivering the mail to the miners.[29]

There was much money to be made and lost in California. By mining, haul-ing, selling, and performing various services, Oglesby earned more than $3,000 the first year. He soon tired of protecting his gold dust and deposited it in a bank that failed a month later. Although the loss staggered him, he earned another $1,500 mining in the area and then rejoined his brother-in-law, who had moved to the Coyote diggings near Nevada City, California. The partners built a house and a store. Prather and many of the central Illinois "boys" were beginning to drift back home, often with large earnings. But Oglesby chose to purchase Prather's share, on credit, and continue operating the Nevada City store, only to hear, while seeing Prather off in Sacramento City, that Nevada City and his store had burned. Oglesby placed his loss at $2,500 but turned the setback to his advantage by purchasing supplies in Sacramento and racing back to Nevada City with the materials needed to quickly rebuild his store. He kept the store until August 10, 1851, when he sold it and returned to Illinois via New Orleans with $5,000 in gold. In New Orleans, he was almost separated from his money by a thief who crawled through the transom of his hotel room door in an attempt to steal his money belt. Oglesby awakened in time to save the gold and prevent a third disaster.[30]

While still in California, Oglesby followed news of Decatur land speculation and legal and political developments with great interest. He was aware that land could be bought cheaply, and he believed the central Illinois area would develop rapidly. After paying Prather $1,800 for his share in the California enterprise and freeing the family slave, Uncle Tim, for $267, Oglesby had enough money to begin buying land warrants from Mexican War veterans and from other sources. He purchased about a thousand acres of land, including that which was laid out in town lots in northwest Decatur. Names were chosen for two major new streets: Eldorado, for the California gold mines that supplied the money, and Cerro Gordo, which recalled his role in the Mexican War and the issuance of land warrants to soldiers. When the railroads came to Decatur, the city began growing rapidly. Oglesby's investment returns quickly multiplied so that he accumulated more than $10,000 in less than five years.[31]

Oglesby also made some of his money in his law practice after teaming with Sheridan Wait, who would become his long-time partner and confidant, in 1853. Oglesby was among the Decatur promoters of the "Indiana and Illinois Central Railroad" in 1853, and Oglesby and Wait served as agents in 1854 and 1855. The law firm accepted nearly a hundred cases or collections each year in 1854 and 1855. At first, many of their clients were relatives and much of their correspondence involved collections, but Oglesby and Wait soon developed an important clientele in other cities and states. Oglesby practiced in Macon and Piatt counties, both part of the Eighth Judicial Circuit that Lincoln traversed twice a year. Lincoln took Oglesby's Macon County case, *Patrick Sullivan v. the People,* to the Illinois Supreme Court in 1853. The high court sustained Sullivan's conviction on charges of selling liquor illegally.[32]

During the early 1850s, both Lincoln and Oglesby were busier practicing law and making money than they were practicing politics. Lincoln's political career was quiescent, and the younger Oglesby was still learning the trade. Both kept themselves informed by subscribing to state and national political publications. Oglesby subscribed to both the Whig *Illinois State Journal* and the Democratic *Register* in 1852 and to the Whig *Weekly National Intelligencer* in 1853, as well as the *Congressional Globe*. Both Whigs supported Gen. Winfield Scott for president in 1852. The twenty-eight-year-old Oglesby was chosen as a Whig delegate to the state convention and subsequently made a presidential elector from the Seventh Illinois Congressional District. During the campaign, he spoke in various places in the district. He also spoke in Louisville, Kentucky, on Scott's behalf.[33]

Years before, Lincoln had admonished aspiring politicians to "stay close to the people," a charge Oglesby remembered for the rest of his life. Oglesby, the orphan boy, learned to be one of those people during the first three decades of his life. He was "everyman" because he had done "everything" that the great mass of young Americans had done. He had been a farmer, carpenter, hemp maker, soldier, teamster, miner, merchant, and speculator. But Oglesby, like Lincoln, aspired to more. Their aspirations made them more Whig than egalitarian. They lacked formal education, but their drive enabled them to rise to a profession, as they must have considered the law and politics, yet they never found it difficult to understand the people. Their Whig Party was dying. It had only been successful in electing presidents when it found military candidates who were not identified with party's aristocratic policies. The introduction of the Kansas-Nebraska bill in 1854 set in motion events that would lead to the creation of the new Republican Party and to political careers for Lincoln and Oglesby. Oglesby's political activities, however, would be interrupted in 1856–57 by an extraordinary adventure.

## Notes

1. Wilkie, p. 1. The *Tribune* sent John Locke Scripps to interview Lincoln in 1860. L. S. Dyche, "John Locke Scripps, Lincoln's Campaign Biographer," *JISHS* 17 (Oct. 1924): 333–51.

2. Wilkie, pp. 2–3.

3. Bancroft, pp. 1–3. The birthdates of Oglesby's parents and the date of their marriage are from a transcript held at the Oglesby Mansion in Decatur, Illinois, which is taken from the Oglesby family Bible and a typed manuscript: Michael James Welch, "History of Elkhart" (1979). Jacob's appointment as deputy sheriff is recorded in Order Book 1, page 357, Oldham County Courthouse, LaGrange, Ky.

4. The first three children born to Jacob and Isabel Oglesby were girls. Emiline Brown was born on January 11, 1816, and later married James F. Wilson of Kentucky; Amanda Watson was born on December 7, 1817, and married Henry Prather of Decatur; and Ophelia Willis, born on January 5, 1820, married a Mr. Adamson before marrying Jasper

J. Peddecord of Decatur. All three were to become important in the future Illinois governor's professional and personal development. Jefferson Woodford Oglesby was born on February 21, 1822, and Richard James Oglesby, the second son, on July 25, 1824. Robert Markland Oglesby, born on February 19, 1827, died on April 18, 1848, and is buried in Floydsburg, Kentucky. Oglesby's younger sisters also died prematurely: Sarah Eleanor, born on July 21, 1830, died in Decatur on August 21, 1836, and Mary Isabel, born May 19, 1833, died on July 6, 1833, and is also buried in Floydsburg. Oglesby family Bible transcript; Welch, "History of Elkhart."

5. Bancroft, pp. 3–4; Wilkie, p. 4. "A Schedule of the personal estate of Jacob Oglesby die'd with the appraised value," in Will Book 1 (pp. 307–14), Oldham County Courthouse, LaGrange, Kentucky, includes the item "1 Negro man Tilman at $375." The actual sale was apparently held on August 17, 1833, and it seemed to raise $444.78, excluding the sale of Tilman. Willis Oglesby was the administrator of the estate. The sale's results were reported to the court on October 21, 1833. Tilman was sold to Katharine Rice Bradshaw, widow of John Bradshaw, on January 16, 1840, together with thirteen other slaves valued at $4,973 (Will Book 2, p. 256). I was unable to find a record of the sale of Tilman to James Wilson. It probably took place in another county, because Oglesby reports Mrs. Bradshaw as being from Westport, Kentucky.

6. Jane Martin Johns, *Personal Recollections of Early Decatur, Abraham Lincoln, Richard J. Oglesby, and the Civil War* (Decatur: Daughters of the American Revolution, 1912), pp. 95–98. Wilkie places the family in a log cabin (p. 7).

7. Johns, *Personal Recollections,* pp. 98–99; Wilkie, pp. 7–10.

8. Wilkie, p. 15; *Lincoln Day by Day,* vol. 1, p. 138. Among eyewitnesses to Lincoln's participation in the Whig rally were General Henderson and Judge Scott, as quoted in Ida M. Tarbell, *The Life of Abraham Lincoln,* 2 vols. (New York: McClure, Phillips, 1902), vol. 1, pp. 165–69.

9. Bancroft, pp. 5–6; Wilkie, pp. 9–10; RJO to Ben: Perley Poore, March 4, 1873, Sprague Collection, Chicago Historical Society.

10. Wilkie, p. 10; David Herbert Donald, *Lincoln* (New York: Simon and Schuster, 1995), p. 37; *Sangamo Journal,* Dec. 25, 1845; Richmond, p. 347.

11. RJO to John M. Palmer, July 8, 1898, in John M. Palmer, *The Bench and Bar of Illinois,* 2 vols. (Chicago: Lewis Publishing, 1899), vol. 2, p. 1155.

12. Wilkie, pp. 10–12; Richmond, pp. 125, 128.

13. RJO to H. Prather and J. J. Peddecord, Matamoros, Sept. 9, 1846, typescript, Oglesby MSS.

14. *Sangamo Journal,* Sept. 17, 1846, p. 3, col. 6; RJO to H. Prather, Camargo, Nov. 16, 1846, typescript, Oglesby MSS; K. Jack Bauer, *The Mexican War, 1846–1848* (New York: Macmillan, 1974), p. 83.

15. RJO to J. J. Peddecord, Matamoros, Dec. 12, 1846, and RJO to "Dear Sisters, Henry [Prather] and Wood [W. W.?] Peddecord and Sissies too," Matamoros, Dec. 20, 1846, both in typescript, Oglesby MSS. There was bad blood between Oglesby and "old Pugh," probably dating from Oglesby's perception that Pugh had failed to come to his rescue against the Irish rioters. In letters to his wife, Pugh protested Oglesby's lack of chivalry. From Tampico on March 4, 1847, he wrote: "I would tell Jane Butler and others of the young ladies about Decatur had better keep their letters to themselves. Dick Oglesby has been

writing to her and others and when he gets their answers makes all sorts of fun [of] them especially Jane. He has no principal [*sic*] in such matters." From New Orleans on May 22, 1847, Pugh wrote: "He is in my opinion unworthy of the good esteem of myself or friends. He tells all his courtships and flirtations he has with the young ladies of Macon." Eric Fair gave me a copy of these letters, which are deposited at the University of California, Riverside.

16. Bauer, *Mexican War,* pp. 237–38.

17. RJO to Mrs. Prather and Peddecord, camp near Tampico, Feb. 1, 1847, and RJO to Jas[per Peddecord], March 5, 1847, camp at Tampico, both in typescript, Oglesby MSS.

18. RJO to Friends, camp before Vera Cruz, April 8, 1847, typescript, Oglesby MSS; Bauer, *Mexican War,* pp. 244, 246, 252; Richmond, p. 129.

19. Bauer, *Mexican War,* pp. 260–67. Oglesby expressed concern about "the horrid history of the disastrous black vomit in Vera Cruz" in RJO to Jas[per Peddecord], March 5, 1847, camp at Tampico, typescript, Oglesby MSS.

20. Bauer, *Mexican War,* pp. 260–68; Justin H. Smith, *The War with Mexico,* 2 vols. (New York: Macmillan, 1919), vol. 2, pp. 51–59; "Gov. Oglesby's Application for a Pension," *Journal,* Dec. 1, 1887, p. 2, col. 3. See also Ezra M. Prince, "The Fourth Illinois Infantry in the War with Mexico," in *Transactions of the Illinois State Historical Society for the Year 1906* (Springfield: ISHL, 1906), pp. 172–87. While Oglesby was serving his third term as governor, Santa Anna's cork leg was presented to the state by J. M. Gill of Pekin, Illinois, and was placed in the Memorial Hall. Correspondence suggests that the men of Company D and some "stragglers" made the capture on April 18, 1847. Oglesby is mentioned as among the "gallant Illinois troops who were climbing the main height" to the scene. *Journal,* May 15, 1886, p. 1, col. 3; *Chicago Journal,* Aug. 17, 1886, p. 1, col. 1. The state still has the purported cork leg, and there is also one in the Oglesby Mansion in Decatur.

21. Bauer, *Mexican War,* p. 270; Richmond, p. 129; RJO to Mrs. Prather and Peddecord, camp near Tampico, Feb. 1, 1847, typescript, Oglesby MSS; *Collected Works,* vol. 1, pp. 420–22. That a number of officers and soldiers from the Fourth Regiment had reached home was reported in "Return of Volunteers," *Sangamo Journal,* June 10, 1847, p. 3, col. 7.

22. Abraham Lincoln to William H. Herndon, Feb. 1, 1848, Lincoln to Thomas S. Flournoy, Feb. 17, 1848, July 27, 1848, speech in Congress, and Lincoln to Herndon, June 22, 1848, all in *Collected Works,* vol. 1, pp. 466, 452, 507, and 491.

23. *Journal,* July 6, 1848, p. 3, col. 3, Sept. 27, 1848, p. 4, col. 4, and July 13, 1848, p. 1, col. 4.

24. Wilkie, p. 12.

25. Bancroft, p. 7.

26. The Independent Company was composed of Henry [Sadoris?], [B.] F. Piatt, and George Matsler of Piatt County; T. L. Loomis of Macoupin County; N. W. Peddecord of Dewitt County; and Henry Prather, William Rea, Jacob Hummell, and Oglesby of Macon County. Mildred Eversole, ed., "Richard J. Oglesby: Forty-niner His Own Narrative," *Transactions of the Illinois State Historical Society for the Year 1938* (Springfield: ISHS, 1939), pp. 158–71. The account was originally published in the *Journal* on October 23, 1849 (p. 2, col. 2); see also Bancroft, pp. 17–18. Judge Thad D. Loomis named the same members of the "independent company" but with some variant spellings. Thad D. Loomis, "Oglesby as Gold Hunter," *Journal,* May 1, 1899, col. 2, pp. 3–4.

27. "Richard J. Oglesby: Forty-niner in His Own Narrative," pp. 163–68; RJO to [Ophelia

and G. G. Peddecord and Amanda Prather], from camp near Ft. Kearney, May 20, 1849, typescript in possession of Carolyn Ogen, Champaign, Ill.

28. Bancroft, pp. 24–26.

29. Ibid.

30. Ibid., pp. 26–28.

31. Ibid.; RJO to H. Prather, Sacramento City, Aug. 10, 1850, typescript in possession of Carolyn Ogen; Richmond, p. 121.

32. "OGLESBY & WAIT Attorneys and Counselors at Law, Decatur, Illinois," business cards ran in the *Decatur Gazette* from April 21, 1854 to May 11, 1855. The *Journal,* July 11, 1853, p. 3, col. 1, noted that the books for subscriptions for the stock of the Indiana and Illinois Central railroad had been opened in Decatur under the superintendency of R. J. Oglesby. The estimate of cases comes from "Private Docket, May 1854 to 1856," a ledger book shown to me by Amelia Mulrooney, Decatur, in 1976. For March 2, 1854, see *Lincoln Day by Day,* vol. 1, p. 116; see also *Sullivan v. People,* Macon County Circuit Court (1853); and Illinois Supreme Court (1853), *Lincoln Legal Briefs Quarterly: Newsletter of the Lincoln Legal Papers,* no. 42 (April–June, 1997): n.p.

33. The *Journal* was paid for on July 9, 1852, and the *Register* on February 27, 1852. Receipts in "Business Papers," Oglesby MSS. The *Congressional Globe and Appendix* and the *National Intelligencer* were paid for on December 7, 1853. The *Journal* reported on Oglesby's speeches in Louisville and Vandalia (Sept. 21, 1852, p. 3, col. 1, Oct. 5, 1852, p. 3, col. 1).

# 2. A Young American Abroad

DESPITE HIS LACK of formal education, Richard J. Oglesby had learned from his experiences in the Mexican War and the gold rush that he possessed leadership qualities. His careers as a lawyer and politician were beginning to blossom in an environment that allowed him to rise to his potential. He came to believe that there was something special about Young America that had been denied the rest of the world. Although the term *Young America* was usually associated with Democrats, the name came to apply to a more general movement in the 1840s and 1850s that identified with aggressive nationalism, Manifest Destiny, and sympathy for republican revolution in Europe. It also included the faith, stressed by Whigs, that one could rise to unprecedented heights through individual effort in the context of the world's only democracy. Lincoln and Oglesby would seize the opportunities afforded, which would lead to Lincoln's ascendancy to the presidency and Oglesby's rise to governor of Illinois. For Lincoln, 1854 was a turning point, but the younger Oglesby lacked confidence in his own abilities. Although he displayed considerable political acumen and had even greater financial success in the early 1850s, by 1856 he had decided upon an adventure in self-education: a grand tour of Europe and the Holy Land.[1]

When Stephen A. Douglas pushed through the Kansas-Nebraska bill of 1854, with its explicit repeal of the Missouri Compromise that had forbidden slavery in the territories north of 36 degrees, 30 minutes latitude, Lincoln and a host of northern Whigs and Democrats felt betrayed. Unwilling to see slavery extended further, they believed the Kansas-Nebraska bill was the vehicle for its expansion. They were united in opposition to the bill but not united politically. Lincoln and Oglesby were among those central Illinois

Whigs who were most reluctant to fuse with other anti-Nebraska (those against the extension of slavery) politicians. They were wary of Democrats and radicals, uncertain about the role of nativists and prohibitionists who were attracted to the American ("Know-Nothing") Party, and hopeful that their political ambitions could be realized in the old Whig Party.[2]

In the autumn of 1854, Lincoln began speaking out against the Douglas bill, which, he later asserted, "aroused him as he had never been before." He reentered politics by managing the reelection campaign of Richard Yates, the Whig member of Congress, and by running for the state legislature as a means of strengthening Yates's chances. The first extant letter from Lincoln to Oglesby is a confidential note dated September 8, 1854, imploring Oglesby to refute a charge attributed to Oglesby, that although Yates "passes as a temperate man, he is in the habit of drinking secretly." Lincoln claimed that he had never seen Yates "drink liquor, nor act, or speak, as if he had been drinking, nor smelled it on his breath." No response from Oglesby survives, but Oglesby, himself a drinking man, may have known Yates better than Lincoln did. The charge followed Yates throughout his political career, and alcoholism eventually led to his disgrace and premature death. Whether Yates's defeat in 1854 can be attributed to the intemperance charge or to a lack of anti-Nebraska fusion is unclear, but he and Oglesby seem to have remained friends and business associates.[3]

Lincoln was also interested in defeating Douglas Democrats elsewhere and in thwarting Douglas's control over the legislature that would choose a U.S. senator. On October 16, 1854, Douglas and Lincoln spoke in Peoria. On that same day, Oglesby was answering the incumbent Douglas-Democrat member of Congress, James C. Allen, in Decatur. According to a partisan reporter's dispatch to the Whig *Illinois State Journal,* Allen had concluded a two-hour speech when calls for Oglesby came from the audience. He responded and galvanized the audience; he also "made some very telling remarks upon the misconceptions and false history that had figured in Mr. Allen's speech." Oglesby portrayed the plight of the poor white man in a slave society such as his native Kentucky. Typical of his "stump speech humor," he insisted that he loved Kentucky—"He was glad he was born there and gladder yet that he had left." He then forthrightly condemned slavery. "I hate the damnable institution," he declared. The enthralled correspondent suggested that Oglesby should have been put in the race against Allen.[4]

Although the Whigs had little success in 1854, the Illinois legislature returned an anti-Nebraska majority for the U.S. senatorial contest. Lincoln resigned his legislative seat in order to become eligible for the Senate. Yates and Oglesby were supporting Lincoln, but Oglesby was fearful. On January

27, 1855, Oglesby wrote to Yates that he would go to Springfield and see how the race developed. "The die is not cast but the elements are molten. I am assured that Mr. Lincoln's chance is growing small by degree and you know the rest," he wrote. "I do not like to see him thus prostrated." Oglesby was correct. On the first ballot, Lincoln received forty-four votes to forty-one for the Douglas Democrat; Lyman Trumbull, the anti-Nebraska Democrat, received only four. As Lincoln's votes ebbed in the balloting it became clear that the only way to elect a committed anti-Nebraska man was to support Trumbull. Lincoln then endorsed Trumbull, who was elected on the tenth ballot. Lincoln understated his dismay by writing, "I regret my defeat moderately," but a new, anti-slavery extension party may have begun to look attractive.[5]

The Whig Party was falling down around Lincoln, Oglesby, and other old-line Whigs at a time when the appeal against the extension of slavery was building. In 1855 Lincoln confessed, "I think I am a Whig; but others say there are no Whigs, and that I am an abolitionist. . . . I now do no more than oppose the *extension* of slavery." Anti-extension became the simple unifying principle behind the belated organization of the Republican Party in Illinois. The first broadly based organizational meeting in Illinois took place on Washington's birthday 1856 in Oglesby's hometown. The Anti-Nebraska Editorial Convention was held in Decatur at the suggestion of William Usrey, editor of Decatur's *Illinois State Chronicle,* and Paul Selby of the *Morgan Journal* in Jacksonville. Usrey had been a corporal in Oglesby's company in the Mexican War, and Selby was a close friend of Richard Yates. Some twenty-five other editors endorsed the meeting. Although not editors, Oglesby was a host, and Lincoln managed to "have some business at Decatur at the time of the convention." Selby was elected chair and Usrey secretary of the convention, and Lincoln apparently had a role in drafting a platform that would not be considered too radical. The name *Republican* did not appear in the platform, although the organization called for the Bloomington convention that later organized the Illinois Republican Party. The Decatur convention named a state central committee, and Oglesby was chosen to represent the Seventh Congressional District; Lincoln's law partner, William Herndon, was picked to represent Lincoln's district.[6]

Citizens of Decatur prepared a postconvention dinner for the "Editorial Fraternity" at the Cassell House. E. W. Blaisdell of Rockford rose after the "sumptuous dinner" to thank the hosts. According to Usrey's *Chronicle,* "Mr. Oglesby was loudly called for" and "made a number of witty remarks and concluded by toasting Mr. Abram [sic] Lincoln" as "our next candidate for the U.S. Senate." Acknowledging the "prolonged applause," Lincoln allowed that he was in favor of that sentiment. He responded with a speech during

which he proposed William Bissell, an anti-Nebraska Democrat, for governor. Next, the most influential Whig editor in the state, Edward L. Baker of
the *Illinois State Journal* in Springfield, toasted "Hon. Dick Oglesby, the next
Secretary of State" to loud applause.[7]

The thirty-one-year-old Oglesby seemed to be among the blessed in Young
America. He was a hero of the Mexican War and a forty-niner who had par-
layed his gold dust into a small fortune in real estate; in addition, he had a
thriving law practice and was recognized by Lincoln and others as a rising
political figure. Ironically, his next adventure grew out of a conversation he
had with Stephen A. Douglas concerning the senator's recent trip to Europe
and Asia. Oglesby's wanderlust may yet have been unfulfilled. Perhaps he felt
insecure about his lack of culture and education; he may have been uncertain about his religion or a rejected suitor; or maybe he saw a the "grand tour"
as an opportunity to hone his oratorical and writing skills. It appears that
all these considerations contributed to his decision to make a trip. He resigned
his membership on the anti-Nebraska central committee and made arrangements to leave on a twenty-month journey that would take him to England,
Ireland, France, Prussia, Russia, Greece, Egypt, Arabia, and Palestine. He left
on April 18, 1856, before the founding convention of the Illinois Republicans
and returned in December 1857 in time to reestablish himself before the 1858
congressional elections.[8]

Oglesby polished his literary skills during the trip by reading guide books
and histories; by writing numerous letters, some for publication; and by keeping a trip diary that eventually grew to 160,000 words. His observations were
both descriptive and judgmental. He wrote from the perspective of a proud
"Young American" who disdained monarchy and indolence and believed that
every country should emulate America. Oglesby's overland journey to port
took him through Louisville, where he no doubt visited his relatives, and then
to Washington via Cincinnati, Wheeling, and Baltimore. On a visit to Mount
Vernon, he "cut a hickory cane" as a token of George Washington's home, a
recurring practice that would eventually net him several trunks of souvenirs.[9]

For $65 Oglesby took passage on the steamer *City of Baltimore* in Phila-
delphia on May 15, 1856, and he landed in Liverpool thirteen days later. During the voyage his rhetorical skills were put to use as the drafter of a resolution commending the captain and crew and in making a toast to "the prairie
and the ocean, twin sisters by the decree of the omniscience, separated on
the third day of creation—the land of the swine and the home of the whale."
That attempt at composition may suggest that his quest for culture and lit-
eracy was well advised.[10]

The future governor visited Trinity College in Dublin, the "Four Courts"

of Ireland, the home of John Knox in Edinburgh, the site of the former parliament of Scotland, and St. Paul's Cathedral ("oh what a big unsightly, ugly,
dull thing it is"), the British Museum, Westminster Abbey, Buckingham Palace, and the Houses of Parliament in London. He found the Irish "lean and
lazy" and the British to be temperate drinkers who "undoubtedly love it, but
they are too prudent to indulge."[11]

In Glasgow he heard a speech by Louis Kossuth, the Hungarian revolutionary who had beguiled Young America devotees in the United States, but pronounced him deficient. "He could never be the successful leader of a free
people, or a people struggling to be free," he wrote, because "he lacks the
vim." Visiting Parliament, he listened carefully to Benjamin Disraeli, Lord
Palmerston, and John Russell but was outraged to discover that females could
only observe the proceedings through a pane of glass, "barred from participating in the deliberations of their country's councils." On a visit to the Tower
of London, Prince Oscar of Sweden passed and everyone bowed except Oglesby, who explained, "Sovereigns pay little regard to princes." Nor did the sov-
ereign of Young America stand in awe of Queen Victoria, whom he observed
riding through Hyde Park on June 30. Although many persons "of the lower
order of animals" rushed to her carriage, Oglesby kept his distance. From
about thirty yards away, however, he described her as appearing a little "care
worn" and possessing "no remarkable or distinguishing features either of
person or feature or of intellect." He judged her as a "chubby comfortable
looking lady of about forty years standing."[12]

If democracy was lacking in Great Britain, perhaps he would find more
revolutionary zeal in Paris, where he arrived in time for the Fourth of July.
But alas, it was a dull day with "no flags, no toasts, and no songs." The best
a patriotic American could do was indulge "freely in champagne for a few
hours" and then stroll around the Place de la Concorde, the garden of the
Tuileries, and the Champs Elysees. By July 17 he was off to the great battlefield
at Waterloo, where he could second-guess the Duke of Wellington and Napoleon, recalling his own battles in Mexico but not knowing those to come.
He journeyed to Brussels and on to Cologne ("the dirtiest and foulest city"
in Europe), where eau de cologne had been invented for good, although insufficient, purpose. He next went up the Rhine to Frankfurt and then on to
Erfurt and Leipzig. Leipzig was, at least, "full of music and beer" as well as
homely women. "I shall be content to live in Decatur after seeing Leipzig,"
Oglesby confided to his diary. He reached Berlin on July 25, his birthday. After
eight weeks of travel in Europe, he was ready to pass judgment on the relative courtesy he had encountered: "The English were formally polite, the
French oppressively polite, and the Germans amiably polite." He liked the

Germans because "no favor comes from them reluctantly, and when performed you are not harassed for the pay."[13]

He also liked Berlin because there was a considerable American community there headed by Peter Vroom, the American minister to Prussia. Oglesby presented a letter of introduction from Sen. Lyman Trumbull to Vroom and found him "intelligent and affable." The former New Jersey governor furnished the future Illinois governor with American newspapers ("Bleeding Kansas" dominated the news) and invited him to a "splendid private dinner." Oglesby described how the "old governor had six varieties of the best wines"; how the party "ate, drank, talked, got funny"; and how he fell in love with the ladies present. A bit embarrassed by his "meager dress," Oglesby rationalized that "what I lacked in dress, I made up in drink."[14]

Minister Vroom introduced Oglesby to a number of important Americans who shared his ambition to attend the coronation of Czar Alexander II in Moscow. After but a few days in Berlin, Oglesby joined Col. J. Riley from Texas, appointee to St. Petersburg as American consul, and his wife and two small children for the journey to St. Petersburg. The arms inventor and manufacturer Samuel Colt, married less than two months to Elizabeth Jarvis, was in the group, as were her sister and brother, Hettie and Richard Jarvis. Oglesby remarked that Hettie Jarvis was pretty. They went by riverboat to Stettin, Prussia, on the Baltic Sea and on to St. Petersburg by steamer. When a wind came up, Oglesby and most of the passengers "went to puking," but "the pretty Miss Hettie was too compelled to yield to the fickle goddess of the Baltic." The portly traveler did not feel much better when he landed in St. Petersburg on August 6 and discovered that, by the Russian calendar, it was his thirty-second birthday again. "I feel quite lonely," he wrote.[15]

For the next twenty days, Oglesby observed the splendors of St. Petersburg. There was the Hermitage and the Marble Palace of the Grand Duke Constantine and much more. There were magnificent churches with art treasures "on this earth unparalleled." He observed "Satin and silk, Jewels, rich stones and Diamonds by the Gallon" until his mind was "choked, glutted and satisfied to see no more." Although he observed signs of a "savage nation awakening to the delights of civilization," he feared that Russia was "yet too fond of tinselly and Jewels to be entirely free."[16]

Before leaving St. Petersburg for Moscow and the coronation, Oglesby expanded his circle of acquaintances to include former Connecticut governor Thomas H. Seymour, the chief American diplomat in Russia, who had the title of minister because Young America refused to acknowledge "old-world" diplomatic ranks such as ambassador. In spite of the minister's influence, Oglesby found to his disgust that passports to Moscow could not be obtained without lengthy delays relieved only by "blatant bribery." "You must be fleeced" was the motto of the Russian bureaucrats. He concluded that "of all the countries in the world this must be the most venial and corrupt." Venality notwithstanding, Oglesby took a certain pleasure in his elevated status. He was in intimate company with governors, diplomats, and celebrities. In addition, the "beautiful Mrs. Colt" allowed Oglesby to see the opulent gifts that had been bestowed upon her famous husband by the sovereigns of Europe.[17]

On August 26 (August 13 by the Russian calendar), Oglesby took the night train to Moscow on Russia's only railroad. He quickly toured the Kremlin, where he carefully observed and measured the big bell, the big tower, and the great churches within the walls. Oglesby was among those crowded along the parade route to see the grand procession into Moscow led by the czar and czarina.[18]

"By mere circumstances" (and his friendship with the diplomats), Oglesby obtained a ticket to the Kremlin on the day of the coronation. The royal couple passed within five feet of the traveler from Decatur, Illinois, on their way into the Cathedral of the Assumption. Although Oglesby was willing to wait eight hours for a chance to feast his "eyes on the vain glory and shallow pomp" of the ceremony, he did penitence when he returned to his "virtuous couch and dwelt upon the vanity of all Earthly greatness" at the end of the day. Oglesby did not realize that he had witnessed the coronation of the Russian who would become the "Czar Emancipator" of the serfs in 1861, nor could he have imagined how closely he would be associated with Lincoln, the emancipator of the slaves in 1863.[19]

After again enduring the obligatory "formalities and expected bribes" required to begin his journey back to Berlin, Oglesby was delighted to leave Moscow. His new friends said farewell from the stagecoach station. Minister Seymour presented him with "fine gold and silver wristband holders," and Colonel Colt offered his own coat and a bottle of brandy for the September journey. Oglesby accepted the brandy and began the twelve-day trip to Berlin in an eight-passenger coach. Along the way, he felt "melancholy" as he reflected on Napoleon's retreat after he had witnessed the burning of Moscow from nearby Sparrow Hill. When crossing the Dnieper River, the future major general reflected on Napoleon's great losses at that crossing. When passing Brest, the last city on the old line between Russia and Poland, he pronounced a summary judgment on Russia: "They have no Laws, no justice, no honesty, no improvements, no common sense, no liberty, but they have a Czar, an army, vodka and lice, no vivacity, no morals but laziness and bigotry."[20]

Nor did he have much sympathy for Poland and her inability to maintain independence. "I could not feel free to admire the sons of a nation who were too anxious for counsel and too weak for war" he wrote. He described Warsaw as "the old capitol of that once proud republic, now the humble dependent of a vast and cruel empire, unfit to hold its own destiny." Still, Oglesby found the Polish people "gay, cheerful, kind, and polite." The young women he thought especially pretty in their Paris fashions. As he bade farewell to "this smiling and weeping city of the past," he looked forward to a lengthy stay in "good old Germany."[21]

Oglesby arrived back in Berlin late on September 24, "glad to lay down the carpet and the rags." He immediately looked up his old friends John Chestnut and Minister Vroom and committed himself to stay in Berlin to further his education in language, culture, literature, and government—not to the exclusion of drinking and courting. He established himself in a $9 a month apartment and bought a new suit of clothing. He was thus prepared to sally "out for a good night of recreation" with the foreign community at Minister Vroom's legation. There he found two especially charming young women, a Miss Benson from England and a Miss Hamline from Austria. Oglesby said he was "kept from actually falling in love with either" because each was irresistible. On another occasion he accompanied Laura Kunstler, the young daughter of his German tutor, to a legation dinner.[22]

Oglesby's quest for German language competency was also frustrated. He quickly committed himself to sixty days of German instruction but soon complained, "I was not intended for a close student, it is foreign to my nature to bear confinement." He did, however, continue his lessons with his tutor, Herr Kunstler, who sometimes combined language lessons with tours of museums and other cultural institutions. Yet Oglesby completed at least seventy-five lessons and progressed past 264 pages of a German textbook, *Ollendorf's Method.*[23]

On the cultural and literary front, Oglesby attended the opera, ballet, art galleries, and a lecture on "universal geography" at the University of Berlin by Professor Karl Ritter. He also obtained a copy of Thomas Arnold's three-volume *History of Rome* from the royal library of Berlin thanks to the intervention of Minister Vroom, spent a "day reading Byron," read seventeen chapters of Acts from the Bible, and began making arrangements to travel to Palestine.[24]

He practiced his writing skills by penning letters for publication to the *Decatur Gazette*. He also wrote lengthy descriptions to friends and relatives. He quoted Lord Bacon as saying, "What is worth seeing is worth noting" while conceding that it might be an exercise in "transferring to foolscap all that enters a fool's head."[25]

Oglesby's education in government was enhanced by visits to the German courts, study of the Prussian constitution, and even by participating in the annual wild boar hunt led by King Frederick William IV ("what a magnificent farce the whole affair was"). Political news from the United States was made available through Minister Vroom, who, like most of the diplomatic corps, was a Democrat. Oglesby was probably not shy about expressing his anti-slavery views around Democrats and southerners, but the heated discussions often ended with "a few bowls of Bourbon" or, as on the occasion of the receipt of the news that Democrat James Buchanan had been elected president, with Oglesby buying the champagne. On Oglesby's last day in Berlin, he concluded, "I knew Berlin so well, I have spent many pleasant hours here and yet, I have been a good student."[26]

Oglesby left Berlin on December 30, 1856, on a quest for Christian faith in the Holy Land. On New Year's Day, in a contemplative mood, he described himself in his diary as a "partial unbeliever." He wrote that he would like to have the honest doubt removed. "I might say I am a Christian, the world might believe and respect me, but God would not," he confessed. He expressed "exquisite delight" on seeing Raphael's Madonna in the Dresden gallery. It was, he wrote, "the only Christian representation I have ever seen worth a moment's patience." His democratic impulse seemed to conflict with his religiosity, however, when he declared himself "out of all patience" with a people who allowed themselves to be taxed "to death and nearly naked [while] ardently admiring and loudly proclaiming their love for such perfect Hell" in support of ostentatious galleries.[27]

The young crusader pressed on to Egypt, making brief stops in the important cities of Europe long enough to visit art galleries and sample opinions. He surveyed Prague and Vienna in a week. In Vienna he looked up Minister Henry Rootes Jackson of Georgia and had an "exciting conversation touching diplomacy, religion, morals, governments, great men" and the Mexican War, a shared experience. He reached the port city of Trieste on January 10 and embarked for Alexandria, stopping at Corfu, where he again celebrated New Year's on the old-style Greek calendar. During his six-day voyage he imagined himself "floating along the classic shores of ancient Greece" and noted with interest the bay where Admiral Nelson had won a great naval victory. He had planned to enjoy the trip by reading Byron but confessed that he was "too seasick for romance or poetry."[28]

Oglesby's uneasy condition at sea was replaced by a jolt of confusion when he landed at Alexandria, Egypt, on January 17. He described the "bluster, clatter, pushing, jamming, grabbing and snatching" that travelers had to endure in a setting in which "a dozen outlandish tongues" were spoken. He had never seen such a city in which people of all nations intermingled. There were people of "all colors, from jet black to pale white, all features, from oval to aquiline, all sizes from giants to pygmies" at the crossroads of civilization, he observed. He was impressed at the sight of the two celebrated obelisks, Pompey's Pillar, the catacombs near Alexandria, and the Pyramids near Cairo. Oglesby was simultaneously overwhelmed and scandalized by "these monster monuments" that impressed "never ceasing awe" on the beholder, and yet his republicanism forced him to denounce the monuments as "the works of vain, foolish and hated men." He had only limited sympathy for the more modern British rulers of Egypt, who seemed "to rule where ever they go in many of their customs and whilst they are generally wise they are always exacting to a people they meet or conquer."[29]

Oglesby next embarked on the Holy Land portion of his journey. He joined Chauncy I. Hawley of New York City in hiring a sailboat and crew to reach the ancient city of Thebes up the Nile River, a four-hundred-mile journey that took forty-two days and cost $90. They delighted in observing the tombs and palaces of the great pharaohs, the statue of Memnon, and various sphinxes. The young American followed his usual practice of collecting souvenirs; at the Temple of Karnak he purchased "a mummy hand and cloth scarves." Oglesby read his Bible and found both verification and doubt. He was delighted to find "leeks and onions" growing in locations identified in the Old Testament, but when reading Job he mused that if God had punished such a "just and perfect man," what might he inflict on "the ungodly"?[30]

Oglesby returned to the comfort of Cairo's Hotel d'Orient to plan his next major adventure, a trip across the desert to Palestine via Sinai and Petra. Before leaving the Cairo area, he rode a donkey to see the Pyramids and the Sphinx. In front of the pyramid of Cheops he was awed but prideful that he shared the same view that "Abraham, Jacob and Joseph, Moses and Aaron, Alexander, Caesar, Ptolemy, Jesus, and Napoleon" as well as Mahomet had shared.[31]

On March 20, 1857, Oglesby joined a group of nine young men who, led by the Reverend Dr. Coleman, set out on a sixty-day expedition across the Sinai to Palestine. Oglesby thought the $337 price that each except Coleman had to pay was exorbitant. Neither was he delighted with sharing Coleman's costs, tent, and strict observation of the Sabbath, but the arrangement was the best available to him. The staff consisted of a dozen or so men and thirty-three camels. Coleman and the young adventurers lived "as well as at the best hotels." Oglesby admitted that he was "ashamed of so much luxury," but his privileged status allowed him to "sleep on the narrow strip of land dividing the two great continents; the lands once peopled by Shem and Ham" [the sons of Noah, alleged founders of all races after the great flood], swim across the Red Sea, and collect a bottle of water from the Fountain of Marah where Moses led the Israelites. The best he could do in defense of his republican principles was to warn off a fellow traveler who was in the habit of beating a dragoman by reminding him that he owned only a tenth of the man and that he should not lay a hand on the other nine-tenths of his body.[32]

A major goal of the expedition was to ascend Mount Sinai as Moses had done. The problem was to identify the right mountain, and Oglesby had little faith that Coleman—or anyone else—knew its location. Standing on Jebel Musa, the traditional location, Oglesby demurred that he "felt more foolish than serious, no feeling of emotion, more doubt than faith." Nevertheless, he and Coleman slept on the mountain and read the Ten Commandments as the sun rose the next morning. Oglesby at least was rewarded by the most beautiful sunrise he had ever beheld. After collecting a piece of granite as a souvenir, he climbed to St. Catherine's Convent, where the altar was represented as being built over the burning bush, which had not been consumed (Exodus 3:2). "I could not feel equal to the moment," Oglesby noted, "being haunted with doubt as to the spot." Skeptical though he was, he purchased three boxes of manna, which a guide represented as being gathered from a tree but was, he suspected, baked in the convent. He next climbed Mt. Horeb, the most commanding of the mountains, and again recited the Ten Commandments as insurance that he had been on Mt. Sinai. Again he bought some stone chips and a "shrub" called the "rod of Moses."[33]

On April 18, 1857, Oglesby began a journey northward out of the port of Aqaba, following the "questionable paths of Moses and Mahomet toward the land of Edom" with a caravan of Bedouins guiding a score of foreigners. It was the anniversary of his leaving Decatur, but Oglesby soon judged the extended trip worthwhile. The prize was Petra, "the red-rose city, half as old as time," which had been "rediscovered" in 1812 by a Swiss adventurer disguised as a Bedouin. The guide warned off the travelers, "but young America," as Oglesby put it, "would defy him." Some of the more adventurous souls decided to "fight" for the "sight" if necessary. Oglesby was touched by the approach to Petra. "I felt all that I could feel that the solitude of nature, crowned by so many tender and rugged aspects could compel me to devotion of her God," he wrote. The ancient city was "shut in on all sides by towering mountains, beautiful as rainbows." In approaching the "rose temple," the interlopers had to pay baksheesh to armed ruffians but were allowed to view El Khazneh, "hewn out of sold rock, equaling in finish the finest temples of Egypt or Europe." It was, Oglesby concluded, "the most thrilling sight of my life."[34]

After making a quick examination of Aaron's tomb, arms drawn to ward off Arabs pointing guns at them, the party beat a hasty retreat "to prevent everything from being stolen" or extracted by baksheesh. They took a north-west course out of the wilderness through the area where the Israelites had wandered for forty years. Mindful of history, Oglesby wrote that his group "reached Canaan" after only forty days in the desert. On April 28 they reached Hebron, where "Abraham Isaac and Jacob are buried," reputedly in the "cave of Machpelah."[35]

Oglesby's crusade next took him to the holy cities of Jerusalem and Beth-lehem. He would daily tread on Mt. Zion, the palace of Pontius Pilate, the Garden of Gethsemane, the Mount of Olives, the Church of the Holy Sepulcher, and the "grotto of the Nativity." The latter he pronounced "a pious fraud." He ventured out of Jerusalem to the Dead Sea, where the water tasted "like strong lye" and in which it was impossible to sink. At the Jordan River ford, traditional location of Jesus's baptism, he extracted a bottle of water "to carry home for baptism should I ever become a good Christian" (he was never baptized, but the water would be used in the baptism of his children). His benediction on Jerusalem suggests that the young American's views were not so different from those of earlier crusaders. "Oh Jerusalem, when shall I see the towers again and dwell amid the holy groves now desecrated by the impious herds filling thy streets and desecrating thy walls," he wrote in his diary.[36]

From May 17 to 28, 1857, Oglesby traveled northwest to Mt. Carmel and Haifa, east to "the village of Jesus—Nazareth" and the Sea of Galilee, and northeast to Damascus. If, as for Paul, conversion lay on the road to Damascus, Oglesby found a detour. He was willing to "drink in the scenery" but unwilling "to imitate the foolish admiration of simple, blind, and devoted pilgrims." He was offended by the paucity of truth in the Holy Land, for "to lie in Palestine is no offense." He also noted the hypocrisy of Christian convents that had become hotels, "more profitable than converting hungry Arabs for Christ." He found it difficult to believe that "everything in Palestine, according to monkish tradition, was done in a cave or grotto." It was in Damascus that he parted company with his Christian travel mentor Doctor Coleman. Typical of the partisan Oglesby, who made a career of disagreeing vigorously while retaining friendships both political and religious, he concluded that they would be "good friends for ever."[37]

Weary of "Adams ale" and longing for "a little old Bourbon," Oglesby headed for Beirut and passage to the Mediterranean Sea. On June 10 he embarked for Constantinople, where he was enchanted by yet another vice: "ladies of harem" who possessed "such inexpressible beautiful faces, such heaven-like expression, such perfect gentleness and unresisting submission to fate." "Oh!" Oglesby continued, "such capital eyes, such lips, such esthetic lips, bathed in the mildest and sweetest complexions." But the women were the sultan's fate not Oglesby's, so he had to settle for a Turkish bath and continued sightseeing at the Mosque of St. Sophia and on an excursion through the Bosporus to the Black Sea.[38]

To Oglesby's delight, Athens, the birthplace of democracy, also offered "several very pretty Greek ladies." The city had the Acropolis and Parthenon, clean and paved streets, and courteous people who "act like free men." On July 3 he took his leave of Athens and sailed to Naples. Seasick though he was as he sailed around "the old Republic" of Greece, he felt constrained to toast the eighty-first anniversary of American Independence, "which gave birth to the best nation under the canopy of Heaven" as the "grandest and freest of all nations." In Messina, Sicily, he called upon the American consul, as he had done in Athens and Constantinople, to talk politics in preparation for a reentry into the United States. "The discreet and amiable" Democratic consul offered a "homily on the Whigs and No-nothings" made tolerable by the sharing of "a bottle of old Bourbon, the nectar of my native state," Oglesby joked. Winding his way up the Italian peninsula, he revisited the German states, Paris, and the Netherlands and sailed back to America from Liverpool, arriving in December 1857 after a twenty-month adventure.[39]

When he returned from the mysterious East, Oglesby found willing audiences awaiting his firsthand account. Central Illinois citizens had followed the published letters Oglesby had sent to editor James Shoaff of the *Decatur Gazette* from Liverpool, Warsaw, Berlin, Alexandria, Thebes, Mount Sinai, Hebron, Paris, and Rotterdam. The *Illinois State Journal* noted his return to New York on December 3, 1857, and the editor reported having "had the pleasure of shaking hands of our old friend R. J. Oglesby of Decatur" in Springfield on December 23. The *Journal's* Decatur correspondent reported on February 24, 1858, "Hon. Richard J. Oglesby (or, as he is more familiarly called, 'Dick') has been favoring our citizens with a series of lectures about 'things he saw' during a recent sojourn amid the classic scenes and associations of the far, far East."[40]

Using his diary as a source, Oglesby carefully wrote an extended account of his travels, but he seldom referred to the manuscript while holding forth. Rather "Dick" developed an informal style that was very agreeable to audiences. There seemed to be no limit to the public's appetite for his talks, which were filled with asides and a few profanities. By Gen. U. S. Grant's account, Oglesby once offered a one-hour lecture on the Holy Land but took two and one-half hours for a "little preliminary description of his adventures in Europe." The enthusiastic audience returned the next night, but he did not progress past his adventures in Russia. When they demanded his return for a third night, he discussed Egypt and the Pyramids. After three hours had elapsed, he looked at his watch and exclaimed, "Well, here it is eleven o'clock, and I'll be damned if I have got to the Holy Land." According to Vice-President Adlai E. Stevenson, Oglesby encouraged give-and-take. In one case he remembered a questioner who asked, "Who built the Pyramids?" Oglesby quickly responded, "Oh damn it, I don't know who built them. I asked everybody I saw in Egypt and none of them knew."[41]

Lincoln heard Oglesby's Holy Land speech in Bloomington and remarked to Judge David Davis, "Here we see a young man who has been at the Pyramids, and stood on the ground where the Messiah and Abraham stood, and this seems to bring the human family a little closer together."[42] It was a favorable comment that presaged Oglesby's political involvement with the Rail-Splitter.

The trip abroad changed Oglesby's life and enhanced his career. His Holy Land speech became his hallmark for the rest of his life, a nonpolitical address that contributed to his political persona. The success of his travel talks advanced his confidence and his technique in making political speeches, and he became one of the most celebrated political stump speakers in the Midwest. If Oglesby was inhibited by his limited education and lack of culture, his grand tour provided him with the trappings of an educated person. His quest for religious faith, however, was burdened by unresolved doubt. His travelogs gained him instant fame and status, and his law practice would thrive. He became one of Decatur's most eligible bachelors—a situation soon to be resolved.

## Notes

1. A useful definition of "Young America" may be found in Richard B. Morris, ed., *Encyclopedia of American History* (New York: Harper and Row, 1965), pp. 215–16.

2. William E. Gienapp, *The Origins of the Republican Party, 1852–56* (New York: Oxford University Press, 1987), p. 122.

3. *Collected Works,* vol. 4, p. 67; Abraham Lincoln to RJO, Sept. 8, 1854, in *The Collected Works of Abraham Lincoln, Supplement, 1832–1865,* ed. Roy P. Basler (Westport: Greenwood Press, 1974), p. 24.

4. *Journal,* Oct. 21, 1854, p. 2, col. 1.

5. RJO to Richard Yates, Jan. 27, 1855, Yates Collection, ISHL; Lincoln to Elihu B. Washburne, Feb. 9, 1855, in *Collected Works,* vol. 2, p. 306.

6. Abraham Lincoln to Joshua F. Speed, Aug. 24, 1855, in *Collected Works,* vol. 2, p. 321; Otto R. Kyle, "Mr. Lincoln Steps Out: The Anti-Nebraska Editors' Convention," *Abraham Lincoln Quarterly* 5 (March 1948): 25–31. William J. Usrey is listed as a corporal in Company C, Fourth Regiment (Richmond, p. 128); see also the *Journal,* Feb. 27, 1856, p. 2, col. 2.

7. Kyle, "Mr. Lincoln Steps Out," pp. 32–35; *Collected Works,* vol. 2, p. 333; Paul Selby,

"Editorial Convention, February 22, 1856," *Transactions of the McLean County Historical Society,* 3 vols. (Bloomington: Pantagraph Printing and Stationery Co., 1900), vol. 3, pp. 30–43.

8. Douglas's European trip of 1853 is described in Robert W. Johannsen, *Stephen A. Douglas* (New York: Oxford University Press, 1973), pp. 382–86. Banton asserts (p. 87) that Douglas told Oglesby about his trip in the fall of 1855. That Oglesby took the trip to overcome his lack of education is suggested in E. T. Coleman, "The Story of Decatur," *Decatur Review,* Dec. 23, 1923, p. 3, col. 5. Another possible motive was given by Judge Thad D. Loomis soon after Oglesby's death. Loomis, who was with Oglesby during the gold rush, revealed that Oglesby had expected to marry when he returned from the goldfields, "but his sweetheart had been united to some one else . . . and through disappointment, he made a trip to Asia and the Holy Land." "Oglesby as a Gold Hunter," *Journal,* May 1, 1899, p. 2, cols. 3–4.

9. Richard J. Oglesby, "Journal of Trip to Europe and the Middle East, April 18, 1856–July 10, 1857," Oglesby MSS. The "Trip Diary" used here was apparently edited by Emma G. Oglesby, Oglesby's second wife, and their daughter Felicite in 1900. Some members of the family seem to be in possession of some of the original journals. A sample comparison of a typed version of the original and the edited version suggests that the edited version used here is fairly faithful to the substance of the original. Materials that might have embarrassed the governor's wife and daughter were not omitted. The editors seemed more interested in correcting spellings and transcribing Oglesby's original notes than in protecting themselves or him. On occasion, they reduced lengthy or redundant descriptions but tended to keep his strong opinions in the text.

10. Entries for May 15, 28, 1856, "Trip Diary."

11. Entries for June 6, 16, 17, 19, 1856, "Trip Diary."

12. Entries for June 12, 26, 27, 30, 1856, "Trip Diary."

13. Entries for July 2–25, 1856, "Trip Diary."

14. Entries for July 28–31, 1856, "Trip Diary."

15. Entries for Aug. 1–6, 1856, "Trip Diary." Evidence that Oglesby was "portly" comes from photographs and from a May 27, 1881, entry in his diary, wherein he says he weighed two hundred pounds in 1851 and 230 to 240 "most years." The 1881 Diary was written on the unused pages of "General Order Book, April–July 1863," Oglesby MSS.

16. Entries for Aug. 6–13, 1856, "Trip Diary."

17. Entries for Aug. 14–24, 1856, "Trip Diary."

18. Entries for Aug. 25–29, 1856, "Trip Diary."

19. Entries for Aug. 26–29, 1856, "Trip Diary."

20. Entries for Sept. 12–19, 1856, "Trip Diary." Oglesby carried Count Gurowski's *Russia as It Is* through Russia, "much to the terror of my friends and my own gratification," and that may help explain his phobia about that country.

21. Entries for Sept. 19–22, 1856, "Trip Diary."

22. Entries for Sept. 24–Oct.22, 1856, "Trip Diary." Laura Kunstler died at age seventeen in 1858. C. F. Kunstler, Berlin, to RJO, Decatur, May 17, 1858, Oglesby MSS.

23. Entries for Sept. 26, Oct. 14, Dec. 5, 1856, "Trip Diary."

24. Entries for Oct. 5, 9, Nov. 5, 12, 1856, "Trip Diary."

25. Entries for Oct. 16, 20, 1856, "Trip Diary."

26. Entries for Nov. 3, 15, Dec. 3, 30, 1856, "Trip Diary."

27. Entries for Dec. 31, 1856, Jan. 1, 1857, "Trip Diary."

28. Entries for Jan. 2, 5, 8, 12, 14, 17, 1857, "Trip Diary."

29. Entries for Jan. 17, 19, 20, 30, 1857, "Trip Diary."

30. Entries for Jan. 22, 23, 27, Feb. 15, 19, 21, March 2, 8, 9, 1857, "Trip Diary"; Mark A. Plummer, "Robert G. Ingersoll on Leeks and Onions in the Holy Land," *Illinois Quarterly* 43 (Fall 1980): 5–10.

31. Entries for March 9, 11, 12, 18, 1857, "Trip Diary."

32. Entries for March 20, 22, 26, 29, 1857, "Trip Diary." The story of the Fountain of Marah is found in Exodus 15:23. Shem and Ham are identified in William P. Barker, *Everyone in the Bible* (Westwood: Fleming H. Revell, 1966), pp. 120, 319.

33. Entries for April 3, 6, 7, 8, 9, 1857, "Trip Diary."

34. Entries for April 18, 21, 22, 1857, "Trip Diary"; *Everyday Life in Bible Times* (Washington: National Geographic Society, 1967), p. 396.

35. Entries for April 22, 24, 25, 27, 28, 29, 1857, "Trip Diary."

36. Entries for May 2, 3, 7, 10, 11, 17, 1857, "Trip Diary."

37. Entries for May 17, 18, 21, 22, 24, 26, 28, 1857, "Trip Diary."

38. Entries for June 3, 10, 17, 19, 20, 21, 1857, "Trip Diary."

39. Entries for June 25, 28, July 1, 3, 4, 5, 8, 1857, "Trip Diary"; *History of Macon County Illinois* (Philadelphia: Brink, McDonough, 1880), pp. 127–28.

40. *Journal,* Dec. 3, 1857, p. 3, col. 1, Dec. 24, p. 3, col. 1, news dated Feb. 24 published on March 2, 1858, p. 2, col. 2.

41. Wilkie, pp. 13–14; Adlai E. Stevenson, *Something of Men I Have Known* (Chicago: A. C. McClurg, 1909), p. 347.

42. Wilkie, pp. 13–14; Walter B. Stevens, "How Lincoln Introduced Oglesby," *St. Louis Globe-Democrat,* Jan. 24, 1909, from a typed copy in the Sandburg Collection, University of Illinois at Urbana-Champaign.

## 3. The Rail-Splitter

As a young man, Richard Oglesby participated in the Mexican War and the gold rush, observed the crowned heads of Europe, became familiar with the monuments of antiquity, and learned how to be at ease with politicians who had been appointed to diplomatic posts in Europe. Upon his return home, it was his destiny to continue to be involved in the important happenings of history, especially those pertaining to Abraham Lincoln. During the Lincoln-Douglas debates of 1858, Oglesby was a Republican candidate for Congress and among those who shared the platform in the Charleston debate. By the presidential campaign of 1860, Oglesby was a candidate for the Illinois senate. More important, he originated the rail-splitter slogan used for Lincoln during that campaign.

In a letter dated April 20, 1858, Oglesby summarized his activities in Illinois to a friend from Berlin, Peter Vroom, the former governor of New Jersey who had recently returned to that state after serving as U.S. minister to Prussia. He reported that he had reentered law practice and was giving his Holy Land speeches. He also confided that Sen. Stephen A. Douglas was bent upon reelection and might succeed if he would "come a little nearer the line [in opposition to the extension of slavery] but he must and I think will cross over in time." Oglesby said nothing about running for Congress. "I am endeavoring to avoid political excitement," he wrote. He was avoiding political excitement by concentrating on his nonpartisan travel speeches that also served to give him name recognition, a potential political tool. Lincoln may have adopted a similar tactic early in the campaign, because he was also giving a nonpartisan speech on "Discoveries and Inventions."[1]

Two days after Oglesby wrote to Vroom, Abraham Lincoln was present at the Champaign County Circuit Court. Oglesby later recalled that he met with Lincoln in Urbana to discuss political strategy for the fifteen-county Seventh Congressional District of east central Illinois. It was a district that had given the Democrats a five-thousand-vote majority in 1856 and contained many old Henry Clay Whigs from Kentucky and Tennessee. An important question to Lincoln and to a congressional candidate was the issue of slavery and race. Most old Democrats and Whigs were anti-abolitionist, although most also opposed the extension of slavery into Kansas and the territories. Oglesby was a little more candid than Lincoln in his anti-slavery views. According to Oglesby's account, written years later, Lincoln advised moderation by proclaiming, during a walk with Oglesby, "Remember, Dick, to keep close to the People, they are always right and will mislead no one."[2]

Oglesby's trip abroad had begun in 1856, immediately before the formation of the Illinois Republican Party. He returned twenty months later without having worked through the transition from Henry Clay Whig to Republican. Because the Whig Party had disintegrated during Oglesby's absence and because Republicans were viewed as radicals by the old-line Whigs of the district, the party was slow to organize for the congressional race. Thus Oglesby began his congressional campaign as an independent. On May 8, however, the Republican *Illinois State Journal* noted that the *Decatur Chronicle* had announced that Oglesby was a candidate for Congress "subject to the decision of the seventh district Republican Convention." Apparently, he became the Republican candidate by default. On June 16, Oglesby was appointed to the state's Republican resolutions committee as a representative of the Seventh District. It was at the Springfield convention that Lincoln, perhaps ignoring his own advice about following the people, made his immoderate "House Divided" speech, which he would have to mitigate during the Lincoln-Douglas debates, especially in Charleston, the Seventh District's debate site.[3]

By July 1858 Oglesby was actively campaigning to represent the Seventh District in the U.S. Congress. The Democracy (Democrats), according to Republican gossip reported to Lincoln, had "become alarmed at the enthusiasm for Oglesby." Lincoln's correspondent thought that Oglesby might "stand a slight chance of beating" James C. Robinson, a Mexican War veteran from Clark County, should Robinson be nominated. On August 11, the Democratic Seventh Congressional District convention, controlled by Douglas men, did nominate Robinson.[4]

On July 24, 1858, Lincoln challenged Douglas to a series of debates. Douglas agreed to a debate in each of the seven congressional districts where the two had not already debated (thus Chicago and Springfield were excluded). Lincoln thought the terms whereby Douglas would have the first and the last word unfair, but on July 31 he accepted. On August 23 Robinson sent Oglesby a list of seven speaking engagements he had scheduled between August 30 and October 2 and challenged him to be present to discuss "the political issues upon which the present canvass is being made." Oglesby objected that the dates were inconvenient and not in accord with the usual practice of conducting political gatherings in conjunction with the sessions of circuit courts. He did find two or three dates on the list to which he did not object, so several formal debates and some informal ones were held between Oglesby and Robinson. Oglesby later recalled that during one of the debates at Marshall in Clark County, Robinson was prepared to press the burden of being a Republican on Oglesby. Oglesby, finding his "position as an independent candidate was untenable" and "not congenial to my feelings," preempted Robinson's speech by "taking strong Republican ground." He recalled making the decision "without consulting my friends." Oglesby was ever after committed to the Republican Party.[5]

In 1858 the Democratic Party was fractured between Douglas Democrats and Buchanan-administration Democrats, and the Republican Party was struggling to formulate a coalition among Whigs, American (Know-Nothings), and anti-Nebraska Democrats. Some Republicans and Whigs, including Horace Greeley of the *New York Tribune* and Kentucky's Whig senator John J. Crittenden, thought Douglas had come close enough to "the line" (by opposing the plans of James Buchanan's administration to force Kansas into the Union as a slave state) to merit their support. The Republican strategy in Illinois was to encourage a split among Democrats while consolidating the Republican Party. Oglesby had to be brought into line with that strategy. As Henry C. Whitney, one of Lincoln's confidants, wrote to him on July 24, Oglesby "bears down on the Administration too much," and Whitney suggested that Lincoln should "talk to him about it."[6]

If the Democrats could be split while the Republicans captured the center of the political spectrum by consolidating the moderates, victory would be certain. The goal was to hold the moderates, including many old-line Whigs, by down-playing abolitionism and equality and portraying Republicans as the party most likely to prevent the extension of slavery into the territories. Oglesby had an unexpected opportunity to contribute to the consolidation goal while visiting Springfield on August 28. A large meeting of "Republicans, Americans, and Whigs" had been scheduled for the Capitol rotunda to hear Sen. Lyman Trumbull, who "was excused by reason of hoarseness." According to the *Journal*, the Republican organ, "The vacuum was ably and acceptably filled" by Judge John M. Palmer and "Richard J. Oglesby, esquire of Macon, who happened to be in the city, and who was successfully called upon by the audience." Oglesby's speech was described as "spirited and to the point, as was abundantly testified by the hearty cheers."[7]

During September, Lincoln spent considerable time in Oglesby's congressional district. Train connections often brought him through Decatur, and on September 6 he was escorted by a trainload of supporters from Decatur to a meeting in Monticello, probably arranged by Oglesby. Lincoln spoke for three hours. The next morning he spoke to an audience of a thousand in Mattoon. Later in the day in Paris in Edgar County, Lincoln spoke for two hours. The presence of the abolitionist Owen Lovejoy in Paris was inconsistent with Republican strategy, but he was loudly called for after Lincoln's speech. Lovejoy spoke again in the evening to the approbation of the *Chicago Tribune,* which reported that the citizens of Edgar County had discovered that he did not wear "horns and a tail." Oglesby was the featured speaker at the Edgar County courthouse that night. "'Dick' made a slam bang speech about an hour and a half in length," the *Tribune* reported.[8]

Oglesby probably followed Lincoln to Jonesboro for the third Lincoln-Douglas debate, held on September 15 at the southern-most site of the debates and before the smallest crowd, 1,200 citizens. Douglas pictured Lincoln as a "Black Republican," pressed him to admit the equality of the races, and continued to chide him about the "House Divided" speech. Lincoln could not win the election unless he could distance himself from the black Republicans (abolitionists), deny that he believed in the equality of the races, and explain away his prediction that the house (Union) would be divided. Jonesboro, already committed to the Democracy, was not very important, but Charleston and Oglesby's Seventh Congressional District were vital to his election. The election would be determined across central Illinois. If most Republican candidates for the legislature from the Seventh Congressional District, heavily populated with former Kentucky Whigs, could be elected, Lincoln would be victorious in the election for U.S. Senate that would take place in the state legislature in January.[9]

The Charleston debate of September 18 was a spectacle. Both sides agreed that more than twelve thousand attended the event at the fairgrounds. The Charleston site excelled in what one paper called the "display of the etceteras of a great campaign." Among the "etceteras" were processions accompanying both Lincoln and Douglas, who came from the rail junction at Mattoon. The streets were overhung with "national flags, banners, and all manner of artistic devices which could be pressed into political service." One banner "sketched an emigrant wagon, drawn by two yoke of oxen" and was labeled "Abe's entrance into Charleston thirty years ago." People arrived "on horseback and muleback, in wagons, in freight trains and on foot." The two sides sponsored parades composed of "carriages, horsemen, bands of music" and a "mammoth car" covered with slogans: "LINCOLN, OGLESBY, MARSHALL, AND CRADDOCK," "We Link-on to Lincoln," and "our mothers were for Clay." "Thirty-two splendidly dressed young ladies," each representing a state of the union, adorned the large Republican wagon. One Democratic banner, proudly reported by the *Chicago Times,* read: "This government was made for white men—Douglas for Life."[10]

Perhaps heeding his own advice to "keep close to the people," Lincoln decided to face the equality question head-on at Charleston. Here he had the advantage of speaking the first and the last words under the arrangement whereby the debaters alternately opened the debates by speaking for one hour, followed by an hour-and-a-half answer and then a half-hour rebuttal. Lincoln knew he could not win if Douglas forced him to admit the equality of the races. He immediately confronted the question in his homespun way by noting that "an elderly gentlemen called upon me to know whether I was really in favor of producing a perfect equality between the negroes and white people." Lincoln then answered that question: "I will say then that I am not, nor ever have been in favor of bringing about in any way the social and political equality of the white and black races (applause)." He also said he opposed "making voters or jurors of negroes" or allowing intermarriage between the races. He went on to assert, "There is a physical difference" between the races "which I believe will for ever forbid the two races living together on terms of social and political equality." He did, however, "not perceive that because a white man is to have the superior position the negro should be denied everything." Every man was entitled to the fruits of his labor. Lincoln joked that Douglas did not "understand that because I do not want a negro woman for a slave I must necessarily want her for a wife (cheers and laughter). I can just let her alone."[11]

Douglas may have feared that Lincoln had preempted his position on white superiority and quickly accused him of having different principles in different parts of the state. Republican principles were "jet black" in the North (where Lincoln had said much about the Declaration of Independence), a "decent mulatto" in the center, and "almost white" in the South, he charged. Douglas then raised the bidding by proclaiming that the government was "made by white men, for the benefit of white men and their posterity forever." In his rejoinder, Lincoln invoked a moral aspect by allowing that states should be able to make citizens of blacks, although he opposed the move for Illinois, and noted that Douglas wanted to extend slavery. He complained that Democrats spoke of "negroes as we do of our horses and cattle." Lincoln answered the "House Divided" charges by explaining that he expected the "ultimate extinction" of slavery—not soon, but "in God's own good time."[12]

Oglesby was among the honored guests who shared the platform with Lincoln and Douglas in Charleston. Also among the platform guests was Orlando B. Ficklin, a Democrat who had served in Congress with Lincoln during the Mexican War. When asked to recall the event to the Lincoln biographer Isaac Arnold, Oglesby remembered not the question of the equality but the dramatic incident during the rebuttal when "Lincoln snatched Orlando B. Ficklin by the coat collar and dragged him to the front of the stand" to deny that Lincoln had voted against appropriating money for supplies for the army in the Mexican War. Ficklin, surprised by the move, recalled that Lincoln had voted for a resolution declaring the Mexican War "unnecessarily and unconstitutionally commenced by the President." Lincoln had, in fact, demanded of President James K. Polk that he identify the "spot" on which American blood had been shed on American soil. But in Charleston he contended that he had voted to supply the army as often as had Ficklin or Douglas. To prove his patriotism, he was anxious to erase the "spotty Lincoln" charge, and he chose that dramatic way to accomplish the goal.[13]

Oglesby's descriptions of Lincoln and Douglas at Charleston, given to Arnold twenty-five years later, are partisan and clouded by the passage of time, but they may be partially corroborated. In 1883 Oglesby wrote that "Douglas was manifestly tiring" and "petulant," whereas "Lincoln was calm—grave and impressive like one who already feels the goal of ambition attained." Only three days after the debate, Oglesby wrote to his law partner that Lincoln's speech was a "most full and complete triumph" over Douglas. The defeat, he added, had taken its toll on Douglas, who "writhed and winced and left the stand in bad humor." Lew Wallace, the future author of *Ben Hur,* was also in attendance. A Douglas Democrat at the time, he nonetheless noted that Douglas's "face [was] darkened by a deepening scowl, and he was angry." Although Wallace initially laughed at Lincoln's appearance, he soon noted that "he was easy and perfectly self-possessed" and concluded that "Mr. Lincoln's speech was a defense of Freedom."[14]

The "etceteras" of the day were far from over. At night the excitement continued at the courthouse, where a quartet of Democratic office-seekers, including Oglesby's congressional opponent James Robinson, held forth at seven o'clock. Oglesby's contemporary account, labeled "private to our mutual friends," describes how "Alone I began a speech in the yard to two hundred faithful. In thirty minutes I had five hundred and in one hour, a thousand." Soon, according to Oglesby's letter to his law partner, the Democratic crowd had left the courthouse, "and I felt that four out of five were for me. . . . It was intensely exciting and I spoke for two hours and ten minutes" as "the crowd screamed 'go on, go on,' and I did so, four glasses of red water took me through." The *Tribune* correspondent was almost as flattering. The Republicans, he said, had organized a meeting four times as large as the Democrats "and were being addressed by Hon. R. J. Oglesby, amid a storm of hurrahs." Oglesby, the reporter wrote, "continued speaking in a powerful strain for about two hours, when the meeting adjourned." Thereafter "the boys" "went and serenaded Mr. Lincoln." Another noncontemporary account asserts that after the rally on the square, Lincoln, Oglesby, John P. Usher, H. P. H. Bromwell, and other Republican leaders gathered at the Charleston home of Thomas Marshall for a conference and "jollification."[15]

After the Charleston debate, Lincoln continued his speaking engagements, often on the heels of Douglas, and the men engaged in three more formal debates at Galesburg, Quincy, and Alton. Lincoln spoke in Sullivan, in Oglesby's district, on September 20 as he continued to focus on the central part of the state. His last campaign speech was on election eve in Decatur, "near his first home in Illinois" where he had split rails and helped build a log cabin.[16]

Meanwhile, Oglesby continued his campaign, sometimes in debates with Robinson or other Democrats, but more often he was "on the stump" alone. He worked the southern counties vigorously in an attempt to reduce the Democratic majority in the portion of his district where Robinson's forces were focusing on Oglesby's Republicanism and abolitionism. In his description of his campaign through Clark County, he wrote that he made eight speeches even though the speeches provoked a swollen throat. He moved on to Majority Point in Cumberland County, where he attracted a crowd of three hundred and spoke for two and a half hours. The *Illinois State Journal* of October 27 noted that Oglesby spoke at Vandalia and was answered by Capt. John Post of Decatur. Years later, Oglesby was fond of telling about his campaign encounter with Robinson in Louisville in Clay County. While Robinson was addressing a crowd, Oglesby borrowed a fiddle from an Irishman and began to play the "Arkansas Traveler." People turned from candidate Robinson and began to dance. Robinson concluded his remarks quickly and "pulled off his coat and commenced dancing with the vim of a dervish." Oglesby thought that Robinson had thereby "recaptured" many of the voters.[17]

The election results showed that Douglas and Robinson had captured enough old-line Whig voters, while minimizing losses to Buchanan Democrats, to be elected. When the new legislature met to choose a U.S. senator, Douglas beat Lincoln by a 54 to 46 count; he had come close enough to "the line" to capture many "Pharisaical old Whigs in the central counties." Oglesby lost to Robinson by a count of 13,588 to 11,760. S. G. Baldwin, the Buchanan candidate, received only thirty-seven votes. Oglesby carried the northern tier of counties in his district, including Logan (Lincoln), his own Macon (Decatur), and Piatt (Monticello) but failed to overcome the Democratic majorities in "Egypt." Lincoln and Oglesby's political house was still divided.[18]

Nevertheless, Republican newspapers found ways to rationalize their defeat by claiming a statistical and moral victory. The sum of the votes for the Republican legislators had been about four thousand more than those polled by the Douglas Democrats, but hold-over state senators and under-represented Republican districts allowed Douglas's reelection by the legislators. The *Chicago Tribune* was quick to note that Republican gains had been made, and it gave Edgar County as an example of how a Democratic district could be captured. "The event has shown what can be done by such men as Richard Moseley, Thos. A. Marshall, R. J. Oglesby, and Abraham Lincoln," the editors asserted. In the previous congressional election in the Seventh District, the Republican candidate had lost by 3,116 votes, whereas Oglesby lost by only 1,828 in 1858. Lincoln emerged from the campaign with a national reputation as a result of his challenge to the more prominent "Little Giant," and Oglesby's reputation as a stump speaker was greatly enhanced by his performance in the campaign.[19]

While in Europe, Oglesby had lamented: "Thirty-two years old, and still unmarried! And so far from home! and so dull the prospect." When he returned to Decatur he still continued to live out of a suitcase, often with his sisters. He boarded at various Decatur hotels. As a prominent lawyer, politician, and orator, his prospects for marriage were no longer dull, however, and he wanted the stability of a family. On March 24, 1859, he married Anna Elizabeth White, with whom he had corresponded while he was overseas.[20]

On the day after Christmas 1859, Oglesby again wrote to Peter Vroom to report on the changes in his life, especially on his marriage. He had been, he marveled, "led by a silken cord to the altar of Heaven and there before his old friends, in a few minutes metamorphosed . . . into a married man . . . and now we are three."[21]

His bride, Anna Elizabeth White, was born on December 6, 1835, in Bainbridge, Ohio, the daughter of Joseph and Mary Ann White. The Whites were a prominent Decatur family, and Anna was described as "one of the belles of the city" when the husky Oglesby came calling. Richard and Anna were married by the Rev. Jonathan Staugher in the White home. Oglesby had withdrawn $60 in gold from his bank "for wedding day festivities," and a four-week honeymoon to Kentucky and Georgia followed. Richard Junior was born on December 19, 1859. Oglesby's life had changed drastically. He reported to Vroom that "he had been seen trudging along under loads of Tin Pans, Cooking Stores, Fruits, Fowls and Fishes and many other Trinkets necessary to regulate a Domestic institution so as to do what the world calls 'keeping house'." Anna's father may have contributed to the purchase of a Decatur house for the couple, but, Oglesby concluded, "I am very glad to have a home but will feel better when it is paid for."[22]

There was also important action on the political front. Richard Oglesby was among a coterie of "Original Lincoln Men" who pushed Lincoln toward the presidency in 1859 and 1860. Most were central Illinois lawyers and politicians who knew Lincoln from the Eighth Judicial Circuit and from the new Republican Party. Jesse Fell, a speculator and founder of the *Bloomington Pantagraph* and Illinois State Normal University, had been in his native Pennsylvania during the Lincoln-Douglas debates and had traveled widely thereafter. He reported to Lincoln that there was keen interest in knowing more about this Abraham Lincoln, and Fell thought that Lincoln might be the perfect compromise candidate for president. Lincoln countered that he was not well known compared to William Seward, Salmon P. Chase, and others. Fell argued, however, that Lincoln's lack of a record could be turned to advantage: "What the Republican party wants, to insure success in 1860, is a man of popular origin, of acknowledged ability, committed against slavery aggressions, who has no record to defend and no radicalism of an offensive character to repel [the voters]."[23]

Fell began to serve as Lincoln's corresponding secretary. He recruited many others who were equally enthusiastic about pushing Lincoln for the presidency. From McLean County, Judge David Davis, who was Lincoln's old friend from the circuit and would later become his unofficial campaign manager, was enlisted, as well as Leonard Swett, William H. Hanna, and William Orme. Fell also recruited Lawrence Weldon from Dewitt County, John M. Palmer of Carlinville, Norman B. Judd of Chicago, Stephen T. Logan of Springfield, and Richard J. Oglesby of Decatur. At about the same time, a caucus was held in the office of Secretary of State O. M. Hatch in Springfield to encourage Lincoln to make the run for president. He professed to doubt his electability but acceded to their wishes.[24]

Fell also solicited an autobiography from Lincoln that was only six hundred words long. It modestly concluded by quoting the ending often given in legal notices concerning horses, cows, and other animals strayed or stolen: "no other marks or brands recollected." In an attached note Lincoln also modestly wrote, "There is not much to it, for the reason, I suppose, that there is not much to me. If any thing be made of it, I wish it be modest, and not go beyond the material." But Fell, as others of his supporters throughout the campaign, did "go beyond the material." That material, expanded sixfold, soon appeared in the newspaper of a Pennsylvania friend of Fell's under the heading "Who Is Abraham Lincoln?" The article was widely quoted in other Republican newspapers.[25]

Lincoln and Davis were acutely aware that they needed an Illinois party united behind Lincoln if he were to have a chance for the presidential nomination. On February 9, 1860, Lincoln wrote to Norman B. Judd, the Republican National committeeman who was feuding with Long John Wentworth in the Chicago mayoralty race: "I am not in a position where it would hurt much for me to not be nominated on the national ticket; but I am where it would hurt some for me to not get the Illinois delegates." Referring to the bitter rivalries within the party in Chicago, he warned, "Your discomfited assailants are most bitter against me; and they will, for revenge upon me, lay to the Bates egg in the South, and to the Seward egg in the North, and go far towards squeezing me out in the middle with nothing."[26]

On February 25, 1860, Davis asked Richard Oglesby to go to Chicago to help Wentworth. Oglesby, Davis thought, would make the "sort of speeches [that] would take better than any body else's." Davis believed more was at stake than the election of the mayor: "Why if Wentworth is beaten I would not give a fig for our prospects in Illinois. And if Illinois is lost, the next Presidential election may be lost." Oglesby apparently convinced Davis that he was needed more in Decatur and did not make the trip.[27]

The state Republican nominating convention was scheduled at Decatur for May 9, 1860, and the Macon County Republican Committee placed Richard Oglesby in charge of the arrangements. In that capacity, he solicited $253 from local sources and arranged for the construction of a "wigwam." The temporary structure was devised by stretching a borrowed canvas tent over a street and two vacant lots and supporting it with adjacent buildings and a temporary wooden framework.[28]

Wigwams symbolized popular involvement in politics, and the symbol was understood in the context of both the state nominating convention in Decatur and the subsequent national convention in Chicago. But something more was needed to place Lincoln in the "man of popular origin" image. Oglesby remembered that his and Lincoln's old Whig Party had won their only national victories when they used effective "common man" slogans. "Old Tippecanoe and Tyler Too," for example, had won the "log cabin" campaign of 1840. Oglesby was in search of such a symbol for Lincoln.[29]

A few days before the Decatur convention opened, Oglesby was talking with John Hanks, Lincoln's mother's cousin, who had worked with the candidate-to-be some thirty years before. What kind of work, Oglesby asked, was Lincoln good at? "Well," Hanks replied, "not much of any kind but dreaming, but he did help me split a lot of rails when we made a clearing twelve miles west of here." Oglesby invited Hanks to join him on a buggy ride to the area the next day to see if the fence rails were still in existence. Hanks was sure he could identify them because, he recalled, they had been cut from black walnut and honey locust trees. Hanks surveyed some of the rails in the area, found stumps that appeared to be the right age and kind, and declared the rails to be the same ones he and Lincoln had mauled when Abe was a young man. They attached two fence rails to the undercarriage of Oglesby's buggy and returned to Decatur, where the rails were hidden in Oglesby's barn. Oglesby apparently consulted with a few delegates but not with Lincoln concerning the use of the rails at the nominating convention. As he recalled, his friends had acquiesced to his scheme by saying, "Go ahead. You can't do any harm, even if you do no good." Two days before the convention opened, however, the *Illinois State Journal*'s correspondent "Viator" reported: "Among the sights which will greet your eyes will be a lot of rails, mauled out of Burr Oak and Walnut, thirty years ago by old Abe Lincoln and John Hanks of this county. They are still sound and firm, like the men that made them. Shall we not elect the Rail Mauler President? His rails like his political record, are straight, sound and out of good timber."[30]

Although it was not the custom for candidates to appear at nominating conventions, Lincoln arrived in Decatur on May 8. "I'm most too much a candidate to be here," he said, "but not enough of one to stay away." When the convention opened the next day, three thousand persons crowded into the nine-hundred-seat wigwam. Lincoln positioned himself inconspicuously in the crowd, but Oglesby arose to announce his presence. According to two contemporaries, Oglesby introduced the "Honest Abe" label for the first time. Lincoln was invited to take a seat on the platform. After his six-foot-four frame was passed horizontally over the crowd, the disheveled Lincoln thanked the convention for its enthusiastic reception. But the best was yet to come. During a lull in the ballot-counting for governor, Oglesby again rose and announced, "An old Democrat of Macon county . . . desire[s] to make a contribution to the Convention." On cue, the crowd shouted "receive it," and John Hanks and Isaac Jennings marched in carrying two fence rails with a placard attached that read, in part, "Abraham Lincoln, the Rail Candidate for President in 1860. Two rails from a lot of three thousand made in 1830 by John Hanks and Abe Lincoln."[31]

A fifteen-minute demonstration erupted during which "the [canvas] roof was literally cheered off the building. . . . Rousing cheers and calls for 'Lincoln' brought 'Old Abe' to his feet." He "scanned the rails a moment with a good humored and quizzical expression of countenance" and addressed the convention. "Well, gentlemen, I must confess I do not understand this: I don't think I know any more about it than you do." He allowed that he had helped build a log cabin and split some rails near Decatur, but he could not swear that these were the identical rails. Nonetheless, he was sure he had split some better than the rough-hewn ones presented. The correspondent for the *Illi-*

*nois State Journal* in Springfield editorialized, "As [the cheers finally subsided] many a delegate in a thoughtful mood contrasted the present position of the noble, self-taught, self-made statesman and patriot, whose name is now mentioned in connection with the highest office . . . of the nation, with that of the humble pioneer and railmaker of thirty years ago." The legend of Lincoln the rail-splitter was born.[32]

The enthusiasm carried over to the second day of the nominating convention. John M. Palmer rose to resolve that Lincoln was the choice of the Illinois Republican Party and the delegates should be instructed to support him as a unit at the Republican National Convention in Chicago. The resolution carried unanimously, but many delegates still doubted Lincoln's chances for nomination. Orville Browning, although friendly to Lincoln, believed that chances of success were better for Edward Bates of Missouri, and various Republicans from northern Illinois believed that Seward had the best chance.[33]

In preparation for the Republican National Convention, Lincoln and the committee on delegates were careful to choose persons who represented various segments of the new party. The delegates at large were David Davis, a former Whig and the whip of the Chicago delegation; Norman B. Judd, a former Democrat and the national committeeman who had staged a coup by winning the convention for Chicago; Gustave Koerner, a German American; and Orville Browning, who was briefly identified with the American (Know-Nothing) Party. Oglesby and others protested the inclusion of Browning, who thought that Edward Bates would be more acceptable to the South. But Lincoln correctly judged that Browning should be with the delegation where they could keep an eye on him rather than on the outside. He trusted Browning's sense of obligation to the unit rule, and he may have been looking ahead to the need to bring Bates's Know-Nothing supporters into the party.[34]

The other eighteen delegates were chosen by congressional districts. In Oglesby's Seventh District, Thomas A. Marshall, the incumbent state senator from Charleston, was chosen. Marshall would help persuade the Maine delegates to support Lincoln on the second ballot at Chicago. William P. Dole, an influential former Indianian who would be instrumental in gaining the votes of Indiana and Pennsylvania in Chicago, took the other Seventh District slot. Oglesby went to Chicago as an alternate at large.[35]

David Davis traveled to Chicago on May 12, four days in advance of the convention, and established a headquarters in two rooms of the Tremont Hotel. Soon the rooms were bulging with more than a dozen energetic Lincoln boosters, the majority from central Illinois. Judge Stephen T. Logan, Leonard Swett, and Jesse Dubois were his chief lieutenants; they were aided materially by Joseph Medill and Dr. Charles H. Ray of the *Chicago Press and Tribune.* Lincoln's friends fanned out and lobbied delegates from the other states. The Illinois men were assigned to states in which they had acquaintances. Indiana, convinced that Seward could not carry their state and sparked by implied promises that Caleb B. Smith would be in Lincoln's cabinet and William P. Dole would be commissioner of Indian affairs, committed its twenty-six votes on the first ballot. Davis, Browning, and Koerner were instrumental in attracting Indiana's delegates. Oglesby probably lobbied individual delegates from Indiana and Kentucky, states where he and Lincoln had lived. Later he related, "We worked like nailers."[36]

On May 18, in the Republican wigwam built especially for the convention, "Honest Abe" Lincoln was nominated for president by Norman B. Judd to the "tremendous applause" of Lincoln's home-state supporters who had packed the arena. William Seward, Simon Cameron, Salmon P. Chase, Edward Bates, and others were nominated. Lincoln's nomination was seconded by Caleb B. Smith and by Columbus Delano of Ohio, who introduced the rail-splitter theme into the convention by proclaiming that Lincoln was "the man who can split rails and maul Democrats." Seward's total vote on the first ballot was 173.5 to 102 for Lincoln. Bates, Chase, and Cameron had about fifty each, with 233 needed to win. Pennsylvania, Maine, and other states added votes for Lincoln on the second ballot as momentum shifted toward him. Near the end of the roll call on the third ballot, enough Ohio votes were changed to give Lincoln the nomination over Seward.[37]

The *Chicago Press and Tribune* reported that Republicans, in celebrating their victory, "collected at the several hotels and shouldering rails marched in joyous triumph through our streets to the cheering music of no less than a score of bands." One observer wrote to his father that "the cry is already 'rails, rails, rails.'" Murat Halstead, a reporter for the *Cincinnati Commercial,* described the scene on the night train from Chicago: "At every station where there was a village, until two o'clock, there were tar barrels burning, drums beating, boys carrying rails, and guns, great and small banging away." In Springfield, the nomination was celebrated with a march on Lincoln's home, firing of cannon, ringing of church bells, and a display of fireworks. Men "went all about the city holding their hats up on the end of a rail, and finally marched into the State House and stacked up the rails on the speaker's stand" and listened to speeches until midnight.[38]

Soon, short-lived newspapers such as Charles Leib's *The Rail Splitter, The Rail Mauler,* and *The Pictorial Rail Splitter* were established. Republican newspapers featured poems and campaign songs. The *Press and Tribune* contributed a song emphasizing "Free Labor and Honest Requital" and "Old Abe, the Rail-Splitter" (to be sung to the tune of "The Star-Spangled Banner"):

This spreading of slavery—work of the devil
At a Democrat's hand may seem ever so grand,
But cannot proceed in this rail-splitting land;
For "Honest Old Abe," uneclipsed at his trade,
Is mauling the rails, and the fence will be made.[39]

Chicago's enthusiasm for the rails was infectious, and delegates from across the North returned to their homes to create rail-splitter clubs, rail-splitter floats, and rail-splitter newspapers. The rail-splitter theme was preponderant at Republican gatherings. Often chairs and gavels were represented as having been made from rails split by Lincoln. Rail fences were constructed around Republican meeting places. Rail-splitters, at work, were often featured on campaign floats.[40]

Democrats countered that Lincoln was the hair-splitter, or the Union-splitter, or the vulgar side-splitter. Whether he split rails or not was immaterial. The *Illinois State Register* remembered that Lincoln was good at a side-splitting story, "especially if there is a vein of vulgarity or impurity in it." It quoted him as having said, "D—n it! I wish I had thought of the rails two years ago— I might now be occupying Douglas's seat in the senate." If Democratic newspapers had been privy to Lincoln's request that Superintendent of Public Instruction Newton Bateman read proof on his May 23 nomination acceptance letter, they might have added the infinitive to the list of objects he split. A poem from the *Indianapolis Sentinel* suggested that Lincoln, like rogues in the South, should be ridden out of town on a rail. By contrast, Douglas was "famed for wisdom marked with wit, Far above the man who's honored for a pile of rails he split." The *Register* also reprinted an item from the *Pike County Democrat,* which noted that the rails Lincoln split were black walnut, and queried, "Is everything with which this [Republican] party concerned to be black?"[41]

When Oglesby returned to Decatur from the Republican National Convention, he found that John Hanks had become a national hero and that the demand for "genuine" Lincoln and Hanks rails was creating a problem of supply. Letters requesting "Lincoln rails" came from Republican newspapermen and party leaders across the nation. Oglesby had a small supply of rails that he intended to distribute free of charge, but when it became necessary for John Hanks to pay the owner of the property for additional rails Oglesby established an account that he labeled "Rail acct with John Hanks." He wrote checks labeled "John Hanks Rail money" to Hanks on May 26 and June 16. The Oglesby account contains the notation "John has recd all the money[.] I have had all the trouble." Because Hanks could not write, Oglesby noted that Hanks had authorized him to "make my mark to all certificates of authenticity of the Lincoln Rails." The records show that Oglesby handled only seventy-two rails of certified authenticity, although other enterprising persons were soon manufacturing hundreds of "genuine Lincoln rails."[42]

Oglesby was very active in Lincoln's campaign, both as a speaker and as custodian of the rail-splitter image. The first of many great Republican rallies was held in Springfield on June 7, and Leonard Swett, Richard Yates, John M. Palmer, and Oglesby spoke to enthusiastic crowds. On June 19, Oglesby, as chair of the Macon County Republican Central Committee, called for a July 7 "ratification" meeting in Decatur. Eight thousand people attended, including two hundred of Springfield's youthful Lincoln Club supporters called "Wide Awakes." Sen. Lyman Trumbull, David Davis, and Leonard Swett spoke in the afternoon. Following a mile-long torch-light parade in the evening, Oglesby presented "a gavel made from a rail split by Mr. Lincoln" to the Springfield Wide Awake Club and made a speech characterized by his friends as "short and neat." The opposition newspaper, however, noted that Dick Oglesby spoke long enough to reveal his "Know Nothing proclivities" by criticizing the Catholicism of Douglas's wife Adele. "Poor Dick," they opined in a charge implying Oglesby was a Deist, one often made against Lincoln as well, "if you have no religion of your own it will not do for you to ridicule the religion of others."[43]

When the Democrats started the rumor that Hanks would not vote for Lincoln, a sixteen-hundred-word letter dated on Independence Day was published over John Hanks's name and asserted that he would indeed vote for Lincoln. The letter was copied in Republican newspapers across the country. In his letter, Hanks asserted that he and Lincoln "were associated together as laborers, sometimes flat-boating, sometimes hog-driving, [and] sometimes rail-making" thirty years before and that he had never known "a man so honest under all circumstances for his whole life." He admitted voting for Douglas in 1858 because of old party ties, but he implied that he had been misled. "Now," he was sure, "as long as I have old Abe to lead me I know that I shall never go very far from the right." Hanks added, "Should he be elected President and find any trouble in steering his new boat he has only to remember how we used to get out of hard places by rowing straight ahead. . . . The tallest oaks in the forest have fallen by his giant arms; he still wields a tremendous maul." He concluded, "Though not a very beautiful symbol of honesty I think the rail a fitting one, and mean to present Abe with one of his own should he be elected." Democrats maintained that the letter was so well composed that some "smart Republican" writer must have written it for Hanks. The document, containing Hanks's mark, is in the Oglesby Family Collection at the Illinois State Historical Library in Springfield. The manuscript is in Oglesby's handwriting, and it bears a notation: "The original John Hanks letter written for him as he stood by and expressed his wishes and gave the facts to me—together we got it up and sent it forth in the Memorable campaign of A.D. 1860 [signed] R. J. Oglesby."[44]

The Democrats quickly countered with a letter from Charles Hanks, John Hanks's brother. Addressed to the Decatur Democratic newspaper the *Magnet,* it was reprinted in the Springfield *Illinois State Register* on July 14, 1860. Charles Hanks charged that his brother had "committed himself to the Decatur politician, who is using him as a tool." The letter asserted that although John's name had been signed to the July 4 letter, "He even yet does not know what is in it, much less did he ever write it." Charles Hanks proclaimed that he remembered Lincoln as "a wild harum scarum boy." Others had to do the lazy boy's work, because "Abe would be rollicking around the country[,] neglecting" his ill parents. Charles also asserted that the rails around the old Lincoln log cabin had burned and been replaced at least three times in thirty years. As to Honest Abe's flatboating career, Charles Hanks charged, "Some young fellers had cut a raft to run down from Jimtown, and Abe, for the fun of the thing, went along instead of staying at home and attending to his own work."[45]

John Hanks and Oglesby considered answering Charles Hanks's letter and wrote to Lincoln on August 23 from Decatur. Their seldom-published letter is printed here in full. It and John Hanks's signature are in Oglesby's handwriting:

> Dear Sir I have been thinking about Charles Hankes letter and a thought struck me that I would answer it in some particulars now. I want you to state to me when and where you first saw Brother Charles. My recollection about the matter is that he never saw you until you moved out to this country in 1830. Please write to me and give me your recollections about it. I shall not use your letter, it shall be assured in my keeping as in your own. Let me know how long your acquaintance had been with Charles Hanks. I am on my way up to Bement to a Republican meeting. What is the prospect since the New York union men have united with the Douglas Democracy. We are in fine spirits here. We are all well used at present. Your sincere friend John Hanks

The reference to New York politics was probably beyond the scope of Hanks's understanding, suggesting that Oglesby had done more than serve as his scribe. Lincoln answered the next day, perhaps indicating the priority he gave to Hanks's rail-splitter theme. He stated that he did not recollect living in the same neighborhood with Charles until they came to Illinois. Lincoln cautioned, however, that his letter should not "be made public by any means."

Hanks put his *X* on no more open letters but turned to making personal appearances at the invitation of Oglesby and others.[46]

An example of the Oglesby and Hanks show transpired in Springfield during what the Republican newspaper heralded as "the biggest demonstration ever held in the west." Recalling the 1840 log-cabin campaign, headlines proclaimed "A Political Earthquake! The Prairies on Fire for Lincoln 75,000 Republicans in Council." An "Immense Procession" featuring dozens of Lincoln Wide Awake Clubs, most with marching bands and a multitude of floats, marched past Lincoln's residence on the way to the fairgrounds. Many floats featured men splitting rails. The Menard County delegation displayed a flatboat, representing Lincoln's New Salem experience. At the fairground, five speaker venues were offered. Senator Trumbull, Wisconsin Sen. James Doolittle, Orville H. Browning, and various candidates for Congress spoke at different stands. Oglesby was assigned to speak at the third stand. The *Illinois State Journal* wrote that he "held an immense crowd for hours and made a telling speech, bristling with sharp points." The *Olney Courier* reported that Oglesby used John Hanks's testimony to bolster Lincoln's rail-splitting image by calling him to the stage and inquiring, "Now John Hanks, in the presence of this vast multitude, I ask you, did you not split three thousand rails with Abe Lincoln in Macon County and navigate a flat-boat from New Salem to New Orleans?" Hanks answered, "We certainly did." The reporter gushed that John Hanks had "showed his honest face to the thousands standing on tiptoe to catch a glimpse of it." He had become "a favorite and thousands" pushed to shake "his hard and horny hand." Similar appearances apparently occurred at Bement and elsewhere. John Hanks was becoming a celebrity.[47]

The Springfield political rally continued into the night, with fireworks and an eight-mile-long torch-light procession. Cong. William Kellogg, Trumbull, Doolittle, and Francis P. Blair from Missouri made speeches at the capitol and at the newly constructed Republican wigwam. The desk at the speaker's stand in the wigwam was described as "a novelty." It was made from a large log, smoothed on top, and into it nine wedges had been driven. The rumor was that it was a log that even "Old Abe couldn't split." The desk was supported by mauls. Sometime during the festivities, Oglesby visited Lincoln's home, where Koerner, Browning, and Judd were among the guests.[48]

On July 18 the Republican Party of the Sixteenth State Senate District (Champaign, Dewitt, Piatt, Macon, Moultrie, Christian, Shelby, and McLean counties) had nominated Oglesby as the party's candidate for state senator. The *Chicago Press and Tribune* pictured him as a reluctant candidate but added, "The importunities of the Republicans of the district, predicated upon the belief that Mr. Oglesby would certainly carry it, while success with another candidate would be doubtful, at last overcame his repugnance for the duty, and he accepted the nomination." The *Tribune* allowed that Oglesby, "who gave the Democracy such a fright" in the 1858 congressional campaign, could win the state senate seat by maintaining his margins of victory in the more northern counties that constitute the Sixteenth District. The newspaper also asserted that "Oglesby's efficiency as a canvasser promises large gains in other parts of the District." The *Tribune* was especially interested in capturing a majority in the state legislature because its candidate, U.S. Senator Trumbull, was up for reelection by the legislature and a close race was expected. The Democracy countered with the nomination of William H. Coler of Champaign.[49]

Oglesby and Trumbull worked the Sixteenth District exhaustively. Trumbull's appointments for speeches between July 27 and August 4 included Bloomington, Clinton, Monticello, Urbana, Sullivan, Shelbyville, and Pana. In Champaign County, Oglesby spoke at Champaign, Urbana, Middleton, St. Joseph, and Sadorus in a three-day swing that began on August 21. The *Central Illinois Gazette* characterized his style of canvassing as "forceful and manly." To a correspondent for the *Illinois State Journal* reporting on a rally at Hickory Grove in Christian County, Oglesby was "an entertaining speaker [who] has the happy facility of commanding the attention of an audience." Fittingly, he reported that the Mechanicsburg delegation to the rally stopped on the way home "at the cabin of a Lincoln railmaker in the woods, and entertained the family with a song." In McLean, the most Republican of the counties in his senatorial district, Oglesby asked for a majority of eight hundred, predicting that the number would bring victory. Rally participants promised a margin of a thousand. Both the plea and the promise would be realized. In the spirit of the great debates of 1858, Oglesby and Coler squared off for joint discussions. A Democratic correspondent for the *Register,* describing an October 9 debate, had railed, "Never have we seen such a scarification inflicted upon any sick man, as Coler gave Richard Oglesby."[50]

But it was Coler who was wounded, especially in the northern counties of the district. McLean County gave Oglesby the one-thousand margin it had promised, and the three other northern-most counties gave him comfortable majorities. In the four southern-most counties of the district, the count was inverted, with Coler polling an eleven hundred majority in Shelby County, the most southern of the counties. The Republican organ in Springfield could exalt that "we are gratified to learn that our glorious Republican friend, Dick Oglesby is elected to the State Senate" from a district that had been Democratic. Oglesby's margin the November 6 election was 244 votes. As he recited thirty years later, he captured more votes (129) than Lincoln in his district, which had given a majority of twelve hundred votes to the Democrats in the previous election. What he did not notice or remember was that Lincoln's plurality was 292 over Stephen Douglas as a result of a scattering of votes for John C. Breckinridge and John Bell. He also remembered carrying his own county by four votes, when, according to a contemporary "official" account, he lost by six. Oglesby's victory gave the Republicans a one-vote majority in the new session of the Illinois senate.[51]

Lincoln's image as Honest Abe, the Rail-Splitter from the West made a major contribution to his election. Even more significant were other factors, including the building of a consensus in the North in opposition to the extension of slavery, certain economic pledges, and Lincoln's ability to keep the Republican Party united while the Democrats were unable to cohere. In the electoral college, 152 votes were necessary to elect. Lincoln received 180; John C. Breckinridge polled 72; Bell, 39; and Stephen A. Douglas, 12. Although Lincoln won all the free states except for New Jersey's split vote and polled 54 percent of the northern popular vote, he could have been denied the prize. Had 25,000 votes out of the 675,000 cast in New York (which had 35 electoral votes) been changed, or had 39,000 voters in California, Illinois, Indiana, and New Jersey (which had 32 electoral votes) not voted Republican, he would not have been elected by the electoral college. With so small a margin it is necessary to examine what role Lincoln and his Democrat opponents played in perpetuating the rail-splitter image.[52]

Many biographers have pictured Lincoln as anxious to forget his rail-splitting, flatboating, and pioneering past. Yet he cheerfully succumbed to Oglesby's rail-splitter scheme, and there is strong evidence that he meant to nurture the image. Although Oglesby did not consult with Lincoln about the presentation of the rails at Decatur, he may have gleaned the idea from Lincoln's March 6, 1860, speech at New Haven, Connecticut, in which he declared: "I am not ashamed to confess that twenty five years ago I was a hired laborer, mauling rails, at work on a flat-boat—just what might happen to any poor man's son [Applause]."[53]

On May 20, 1860, the day following Lincoln's official notification that he had received the Republican nomination, the sculptor Leonard Volk made a cast of Lincoln's hands. By Volk's account, Lincoln explained the scar on his right thumb: "You have heard that they call me the rail-splitter . . . , well, it is true that I did split rails, and one day, while I was sharpening a wedge on a log, the ax glanced and nearly took my thumb off, and there is the scar, you see." In his terse autobiography written in June of 1860 for John L. Scripps's campaign biography, Lincoln wrote of his experience, "Westerly from Decatur," when he and his kin "built a log-cabin, into which they removed, and made sufficient of rails to fence ten acres of ground. . . . These are, or are supposed to be, the rails about which so much is being said just now, though they are far from being the first, or only rails ever made by A." In another passage of the autobiography, describing flatboating on the Sangamon River with John Hanks, Lincoln displays keen bemusement and apparent approval in identifying Hanks as "the same John Hanks who now engineers the 'rail enterprise' at Decatur." In addition, the fact that Lincoln promptly replied to John Hanks's August 23 letter about Charles Hanks suggests an eagerness to support John Hanks and Oglesby in keeping the rail-splitter image alive. In October, a *New York Herald* correspondent reported that Lincoln boasted that Josiah Crawford of Gentryville, Indiana, near where he had lived as a youth, sent him a piece of one of the rails he had split for him in 1825.[54]

President-elect Lincoln visited his stepmother in Coles County in January. On January 28, 1861, he wrote to John Hanks, "I now think I will pass Decatur, going to Coles, on the day after tomorrow—Wednesday, the 30th. of the month. Be ready, and go along." As the train approached Decatur, Lincoln told his companions that he and John Hanks had helped his father, Thomas Lincoln, build a cabin nearby and had made enough rails to fence ten acres of ground. Oglesby apparently did not join Lincoln in Decatur; perhaps both men thought it best not to advertise Oglesby's tutelage of Hanks. John joined the party for the family visit to the Charleston area to see Sarah Bush Lincoln and visit Thomas Lincoln's grave.[55]

While Lincoln was in transit to Washington, Richard Oglesby wrote to him to ask that he "confer some mark of respect upon" John Hanks, presumably an appointment. Hanks apparently wanted to be an Indian agent. Oglesby sermonized the president-elect: "No attribute of nature is more beautiful when fully illustrated than the acknowledgement of former relations in life when one may be supposed to have forgotten them by reason of advancement to and power in Earthly Honors." As Lincoln was aware, Oglesby put it, "the difficulty I plainly see will be to overcome the misfortune Mr. Hanks labors under of not knowing how to write." Lincoln did consider an appointment, according to Henry Clay Whitney, who quoted him as saying that John Hanks was a "thoroughly honest [man] whose son had a tolerable education, and might be his clerk." But no political appointment was forthcoming, although Hanks attended the president's inauguration in Washington and visited the White House several times. When the war began, he enlisted, although overaged, as a teamster in the Illinois regiment commanded by Col. U. S. Grant. The next time he encountered Cousin Abraham was at Lincoln's funeral and burial in Springfield.[56]

Some Republicans, many foreign observers, and most Democrats found the image of a rail-splitter as president foolish. The *New York Times* wrote: "Some of Lincoln's Republican friends, in their earnest desire to excite the enthusiasm of the nation by detailing the exploits of 'honest old Abe' with a maul and a wedge, certainly make a rather comical figure." The *Times,* which had supported Seward, thought the 1840 log-cabin symbol was out of date, demagogic, and not "per se picturesque." It was one of the "constant perils of a Democracy that third-rate party caciques are always prone to play the sycophant to labor," the paper noted. The *Times* tried to absolve Lincoln by supposing that he would feel "a desire to kick the supporter, who should put forward his rail-splitting experiences as a reason for his election." Horace Greeley's *New York Tribune* was less fastidious: "Let us put these [rails] entirely out of the account, and judge Mr. Lincoln solely by his intellectual and political record." As the election neared, however, Greeley, in an editorial headed "Rail-Splitter," argued that Lincoln exemplified Republicanism by being born in poverty, splitting rails, and reading by firelight in a rude log cabin. "That he split rails is of itself nothing, that a man who at twenty was splitting rails for a bare living is at fifty the chosen head of the greatest and most intelligent party in the land . . . that is much, is everything."[57]

The British, who were anti-slavery but prone to characterize Americans as uncouth, found validation for that viewpoint in the wide use of the rail-splitter sobriquet by Lincoln's supporters. The British minister to Washington, Lord Lyons, characterized Lincoln as a "rough farmer—who began life as a Farm Labourer—and got on by a talent for stump speaking." The aftermath of the rail-splitter campaign was that the British viewed Lincoln as "shambling, unkempt, and uncouth." The aristocratic *London Times* and the humor magazine *Punch* led the way in picturing him as boorish.[58]

Democrats were incredulous about Lincoln the rail-splitter. They ridiculed that image, which they came to label as "Raillery." According to one newspaper, Lincoln's rails were "like the Republican Party, as crooked as a dog's hind leg." The *Illinois State Register* published more than forty items during the campaign that were disparaging to Lincoln the rail-splitter, although perhaps they were insulting to others with humble backgrounds as well. Another Democratic newspaper took the line that splitting rails was Lincoln's only qualification for president "aside from his personal beauty." The Democrat humorist Artemus Ward contributed a parody in which he pretended to be a member of the Republican notification committee. "Mr. Lincoln Sir, you've been nominated, Sir for the highest office, Sir." "Oh, don't bother me," Lincoln replies, "I don't want to be pestered with no stuff about conventions . . . I've only got two hundred thousand rails to split before sundown."

A comparative reading of Republican and Democratic newspapers in Springfield suggests that the Democrats were more interested in ridiculing the rail-splitter image than the Republicans were in promoting it.[59]

Oglesby was a junior partner in Abraham Lincoln's rise to power, yet his "rail enterprise" played a major role in Lincoln's election in 1860. Without his explicit warrant, Oglesby contrived a powerful image for Lincoln as a man of the people. The presentation of the rails at the Republican state nominating convention in Decatur elicited great enthusiasm. The rail-splitter furor influenced the Republican National Convention and the election campaign. Although Lincoln was proud to have escaped from his backwoods environment, he quickly recognized the salutary effect of the rail-splitter symbol and discreetly encouraged its use. The Democrats, by protesting too much, magnified the image of Lincoln as a "man of popular origin." Lincoln's victory brought despair to the Democrats. The *Register* copied one article that fearfully predicted: "The Wicked have triumphed—slavery is to be abolished on the 5th of March—white men will take back seats, and the railsplitter—oh, we forgot—Mr. Lincoln will preside over the destinies of this country." Under threat of the secession of the southern states, what use was a rail-splitter president. Was he the "Union-splitter" as well? Had he ever reunited "a log after he had rent it in twain"?[60]

## Notes

1. RJO, Decatur, to Peter Vroom, Trenton, N.J., April 20, 1858, Chicago Historical Society. Lincoln first delivered his "Discoveries and Inventions" speech in Bloomington on April 6, 1858. Wayne C. Temple, "Lincoln the Lecturer, Part 1," *Lincoln Herald* 102 (Fall 1999): 101.

2. Wilkie, p. 15; *Lincoln Day by Day,* vol. 2, pp. 213–14.

3. *Journal,* May 8, 1858, p. 2, col. 3, and June 16, 1858, p. 2, col. 4.

4. Augustus H. Chapman to Abraham Lincoln, Charleston, July 24, 1858, as quoted in Charles H. Coleman, *Abraham Lincoln and Coles County, Illinois* (New Brunswick: Scarecrow Press, 1955), pp. 169–70; *Journal,* Aug. 14, 1858, p. 3, col. 1. See also Henry Lee Payne, "Richard J. Oglesby: Politician and Soldier to 1865," M.A. thesis, University of Illinois, 1961.

5. *Lincoln Day by Day,* vol. 2, pp. 222–23; James C. Robinson to RJO, Aug. 23, 1858, Oglesby MSS; Wilkie, p. 14.

6. Henry Clay Whitney to Abraham Lincoln, July 24, 1858, microfilm reel 3, item 1045, Robert Todd Lincoln Collection, LC.

7. *Journal,* Aug. 30, 1858, p. 3, col. 1.

8. *Chicago Press and Tribune,* Sept. 11, 1858, p. 2, col. 5.

9. Bancroft, p. 29.

10. *Chicago Press and Tribune,* Sept. 21, 1858, p. 4, col. 2. A *Chicago Times* article of September 21, 1858, is quoted in Edwin E. Sparks, *The Lincoln-Douglas Debates of 1858,* vol. 3 of *Collections of the Illinois State Historical Library,* (Springfield: ISHL, 1908), p. 312. The

"emigrant wagon" report is from the *Chicago Democrat,* Sept. 22, 1858, as cited in Sparks, *Lincoln-Douglas Debates,* p. 311. Thomas A. Marshall and William W. Craddock, both from Coles County, were the successful candidates for the state senate and house of representatives, respectively, according to Coleman, *Abraham Lincoln and Coles County, Illinois,* pp. 168–69, and John Clayton, *The Illinois Fact Book and Historical Almanac, 1863–1968* (Carbondale: Southern Illinois University Press, 1970), p. 222.

11. *Collected Works,* vol. 3, pp. 145–46.

12. *Collected Works,* vol. 3, pp. 176, 177, 179, 181.

13. RJO to Isaac N. Arnold, March 7, 1883, Arnold Collection, Chicago Historical Society; *Collected Works,* vol. 3, pp. 182–83.

14. RJO to Isaac N. Arnold, March 7, 1883, and RJO to Sheridan Wait, Sept. 21, 1858, both in Otto R. Kyle, *Abraham Lincoln in Decatur* (New York: Vantage Press, 1957), 98; Lew Wallace, *An Autobiography,* 2 vols. (New York: Harper and Brothers, 1906), vol. 1, pp. 254–55.

15. RJO to Sheridan Wait, Sept. 21, 1858, in E. T. Coleman, "The Story of Decatur," *Decatur Review,* May 18, 1924; *Chicago Press and Tribune,* Sept. 21, 1858, p. 4, col. 2; Coleman, *Abraham Lincoln and Coles County,* pp. 184–85.

16. *Lincoln Day by Day,* vol. 2, pp. 229, 235.

17. RJO to Sheridan Wait, Sept. 21, 1858, in *Decatur Review,* May 18, 1924; *Journal,* Oct. 27, 1858, p. 3, col. 2; Wilkie, p. 14.

18. Kyle, *Abraham Lincoln in Decatur,* p. 98; David Davis to Abraham Lincoln, Nov. 7, 1858 (lamenting loss of Whigs), in Willard L. King, *Lincoln's Manager David Davis* (Cambridge: Harvard University Press, 1960), p. 126; *Chicago Press and Tribune,* Nov. 18, 1858, p. 1, col. 1.

19. *Chicago Press and Tribune,* Nov. 8, 1858, p. 2, col. 2. The election figures are from Lusk, pp. 34, 44, 103.

20. Receipts, Oglesby MSS. Oglesby sent notes to Miss Kline, Miss Lutril, Mrs. Edmundson, and Miss White on August 23, 1856. See entry for Oct. 20, 1856, in Richard J. Oglesby, "Journal of Trip to Europe and the Middle East, April 18, 1856–July 10, 1857," Oglesby MSS.

21. RJO to Hon. Peter D. Vroom, Decatur, Dec. 26, 1859, Oglesby MSS. Oglesby also wrote about changes in his law practice: "The firm of [Albert J.] Gallagher, Wait and Oglesby transfused itself into Oglesby and [Sheridan] Wait on the 1st of Sept. last as it used to be in 1856." The firm's Letterpress Book, July 1860–April 1862 (Oglesby MSS), shows that Oglesby increasingly turned his cases to his partner. He was licensed to practice law in the U.S. District Court on February 12, 1860 (Oglesby MSS), but apparently did not try any cases. He tried his last case in any court in November 1860 (John M. Palmer, *The Bench and Bar of Illinois: Historical and Reminiscent,* 2 vols. [Chicago: Lewis Publishing, 1899], vol. 2, p. 1155).

22. Michael James Welch, "History of Elkhart" (1979); transcript, Oglesby family Bible; "Richard J. Oglesby's Parents and Family," *Oglesby Mansion News,* Feb. 1982; Banton, p. 91; canceled check on Peddecord, Burrows & Co. by RJO, March 24, 1859, for $60 in gold, Oglesby MSS; and E. T. Coleman and Others, "History of Macon County," ch. 31 (photocopy provided by Amelia Mulrooney, Decatur, Ill.). From the John Whitney estate, Oglesby bought block 5, lots 1–4 in the Western Addition, on September 28, 1859, for $2,600 (Macon County Recorder of Deeds, book 34, p. 233).

23. William Baringer, *Lincoln's Rise to Power* (Boston: Little, Brown, 1937), p. 67. Other Original Lincoln Men, as listed under "Illustrations," were O. H. Browning, Judge David

Davis, Leonard Swett, Jesse K. Dubois, Norman B. Judd, William H. Herndon, John M. Palmer, Ozias M. Hatch, Stephen T. Logan, Gustavus Koerner, Ward Lamon, and Jesse Fell.

24. Harry E. Pratt, "Abraham Lincoln in Bloomington," *JISHS* 29 (April 1936): 65.

25. Jesse W. Fell, in *The Lincoln Memorial: Album—Immortelles,* ed. Osborn H. Old-royd (New York: G. W. Carleton, 1882), p. 475; *Collected Works,* vol. 3, p. 511.

26. *Collected Works,* vol. 3, p. 517.

27. James T. Hickey, "Oglesby's Fence Rail Dealings and the 1860 Decatur Convention," *JISHS* 54 (1961): 6.

28. Richmond, p. 66. Hickey confirms Oglesby's role by listing the subscriptions Oglesby recorded ("Oglesby's Fence Rail Dealings," pp. 19–20). Baringer cites the *Chicago Press and Tribune,* April 23, 1860, on Oglesby's appointment to provide a Decatur meeting place (*Lincoln's Rise,* p. 181).

29. Allan Nevins, *The Emergence of Lincoln,* 2 vols. (New York: Charles Scribners' Sons, 1950), vol. 2, p. 244.

30. Baringer, *Lincoln's Rise,* p. 184; William Baringer, "Campaign Techniques in Illinois—1860," *Illinois State Historical Society Transactions for the Year 1932* (Springfield: ISHL, 1932), pp. 222–25; Jane Martin Johns, "The Nomination of Abraham Lincoln to the Presidency: An Unsolved Psychological Problem," *JISHS* 10 (1917–18): 565; *Journal,* May 7, 1860, p. 2, col. 2. Some "rail-splitter" material appears in Mark A. Plummer, "Lincoln and the Rail-Splitter Election," *Lincoln Herald* 101 (Fall 1999): 111–16.

31. Jewell H. Aubere, "A Reminiscence of Abraham Lincoln: A Conversation with Speaker Cannon," *World's Work* 13 (Feb. 1907): 8528, as cited in Wayne C. Temple, "Lincoln's Fence Rails," *JISHS* 47 (1954): 24; Baringer, *Lincoln's Rise,* p. 184; Temple, "Lincoln's Fence Rails," p. 26; Baringer, *Lincoln's Rise,* pp. 184–85. According to some sources, the sign mistakenly said "Thomas Hanks" rather than "John Hanks." John Hanks was illiterate and might not have known the difference. Isaac D. Jennings has been identified as the other rail-carrier (Temple, "Lincoln's Rail Fences," p. 26n25; Richmond, p. 67). Richmond lists Jennings as being sheriff of Macon County from 1872 to 1876 (p. 151). A letter from Sen. Shelby Cullom to William E. Mitchell, from Washington and dated September 11, 1894, recalls Oglesby speaking of "Honest Old Abe" or "Honest Abe" for the first time. Sen. John M. Palmer, who played an important role in Lincoln's nomination at the Decatur convention, agreed.

32. Johns, "The Nomination of Abraham Lincoln," pp. 561–67; Correspondent "Illinois," from West Urbana, May 28, 1860, in *New York Daily Tribune,* June 8, 1860, p. 6, col. 3; *Journal,* May 11, 1860, p. 2, col. 2.

33. *Chicago Press and Tribune,* May 11, 1860, p. 1, col. 2; Baringer, *Lincoln's Rise,* p. 186; *Browning Diary,* vol. 1, pp. 405–6.

34. King, *Lincoln's Manager,* pp. 135, 182; *Chicago Press and Tribune,* May 10, 1860, p. 1, col. 2; Carl Sandburg, *Abraham Lincoln: The Prairie Years,* 2 vols. (New York: Harcourt, Brace, 1926), vol. 2, p. 332; Ida M. Tarbell, *In the Footsteps of Lincolns* (New York: Harper and Brothers, 1924), pp. 345, 391; *Browning Diary,* vol. 1, p. 406.

35. The *Journal,* May 12, 1860, p. 2, col. 5, lists the delegates and alternates at large.

36. For details of the convention, see Murat Halstead, *Three against Lincoln: Murat Halstead Reports the Caucuses of 1860,* ed. William B. Hesseltine (Baton Rouge: Louisiana State University Press, 1960), pp. 141–84; see also Baringer, "Campaign Techniques in Illinois—1860," p. 229; and Ida M. Tarbell, *The Life of Abraham Lincoln,* 2 vols. (New York: McClure, Phillips, 1902), vol. 1, p. 345.

37. Halstead, *Three against Lincoln,* pp. 161–72.

38. *Chicago Press and Tribune,* May 19, 1860, p. 4, col. 8; M[urat] H[alstead] in the *Chicago Press and Tribune,* May 22, 1860, p. 1, col. 2; Elbridge Atwood, Springfield, to Alice M. Atwood, Jackson, Mich., May 27, 1860, Elbridge Atwood Collection, ISHL.

39. Microfilm newspapers, July 21, Sept. 3, 1860, ISHL; "The Rail Splitter," *Lincoln Lore,* no. 1445 (July 1958), 1–3; Jesse Clement, "A Lincoln Lyric," *Chicago Press and Tribune,* May 28, 1860, p. 3, col. 3.

40. Temple, "Lincoln's Fence Rails," pp. 28–33; J. H. Burnham to Father, May 19, 1860, as cited in Reinhard H. Luthin, *The First Lincoln Campaign* (Cambridge: Harvard University Press, 1944), p. 182; H. Preston James, "Political Pageantry in the Campaign of 1860 in Illinois," *Abraham Lincoln Quarterly* 4 (1947): 320–21.

41. *Register,* May 26, 1860, p. 2, col. 3, June 4, 1860, p. 2, col. 4, June 7, 1860, p. 2, col. 1, July 2, 1860, p. 2, col. 3, June 27, 1860, p. 4, col. 1 (poem from the *Indianapolis Sentinel*), and June 29, 1860, p. 4, col. 1. In Springfield, where a visit from the Prince of Wales was impending, some of the boys began calling the Lincolns' eldest son Robert Todd the "Prince of Rails," a nickname that stuck with him for some time. Temple, "Lincoln's Fence Rails," pp. 29, 31, 32. Bateman found that Lincoln had split an infinitive by writing "to not violate [the Republican platform]" when he should have said "not to violate." "So you think I better put those two little fellows end to end, do you"? Lincoln reportedly mused. Don C. Seitz, *Lincoln the Politician: How the Rail-splitter and Flatboatman Played the Great American Game* (New York: Coward-McCann, 1931), p. 181; see also *Recollected Words of Abraham Lincoln,* comp. and ed. Don E. Fehrenbacher and Virginia Fehrenbacher (Stanford: Stanford University Press, 1996), p. 24.

42. Oglesby MSS; Hickey, "Oglesby's Fence Rail Dealings," pp. 9–10, 16–18. James Lawrence of Trenton, N.J., wrote to his son William in Illinois on July 11, 1860: "We are all Lincoln men or Rail Maulers here. When you get ready to come east go to the Woods and cut all the black walnut sprouts you can. They will make nice Canes & say that they were from Abe's farm, and they would sell like hot cakes." Lawrence Collection, Illinois Historical Survey, University of Illinois at Urbana-Champaign.

43. Wayne C. Williams, *A Rail Splitter for President* (Denver: University of Denver Press, 1951), p. 100; Oglesby Ledger Book, shown by Amelia Mulrooney, Decatur, Ill., Dec. 12, 1976; *Journal,* July 10, 1860, p. 3, col. 3; *Decatur Gazette,* July 11, 1860, p. 3, Miscellaneous Papers, roll 294, ISHL.

44. Marilyn Gahm Ames, "John Hanks: Lincoln's Rail Splitter Cousin," M.A. thesis, Illinois State University, 1974, pp. 47–52, cites the complete Hanks-Oglesby letter of July 4, 1860, and offers a thorough account of the Hanks-Oglesby relationship. Williams, *A Rail Splitter for President,* p. 99.

45. Ames, "John Hanks," pp. 52–56; *Register,* July 14, 1860, p. 2, col. 3.

46. John Hanks to Abraham Lincoln, Aug. 23, 1860, Presidential Papers microfilm reel 8, no. 3585, Abraham Lincoln Papers, LC; Lincoln to John Hanks, Aug. 24, 1860, in *Collected Works,* vol. 4, p. 100.

47. *Journal,* Aug. 9, 1860, p. 2, cols. 2–5; *Olney Courier* quoted in *Journal,* Aug. 14, 1860, p. 1, col. 2.

48. *Journal,* Aug. 9, 1860, p. 3, cols. 2–5, Aug. 8, 1860, p. 3, col. 4; Elbridge Atwood to Alice M. Atwood, Jackson, Mich., Aug. 5, 1860, Elbridge Atwood Collection, ISHL; Col. Risdon

M. Moore, "Mr. Lincoln as a Wrestler," *Transactions of the Illinois State Historical Society for 1904,* no. 9 (1904): 334; *Browning Diary,* vol. 1, p. 422.

49. *Chicago Press and Tribune,* July 23, 1860, p. 2, col. 2.

50. Henry Lee Payne, "Richard J. Oglesby: Politician and Soldier to 1865," M.A. thesis, University of Illinois at Urbana-Champaign, 1961, citing the *Central Illinois Gazette,* Aug. 15, 29, 1860; David Davis to RJO, Bloomington, July 12, 13, 1860, Oglesby MSS; *Bloomington Daily Pantagraph,* Nov. 21, 1860, p. 3, col. 2; *Register,* Oct. 15, 1860, p. 2, col. 2, quoting the *Bloomington Statesman.*

51. *Journal,* Nov. 8, 1860, p. 2, col. 2; Bancroft, pp. 29–30; Wilkie, p. 14; Howard W. Allen and Vincent A. Lacey, *Illinois Elections 1818–1990* (Carbondale: Southern Illinois University Press, 1992), pp. 144–45.

52. Gabor S. Boritt, "Was Lincoln a Vulnerable Candidate in 1860?" *Civil War History* 27 (March 1981): 32–48. Boritt is more interested in the "Honest Abe" versus the "Tricky Old Abe" image than in the rail-splitter image.

53. David Herbert Donald, *Lincoln* (New York: Simon and Schuster, 1995), p. 243; Stephen B. Oates, *With Malice toward None: The Life of Abraham Lincoln* (New York: Harper and Row, 1977), p. 4; J. G. Randall and Richard Current, *Lincoln the President,* 4 vols. (New York: Dodd, Mead, 1945–55), vol. 1, p. 151; Henry Clay Whitney, *Life on the Circuit with Lincoln* (1892, repr. Caldwell: Caxton Printers, 1940), p. 466; *Collected Works,* vol. 4, p. 24.

54. Leonard Volk, "The Lincoln Life-Mask and How It Was Made," *Century Illustrated Monthly Magazine* 23 (Dec. 1881): 228; *Collected Works,* vol. 4, pp. 64, 65, 100; Temple, "Lincoln's Fence Rails," pp. 20–34; *Lincoln Day by Day,* vol. 2, p. 292, quoting the *New York Herald,* Oct. 20, 1860.

55. *Collected Works,* vol. 4, p. 181; Ames, "John Hanks," pp. 59–60, citing John M. Lansden, "Abraham Lincoln, Judge David Davis and Judge Edward Bates," *JISHS* 7 (April 1914): 56–58.

56. RJO to Hon. A. Lincoln, Springfield, Feb. 17, 1861, Oglesby MSS; Whitney, *Life on the Circuit,* p. 419; Coleman, *Abraham Lincoln in Coles County,* pp. 213–14; Edwin David Davis, "The Hanks Family in Macon County, Illinois (1828–1939)," *Papers in Illinois History and Transactions for the Year 1939* (Springfield: ISHS, 1940), p. 139.

57. *New York Times,* June 14, 1860, p. 4, col. 4; *New York Tribune,* May 24, Oct. 23, 1860, as cited in Herbert Mitgang, *Lincoln as They Saw Him* (New York: Rinehart, 1956), p. 185 (quotations); Harlan Hoyt Horner, *Lincoln and Greeley* (Urbana: University of Illinois Press, 1953), pp. 183–84.

58. Lord Richard Lyons to Lord John Russell, July 23, 1860, as cited in Randall, *Lincoln the President,* vol. 2, p. 32; Merrill D. Peterson, *Lincoln in American Memory* (New York: Oxford University Press, 1994), pp. 24–25.

59. Melvin L. Hayes, *Mr. Lincoln Runs for President* (New York: Citadel Press, 1960), pp. 131, 135; *Register,* Aug. 15, 1860, p. 1, col. 1; Charles F. Browne, *Artemus Ward in London* (New York: Carleton, 1865), p. 222.

60. *Register,* Nov. 17, 1860, p. 2, col. 2 (quoting *Western Pluck*) and Dec. 22, 1860, p. 1, col. 1.

# 4. And the War Came

FROM THE TIME of his election in November until his inauguration on March 4, 1861, Lincoln maintained his policy of public silence on the issue of secession. Meanwhile, led by South Carolina, the states of the Deep South seceded. The *Illinois State Register* complained, via the reprinting of an article from the *Ohio Statesman,* that Lincoln had become the Union-splitter through his silence. It argued that all that was required to prevent "the catastrophe of a severance of a hitherto united, happy and prosperous country" was to announce that he would not allow the use of "an abolition wedge to split the Union asunder." Lincoln and most Republicans would allow slavery to exist where it was already established, but they believed that the South had lost the election and now wished to blackmail the party into granting endless concessions to preserve the Union.[1]

Richard Oglesby arrived in Springfield on January 5, 1861, two days in advance of the opening of the legislative session. The Republicans enjoyed a 13-to-12 lead in the senate and a 40-to-35 majority advantage in the house. The Republican victory contributed to the large turnover in both houses; twelve newcomers in the senate and twenty-six in the house. On Saturday night, January 5, the Republicans caucused to select legislative officers and staff. Oglesby's rotund neighbor from Coles County, Thomas A. Marshall, was slated for senate president pro tem, and Shelby M. Cullom of Sangamon County was chosen as speaker of the house.[2]

The Twenty-second General Assembly was no ordinary legislative session. Two days after it opened on January 7, Mississippi seceded from the Union. All of the states of the Deep South would pass ordinances of secession before the legislature adjourned in February. The senate proceeded to organize and choose its committees, and Oglesby was appointed to six of the twenty standing ones: judiciary, public roads, township organization and counties, and state institutions. He also chaired the education and military affairs committees. In addition to routine fiscal matters, the General Assembly was responsible for the election of a U.S. senator, legislative and congressional reapportionment, militia reorganization, and calling a constitutional convention—all highly partisan issues. Reflecting the secession crisis, legislators would also have to resolve the issue of participation in the Virginia Peace Convention.[3]

Lyman Trumbull was reelected to the U.S. Senate by a joint session of the legislature as President-elect Lincoln looked on. The vote was fifty-four for Trumbull to thirty-six for Samuel J. Marshall, Oglesby voting with the majority. He had opposed Trumbull in favor of Lincoln in 1854 and would attempt to unseat him in 1866. But Trumbull had worked hard for Oglesby's election. Oglesby's victory enabled the Republicans to organize the Illinois senate with a one-vote majority. Without that narrow victory, the Democrats would likely have delayed the reelection of Trumbull and obstructed reapportionment. Unrepresentative apportionment, the Republicans remembered, had contributed to Lincoln's defeat by Stephen A. Douglas in 1858.[4]

Gov. Richard Yates used his inaugural address on January 14 to demand that secession of the southern states be overridden. The *New York Herald* thought Yates's speech "so radical as to make it altogether improbable" that it represented Lincoln's views, but Lincoln silently shared Yates's opinion, if not his parlance, concerning the preservation of the Union. Oglesby voted with the majority to print ten thousand copies of Yates's speech in English and another three thousand in German. Illinois Democrats countered two days later with a party convention. The five hundred delegates were divided, but they adopted resolutions that counseled extensive compromise and warned that coercion of the seceded states might cause a civil war.[5]

Republican and Democratic senators managed to maintain some civility during the session, but the tension was tangible. The State Board of Education and Bloomington city officials invited the legislature to attend the formal opening of the recently completed edifice at Illinois State Normal University. Oglesby, as senator representing the Bloomington area, pushed for acceptance. The shared festivities might break the tension and smooth the way for appropriations for the state's only public university. After assurances that the entire weekend would be complimentary and that no appropriations were mandated by attendance, the senate agreed to the trip. On January 24, more than four hundred persons, including legislators, their families and invited guests, and a Springfield band, boarded the special train furnished by the St. Louis, Alton, and Chicago Railroad. The train took them to "the junction" located about eight hundred yards from the Normal University. During the afternoon the guests watched students perform and marveled at the modern features of the $145,000 building, built largely by pledged subscription, some of which remained unpaid. Governor Yates, Speaker Cullom, and Sen. William H. Underwood made congratulatory remarks. Oglesby's speech, "besides being replete with humor and wit, was an earnest and eloquent plea in behalf of the Normal School." The guests were then transported to Bloomington, where they enjoyed a "grand jollification." Their "sumptuous dinner" consisted of ninety-six menu items accompanied by "a sparkling fluid, which gave spirit to their wit and sparkle to their sentiments." A magnificent ball attended by the "beauty and chivalry of Bloomington" rounded out the evening. A month later, Oglesby hailed the passage of an appropriations bill he had shepherded through the senate for the benefit of Illinois State Normal University.[6]

The Virginia legislature called upon the states to send commissioners to a February 4 meeting in Washington, D.C., in an effort to avoid war. Lincoln and Yates preferred not to send representatives from Illinois, fearing that the principle of non-extension of slavery might be challenged. Public sentiment, however, seemed to favor doing something. The General Assembly's response was to push through a joint resolution calling for the appointment of five commissioners. The Republican majority, with Thomas Marshall and Oglesby taking the lead in the senate, insisted upon placing the appointments in Governor Yates's hands. In an extensive debate on February 1, Oglesby asked the Democrats to trust the newly elected "dominant party" to assume the responsibility for which it had been elected. Oglesby asserted, however, that he would not yield to "the mere braggart threat of dissolving the Union." Although he feared civil war as having "more terror for me than any other calamity which has beset the progress of mankind," he felt that he must stand on principle and not allow the southern states to "break up the Union, pull down the fair fabric of our government, tear the national flag into shreds and trail the stars and stripes in the dust." Marshall and Oglesby were congratulated by the Republican *Illinois State Journal* for their "gallant" stand. Governor Yates appointed five representatives who were acceptable to Lincoln, all of whom were labeled as "irrepressible conflict boys" by the Democrats. Nothing came of the Virginia conference because neither the Republicans nor the states of the Deep South would compromise.[7]

There was routine business enough to occasionally divert the Illinois senate from the national crisis. Because there were no effective general incorporation laws, each organization—towns, school districts, banks, seminaries, insurance companies, and railroads—required special legislation. Oglesby introduced dozens of private bills, including those to incorporate the Terre Haute and Alton Railroad, certain banks, insurance companies, and stock companies; to charter several school districts and colleges; and to amend the charters of Decatur and Mattoon and grant charters to the cities of Hyde Park and Pana. The legislature also held the power to decide matters dealing with individual rights and privileges. On February 4 the senate passed "An Act to protect married women in their separate property," which the governor subsequently signed into law. The vote in favor of passage was fourteen yeas and eight nays. Oglesby voted on the losing side. Although no record survives to explain his vote, he was perhaps influenced by his law practice or by his wealth and recent marriage.[8]

One key to Oglesby's popularity, even among political opponents, was that he frequently inserted humor into the proceedings in times of great tension. In early February, he introduced an emergency measure to change the name of a man who had been using his stepfather's surname. When the man's fiancée discovered the discrepancy, she demanded a legal change in advance of the wedding, which was scheduled for the day after Oglesby introduced the legislation. Oglesby warned that if the bill failed "the wedding would be broken up and the Union dissolved." The ayes prevailed, and the chair announced, "The Union is saved."[9]

Two politically charged issues that became implicitly connected were reapportionment and calling a constitutional convention. Democrats wanted to postpone reapportionment until after the next election. Although reapportionment was legally required, they argued, it would be prudent to wait for data from the 1860 census. Republicans, although conceding that an 1860 referendum required calling a constitutional convention, contended that it would be prudent to wait until the national crisis had passed. Oglesby took a leading role in the debates over reapportionment. His district, which usually voted Democratic, was to be changed to a Republican majority by reassigning the southern counties. Oglesby mirthfully admitted his delight with the bill when he remarked, "I have lived all my life under democratic domination . . . until absolutely I have got sick and tired of it. This is the first chance I have ever had to get out, and I intend to get out if I possibly can" he concluded as laughter erupted in the senate chamber. William H. Underwood, the Democratic leader, although professing to "take this thing in perfect good humor," caustically remarked that Marshall and Oglesby, "both well fed, sleek and corpulent men," had obviously suffered little under Democratic rule. He then compared his "friends from Coles and Macon" to "the fat man Brutus, who gave the unkindest cut of all" to Julius Caesar, not unlike that administered by Marshall and Oglesby in striking "their dagger into the democratic party." The Republican Party prevailed by controlling the redistricting of the Illinois house and senate as well as the congressional districts. They also reluctantly passed legislation calling for an election of delegates to a constitutional convention set for November 1861. The Democrats, believing they could capture the convention and overturn the reapportionment, allowed the reapportionment measure to become law without obstructing the session.[10]

As chair of the committee on military affairs, it was Oglesby's responsibility to respond to the governor's call for a more forceful militia law. Oglesby pronounced the militia system as "entirely inadequate to a state of war" and "too complex and burdensome for peace." For want of time to devise a new system in the context of an "agitated and overheated land" (and because the Democrats threatened to obstruct its quick passage), he and his committee unanimously decided to hold it over to the next session. He prophetically assured the senate, however, that "if after all efforts to stay the present unhappy agitation bordering on insanity in the southern portion of the United States, whereby the blessings of peace are seriously threatened," should lead to a call of arms for all patriots, "the whole country having the love of the Union at heart, would rise *en masse,* and disregarding the hindrances of a militia law, volunteer their service to the proper authority of the state speedily and without delay." The Illinois General Assembly adjourned on George Washington's birthday.[11]

Lincoln left Springfield on his circuitous journey to Washington on February 11. Among those invited to join the traveling party were Ward Hill Lamon and David Davis. Leonard Swett would meet the group in Pittsburgh. These Eighth Judicial Circuit lawyers would become Oglesby's conduit to the president. On January 31 he had written to the president-elect to solicit the Paris consulship for Lamon, but Lamon's appointment as marshal for the District of Columbia was even more advantageous to Oglesby in the long run because of Lamon's frequent contact with the president. On April 3 Oglesby wrote to "Hill," asking that he either show the letter to Lincoln or convey its content orally. Oglesby was supporting William Usrey, the editor of the Decatur Republican newspaper, for postmaster. Usrey, however, was not appointed postmaster, nor was John Hanks appointed an Indian agent as Oglesby had requested in a February 17, 1861, letter written directly to the president. Lincoln, in a period of crisis, had neither time nor positions enough to satisfy the multitude of his supporters. Even Judge Davis, his political manager, had to wait a year for an appointment to the Supreme Court.[12]

News that the new Confederacy had fired on Fort Sumter at Charleston, South Carolina, on April 12, outraged most northerners, Republicans and

Democrats alike. Men, women, and children turned out for town meetings "united in the utterance of loyal sentiments, amid the singing of patriotic songs and enthusiastic cheers." As Oglesby had predicted, "the whole country" seemed willing to volunteer for service. He rushed forward in an attempt to recruit the first Illinois regiment of the six requested under Lincoln's call for seventy-five thousand ninety-day volunteers.[13]

Governor Yates called the legislature into a special session to convene on April 23. Oglesby began dividing his time between the legislature and nearby Camp Yates, where his men were being mustered into service. Yates's special message to the legislature called for an appropriation of $3 million to support the recruitment of the six regiments requested by the federal government as well as an additional ten regiments. The militant governor declared that party distinctions had disappeared overnight and that "men of all parties, by thousands, are begging for places in the ranks, and every village and hamlet resounds with the beat of drum and clangor of arms." He prophetically forecast, "Our people will wade through seas of blood before they will see a single star or a solitary stripe erased from the glorious flag of our Union." Some Democrats objected to the military bill being proposed, but Sen. Stephen A. Douglas rushed to Springfield to promote the arming of Union troops. On April 25 he quietly pressured Democrats into agreement. That night, Douglas addressed the legislature and demanded undivided loyalty to the Union. He warned his fellow Democrats not to allow their recent political defeat to convert them "from patriots to traitors." The shortest way to peace, he asserted, "is the most stupendous and unanimous preparation for war." The legislature increased the war appropriations to $3.5 million, strengthened the militia bill that Oglesby had deferred in the regular session, and defined and fixed a penalty for treason. On May 3, the legislature adjourned after singing "The Star-Spangled Banner" and taking an oath of allegiance.[14]

In less than two weeks after President Lincoln's call for troops, Oglesby had recruited ten companies from central Illinois, including two from Decatur. The regiment was mustered into service on April 25 while he was still serving in the Illinois senate. The next day, he resigned from the committee on military affairs in order to devote more time to the regiment. Thereafter he voted only sporadically in the senate. Meanwhile, former Springfield mayor John Cook rushed his regiment into service. A dispute followed as to which regiment was first to muster. Yates ratified an arrangement whereby the Springfield regiment would be designated as the Seventh Infantry Regiment (the first six numbers were not used "in token of respect to the six Illinois regiments" in the war with Mexico), but Oglesby would be listed first among the volunteer regimental commanders, behind only Gen. Benjamin Prentiss, who was designated as the brigade commander. Oglesby accepted command of the Eighth Illinois Infantry, but the date-of-rank dispute surfaced with each of his subsequent promotions. His "date of rank and enlistment" on the three-month regiment is listed as May 3, 1861, the same day the legislature adjourned. The roster of the reenlisted three-year regiment, however, "corrects" the date to April 25. Colonel Oglesby's selection as regimental commander was consistent with the general practice of appointing veterans of the Mexican War, said to have "standing and influence in one party or the other, and supposed military knowledge and adaptability to the service."[15]

Cairo, Illinois, at the junction of the Ohio and Mississippi rivers and the Illinois Central Railroad, was recognized as a critical site by the War Department. On April 19, Simon Cameron, secretary of war, perhaps alarmed that Kentucky Governor Beriah Magoffin had answered Lincoln's call for troops by emphatically asserting that "Kentucky will furnish no troops for the wicked purpose of subduing her sister Southern States," had telegraphed Governor Yates to send four regiments to protect Cairo. Northern Illinois militia, "indifferently armed with rifles, shot-guns, muskets and carbines," had been hastily transported by rail to Cairo, arriving on April 23. Oglesby's Eighth Infantry was among the regiments ordered to relieve that temporary unit. The regiment arrived there on April 28 and would complete its three-month enlistment at that post.[16]

The *Illinois State Register* reported that Colonel Oglesby's regiment was "loudly and enthusiastically cheered" as the men departed the Springfield depot. At Decatur, the two local companies were allowed to detrain for an emotional farewell ceremony at Central Park. More than a hundred women of the city had hastily sewn a silk flag for the regiment; no one was allowed to sew more than a few stitches. Hattie White, Oglesby's sister-in-law, held the flag as he "made a speech of such fervid eloquence that people went wild." On command, the companies marched back to the cars, accompanied by two drums and a fife.[17]

Oglesby and the men of the Eighth Illinois Regiment were spoiling for a fight, but none was forthcoming despite his provocative attempts to challenge Confederates in "neutral" Kentucky. The regiment suffered through three months of hot weather, drill, and patriotic speeches amid recurrent rumors of attacks coming from Kentucky. Because the men were unaccustomed to the discipline of the army, Oglesby lectured his volunteers on the necessity of following orders: "You are no longer mere men, you are soldiers. Your captain's uniform marks him as your superior even though he may once have been your bootblack. Your duty is to obey orders." One of the more difficult orders to enforce was an instruction from General Prentiss of May 9, 1861,

directing that each soldier should bathe twice a week. The troops also had
to endure a dress parade each evening. On June 13 they were rewarded by a
favorable review conducted by Gen. George B. McClellan, who was on a tour
of inspection.[18]

William Howard Russell, correspondent for the *Times* of London, visited
Cairo on June 19, 1861, and his dispatches offer a glimpse of Oglesby and the
men. He was in a party with Cong. Elihu Washburne, General Prentiss, and
Oglesby. The men called for speeches, "as civilian soldiers command their
Generals on such occasions." When Oglesby was summoned, Russell wrote,
"The tall, portly, good humoured old man stepped to the front, and with
excellent tack and good sense, dished up in the Buncombe style, told them
the time for making speeches had passed" and that it was time for fighting.
In another dispatch, Russell maintained that Oglesby was typical of the commanding officers of the volunteer regiments. He described him as an "excellent, kindly, and shrewd old man . . . who raised himself from obscurity . . .
in spite of a defective education." "Apparently," Russell continued, "he is
selected to be a colonel because he can make good, homely, telling speeches
to the men." Russell seemed surprised that the soldiers could parade "with
precision and rapidity." The officers, however, "did not seem very quick."[19]

Oglesby's "time for fighting" speech was not idle talk. On June 12 he had
commanded two companies of soldiers loaded on the steamer *City of Alton*
for a reconnaissance down the Mississippi. His orders precluded landing on
the Kentucky shore, but upon seeing a rebel flag near Columbus, Kentucky,
engine trouble was discovered and the ship briefly anchored near the shore-
line. Oglesby forbade his men disembarking, but, as the correspondent of the
*Illinois State Journal* reported, "the noble hearted Captain Barnes, the commander of the boat, not being subject to any orders rushed into the town"
and "tore down the rebel flag and bore it in triumph to Col. O." Oglesby, in
turn, presented the flag to General Prentiss, who responded with a patriotic
speech. Rumors soon arrived from Kentucky that the secession flag incident
would be revenged if ever Colonel Oglesby fell into Confederate hands. The
next test for Oglesby's martial spirit was to persuade his men to reenlist for
three years. In the face of mud, malaria, humidity, and stifling heat combined
with delayed pay and lack of opportunity to face the enemy, he could only
spur about half the regiment to reenlist. The new three-year Eighth Regiment
accepted recruits and mustered in on July 25, 1861.[20]

Years later, when Ulysses S. Grant was president of the United States and
Oglesby was a U.S. senator from Illinois, the two would reminisce about their
first meeting, which took place in Cairo on September 4, 1861. The incident
also appears in Grant's memoirs. Oglesby was temporarily serving as the

commander of the forces at Cairo. Grant, who was waiting for his new general's uniform to be shipped to him, entered the city in civilian clothes. Arriving at Oglesby's headquarters in the St. Charles Hotel, he was introduced to Oglesby, who did not clearly hear the introduction and assumed that Grant was another of the flock of refugees or merchants seeking favors. Grant, "dusty and unshaven" by Oglesby's account, asked for pen and paper. Although Oglesby thought it "cheeky" of an unidentified civilian to make such a request, he complied, and Grant wrote out an order assuming command. Oglesby tried to apologize by remarking, "Why, Great God, are you General Grant: I thought it was a refugee. The last time I saw a general, in the Mexican war, he was in uniform—for that reason, excuse me General: I did not recognize you."[21]

Gen. John C. Frémont's enlargement of Grant's Department of Southeast Missouri to include Cairo and environs was timely. On September 3, Confederate general Gideon Pillow broke Kentucky's neutrality and occupied the strategic high ground above the Mississippi River at Columbus, Kentucky. Grant then occupied Paducah at the junction of the Ohio and Tennessee rivers. He also began probing southward along the Mississippi River toward Belmont, Missouri, across the river from the Confederate-fortified bluffs at Columbus. From Cairo he could cope with threats from both sides of the river and prevent the massing of the forces of General Pillow east of the river with Gen. Jeff Thompson on the west.[22]

From September 10, 1861, until October 1, Oglesby commanded a force based at Norfolk, Missouri. Grant sent him on repeated reconnaissance missions toward Belmont, often in conjunction with a Union gunboat and also ordered similar missions to the west of Cairo toward Charleston, Missouri, in order to ascertain the position of Pillow and Thompson. Although Grant wished to move on Columbus, he was under-strength. As many as one-sixth of his troops were ill, and Frémont was unwilling to divert troops from southwestern Missouri where Union forces had been defeated at Wilson's Creek near Springfield. Oglesby was successful in capturing a few Confederate prisoners and probing behind the lines, but he was under orders not to engage the enemy in force. Despairing of immediate reinforcements and concerned about rumored movements of Thompson in Missouri, Grant ordered Oglesby on October 1 to withdraw from Norfolk to Bird's Point. As he explained to Oglesby, it was "the better part of valor to be prudent." Oglesby was to assume command of the large camp at Bird's Point across the Mississippi River from Cairo, from whence he could move either west or south to engage the enemy.[23]

Acting on information supplied by a Confederate deserter, Grant ordered

Oglesby to send a thousand men to Charleston, Missouri, about ten miles to the west, to disrupt the supposed route of Jeff Thompson, rumored to be leaving Belmont. Oglesby sent 1,150 infantry and 100 cavalry, but Thompson did not appear. He had moved southwest from Belmont to New Madrid. Meanwhile, Grant and John A. McClernand had to deal with the frustrations of their volunteer soldiers. Before leaving Norfolk, Oglesby's men had, according to information Grant relayed to his superiors, wantonly burned the steam ferry. On October 9, Grant recommended assessing the entire command double the damage. On that same day, McClernand, in overall command of Cairo and vicinity, ordered the closing of all "tippling and other disorderly houses." Oglesby may have avoided some of the immediate embarrassment inflicted by his men by taking a ten-day furlough. In Decatur, he saw his two-month-old daughter Anna Elizabeth for the first time. He was also welcomed by his wife Anna and their twenty-two-month-old son Dickie. When Oglesby returned to duty about October 17, he found that Grant had reorganized the troops into brigades, and he was assigned to the Second. His new command consisted of his own Eighth Illinois, the Seventh Iowa, and the Twenty-second Illinois, along with Capt. Charles Houghtaling's light artillery—eighty officers and 1,190 infantry and fifteen officers and 258 artillerymen in all. Grant and the men wanted action, and he was organizing to attack should the opportunity present itself.[24]

The opportunity came on November 7, 1861, at Belmont. Orders were received from Frémont in St. Louis on November 1 to make a demonstration on both sides of the river in the direction of Columbus. The next day, Frémont's command ordered Grant to send a force to the St. Francis River, sixty miles west of Cairo, to aid in forcing Thompson to retreat into Arkansas. Showing his aggressive nature, Grant immediately ordered Oglesby to lead an expanded command to destroy Thompson's army. On November 2, Lincoln removed Frémont from his command. Grant apparently learned of the change on November 5, and the next day he embarked with three thousand men on riverboats heading downstream toward Columbus. Taking advantage of the vacuum created by the transition of command in St. Louis, Grant reinterpreted the term *demonstration* and attacked Belmont. His men pushed the outnumbered Confederates away from their camps. While Grant's undisciplined volunteers were celebrating and looking for souvenirs, Confederate reinforcements were ferried across the river from Columbus, and Grant was forced to retreat to the boats. He suffered about six hundred casualties, including ninety killed; the Confederates lost 641, including 105 killed.[25]

Meanwhile, Oglesby had promptly obeyed Grant's orders of November 2 and, after taking passage on riverboats upstream to Commerce, Missouri, had marched sixty miles southwest to Bloomfield. The march took them across a miserable swamp, forcing them to construct bridges and upgrade some roads on the way. By the time Oglesby reached Bloomfield, Thompson had fled southward. In Bloomfield, Oglesby received new orders from Grant to turn southward toward New Madrid and to communicate with Grant at Belmont. Oglesby's four-thousand-man force was but one of six columns, on both the Kentucky and the Missouri sides of the river, which Grant had suddenly ordered to parallel his drive toward Columbus. He may have furtively intended to attack Columbus, but his retreat from Belmont negated any further offensive plans. Before Oglesby could turn toward Belmont, and after Grant's retreat, Colonel Oglesby received oral orders via Col. William H. L. Wallace to return to base camp at Bird's Point. Oglesby told Wallace that he would not cross "the terrible swamp . . . again for a reputation." He marched his command northeasterly to Cape Giradeau and returned to Bird's Point by steamship on November 12.[26]

In his memoirs, Grant stated that his purpose in attacking Belmont had been to protect Oglesby's troops from Confederate reinforcements coming from Kentucky to Missouri. He admitted that his actions had been "severely criticized in the North as a wholly unnecessary battle, barren of results." Grant contended, however, "If it had not been fought, Colonel Oglesby would probably have been captured or destroyed with his three thousand men. Then I should have been culpable indeed." Grant's memoirs represent the culmination of his attempts to rationalize the battle at Belmont. He also allowed his staff to rewrite the official record of the battle after he had been appointed as Lincoln's top commander in 1864. In reality, no danger to Oglesby existed, because the Confederates were unwilling to send troops to Thompson in Missouri.[27]

Grant's withdrawal to Cairo and Bird's Point was only temporary. He was still spoiling for a fight, but his next move would have to await the sanction of his new commander, Henry W. Halleck, and the completion of seven armored gunships. In the interim, Grant tried to keep his volunteer soldiers battle-ready and disciplined. As camp commander at Bird's Point, Oglesby administered Grant's orders to punish soldiers who looted, confiscate contraband intended for the Confederates, and keep a careful watch on enemy forces. On occasion, the troops had to turn out for dignitaries such as Oglesby's friend, the newly appointed U.S. senator Orville H. Browning, who visited Oglesby at Bird's Point on November 21. Oglesby also kept in touch with David Davis. During the three-month interim between the battles of Belmont and Fort Henry, Oglesby served as Bird's Point camp commander until he was granted home leave between Christmas and New Year's. Colonel Oglesby was given command of the first brigade of the First Division on the eve of the Fort Henry expedition.[28]

In early 1862 President Lincoln lamented to Gen. Montgomery C. Meigs: "General, what shall I do? The people are impatient . . . the General of the Army [McClellan] has typhoid fever. The bottom is out of the tub. What shall I do?" Lincoln answered his own question by insisting that his generals take the offensive. Halleck responded by allowing Grant to attack Fort Henry on the Tennessee River at the northern border of Tennessee. Grant combined forces with Flag Officer Andrew Foote, who shipped Grant's army up the Tennessee River to within four miles of Fort Henry. Oglesby's brigade, under McClernand's divisional command, landed on the east bank and slogged through the muddy terrain toward the fort. He and his Eighth Illinois Regiment were ordered forward to reconnoiter. About a mile from Fort Henry they encountered a troop of Confederate cavalry and drove them back, with the loss of one killed on each side. But Foote's ironclads had moved faster than Grant's soldiers. The river fleet forced the surrender of the partially flooded and outgunned fort before McClernand's division could close off the escape road. Two thousand Confederates scampered toward Fort Donelson, twelve miles to the east, to fight again. Fewer than a hundred men were left to surrender. Grant, with Oglesby leading his right front, entered the fort on February 6, 1861.[29]

Grant and his volunteer soldiers may have thought Fort Donelson was also ripe for capture. It was, but Oglesby's brigade was destined to pay a heavy price for the fruits of victory. Oglesby's command, consisting of five Illinois infantry regiments—his own Eighth, the Eighteenth, the Twenty-ninth, Thirtieth, and Thirty-first in addition to several cavalry companies and two artillery batteries—led the way across the land between the rivers. Meanwhile, Foote was to transport some troops north to the Ohio River, back south on the Cumberland River, and then stage another gunboat attack on Fort Donelson. McClernand's division, Oglesby's brigade in the lead, encountered Confederate cavalry under Nathan B. Forrest on February 12 but were able to maneuver into position on Wynn's Ferry Road, south of the fort near Dover, Tennessee. On February 13, Oglesby's men moved closer to the river and to within a few hundred yards of Confederate fortifications. From there, they blocked the main roads south out of the fort. The Confederate forces seemed content to hunker down in their strongly fortified positions. The eager, inexperienced Union troops suffered because they attacked prematurely and because they had abandoned overcoats and blankets on the twelve-mile hike in autumnal weather. On the night of February 13, bitter north winds brought rain, sleet, and three inches of snow. The temperature dropped to twelve degrees Fahrenheit. As Oglesby's official report recalled, "The men stood to arms all night under one of the most persecuting snow storms ever known in this country, without fire and without reliefs." They had also exhausted their rations. One of Oglesby's regimental commanders put it more simply: "The men remained with arms in their hands during the night; the extreme cold and snow forbade their lying down." Valentine's Day witnessed cheers from the Confederate garrison as Foote and his gunboats were disabled by effective battery fire from the fort. McClernand then moved McArthur's brigade to Oglesby's right to tighten the siege by extending the lines nearer to Dover and the river.[30]

Saturday, February 15, was cold and deadly for Oglesby's men. During the night of February 14–15, Confederate generals John B. Floyd, Gideon J. Pillow, and Simon Buckner decided to break out of the Union encirclement by attacking the Union's right flank. Oglesby's brigade, as part of McClernand's division, and John A. McArthur's brigade, were the first to feel Pillow's furious attack. Before Oglesby's troops could finish drinking their coffee and eating a few scraps of hardtack, the only rations available, the attack began. Two Decatur regiments, Isaac Pugh's Forty-first (assigned to McArthur's brigade) and Oglesby's own Eighth, bore the first blow. Of the 613 men of the Eighth, 54 would be killed and 188 wounded, including three officers killed and five wounded. By about 10 A.M., McArthur's brigade had been bent around Oglesby's right flank and began to dissolve. When Oglesby's men ran low on ammunition, a Union regiment from Kentucky was ordered to take their place in the line, but because of confusion of uniforms, "friendly fire" was exchanged with Union troops already in line. It was difficult to find and identify the enemy, which, according to Oglesby's report, "skulked behind every hiding place, and sought refuge in the oak leaves, between which and their uniforms there was so strong a resemblance, our men were continually deceived by them." With no organized unit guarding their right flank and with many of their officers incapacitated, they began to withdraw piecemeal toward the hospital and the ammunition supply.[31]

In his official report, Lt. Col. James B. McPherson, Grant's chief engineer, vouched for "the determined bravery of General McClernand's division, which though forced to fall back after several hours of the most severe fighting, did it, contesting every foot of ground." When the fighting began, Grant was conferring on Foote's gunboat. Fortunately, Gen. Lew Wallace recognized the need to order John M. Thayer's brigade into position to stop the Confederate advance along Wynn's Ferry Road. When Grant finally arrived on the scene in the early afternoon, mass confusion and demoralization on the part of brigades that had borne the blunt of the attack were apparent. He quickly ordered a counterattack that coincided with an inexplicable order given by General Pillow for the Confederates to return to their fortifications. Grant also ordered Gen. Charles F. Smith to attack from the left to reduce the pressure on Grant's right, and Smith managed to pierce some Confederate fortifications. By evening, most of the surviving members of Oglesby's brigade were back in their early-morning positions, tending to half-frozen wounded comrades and dreading the next day.[32]

Dawn brought jubilation to Oglesby's lacerated brigade. They were greeted with white flags flying above the enemy works. Pillow had opened an escape route with his offensive against Grant's right flank, but he and his fellow commanders had failed to order a breakout. On midday of February 15, Pillow had telegraphed his commander, Albert Sidney Johnston, "On the honor of a soldier, the day is ours." Perhaps it was, as Lew Wallace unchivalrously recorded in his memoirs, that "General Pillow's vanity whistled itself into ludicrous exaltation." He may have believed that he could defeat the Yankees any day or that he had forced open the escape door permanently. Overnight, however, the situation changed drastically. The Confederate triumvirate of Floyd, Pillow, and Buckner was in despair. Pillow surmised that Grant had closed the escape route; Floyd reported that Union reinforcements were pouring in by ship; and Buckner believed he could not resist another attack from C. F. Smith in his sector. Buckner argued that surrender was the only alternative, given encirclement by an overwhelming enemy force, depleted ammunition, no hope of reinforcement, and the prospect of three-quarters of the command being destroyed in a breakout attempt. No general, he opined, "had the right to make such a sacrifice of human life." The other generals reluctantly agreed, but they wanted to pass the ignoble task of surrendering down the chain of command from Floyd to Pillow to Buckner. When Buckner, Grant's old army friend, asked for terms, he was shocked at the response: "No terms except unconditional and immediate surrender can be accepted. I propose to move immediately upon your works." There was no choice but to accept. Nathan Forrest refused, however, and led his cavalry through icy fords to escape; Floyd, Pillow, and a few hundred others fled by boat. But some fifteen thousand Confederates were surrendered. Starved for a victory, the North noted that Grant's initials could also stand for Unconditional Surrender or for Uncle Sam. He was gaining fame and was soon aware that his victory had "created a perfect furor through the North." A few days later, however, he reflected to his wife, "These terrible battles are very good things to read about for persons who lose no friends but I am decidedly in favor of having as little of it as possible. The way to avoid it is to push forward as vigorously as possible."[33]

Soon the shattered brigades of Oglesby and others from the right flank paraded into Dover to the tune of Yankee Doodle. Oglesby's men were thankful to be alive but shocked by the grievous loss of their comrades. In the parlance of the war, they had seen the elephant. In Oglesby's brigade, the Decatur regiment had suffered the most casualties: 242. In McClernand's division, Oglesby's brigade endured the most casualties: 853. Among the three divisions under Grant, McClernand's First experienced the most victims: 1,552, or a 20 percent loss from eight thousand troops. Grant's army of 21,500 lost a total of 2,832. Scores more would subsequently die from wounds, pneumonia, and other cold-weather-related ailments.[34]

After the battle, there were recriminations among the vanquished as well as the victors. Floyd and Pillow were shunned by Confederate president Jefferson Davis. Among some of the winners, there were disputes over who should reap the glory. When transmitting former Democratic Congressman McClernand's voluminous report, Grant observed that it was "a little highly colored as to the conduct of the First Division." When he went over his papers years later, Oglesby came upon a copy of McClernand's congratulatory order to his men and penciled on the back of it, "We did the fighting. He did the writing." Neither did McClernand forward Oglesby's report to the war department. Lew Wallace complained in his memoirs that McClernand's report ignored Wallace's help. "All he plausibly can he appropriates to himself," Wallace protested.[35]

From St. Louis, Grant's commander, Henry W. Halleck, telegraphed General-in-Chief George B. McClellan on February 17: "Make Buell, Grant, and [John] Pope major-generals of volunteers, and give me command in the West. I ask this in return for Forts Henry and Donelson." Halleck got his reward a few weeks later when a new department was created by adding Don Carlos Buell's Ohio Department and Kansas to his command. Halleck may have wanted to blunt Grant's newly achieved celebrity by having the three generals promoted simultaneously. Among generals, date of rank was the dominant distinction. Grant, however, had his own patron in Washington, Cong. Elihu Washburne. On the night of Grant's victory at Fort Donelson, President Lincoln nominated Grant as major general. The Senate approved the nomination three days later, with rank from February 16. Washburne immediately telegraphed Grant: "You are appointed Major General." Buell and Pope's promotions were dated March 22. On March 3, 1862, President Lincoln directed the secretary of war to promote to major general those brigadiers who had commanded divisions at Fort Donelson, including John A. McClernand, Charles F. Smith, and Lewis Wallace. Promoted to brigadier general were John Cook, Richard J. Oglesby, William H. L. Wallace, John

McArthur, Jacob G. Lauman, and John A. Logan. The appointments were confirmed on March 22 by the U.S. Senate. Although the appointments were consistent with Lincoln's military policy of rewarding victorious officers, Republican and Democrat, Oglesby readily acknowledged the aid of three of Lincoln's campaign managers, David Davis, Leonard Swett, and Ward Hill Lamon, in securing his promotion. He also wrote to the adjutant general in Washington, asking that his promotion be given rank over John Cook of the Seventh Illinois because he had seniority as a colonel. Oglesby and Cook's date-of-rank dispute would continue into their old age.[36]

After Fort Donelson, Grant's desire "to push forward as vigorously as possible" was stymied by Halleck's need to consolidate his enlarged command. Halleck faulted Grant for his alleged failures to report, his aggressive posture, and the lack of discipline among his victorious volunteer troops. Oglesby had to deal with one example of the lack of discipline in an Irish regiment on St. Patrick's Day on board a transport. An eyewitness reported that there were fistfights all day, most of them among drunken Irishmen. Various officers' attempts to quell the troubles failed. "In stepped 'Old Col. Dick' who yelled out at them in his usual comic way, to stop that riot," and the disturbance quieted. According to the admiring witness, one soldier, "who had been bullying, drinking and fighting all night and morning, concluded he would whip the Col. too." Perhaps remembering the near-fatal incident involving an Irish regiment on a boat in the Mexican War, Oglesby "seized a gun from one of the Guards and stabbed him two or three times in the thigh, making the blood run freely." The soldier retreated.[37]

Between the battles of Fort Donelson and Shiloh, Oglesby was assigned various commands. He was commander of the Fort Donelson post at Dover for several weeks. Hundreds of fugitive slaves were in camp, and some had been used by the Confederates to build the fortifications that had stymied the Union forces. Soon, slave owners were importuning the army for the return of their slaves. Oglesby ruled that a slave could leave camp voluntarily, but his command would not "deliver him to his master or to any men claiming to be his master." The spirit of his orders, he proclaimed, "is not to make us slave catchers." Most Illinois soldiers were fighting for the Union and not yet to end slavery, but they were willing to allow the fugitives to stay in camp as quasi-servants and laborers. On March 7, Grant ordered Oglesby to dismount the fort's guns and the surplus "public and private property" at Fort Donelson and ship them to Cairo. A week later, he ordered Oglesby to take his command, by boat, to join the forces under Gen. Charles F. Smith near Savannah, Tennessee.[38]

Meanwhile, the Confederate forces under Albert Sidney Johnston's command had abandoned their posts at Columbus, Kentucky, and Nashville and had retreated to a line paralleling the northern boundary of Mississippi. Johnston made a fateful decision to concentrate his forces, as he had failed to do before the Donelson debacle, and attack Grant before Buell's army could join him after Buell's occupation of Nashville. Grant, however, was offensive-minded and seemed to ignore the possibility of being attacked. On April 5 he reported to Halleck, "I have scarcely the faintest idea of an attack, (general one) being made upon us." On the same date he granted Oglesby a ten-day leave of absence. Oglesby recalled that Grant had asked him "to return in eight days if possible as he wished to move against Corinth [Mississippi] by that time. He said I could go very well as the Enemy was not near us and he apprehended no attack from them." But Johnston attacked Grant on April 6, at Shiloh Church (Pittsburg Landing), Tennessee. Grant's miscalculation may have saved Oglesby's life, but it cost the lives of hundreds of others. In the bloodiest battle of the war to date, Grant's army suffered 13,047 casualties compared to about 10,700, including Johnston, for the enemy. Oglesby's old brigade lost 580 men, and the new commander was wounded. The new brigade, to which Oglesby had been assigned on April 2, lost 535 men, and its acting commander was mortally wounded. Although the North rejoiced at the victory (the Confederates had retreated), the troops from Illinois mourned as casualty lists were published.[39]

Oglesby must have been mortified by his absence at the battle. Two years later during the heated gubernatorial campaign, the editor of the Springfield Democratic newspaper recalled having dined with Oglesby in Cairo on the opening day of the battle of Shiloh. Oglesby, whom the newspaper referred to as "the miscegen[ation] candidate," was asked if a battle was imminent. "Of course," he flippantly replied. "What else brings so many officers away just at this time?" When Oglesby returned to the front near Corinth, Mississippi, he was given command of the Second Brigade of Gen. Thomas A. Davies's Second Division. By Oglesby's account, "I was now separated from my old Regt and Brigade, as Genl Grant persisted in the opinion that in all cases of promotions of Colonels, it was the best policy to separate them entirely from their old commands." He may have felt that he must display unflinching bravery in the next battle. After the great bloodletting at Shiloh, the Union forces moved gingerly toward Corinth, the strategic rail crossing that was the objective of the campaign. Grant reported to his wife on May 31, "Corinth is now in our hands without much fighting." The Confederates had retreated to Tupelo.[40]

During the summer of 1862, Oglesby was intermittently a brigade commander, commander at Corinth, and acting division commander. His load was lightened by the appointment of his Decatur law partner and confidant Sheridan Wait as his assistant adjutant general. Oglesby's routine included writing letters of recommendation for promotions, especially for surviving members of his Decatur regiment; responding to complaints about his "stinking camp"; and making patriotic speeches. He recommended the Eighth Regiment's assistant surgeon to Governor Yates for promotion by writing, "He will cut off a soldiers leg or a traitors head at a blow and with equal skill in the shortest possible time." After a medical officer complained to Oglesby's commander about the stench around his camp, Oglesby was reprimanded for his answer: "If he smelled any stink around my camp it was one of his own creating." His oratorical skills also came into play. One soldier from the Seventh Illinois reported, "On the Fourth of July we had a soldier's celebration, a barbecue and a grand dinner . . . we are also favored on the occasion with a good, wholesouled speech from General Oglesby." A soldier of the Fifty-second Illinois shared the sentiment: "Oglesby is a merry whole souled man, and [Brig. Cmdr. Pleasant A.] Hackleman is fully as good." In three months, the two "whole souled" generals would be carted off the battlefield in the same ambulance.[41]

Oglesby almost dodged the bullet again in the October 3 opening of the battle of Corinth. On July 30 he presented a surgeon's certificate of disability and asked for a twenty-day leave. He wrote to inform Grant's headquarters that he was unfit for duty. His request was refused, but it was apparently forwarded to Halleck. On September 4 Oglesby was granted "fifteen days absence owing to his disability." The "disability" was probably diarrhea, but a more compelling reason for the request may have been the illness of his year-old daughter Anna, who died on September 6, 1862. Another daughter was probably conceived during his brief leave. Olive would be born on June 17, 1863.[42]

Although the bloody battle of Corinth involved a total of more than forty thousand troops, contemporary and subsequent historians and biographers have often either overlooked it or confused it with the battle of Shiloh. In early 1868, Isaac N. Arnold, a prominent Lincoln biographer, wrote to Oglesby to ask if some mistake had been made in recording October 1862 rather than April as the date Oglesby had been shot. The reply was terse: "On the 3rd and 4th of October 1862, the terrible battle of Corinth was fought under the immediate command of Gen. [William S.] Rosecrans, in which battle on the afternoon of the first day, leading a charge of my small Brigade, I was mortally wounded, but as you are aware, have not yet died."[43]

In September 1862 Confederate generals Earl Van Dorn and Sterling Price were ordered to attack Grant's forces along the Mississippi-Tennessee border to prevent Union forces from being shifted toward Nashville and beyond, where Confederate general Braxton Bragg was mounting a major offensive. Price attacked Iuka, Mississippi, with seventeen thousand troops on September 19, 1862, but was unable to sustain the attack. Combining forces with Van Dorn, the Confederates next attacked Corinth. In late September, Oglesby returned to his command of the Second Brigade of Thomas A. Davies's Second Division of the Army of West Tennessee stationed in Corinth. Major General Rosecrans headed the Union forces in the area. Through detachment and attrition, the brigades were vastly under strength. Oglesby's brigade counted only 720 effectives, a number less than full strength for a single regiment. The other two brigades, Gen. Pleasant Hackleman's with 1,097 men and Col. Silas Baldwin's with 1,117, were also grossly under strength. With reduced size, brigade commanders acted more like regimental leaders who were expected to be seen near the front.[44]

On October 3 Confederate forces attacked Corinth from the northwest along the road from Chewalla, Tennessee. Grant and Rosecrans were uncertain what city the enemy would attack and thus were slow to send reinforcements. The attack was largely funneled into a V-shaped area bounded by the Memphis and Charleston Railroad, which followed a northwestward line, and the Mobile and Ohio Railroad, which ran due north. The railroads intersected in Corinth. Slow to come to Corinth, Rosecrans gave very few directions to David S. Stanley, Thomas Davies, and Charles Hamilton, his division commanders.[45]

At 9 A.M., Oglesby's brigade, as a part of Davies's division, formed a line of battle about a mile and a half north of Corinth and on the west side of the Mobile and Ohio Railroad line. Finding no enemy but hearing cannon fire to the north, they pushed forward to the old earthworks that the Confederates had built during their occupation of the city. The Confederates attacked at about 10. Davies's thin line was not sufficient to halt the attack, and there were gaps on their flanks. He ordered his men to fall back so that the width of the line between the railroads would be compacted. During the retreat, the men often established temporary lines to slow the Confederate push. The "retrograde" movements were sometimes haphazard as some men broke ranks and fled. Davies came up and established a rallying point where Hackleman and Oglesby could reorganize. Oglesby, chagrined by the retreat and perhaps remembering that he had escaped the carnage at Shiloh, shouted to his troops: "Men, we are going to fight them on this ground. If there's dying to be done, men, I pledge to you my word I'll stay with you and take my share of it." Davies, however, ordered his division to fall back a few hundred yards more to more defensible terrain about 725 yards in front of Battery Robinett in Corinth. On the left of this new line was a single white house that became the sighting point as well as the designation of the line.[46]

By the time that line was established at about 3 P.M., enemy fire, fatigue, heatstroke, and terror at being overrun had reduced Oglesby's brigade to 576 men. Davies ordered a counterattack. Oglesby believed that his thin line was all that stood between the Confederates and the capture of Corinth. Speaking for his men in a report he filed in March 1864, Oglesby wrote: "It was inspiring to behold the soldier shaking off hesitation, doubt and dismay as the nobler and irrepressible emotions of the soul rose to true heroism and bounding into the region of loftiest manhood drove him on to victory and to death."[47]

All three of Davies's brigade commanders were at the front. All were shot. General Hackleman suffered what was to be a mortal wound, and Col. Silas D. Baldwin was slightly wounded in the hand. He was later cashiered for leaving his men both at Fort Donelson and Corinth. A one-ounce minié ball struck Oglesby under the left armpit above the heart and pierced his lungs as he was speaking with Col. Augustus Chetlain. Oglesby recalled that he felt no pain at first but knew he had been hit because he was gasping for breath and weakened. Chetlain summoned an ambulance. Davies's report quoted the bleeding Oglesby as having said, "Never mind me; look yonder (pointing to the enemy); I have lived to see my troops victorious." Oglesby's recollections were similar. In 1864 he remembered, "I received almost my death wound but thank God, as I turned from the field as I thought dying—I beheld with a joy my soul cannot express the lines of the enemy breaking as our flag was advancing. I saw no more of the battle of Corinth." The Union counterattack was short-lived, however. Rosecrans ordered a retreat to the prepared positions in Corinth, where fierce fighting would resume the next day. Rosecrans mobilized various scattered units and carried the battle on October 4. Oglesby's brigade suffered 333 casualties, or a 46 percent loss; Davies's division 976, or 30 percent; and Rosecrans's army had 2,520 casualties, including 27 officers killed and 115 wounded out of 21,147 engaged (a 12 percent loss). Like Fort Donelson, Oglesby's brigade led the army in terms of the relative casualties. The Confederates suffered almost identical losses from a number similar to Rosecrans's army but were forced to retreat in disarray.[48]

The ambulance carrying Oglesby picked up General Hackleman along the way to Corinth. Only after the vehicle had crossed a corduroy bridge did Oglesby's pain begin. That night, General Davies came to visit his wounded brigade commanders in the makeshift hospital in Corinth's Tishomingo Hotel. He found them all in the same room. Hackleman died in Davies's presence, and "General Oglesby was undergoing most excruciating pain." His misery increased when the hospital had to be temporarily evacuated when the Confederates threatened the town. On October 4 Rosecrans telegraphed Grant: "Brig General Hackleman fell bravely . . . Genl Oglesby dangerously wounded." On October 9 Dr. John Holston, medical director of the Army of the Tennessee, telegraphed Oglesby's prognosis to Grant: "I have scarcely any hope—The Ball is not found, and interferes seriously with the most important functions of life respiration and circulation—his ease is deceptive." Holston followed up on the next day by a wire: "Genl Oglesby case I had re-examined by surgeon Norman Gay this morning. Pulse 120 lying down breathing forty in the minute—Great distress-the doctor agrees with my opinion telegraphed yesterday—no reasonable hope of recovery."[49]

On the morning after the Confederates had been repulsed by Rosecrans's army at Corinth, Grant telegraphed General Halleck in Washington: "Genl Oglesby dangerously wounded." On October 8 Lincoln congratulated Grant on his recent victories. He added that he was "very anxious to know the condition of Gen. Oglesby, who is an intimate personal friend." Grant replied: "Genl Oglesby is shot through the breast & ball lodged in spine. Hopes for his recovery."[50]

## Notes

1. *Register,* Dec. 22, 1861, p. 1, col. 1; see also New York *Herald,* Jan. 28, 1861, cited in *Collected Works,* vol. 4, pp. 175–76.

2. *Journal,* Jan. 5, 1861, p. 4, col. 3, Jan. 7, 1861, p. 3, col. 2; Moses, vol. 2, p. 637.

3. *Register,* Jan. 9, 1861, p. 2, col. 2.

4. Moses, vol. 2, p. 638; *Register,* Jan. 10, 1865, p. 3, col. 1, Jan. 15, 1861, p. 3, col. 5; *Journal,* Jan. 10, 1861, p. 2, col. 1. Both the *Journal* and the *Register* printed daily summaries of the proceedings of the General Assembly. Similar accounts are in the *Journal of the Senate of the Twenty-second General Assembly of the State of Illinois at Their Regular Session, Begun and Held at Springfield, January 7, 1861* (Springfield: Bailhache and Baker, Printers, 1861).

5. Moses, vol. 1, pp. 639–40; *New York Herald,* Jan. 14, 1861, as quoted *Lincoln Day by Day,* vol. 3, p. 5; Arthur Charles Cole, *The Era of the Civil War 1848–1870* (Springfield: Illinois Centennial Commission, 1919), pp. 255–56.

6. *Register,* Jan. 12, 1861, p. 2, col. 3; *Journal,* Jan. 14, 1861, p. 2, cols. 2–3, Jan. 26, 1861, p. 2, cols. 4–6; Helen E. Marshall, *Grandest of Enterprises: Illinois State Normal University, 1857–1957* (Normal: Illinois State Normal University, 1956), pp. 67–69.

7. Cole, *Era of the Civil War,* pp. 257–58; *Register,* Feb. 4, 1861, p. 3, cols. 3–4; *Journal,* Feb. 4, 1861, p. 2, col. 1.

8. *Register,* Jan. 12–Feb. 23, 1861. The legislative summaries usually appeared on page 3. The separate property bill vote is in the *Illinois Senate Journal,* 22d sess., Feb. 4, 1861, p. 251.

9. *Register,* Feb. 7, 1861, p. 2, col. 6.

10. *Register,* Jan. 23, 1861, p. 2, col. 5, Jan. 24, 1861, p. 3, col. 3; Cole, *Era of the Civil War,* p. 259.

11. *Register,* Feb. 25, 1861, p. 2, col. 1; *Illinois Senate Journal,* 22d sess., Feb. 22, 1861, pp. 644–45.

12. RJO to Abraham Lincoln, Springfield, Jan. 31, 1861, and RJO to W. H. Lamon, Decatur, April 3, 1861, both in the Ward Hill Lamon Collection, Huntington Library; RJO to Lincoln, Feb. 17, 1861, Oglesby MSS.

13. Moses, vol. 2, p. 641.

14. *Illinois Senate Journal, Special Session,* April 23, 1861, pp. 8, 10; Robert W. Johannsen, *Stephen A. Douglas* (New York: Oxford University Press, 1973), pp. 866–67; Moses, vol. 2, p. 643.

15. *Illinois Senate Journal, Special Session,* April 26, 1861, p. 19. General Order No. 89, Illinois Adjutant General's Office, Springfield, May 20, 1861, addressed to Col. William H. L. Wallace, reads: "It is the order of the Commander-in-Chief that the following shall be the number and rank of the Colonels of the Six Regiments raised and organized under the call for volunteers by the Governor April 16, 1861. 7th Regiment John Cook Colonel 3d; 8th di[tto] Richard J. Oglesby's 2nd." Benjamin M. Prentiss (Tenth Regiment) was listed first because he was to be brigade commander. Wallace-Dickey Collection, ISHL; Moses, vol. 2, pp. 649, 645; *Register,* April 26, 1861, p. 3, col. 1; *Report of the Adjutant General of the State of Illinois,* 8 vols. (Springfield: Phillips Bros. State Printers, 1900–1901), vol. 1, pp. 273, 388.

16. *Report of the Adjutant General of the State of Illinois,* vol. 1, pp. 7, 8; *Register,* April 29, 1861, p. 3, col. 2, April 30, 1861, p. 3, col. 2.

17. *Register,* April 29, 1861, p. 3, col. 2; E. T. Coleman, "The Story of Decatur: First in War," *Decatur Review,* Feb. 26, 1924.

18. Coleman, "The Story of Decatur"; B. M. Prentiss to RJO, Camp Defiance, May 9, 1861, Oglesby MSS; *Journal,* June 18, 1861, p. 2, col. 3.

19. William Howard Russell, *My Diary North and South* (1863, repr. New York: Harper, 1954), p. 177; "Russell at Cairo," unidentified newspaper clipping, Oglesby MSS.

20. *Journal,* June 17, 1861, p. 2, col. 3, June 18, 1861, p. 2, col. 3; *Report of the Adjutant General of the State of Illinois,* vol. 1, p. 428.

21. Ulysses S. Grant, *Personal Memoirs of U. S. Grant,* 2 vols. (New York: Century Company, 1885–86), vol. 1, p. 264. Oglesby's account, in "Grant Takes Command at Cairo," *JISHS* 39 (June 1945): 242–44, varies on some of the details. Another account is *Recollections of John McWilliams; His Youth, Experiences in California and in the Civil War* (Princeton: Princeton University Press, 1929), pp. 121–22. Noting that Grant was in Cairo on September 2, John Y. Simon doubts that he would wait two days after his arrival to take command. It may be that the incident did take place on September 2, but the more specific, detailed published order was not written until September 4 (*Grant Papers,* vol. 2, p. 184n). The official order is in *Official Records,* ser. 1, vol. 3, p. 47.

22. Bruce Catton, *Grant Moves South* (Boston: Little, Brown, 1960), pp. 58–61.

23. *Grant Papers,* vol. 2, pp. 235, 236, 245, 246, 252, 280, 292, 314, 315, vol. 3, pp. 5–6; Nathaniel Cheairs Hughes, Jr., *The Battle of Belmont* (Chapel Hill: University of North Carolina Press, 1991), p. 5.

24. *Grant Papers,* vol. 3, pp. 6, 12, 29, 388; McClernand, General Order No. B, Camp Cairo, Oct. 9, 1861, Oglesby MSS; *Official Records,* ser. 1, vol. 3, pp. 533, 558.

25. John Y. Simon, "Grant at Belmont," *Military Affairs* 45 (Dec. 1981): 161–66; Kenneth

P. Williams, *Lincoln Finds a General*, 5 vols. (New York: Macmillan, 1952), vol. 3, pp. 75–81; Hughes, *The Battle of Belmont*, pp. 51–52, 184–85.

26. *Official Records,* ser. 1, vol. 3, pp. 256–57; Hughes, *The Battle of Belmont*, pp. 46, 47, 55.

27. Grant, *Personal Memoirs*, vol. 2, p. 281; A. L. Conger, *The Rise of U. S. Grant* (1931, repr. Freeport: Books for Libraries, 1970), appendix A, "Belmont in the Memoirs," chronicles the eleven accounts given progressively by Grant. Hughes, *The Battle of Belmont*, pp. 192–97; Simon, "Grant at Belmont," p. 165.

28. Catton, *Grant Moves South*, pp. 101–3; General Orders, July 1861–April 1862, Oglesby MSS; Richard Oglesby, "Report to Lorenzo Thomas, Adjt. Gen. of the Army," March 1864, typescript, Oglesby MSS, pp. 2–3; entry for Nov. 21, 1861, *Browning Diary,* vol. 1, p. 510; David Davis to RJO, Oct. 27, 1861, Oglesby MSS.

29. Catton, *Grant Moves South*, pp. 141–45. Lincoln's January 10, 1862, statement to Meigs is quoted in *Recollected Words of Abraham Lincoln,* comp. and ed. Don E. Fehrenbacher and Virginia Fehrenbacher (Stanford: Stanford University Press, 1996), p. 328. See also "Report of Brig. Gen. John A. Logan," Feb. 10, 1862, *Official Records,* ser. 1, vol. 7, pp. 126–31.

30. "Report of Col. Richard J. Oglesby, Eighth Illinois Infantry, Commanding First Brigade," Feb. 20, 1861, *Official Records,* ser. 1, vol. 7, pp. 183–85; Benjamin Franklin Cooling, *Forts Henry and Donelson: The Key to the Confederate Heartland* (Knoxville: University of Tennessee Press, 1987), pp. 122–46; "Report of Capt. Samuel B. Marks, Eighteenth Illinois Infantry," Feb. 22, 1862, *Official Records,* ser. 1, vol. 7, p. 190; "Report of Brig. Gen. John A. McClernand," Feb. 28, 1862, *Official Records,* ser. 1, vol. 7, pp. 170–82.

31. "Report of Col. Richard J. Oglesby," pp. 185–87; "Report of Brig. Gen. John A. McClernand," pp. 175–78; "Report of Lieut. Col. Frank L. Rhoads, Eighth Illinois Infantry," Feb. 18, 1862, *Official Records,* ser. 1, vol. 7, pp. 188–89.

32. "Report of Lieut. Col. James B. McPherson, Chief Engineer," Feb. 25, 1862, *Official Records,* ser. 1, vol. 7, p. 163; Cooling, *Forts Henry and Donelson,* pp. 171–98.

33. Cooling, *Forts Henry and Donelson,* pp. 175, 182, 209; Edwin C. Bearss, *Unconditional Surrender: The Fall of Fort Donelson,* National Park Service (reprint pamphlet); Ulysses S. Grant to Julia Dent Grant, Ft. Donelson, Feb. 22, 24, 1862, in *Grant Papers,* vol. 4, pp. 271, 284.

34. Cooling, *Forts Henry and Donelson,* p. 213; "Casualties in the Army Commanded by Brig. Gen. U. S. Grant, at the Siege of Fort Donelson, Tennessee," Feb. 12–16, 1862, *Official Records,* ser. 1, vol. 7, pp. 167–69.

35. Grant's cover letter for Brig. Gen. John A. McClernand, "Report, Ft. Donaldson," April 21, 1862, *Official Records,* ser. 1, vol. 7, p. 170; copy of McClernand's congratulatory order, Feb. 17, 1862, Oglesby MSS; RJO to John A. McClernand, Feb. 22, 1864, McClernand Collection, ISHL; Lew Wallace, *An Autobiography,* 2 vols. (New York: Harper and Brothers, 1906), vol. 1, p. 408n.

36. *Official Records,* ser. 1, vol. 7, p. 628; *Collected Works,* vol. 5, p. 142; *Grant Papers,* vol. 4, pp. 272–76; RJO to Ward Hill Lamon, Washington, D.C., March 25, 1862, Lamon Collection, Henry E. Huntington Library; RJO to L. Thomas, Cairo, April 7, 1862, Records of the Adjutant General's Office, Letters Received, 1805–89, 382 B 1864, Record Group 94, National Archives.

37. Ira A. Batterton, March 17, 1862, Batterton Papers, microfilm, ISHL.

38. Cited in Cooling, *Forts Henry and Donelson,* p. 248; Ulysses S. Grant to RJO, March 7, 14, 1862, in *Grant Papers,* vol. 4, p. 333.

39. Ulysses S. Grant to Henry W. Halleck, Savanna[h, Tenn.], April 5, 1862, in *Grant Papers,* vol. 5, p. 14; "Casualties at Pittsburg Landing, or Shiloh, Tenn., April 6–7, 1862," *Official Records,* ser. 1, vol. 10, pt. 1, p. 100.

40. *Register,* June 7, 1864, p. 4, col. 1, June 4, 1864, p. 1, col. 1; Oglesby, "Report to Lorenzo Thomas," p. 8, Oglesby MSS; *Grant Papers,* vol. 5, p. 134.

41. Sheridan Wait to R. S. Whiting, St. Louis, April 23, 1862, Oglesby and Wait Letterpress Book, July 1860–April 1862, Oglesby MSS; RJO to Richard Yates, Aug. 19, 1862, Yates Collection, ISHL; RJO to E. O. C. Ord, July 9, 1862, and Ord to RJO, July 12, 1862, Oglesby MSS; D. Lieb Ambrose, *History of the Seventh Regiment Illinois Volunteer Infantry* (Springfield: Illinois Journal, 1868), p. 82; John S. Wilcox to Wife, July 4, 1862, Wilcox Collection, ISHL.

42. Richard Oglesby to John A. Rawlins, July 30, 1862, Oglesby MSS; *Grant Papers,* vol. 5, p. 3.

43. Richard Oglesby to I. N. Arnold, Chicago, Feb. 19, 1868, Letterpress Book, 1866–69, Oglesby MSS.

44. Peter Cozzens, *The Darkest Days of the War: The Battles of Iuka and Corinth* (Chapel Hill: University of North Carolina Press, 1997), p. 162.

45. Cozzens, *The Darkest Days,* p. 158 and pp. 141, 167 (maps); Albert Castel, "Victory at Corinth," *Civil War Times Illustrated* 17 (Oct. 1978): 12–23.

46. Cozzens, *The Darkest Days,* pp. 165–98; "Report of Brig. Gen. Thomas A. Davies . . . October 3–12," *Official Records,* ser. 1, vol. 17, pp. 252–56.

47. "Report of Brig. Gen. Thomas A. Davies," ser. 1, vol. 17, p. 255; RJO Report, Washington, D.C., March 1864, National Archives; Cozzens, *The Darkest Days,* p. 196.

48. *Official Records,* ser. 1, vol. 17, pt. 1, p. 256; *Grant Papers,* vol. 7, p. 305n. Davies may have been too enamored with including dying statements in his official report. He quoted Hackleman as saying, "I am dying, but I die for my country. If we are victorious, send my remains home; if not, bury me on the field." Col. James Baker's last words were purported to be "I die content. I have seen my regiment victoriously charging the enemy." "Report of Brig. Gen. Thomas A. Davies," ser. 1, vol. 17, pt. 1, p. 256; Oglesby, "Report to Lorenzo Thomas," p. 11; "Report of Casualties," *Official Records,* ser. 1, vol. 17, pt. 1, pp. 173–76; Cozzens, *The Darkest Days,* p. 207.

49. Bancroft, 30; *Official Records,* ser. 1, vol. 17, pt. 1, p. 257; *Grant Papers,* vol. 6, pp. 115n, 144n.

50. Ulysses S. Grant to Henry W. Halleck, Oct. 5, 1862, Abraham Lincoln to Grant, Oct. 8, 1862, and Grant to Lincoln, Oct. 10, 1862, all in *Grant Papers,* vol. 6, pp. 116, 143.

# 5. Fire in the Rear

THE OCTOBER 9 edition of the Republican *Illinois State Journal* carried an article headed "GEN. OGLESBY IS DEAD." His long-time critic the Democratic *Register* praised the fallen "gallant officer." Gen. William Orme, a close friend from Bloomington, lamented to his wife Nannie, "So fall the good and brave—No better man was in the army than Dick Oglesby—But he has gone and many more will pay the same penalty before this unholy war is ended." Within a week, however, Oglesby could profess to be "greatly amused at the obituaries written of him." Yet his recovery was doubtful.[1]

Oglesby's improbable recovery may be credited to his rank, the skill of his physician, his physical fitness, and good luck. According to the memoirs of Dr. Silas T. Trowbridge, Oglesby asked Ulysses S. Grant on October 6 to send Trowbridge to treat him. Grant readily agreed to allow Oglesby's old Eighth Illinois surgeon to make the fifty-five-mile trip from Jackson, Tennessee, but Grant warned the doctor that the rail lines had been interrupted from Bethel to Corinth. Armed with Grant's orders, the Decatur doctor began the journey and found, to his relief, that the Bethel to Corinth line had been reopened. Trowbridge recalled arriving at Oglesby's side at 10 P.M. on October 6. He found Oglesby "pale, haggard and in much distress, incapable of lying down, with a pulse of 136 per minute, respirations very laborious, guarded, catching and 42 per minute." He also noted that Oglesby was "expectorating small quantities of arterial and much larger amounts of venous blood . . . excretions from the kidneys and bowels almost suspended, and [he was] compelled to sit in a semi-recumbent posture in a rocking-chair." Trowbridge observed that the musket ball had entered Oglesby's left side "at the lower and back part of the armpit (Axilla) . . . ranging directly towards the center of the lungs." The doctor concluded, "The ball had passed between the coastal and pulmonary pleura, and lodged in the body of the four dorsal vertebra" and that "the ambulance ride probably disengaged it, and it fell upon the Diaphragm."[2]

Trowbridge gave Oglesby hope by noting that people who lived for several days after a wound often recovered. A conflict soon ensued between Dr. John G. F. Holston, medical director of the Army of the Tennessee, and Trowbridge concerning Oglesby's prognosis. Holston believed that Oglesby would die, and he wished to make him comfortable and to allow him to indulge his appetite for beefsteak and wine augmented with opium. Holston asserted that although there was "scarcely any hope," Oglesby's "Medical attendants [Dr. Trowbridge and staff] feel sanguine of his recovery." Trowbridge used Grant's written orders to overrule the higher-ranking surgeon and prescribed a light diet and morphine to quiet his pain. His pulse came down to 112, and his respiration to 28 per minute. Oglesby soon became jaundiced, but he gradually improved enough to be moved. His wife, sister, and brother-in-law came to retrieve him. On October 11, Grant's headquarters issued orders that read: "Brig General R. J. Oglesby, having been dangerously wounded at the late battle of Corinth, has leave of absence, for the purpose of proceeding to Decatur, Illinois, where he will report by letter to these Headquarters." Trowbridge and Oglesby's staff were allowed to accompany him. A boxcar was rigged for the trip to Decatur, a thick mattress on its floor upon which was placed a rocking chair in a semi-inclined position for Oglesby's comfort.[3]

On November 11, 1862, Sen. Orville H. Browning paid the wounded Oglesby a visit in Decatur. Browning was upset with the issuance of Lincoln's Preliminary Emancipation Proclamation, which, he correctly believed, would cost him reelection to the Senate. Oglesby, according to Browning's diary, agreed that most soldiers "cared nothing about the negro, or party politics— They wished to put down the rebellion, restore the Union, and restore the authority of the constitution and laws and let all other questions alone." Oglesby also expressed his opinion of Grant's generalship. He said that a great injustice had been done to Grant by the charge of drunkenness, "that he once had been dissipated and sometimes drank a little now, but did not get drunk." Oglesby thought Grant "personally brave and anxious to discharge his duties as a soldier, but was not a very able Genl." In Oglesby's experiences at Cairo, Fort Donelson, and Corinth, Grant had seemed incapable of moving large numbers of troops simultaneously. Rather, he would "leave them to go in pell-mell if they chose to do so." Grant apparently thought well of Oglesby, although he had joked to his adjutant that the greatest punishment that could be inflicted upon Oglesby would be enforced silence. Ten days before

Oglesby's conversation with Browning, Grant had recommended him for promotion to major general. He was nominated on February 9, 1863, and confirmed on March 9 to rank as a major general from November 29, 1862. Soon after the rank was confirmed, Oglesby wrote to Ward Hill Lamon, marshal of the District of Columbia, to thank him, Leonard Swett, and Supreme Court Justice David Davis for their unsolicited effort in securing his promotion "from pure motives of personal attachment and kind old remembrances." He added a note intended to be passed along to Lincoln: "Do not forget to remember me to the President cordially. May God spare his life many years yet. I hope he never despairs or falters under his heavy burden."[4]

During Oglesby's convalescence in Decatur, Doctor Trowbridge made monthly reports concerning his condition. On October 31, 1862, he wrote that Oglesby was recovering slowly and that he would eventually recover. A month later he reported that he was "slowly progressing." On December 31, Trowbridge reported that the wound had healed but "the ball not extracted" and "he is not yet fit for duty." Oglesby, however, was so distressed by the perceived lack of enthusiasm for the war effort and the emergence of "semi-traitors" in Illinois that he chose to make a speech before the Union Party's mass meeting being held in the Hall of Representatives in Springfield on the evening of January 9, 1863. According to the *Illinois State Journal,* Oglesby came from his "invalid couch" against the advice of his surgeons and "spoke with great difficulty" at the "Grand Union Demonstration."[5]

"As a citizen and a soldier," he began, "entirely relieved from the domination of party, simply and purely as a honest Union man" and being presently "unfit for duty in the field," he thought "the next best thing to opposing treason in the field would be to go to a good Union meeting." He called for "self-sacrificing patriotism" to counter talk of "concession and compromise with the armed traitors who are waging war against us." Prosperity could wait until there was "a country and Government under which that prosperity can be enjoyed (Cheers)." Oglesby conceded that the Confederates were "brave and determined." It was, however, "their chief and nearly their only excellence," because they "conspired against us and tried to destroy our national existence and blast forever our hopes and the hopes of the civilized world in a Republican form of government." He called for support for Union troops who stood "shoulder to shoulder, differing in politics but united in love of country, covered with the blood of battle." Oglesby's prayer was that he would never have to live in a divided land. To allow dissolution of the country would show Americans as an "ignominious and contemptible people, unable to maintain the charge which God and Washington gave" them. In a statement reminiscent of Lincoln's advice to "stay close to the people," Oglesby asserted that people "may be misled and discouraged for a time, but they will always come out right." When a fire alarm was sounded outside the building, he laughed it off and blamed the Copperheads, who were also responsible the "fire in the rear" of the war effort.[6]

Visibly weakened by his speaking effort, Oglesby shifted his subject to a defense of Lincoln and the Emancipation Proclamation. Lincoln was a "great and good man" whose integrity was beyond reproach. Of the Emancipation Proclamation, Oglesby asserted, "This proclamation is a great thing, perhaps the greatest thing that has occurred in this century. It is too big for us to realize." Beyond the freeing of the slaves, it was a "tremendous thing" because it could "assist in depriving the proud rebel of the services of his slave—by whose labor he is daily fed and supported in his work of death, devastation and treason." Oglesby agreed with Lincoln that the Union could not be saved by conventions or by an armistice; "nothing but hard fighting and a good thrashing" would suffice. The "carnage will be terrible," he admitted. "It is awful to witness, but upon our side it is for country, for liberty, for Union, for freedom, for history and for our blessed posterity for all time to come and we will never fail unless the public sentiment becomes perverted and I believe in God it never will." Oglesby concluded on a lighter note by pointing out that he had been accused of being among those who helped bring about the war. Recalling his role in the election of Lincoln, he retorted, "I don't think I did much to bring it on. I may have pitched in a rail or two, or something of that kind (laughter)." In any event, if his life was spared and his health restored, he intended "to have something to do with winding it up."[7]

Oglesby was anxious, perhaps too anxious, to return to the front. In his monthly report on January 31, 1863, he said he might be able to return to field duty at the end of February and could do light duty even sooner. In next month's report, he stated that he wanted to be assigned to the Department of the Tennessee under Grant but noted that he was still "quite feeble and seriously affected by Rheumatism." On April 1 he joined Grant at Young's Point opposite Vicksburg. Grant assigned him to command the left wing of the Sixteenth Army Corps, with headquarters at Jackson, Tennessee. His immediate commander was another citizen-soldier, Stephen A. Hurlbut, whose headquarters were at Memphis. Sheridan Wait, Oglesby's law partner, returned to duty with Oglesby and Lt. Samuel Caldwell, Oglesby's future gubernatorial secretary, who had been transferred from McClernand's staff to rejoin him. During Oglesby's convalescence, Grant had shifted most of his forces from Tennessee and northern Mississippi to the swamps of the Mississippi River in the vicinity of Vicksburg. Hurlbut and Oglesby's task was to maintain communications along the Memphis and Charleston Railroad from the Mississippi to Corinth, report on enemy troop movements, harass enemy supply lines, and maintain the threat of an attack from the North as a screen for Grant's operations around Vicksburg. A welcome additional assignment was to expedite the recruitment and training of black regiments in his area of command.[8]

Oglesby's three months of active duty corresponded with Grant's shift of operations to the area below Vicksburg, a period that included Grant's defeat of Gen. Joseph Eggleston Johnston's army near Jackson, Mississippi, and his successful siege of Vicksburg. Gen. Grenville M. Dodge, future builder of the Union Pacific Railroad, was the field commander under Oglesby who collected intelligence and harassed enemy supply lines. He directed an attack on Johnston's supply lines in northern Alabama that was supposed to be coordinated with the daring Abel D. Streigh raid in Alabama. Streigh, who had been sent by Gen. William S. Rosecrans from Nashville, was captured by Confederate general Nathan B. Forrest. These movements, however, may have masked the spectacular raid of Benjamin H. Grierson along the length of Mississippi, which in turn disguised Grant's intentions around Vicksburg. Grierson's successful raid originated from LaGrange, in Oglesby's command, on April 17 and concluded at Baton Rouge, Louisiana, on May 2.[9]

Oglesby played an enthusiastic role in the recruitment of blacks into the Union army. With the advent of the draft in March 1863, the recruitment of African Americans became more palatable to the public and to the army. Lorenzo Thomas, adjutant general of the army, was ordered to expedite the recruitment of "colored" regiments, and he arrived in the area a few days after Oglesby assumed command. General Dodge took the lead in organizing black troops by applying for permission to raise two African American regiments and staff them with officers from his own division. Oglesby endorsed his proposal by testifying that he had "personally inspected a company of African soldiers and found them in a good state of discipline, well drilled and quite familiar with the manual of arms." On May 16, Thomas visited Corinth, within Oglesby's jurisdiction, where there was an abundance of black refugees. He made a statement concerning the new policy of recruiting blacks, and Oglesby made a speech that an observer described to his wife as "characteristic of the man, full of truth, sense, and humor." Oglesby told General Dodge that he would "have full power to raise all the colored regiments you wish." On May 18 Oglesby published General Orders No. 8, which listed the procedures to be followed in facilitating the organization of colored regiments. Restrictions upon "the free ingress of persons of color" into Union lines were rescinded. Officers and noncommissioned officers were allowed to be detached from their regular regiments for the purpose of collecting and organizing "colored persons into regiments and companies." Division commanders were charged with selecting white officers from the old regiments to command the newly organized black troops and requisition necessary supplies. Oglesby also ordered his aide-de-camp Samuel Caldwell to facilitate the organization of colored regiments. By the end of the year, Thomas could boast that he had recruited twenty regiments of African Americans.[10]

Oglesby the citizen-soldier may have come into conflict with Grant the professional soldier in the context of the court-martial and dismissal of Col. Silas D. Baldwin of Chicago. Baldwin had been charged with deserting his troops at the battles of Fort Donelson and Corinth. Knowing the pressures and fears of those battles, Oglesby may have been ambivalent about the court-martial of a fellow brigade commander. Of the three wounded brigade commanders in Gen. Thomas A. Davies's division at Corinth, Baldwin had been least seriously hurt but chose to leave the field with only an injured hand. Oglesby wrote a letter of introduction to President Lincoln for Baldwin's wife so she could plead her husband's case. That letter, dated April 21 and from his headquarters in Corinth, made no case for Colonel Baldwin but rather stated that Mrs. Baldwin was "entitled to respectful attention as she is an excellent Lady—was very kind to me at the time I was wounded here six months ago." Whether Lincoln received her or not is unclear, but, acting on a petition of several Chicago newspapermen and politicians including Isaac N. Arnold, Lincoln removed the "disability" created by the cashiering so Governor Yates could appoint Baldwin to command a new regiment. The new appointment was subsequently revoked, however, and with Lincoln's approval, by Secretary of War Edwin M. Stanton.[11]

Oglesby was beginning to have doubts about the wisdom of his return to field duty. He found it difficult to ride a horse, and his wound, he said, although seemingly healed, "constantly harasses and annoys me." Another concern was the health of his pregnant wife Anna. On June 16 he wired Hurlbut, "My wife is seriously ill, is there any objection to my visiting Memphis a day or two to find out about it?" Anna Oglesby gave birth to Olive the next day. A week later, Oglesby submitted his letters of resignation to the army and to President Lincoln. His letter to the adjutant general declared that he was resigning "without a single grievance or without complaint of a single act of injustice from our generous government" because "my health seems fully to require it." On June 25 Oglesby sent a copy of his letter of resignation to President Lincoln and drafted a cover letter to thank the president for his confidence. For reasons of his health and family, he said, he wished "to retire from the service after twenty-six months devotion to it." He also asked that Maj. Sheridan Wait be allowed to retire. Grant, in the final stage of the siege of Vicksburg, offered a six-month leave and bucked the decision to Washington. His endorsement asserted that Oglesby had been a valuable officer whose disability had originated "from a wound received whilst gallantly serving the cause of the Union." Oglesby apparently accepted the leave and was issued orders allowing him "to go beyond the limits of the Department to await notification of the action of the President." On July 6 Lincoln endorsed Oglesby's letter of resignation: "I wish Gen. Oglesby to be obliged—by a leave of absence, rather than an acceptance of his resignation, if that would be a greater kindness."[12]

Oglesby published his final order to his men on July 6, 1863. "Fellow soldiers," he wrote, "I part with you with much regret. I have known your suffering, and with pride have witnessed your devotion to our common and noble cause. . . . Faithful soldier, thou hast served thy country well." He promised to oppose every man who did not in "thought and soul" sustain them at home. To the traitors who foolishly waged the war, it was just retribution that they "should at last meet face to face the black race of the south . . . and tremble before the men proclaimed by them to have no rights." Oglesby's determined rhetoric was copied in the *New York Times* and the *Illinois State Journal*. His work finished and his command safely in the hands of his friend General Dodge, Oglesby had much to celebrate. News of the fall of Vicksburg had been received in Memphis, he was a new father, and he would be going home soon. When he checked out of his Memphis hotel on July 7, his bill included a $12.50 charge for his room and $10 for whiskey.[13]

It brought Oglesby great pleasure to be home in Decatur with Anna Elizabeth and their three-year-old son Richard and baby daughter Olive. The editors of the *Illinois State Journal* greeted him as one of the country's "truest, bravest, and most patriotic servants." The resignation of Major Wait, Oglesby's assistant adjutant and business partner, was accepted, and he and Oglesby transacted some business during Oglesby's six-month leave. Then Oglesby set out to fulfill his promise to his troops to oppose those who were not behind them in "thought and soul." He made patriotic speeches where support for the war seemed to be lagging across central and southern Illinois. He opened his tour on July 23 in his hometown, where "he held the vast concourse spell-bound for over two hours, during which time he poured hot shot into the dastardly home traitors." He made a similar speech in "Egypt" (southern Illinois) at Duquoin, where antiwar sentiment ran high. He also spoke at grand union meetings in Charleston, Shelbyville, Mt. Zion, Sullivan, Clinton, Springfield, and Bloomington.[14]

According to the reminiscence of a former resident of Long Creek, Oglesby's defiance of Copperheads was fearless. He was returning from a "black

Republican" (abolitionist) rally in Sullivan when his buggy was detained by a crowd of Democrats who were holding a rally at Long Creek near Decatur. Cong. John R. Eden had been advising resistance to the draft, and hurrahs had gone up for an Ohio Copperhead, Clement Vallandigham. Many in the crowd were armed. When they blocked Oglesby's passage, he rose in the buggy and made a speech. The observer noted that he had heard many speeches, but "for bitter invective, blighting sarcasm and abundance of vigorous adjectives, we never, before or since, heard Dick Oglesby's twenty minutes speech on that occasion equaled." Oglesby had a "somewhat fluent use of forcible profanity" by which he damned Eden for leading the crowd to hell. He concluded, "Copperheads, as you are, you dare not injure a hair of my head; for if you did, there would not be a house or a panel of fence left standing from one end of Long Creek to the other." The stunned crowd then allowed Oglesby to ride on as "silence reigned supreme."[15]

Oglesby's speeches were part of a larger campaign intended to neutralize the antiwar sentiment that had escalated since the issuance of the Emancipation Proclamation, the inauguration of the draft, and the suspension of the writ of habeas corpus. The great Union victories at Gettysburg and Vicksburg in July 1863 brought expectations for a speedy end to the war. That faction of the Democratic Party known as the Peace Democrats called for an armistice based upon compromise that would leave slavery, if not the Union, in place. Republicans and "War Democrats," having invested their blood and treasury, wanted a completely restored Union. Illinois Unionists scheduled a mass demonstration of "unconditional" Union men to be held at the former fairgrounds in Springfield on September 3, 1863. The chair of the arrangements committee, James C. Conkling, solicited a speech from the president. Lincoln, anxious to build support for a final push to win the war and restore the Union, agreed to come "or send a letter—probably the latter." The reading of Lincoln's letter was the keynote at the great rally. He praised all those who were unconditionally devoted to the Union. To his opponents, he argued that either the rebellion must be suppressed or the Union broken. He asserted that the Emancipation Proclamation and the arming of blacks would shorten the war. "You say you will not fight to free negroes," he chided. "Some of them seem willing to fight for you; but, no matter. Fight you, then, exclusively to save the Union." As to reneging on emancipation, he explained, "The promise being made, must be kept." The letter was published in most of the newspapers of the country. The *New York Times* especially praised it, and the *Chicago Tribune* called it "one of those remarkably clear and forcible documents that come only from Mr. Lincoln's pen."[16]

The *Tribune* featured the Springfield "Grand Rally of the Masses" for several days. The newspaper reported that fifty to seventy-five thousand had attended, and its headline proclaimed "The Prairies on Fire with Loyalty." Trainloads of citizens came to Springfield to participate, a grand procession was staged to lead the crowd from the square to the fairgrounds, and six platforms were set up to accommodate twenty-five distinguished speakers. After Lincoln's letter was read, other statements from prominent Unionists were recited. Senators Trumbull, J. R. Doolittle of Wisconsin, Henry Lane of Indiana, and Zachariah Chandler of Michigan made speeches at the various venues. Several War Democrats, including Gen. John McClernand and I. N. Haynie, Oglesby's future Illinois adjutant-general, spoke. Oglesby was the featured speaker at Stand Number One. The *Chicago Tribune* commented that no poor speeches were made, but it singled out Oglesby's effort as "marked by all the logic, philosophy, and eloquence of the true statesman and patriot." The correspondent reported that the "masses" were so enthralled and entertained by Oglesby that they were reluctant to allow him to stop after he had spoken for three hours. "A truer or better man never breathed than Gen. Richard Oglesby," the reporter effused.[17]

Oglesby's speech embellished Lincoln's concerns but in less guarded and more extended rhetoric. He opened by invoking the patriotism of the audience: "We are here for a great and noble purpose. We are assembled with no selfish feelings. We have come here to manifest our love for our country, and our love to God. We are happy." Who is not happy? he asked rhetorically and replied that it was the Copperheads, "in sympathy with traitors in this monstrous and wicked rebellion." He perceptibly stated that the "political aspect" of the time was "more serious than the war." He asserted that after Gettysburg and Vicksburg, the Confederacy could no longer attack. "Their object now is to prolong the war," he maintained, "until the North should weary of it." Reflecting Lincoln's reasoning, he defended emancipation and the enlistment of black soldiers as being both right and expedient. Rather than have them build forts for the enemy, as he had seen at Fort Donelson to his command's grief, it was best to use African Americans for the Union cause. Oglesby rephrased Lincoln's challenge to those who would not fight to free blacks by suggesting that the former slaves might not be needed if the white "opposers" ("cowards" he charged) were willing to enlist and fight. After blacks "have fought for and benefited us, can we reduce them again to slavery?" he asked. The crowd answered, "Never, no never." "The secesh [secessionists] began this war, and we will settle it," Oglesby thundered. The Springfield opposition newspaper, the *Illinois State Register,* used excerpts from the speech of "One Oglesby, a small-potato politician from Decatur" to prove that the Republicans were "Fearful of Peace." The Republican newspaper, in return, objected to the *Register*'s "ineffable, mean, and contemptible assault upon one of the truest and most noble and patriotic citizens of Illinois."[18]

At the expiration of his six-month leave of absence, Lincoln and Secretary of War Stanton found appropriate work for the wounded major general in Washington. On January 13, 1864, he was ordered to preside over the court-martial of Surgeon General William Hammond. The location of the assignment was auspicious for Oglesby. He could perform a necessary function for the army, reconnect with Abraham Lincoln, insert himself into the Washington power structure and society, make some money on the side, and enhance his chances of being nominated as governor. The court usually met only from noon until 4 P.M. on three days a week. Oglesby boarded a block from the White House at Willard's Hotel, where most important visitors stayed, and began expanding his contacts. The effervescent major general's hotel bills usually included a substantial amount for champagne.[19]

Surgeon General Hammond had instituted many medical reforms in the army, including the waiving of much of the red tape involved in buying medical supplies. Old-guard surgeons came to oppose him; more important, he lost the support of Secretary of War Stanton. His enemies saw him as tactless and pompous; even some of his friends conceded that he was impulsive and "not always wise or prudent." When Stanton appointed a physician hostile to Hammond as medical inspector general, and after an acting surgeon general was appointed while Hammond was on an ordered inspection trip to the West, Hammond asked for a court-martial to clear his name. On the day after Christmas 1863, Lincoln ordered: "Let the Surgeon General be put upon trial by a court, as suggested by Judge Advocate General [Joseph Holt]." Brigadier General Hammond was charged with "disorders and neglect to the prejudice of good order and military discipline" and "Conduct unbecoming an officer and a gentleman to the prejudice of military discipline." The specifications included "wrongfully and unlawfully" contracting for the purchase of inferior blankets and beef. Major General Oglesby and several brigadier generals were assigned to the case. A former member of Congress, Maj. John A. Bingham, prosecuted. Oglesby convened the court-martial on January 19, and it continued beyond his resignation on May 26, 1864. Hammond was found guilty of some of the specifications and dismissed from the service on August 18, 1864.[20]

About three weeks after the court-martial convened, Oglesby reported to a political friend that official duties had kept him too busy either to see Washington or to learn "the tricks of politicians." Soon reunited, however, with Lincoln's political managers from central Illinois, including Supreme Court Justice David Davis, Marshal of the District of Columbia Ward Hill Lamon, and Lincoln's roving emissary Leonard Swett, he began "working the wires." The four old friends attended the funeral of Capt. Charles E. Orme, also from central Illinois, on January 31. Oglesby and Swett met with Lincoln on March 29 concerning the expanded use of the money from the 2 percent fund, which allotted revenues to the states from the sale of federal land. Oglesby's memo on the meeting ended: "After some pleasant conversation with him upon several other subjects Mr. Swett and myself left him." Oglesby had the president's confidence concerning selected appointments. He endorsed, for example, Oglesby's recommendation that Capt. Frank L. Hays be made paymaster: "If it can be consistently done, let it be done." It was done, and Hays was appointed on April 7. Oglesby apparently widened his circle of friends to include Secretary of State William H. Seward and Secretary of War Stanton. David Davis introduced Oglesby to Seward, who came to admire his verve. Oglesby also associated with members of Congress, especially the Illinois Republican delegation. General Grant thought he was well enough connected to serve as a direct conduit to Henry Wilson and John Hale of the Senate Military Affairs Committee in support of a promotion to brigadier general for his adjutant, John A. Rawlins.[21]

Oglesby was among those who persuaded the president to attend a Christian Commission Fair at the Patent Office on February 22, 1864, to benefit the families of District soldiers. The *Washington Evening Star* reported that President Lincoln and his son Robert were seated on the stage, and Mary Todd Lincoln, "accompanied by the soldierly looking Gen. Oglesby," was seated immediately in front of the stage. After several speeches were made, Lincoln was called upon to speak, and he made an impromptu talk that was a fumbling apology for not making a speech. When the president rejoined Mrs. Lincoln and Oglesby, Mary Lincoln told her husband that it was the worst speech she had ever heard and that she "wanted the earth to sink and let me through." Oglesby reported that no one spoke during the carriage ride back to the White House.[22]

There was time enough and money to engage in questionable speculative ventures while Oglesby was in Washington. Other than his duties as head of the Hammond court-martial, he considered himself free to pursue his personal financial and political gain. In March and April, he attended congressional committee meetings dealing with an increase in the whiskey tax. He then relayed information concerning the potential rates to Charles H. Ray, who was an editor of the *Chicago Tribune,* and to a New York broker. At issue was whether existing stocks of whiskey would be taxed or only those produced after passage of the tax bill. If present stocks were not subject to the increased tax, their value would increase to near the taxed price on new stocks. Thus, speculators who knew in advance the size of the tax and whether present stocks would be taxed could purchase whiskey and wines and expect to make large profits. Oglesby invested an initial $1,500 with Ray to buy 480 barrels of spirits on margin through Rumsey Brothers and Company of Chicago. He used the financial services of the banking office of J. Young Scammon, a political supporter, for loans and to collect and disperse his profits. Oglesby and Ray appear to have run their account with Scammon up to $32,811.78. When the agents sold Oglesby and Ray's holding, they remitted $8,065.11 to Oglesby's banker. Scammon reported to Oglesby that his balance, less remittance for certain obligations, was $3,883.45. Oglesby later urged Lincoln to allow Ray to trade in cotton, whiskey, and other scarce commodities in the South. Lincoln acquiesced and Grant cooperated, but Ray apparently made little money.[23]

Oglesby was involved in a similar scheme involving a New York speculator. Lockwood and Company of New York purchased five hundred barrels of whiskey for Oglesby without a deposit. Anticipating a profit from the insider information, the broker wrote to Oglesby on April 13, "I hope to send you a check for a handsome sum." Although Oglesby thought his correspondent sold too quickly because he did not trust the information Oglesby was sending, he did make a $1,171.53 profit. When the agent learned that Oglesby was going to visit Grant's army at the front, he wrote, "If you can give me [coded telegraphic] information on the result of the first engagement between Grant and Lee before it is known in Wall Street I can make you something handsome on stocks on gold." Oglesby visited the front in late April, but there is no evidence that he relayed any information.[24]

By early 1864, Oglesby had set his sights on running for governor. On February 5, he wrote to a supporter in Bloomington that people "both here and in Ills" thought "it proper if not necessary" that he should be the candidate of the Union (Republican) Party for governor of Illinois. He modestly confessed that he possessed no special qualities that fit him for that high place, but "I am almost afraid I am too small to reject such an offer." Serious efforts were being made in Washington to "rout out Mr. Lincoln," but the attempt would fail because "Lincoln is already the candidate of the people and [he] will certainly be reelected." Reflecting again on Lincoln's axiom to trust the people, Oglesby added, "Politicians cannot withstand the current of popular opinion. They can fall in behind and steer a little—some times put it off the right course, but seldom however." Endorsements for Oglesby came in early. In January the Charleston, Illinois, *Plaindealer* prophetically endorsed "a complete ticket": Abraham Lincoln, Andrew Johnson, and Richard Oglesby. The *Bloomington Pantagraph* declared for Oglesby in January.[25]

The other potential candidates for governor were State Auditor Jesse Dubois, Adjutant General A. C. Fuller, and Maj. Gen. John M. Palmer. Joseph Gillespie, a discerning political observer and confidant of Palmer, fairly summarized the attributes of the candidates ten months in advance of the election: "Oglesby would start with the advantage of being a talented, popular, high-souled fellow, overflowing with courage and patriotism, marked and maimed with an honorable wound in the defense of his country. . . . This would be hard to beat." Gillespie saw Dubois as "a capital fellow" who "has done his duty nobly but he is rich and rather old and his personal qualities are not known to as wide a circle as is the fame of his competitors." Fuller "is not much spoken of, although his services are highly appreciated." Gillespie's choice, General Palmer, took himself out of the competition, in part from concern that he could not feed his large family on the miserly $1,500 salary ("one forth my present pay"). He also wrote that the honors of being governor were "imaginary."[26]

Gillespie had correctly predicted that in the election "the military will prevail over the civil" candidates. On February 16, one alarmed backer of Jesse Dubois wrote to Lincoln, ostensibly asking him to intervene in order to avoid an ugly contest between Dubois and Oglesby. Knowing that Dubois was Lincoln's Springfield neighbor, had named a son for Lincoln, and had been a principal manager for Lincoln's nomination in 1860, Illinois secretary of state Ozias M. Hatch thought he might intercede on Dubois's behalf. Dubois may have lost some of his stature with Lincoln, however, by his recurring complaints about Lincoln's appointments, particularly that of Lincoln's brother-in-law. On February 23, the day after he had been with Oglesby at the Christian Commission Fair, Lincoln tersely replied, "I would be very glad, but really I do not perceive how I can reconcile the difficulty you mention." Lincoln liked Oglesby, and he probably thought a military hero would be more apt to help him carry the state than would a "rich and rather old" state office-holder. On March 14, Palmer wrote to his wife Malinda that "based upon long knowledge of men," the canvass has already been arranged, and "General Oglesby is to be the Union candidate" for governor. Palmer's wife replied, "General Oglesby has been to Washington and all around with other generals, working the wires." On April 15, Dubois made another desperate appeal to Lincoln, claiming that he was the only candidate who was openly supporting Lincoln for reelection but that he found himself "opposed by the whole military and official Patronage of the General Government." Lincoln did not reply.[27]

In late April and early May, Oglesby received endorsements from several county conventions. His home county, Macon, endorsed him for governor and selected their delegates to the state convention, including his law partner Sheridan Wait and several other close friends. The *Chicago Tribune* maintained a preconvention neutrality, but in its April 20 edition characterized Oglesby as "a generous, noble-hearted, courteous gentlemen" who "at once commands the respect and esteem of all who know him." The editor continued, "His bitterest enemies, politically—for he has no other—honor his patriotism, his sterling integrity, his ripe judgment, and his commanding abilities . . . at the ballot box." By May 3 he was ready to allow Republican newspapers to publish a letter he had written to a supporter stating that he would accept the nomination for governor were it offered. To be sure that political matchmakers would not put him off the gubernatorial track by nominating him for Congress, he added that he would "not in any event" be a candidate for Congress. Inspired by his "commanding qualities at the ballot box" and his availability, many more county conventions soon fell in line.[28]

According to a story Oglesby told in a later campaign, Lincoln and Stanton asked him to visit Grant, who was taking heavy casualties in his spring 1864 campaign against Richmond. He told Grant that the president had "sent me to talk a little with you." Grant, according to Oglesby's account, was optimistic about both the eastern and western fronts. "Said he, 'Oglesby, I tell you I shall conquer this man Lee,'" and Gen. William T. Sherman, he thought, would win in the West. Before leaving for home to witness the state's Union Party convention, Oglesby also ventured to New York City, where he was fortuitously invited to speak at a "Great Lincoln Rally" on May 13. As he reported it in Chicago, New York Republicans "gobbled him up" and made him speak at the Cooper Institute, "a sanctified place" where Lincoln had made a critical speech in the 1860 campaign. He was introduced as the next governor of Illinois. The "finely" uniformed Oglesby praised Lincoln as "the people's man" who was "faithful, constant and devoted to his labor for the saving of his country." A correspondent from the *Chicago Journal* reported that Oglesby seemed to be suffering "from an infection of the lungs, caused by a rebel bullet" but that he spoke for almost an hour and a half. His speech was a "masterpiece of solid argument" that "enlisted the plaudits of the audience." The next speaker, Illinois Cong. Isaac Arnold, suggested that the "Illinois Rail Splitters" (presumably Lincoln, Grant, and Oglesby) would strike "still harder" blows at slavery and the Confederacy.[29]

Oglesby returned to Illinois a few days before the Union Party's state convention, and was among those who pushed to call it the Union, rather than Republican, convention. He recognized, as did the national party, that the loyal War Democrats were needed to unite a majority in favor of seeing the war through. After a few days with his family in Decatur, Oglesby registered at Springfield's St. Nicholas Hotel and began lobbying for the gubernatorial nomination. The convention convened on May 25 at the state capitol. An informal ballot for governor tallied Oglesby, 283; Allen C. Fuller, 220; Jesse K. Dubois, 103; and John M. Palmer, 75. On the next ballot Oglesby's total jumped to 358, a majority. A motion was passed to make the vote unanimous for Oglesby. William Bross of the *Chicago Tribune* was nominated to be lieutenant governor. A committee ushered Oglesby in, and a speech was demanded. After complimenting the other contenders and presiding officer Andrew Jackson Kuykendall, a War Democrat, and also praising Lincoln, "that God-like man," he launched a "soul stirring speech, replete with patriotism." "We must stop this war," he asserted. "We must do it by annihilating this rebellion. We must drive treason from our soil and put the traitors under forever." There was some difficulty with the first draft of the party platform, which could be read as only a "quasi endorsement" of the administration. The resolution was tabled, and a new platform committee decreed unconditional support and endorsed Lincoln for renomination. The endorsement, coupled with similar endorsements from other state conventions and legislatures, drove Lincoln's renomination at the Union Party National Convention in Baltimore on June 8.[30]

Reaction to Oglesby's nomination by the Democratic press was contemptuous. They labeled him as "the Miscegen[ation] candidate," a "remorseless blackguard," a lover of "rot gut whisky," and a "blatant, brainless and blasphemous braggart." Lincoln's hometown Democratic newspaper took exception to Oglesby's statement that had there been no slavery there would have been no war. That statement, it charged, would have been more correct had the word *Lincoln* been substituted for *slavery* as the cause of the war. When a Democratic newspaper charged that Oglesby's career was undistinguished, the Republican *Illinois State Journal* countered by reciting his extensive achievements and by concluding that the opposition publication had attacked Oglesby because he had attacked its friends, the rebels. For Republican newspapers, Oglesby was "a brave and intrepid soldier, who bears scars which attest his sturdy patriotism; a statesman of generous and liberal principles" who "will blaze like a comet in his canvass against the traitors at home." "His election is an assured event," they forecast.[31]

The carnage that transpired during the summer of 1864 made Oglesby and Lincoln's election less than an "assured event." It also intensified the belligerence between Republicans and Democrats. The country had entered 1864 with high hopes that the war would end during the summer. Grant's appointment in March as commander of the Union armies was initially popular, but the casualty figures in Virginia were staggering. More than fifty thousand soldiers were killed or wounded from the Battles of the Wilderness on May 5, 1864, to the stalemate at the Battle of the Crater on July 30. No end was in sight. The draft was becoming a real threat as Lincoln called for five hundred thousand more soldiers. The Peace Democrats thought the bloodbath could be stopped if only Lincoln would renounce abolition. The *Register* wrote on July 26 that "a vote for Abraham Lincoln is a vote for war, for murder, for the impoverishment of our people now and forever, because he will not abate one jot of his determination to employ the armies of the union to wipe out slavery." The *Cairo Democrat* asked, "How much more will the freemen of America stand for from the usurper and tyrant who is only fit to split rails?" Republicans argued that there was no turning back, and they became more adamant against the rebels and the Copperheads. Some Democrats formed secret societies to sabotage the war effort, but their attempts were minimized by their optimism that they could win the elections. Republicans used Union Leagues, intent upon protecting loyal citizens and suppressing disloyal elements.[32]

The formal political campaign did not begin until late August, but Oglesby found numerous opportunities to speak during the desperate summer months. He addressed furloughed soldiers and ratification rallies supporting Lincoln's nomination. Oglesby had resigned his commission as major general, effective on May 25, the date of his nomination, but the men of his old brigade wished to honor him with public presentation of an "elegant sword" in honor of his leadership at Corinth. The *Journal* crowed that the celebration demonstrated "that the hearts of the soldiers still beat enthusiastically for their old commander—and next Governor of Illinois." A Lincoln and Oglesby club was formed in Chicago, and G. P. A. Healy, the most distinguished of the Lincoln portrait painters, commenced a likeness of General Oglesby.[33]

A meeting of the Union Party's State Central Committee, charged with making speaking appointments for the candidates, was called for the Tremont House in Chicago on July 12, 1864. Oglesby was assigned to begin a campaign tour at LaSalle on August 25. He appeared in more than forty cities, usually speaking for more than two hours. The travel pattern was to begin in the north and swing around the state counter-clockwise, ending in the vital central Illinois area. The brief notes Oglesby prepared for twenty of the speeches have been preserved. They usually included a few complimentary words about the host city. He would then jot down key phrases that served as an outline. In most locations he discussed the causes of the war, the unconstitutionality of secession, the illusion of a negotiated peace, the treachery of the Copperheads, the righteousness of Lincoln and of emancipation, the efficacy of black soldiers, Confederate mistreatment of captured soldiers, and, finally, he urged devotion to flag and country.[34]

Oglesby's contemporaries left varying judgments, influenced by their party and class, of his speaking prowess, but all agreed that he was a formidable stump speaker, perhaps the best in the West. Nineteenth-century historians Alexander Davidson and Bernard Stuve described him as "a fine appearing affable man, with regular, well defined features and rotund face. . . . His physical appearance is striking and prepossessing, while his straight-out, not to say bluff, manner and speech are well calculated to favorably impress the average masses." He was "ardent in feeling and strong in party bias." They recalled his use of "abundant homely comparisons of frontier figures, expressed in the broadest vernacular and enforced with stentorian emphasis." They surmised that "he delights a promiscuous audience beyond measure." Another observer who found Oglesby crude while noting that Illinois citizens saw him as "eloquent" was Ernest Duvergier de Hauranne. The French writer was touring Galena on September 5, 1864, when he happened on to a Union Party rally. Oglesby's speech, he reported, began "not without some charm and with a certain dignity of manner," but soon "he began to shake his fists, stamp his feet, rocked back and forth and waved his arms around like an epileptic." Hauranne complained that the speaker harangued for two hours as he "heaped all the abusive words of a tavern vocabulary upon an imaginary adversary." After observing the approbation of the crowd, Hauranne surmised that the "honorable orator sacrificed merely to the popular taste," for western Americans seemed to like "big chunks of crude and raw meat." Cong. Elihu B. Washburne of Galena later credited Oglesby's speech as the turning point in the campaign in gaining a large victory in Galena and environs.[35]

John Moses, private secretary to Civil War governor Richard Yates and later secretary of the Chicago Historical Society, remembered Oglesby for possessing a "clean shaven, expressive face" and for his "bluff, hearty, western manner." Moses described Oglesby's rotund body as "a physique of symmetrical and commanding proportions." He recalled that Oglesby's "strong feelings and resonant voice, his homely metaphors and vigorous denunciations, his humorous sallies, forcible reasoning, and earnest, even passionate manner, carried his hearers along the current of his thoughts." Moses thought Oglesby's "impetuous eloquence" served the Republican Party and the cause of the Union well. He was "a man of no ordinary powers," he concluded. One anonymous critique, provided by Oglesby's son a generation later, marveled at Oglesby's effective word choice. After reading Oglesby's travel writings and some of his speeches, the critic noted that Oglesby "liked open vowels and rounded syllables" and that he spoke "rhythmically." It was "like formal blank verse" and similar to Lincoln's speeches the analyst posited.[36]

Another next-generation admirer of Oglesby's oratory was Joseph G. Cannon, speaker of the U.S. House of Representatives. For the *Saturday Evening Post,* he recalled Oglesby's dauntless actions in the 1864 campaign at the Charleston, Illinois, courthouse. On March 28, 1864, Copperheads had attacked furloughed soldiers, and several people were killed in what became known as the "Charleston Riot." Against the wishes of Oglesby's protective friends, he insisted on speaking at the exact site where the soldiers had been killed. According to Cannon, Oglesby marched up to the speaker's stand and opened with: "I smell blood! I smell the blood of Union soldiers, here foully murdered by disloyal citizens, your neighbors and mine, shot in the back by as damnable cowards as ever wore the form of human beings." No one challenged the bellicose candidate as he completed his speech defending Lincoln and calling for unconditional patriotism.[37]

The Democrats were divided and delayed in holding their national convention. They finally met in Chicago on August 29 and adopted a "peace" platform, declaring the war a failure and calling for cessation of hostilities. Trying to appease both factions, they selected a "war" candidate, Gen. George B. McClellan, and a "peace" candidate for vice president. A week later, Illinois Democrats nominated Oglesby's 1858 congressional opponent, James C. Robinson, for governor and S. Corning Judd, a prominent Copperhead, for lieutenant-governor. No representatives of the War Democrats were nominated for state office. Robinson was "unabashedly for peace at any price." Certain Illinois Democrats secretly solicited support for Robinson from Confederate agents working from Canada. Capt. Thomas H. Hines, for example, collected receipts for $50,000 to be used by the Illinois Democratic Party to promote the election of Robinson.[38]

The campaign between Robinson and Oglesby was short and furious. Fortunately for Oglesby, many War Democrats came to realize that an armistice would mean disunion. The War Department gave furloughs to many officers who supported the Union. To the consternation of the Illinois Democratic Party and its organ the *Illinois State Register,* Maj. General John A. Logan came home to campaign for Oglesby and against his former law partner, Peace Democrat William J. Allen, who was running for Logan's old congressional seat. Another southern Illinois Democrat, Gen. I. N. Haynie, also stumped for the Union Party ticket. Many other War Democrats followed, including the erudite Ingersoll brothers, Cong. Ebon and former Col. Robert. Maj. Gen. John M. Palmer also joined the campaign in the critical month of October. More consequential than the canvass were timely battlefield victories. Mobile fell in August, Atlanta in September, and the Shenandoah Valley in October, thus discrediting the Democratic platform's assessment of the war as a failure. The end was now in sight. Oglesby led the Illinois Republican ticket by beating Robinson 190,376 to 158,701. He polled a few hundred more votes than the Lincoln-Johnson ticket.[39]

Emboldened by victory in the November 8 elections, Oglesby wrote Lincoln a four-page letter congratulating him on his reelection. Oglesby recapped his unflinching loyalty to the president in the late campaign and described his impatience with those who took exception to some of his policies. Paradoxically, he then proceeded to lecture the president on his excessive "leniency to traitors" and Copperheads. Oglesby thought modifications in Reconstruction policy should tend toward limiting, not increasing, the privileges to the rebels. He wrote that the people had faith in the president, but "there is manifestly a verry [sic] general disposition amongst the people to compel the rebels to submit humbly to the Laws without a single indulgence." The governor-elect concluded by expressing the hope that the president would be blessed with good health and be permitted to serve for another four years. Oglesby could not have known that a wrathful rebel would soon take the life of the president. Nor could he have known that he would be at Lincoln's deathbed and that the "icon" of the martyred president would be imprinted on him for the rest of his life.[40]

## Notes

1. *Journal,* Oct. 9, 1862, p. 2, col. 1; *Register,* Oct. 8, 1862, p. 2, col. 1; Gen. William Orme to Nannie L. Orme, Oct. 9, 1862, Orme Papers, ISHL.

2. "Saving a General," *Civil War Times Illustrated* 11 (July 1972): 20–25, excerpted from Silas Thompson Trowbridge, *Autobiography of Silas Thompson Trowbridge, M.D.* (Vera Cruz: Published privately, 1872).

3. "Saving a General," p. 11; E. T. Coleman, "The Story of Decatur," *Decatur Review,* March 14, 1924, p. 3, cols. 5–7; John G. F. Holston to Ulysses S. Grant, Oct. 9, 1862, in *Grant Papers,* vol. 6, p. 144n; Special Order 218 issued by John A. Rawlins, Oct. 11, 1862, in *Grant Papers,* vol. 6, p. 145n.

4. *Browning Diary,* vol. 1, pp. 583–84; Ulysses S. Grant to Henry Halleck, Nov. 11, 1862, in *Grant Papers,* vol. 6, p. 145. On July 30, 1863, Rawlins, en route to Washington, wrote to Grant, "had one day I could scarcely talk, which I suppose would make you think of me as you did of Dick Oglesby, that it was terrible punishment" (*Grant Papers,* vol. 9, p. 81n). RJO to Ward Hill Lamon, March 24, 1863, in Ward Hill Lamon, *Recollections of Abraham Lincoln, 1847–1865* (Washington, D.C.: Published by the Editor, Dorothy Lamon Teillard, 1911), p. 330.

5. S. T. Trowbridge, Decatur, to Lorenzo Thomas, Adj. Gen., Washington City, Oct. 31, Nov. 30, Dec. 30, 1862, Oglesby MSS; *Journal,* Jan. 10, 1863, p. 2, col. 1.

6. *Journal,* Jan. 13, 1863, p. 1, cols. 1–4. Lincoln was also concerned about disloyalty in

the Northwest. In January 1863 he expressed concern about the "fire in the rear" to Charles Sumner. See *Memoir and Letters of Charles Sumner,* 4 vols. (Boston: Roberts Brothers, 1877–93), vol. 4, p. 114.

7. *Journal,* Jan. 13, 1863, p. 1, cols. 1–4. Other efforts by Oglesby to rally support during his convalescence in Decatur are vividly described in Robert D. Sampson, "'You Cannot Kill Off the Party': The Macon County Democracy in the Civil War Era," *JISHS* 2 (Winter 1999): 246–72.

8. RJO to Lorenzo Thomas, Adj. Gen., Washington, Jan. 31, Feb. 28, 1863, Oglesby MSS; Department of the Tennessee Special Orders 91, *Official Records,* ser. 1, vol. 24, p. 165; Samuel Caldwell to John McClernand, April 2, 1863, McClernand Papers, ISHL.

9. Telegrams Received, April 10, June 30, 1863, Oglesby MSS.

10. Oglesby endorsement of Dodge proposal, May 4, 1863, Oglesby MSS; John S. Wilcox, HQ 52d Ill. Vol., Corinth, to Lottie Wilcox, May 16, 1863, Wilcox Collection, ISHL; General Orders Nos. 8 and 7, both May 18, 1863, General Order Book, Oglesby MSS; Dudley Taylor Cornish, *The Sable Arm: Negro Troops in the Union Army, 1861–1865* (New York: Longmans, 1956), p. 114.

11. RJO to Abraham Lincoln, April 21, 1863, Miscellaneous Files, Fifty-seventh Illinois Volunteers, ISA; Memorandum concerning Silas D. Baldwin, May 31, 1863, acting on a petition signed by seven Chicago citizens, May 13, 1863, in *Collected Works of Abraham Lincoln, Supplement 1832–1865,* ed. Roy P. Basler (Westport: Greenwood Press, 1974), pp. 189–90.

12. RJO, LaGrange, Tenn., to Stephen A. Hurlbut, Memphis, June 16, 1863, RJO to Lorenzo Thomas, June 23, 1863, and RJO to Abraham Lincoln, June 25, 1865, all in Oglesby MSS. For the endorsements of Grant, Lincoln, and Rawlins, see *Grant Papers,* vol. 8, p. 568.

13. General Order No. 21, Memphis, July 6, 1863, General Order Book, Oglesby MSS; *New York Times,* July 27, 1863, p. 3, col. 3; *Journal,* July 20, 1863, p. 3, col. 3; House Bill, Memphis, July 7, 1863, Oglesby MSS.

14. *Journal,* July 10, 1863, p. 2, col. 1, July 25, 1863, p. 2, col. 3, July 16, 1863, p. 3, col. 3, Aug. 10, p. 2, col. 1, Aug. 11, 1863, p. 2, col. 3, Aug. 26, 1863, p. 2, col. 1, Aug. 24, 1863, p. 3, col. 3, Sept. 28, 1863, p. 3, col. 3, Sept. 24, 1863, p. 3. col. 3, Sept. 7, 1863, p. 2, col. 2, and Nov. 16, 1863, p. 3, col. 3. While on leave, Oglesby purchased blocks 2–6 and 12–24 in Carvers Addition in Decatur for about $6,000 on November 20, 1863 (Oglesby MSS).

15. *Journal,* Jan. 7, 1889, p. 2, col. 3; *Decatur Herald and Review,* Dec. 19, 1965.

16. James C. Conkling to Abraham Lincoln, Aug. 14, 1863; Lincoln to Conkling, Aug. 20, 26, 1863, in *Collected Works,* vol. 6, p. 399n; *Collected Works,* vol. 6, pp. 399, 406–10; David Herbert Donald, *Lincoln* (New York: Simon and Schuster, 1995), pp. 456–57.

17. Camilla A. Quinn, *Lincoln's Springfield in the Civil War,* Western Illinois Monograph Series no. 8 (Macomb, 1991), pp. 51–52; *Chicago Tribune,* Sept. 5, 1863, p. 1, cols. 1, 2, Sept. 7, 1863, p. 2, col. 2.

18. *Journal,* Sept. 4, 1863, p. 3, col. 1, Sept. 11, 1863, p. 3, col. 3; *Register,* Sept. 10, 1863, p. 2, col. 1.

19. *Journal,* Jan. 18, 1864, p. 1, col. 3; bill from Willard's Hotel, Jan. 31–May 10, 1864, Oglesby MSS.

20. George Worthington Adams, *Doctors in Blue* (New York: Henry Schuman, 1952), pp. 40–41; Proceedings of the Court-Martial of Gen. William Hammond, case MM 1430,

Record Group 153, Records of Judge Advocate General, National Archives; printed copy of "Charges and Specifications Preferred against Brigadier General William A. Hammond, Surgeon General United States Army," Oglesby MSS; *Journal,* Jan. 18, 1864, p. 1, col. 3; *Collected Works,* vol. 7, pp. 94–95; see also Louis C. Duncan, "The Strange Case of Surgeon General Hammond," *Military Surgeon* 54 (Jan.–Feb. 1920): 98–114, 252–67. A reinvestigation of Hammond's case was ordered by Congress in 1878, and he was restored to rank on the retired list.

21. RJO to William H. Hanna, Bloomington, Feb. 5, 1864, and Davis to Son, Feb. 7, 1864, both in Davis Family Papers, ISHL; "Substance of Conversation with Mr. L in Regard to the Claim of Ills to the Two Per Cent Fund, Tuesday Evening, March 29, 1864," Oglesby MSS; Abraham Lincoln to Edwin M. Stanton, March 11, 1864, in *Collected Works, Supplement 1832–1865,* ed. Basler, p. 230; Ulysses S. Grant, to RJO (telegram), April 10, 1864, and RJO to Grant (telegram), April 11, 1864, both in *Grant Papers,* vol. 10, p. 260n. Rawlins was confirmed on April 14.

22. *Washington Evening Star,* Feb. 23, 1864, p. 2, col. 5; Carl Sandburg and Paul M. Angle, *Mary Lincoln, Wife and Widow* (New York: Harcourt, Brace, 1932), p. 112; Justin G. Turner and Linda Levitt Turner, *Mary Todd Lincoln: Her Life and Letters* (New York: Alfred A. Knopf, 1972), p. 184; Sydney Kramer, "Lincoln at the Fair," *Abraham Lincoln Quarterly* 3 (Sept. 1945): 340–43; "From My [Carl Sandburg] Interview with Joseph W. Fifer, Bloomington, 1924," Sandburg Collection, University of Illinois at Urbana-Champaign.

23. "Accounting by Rumsey Brothers" to RJO, Chicago, Rumsey to RJO, March 25, April 9, April 15, April 20, 1864, and J. Young Scammon to RJO, April 26, 1864, all in Oglesby MSS; "The Whiskey Tax," *Chicago Tribune,* May 3, 1864, p. 1, col. 2; Abraham Lincoln to Ulysses S. Grant, Feb. 11, 1865, in *Collected Works,* vol. 8, pp. 288–89n (quoting RJO, Jan. 17, 1865, to Lincoln on Ray's behalf); see also Dr. Emmet F. Pearson, "Dr. Charles Henry Ray: Illinois Medical Truant, Journalist, and Lincoln King-Maker," *Journal of the American Medical Association* 228 (April 1974): 484–90.

24. Lockwood and Co. to RJO, Willard's Hotel, Washington, April 13, 28, 1864, and RJO to Lockwood and Co., April 18, 22, 1864, Oglesby MSS. Oglesby may also have been speculating in cotton. The *Browning Diary* (vol. 1, p. 633) includes a cryptic entry for March 12, 1864: "In the morning went to the Treasury Department about Oglesby's cotton." Entries for a passbook account with Peddecord and Burrows, Decatur, show a $2,000 deposit from New York on April 12, 1864, and another on May 20 for $4,000. Other May 27 deposits totaled $3,883.67 (Oglesby MSS). A May 30, 1864, voucher from the Adjutant General's Office shows that Oglesby was paid $360.94 for service from May 1 to his resignation on May 26, 1864 (Oglesby MSS).

25. RJO, Court-martial Rooms, Washington City, D.C., to W. H. Hanna, Bloomington, Feb. 5, 1864, Davis Family Papers, ISHL; *Journal,* Jan. 15, 1864, p. 3, col. 4 (quoting the *Charleston Plaindealer*) and Jan. 28, 1864, p. 4, col. 1 (quoting the *Bloomington Pantagraph*).

26. Joseph Gillespie to John M. Palmer, near Christmas 1864, and Palmer, Chattanooga, to Malinda Palmer, Jan. 30, 1864, quoted in George Thomas Palmer, *A Conscientious Turncoat: The Story of John M. Palmer, 1817–1900* (New Haven: Yale University Press, 1941), pp. 130, 133.

27. O. M. Hatch to Abraham Lincoln, Feb. 23, 1864, in *Collected Works,* vol. 7, pp. 201–2; Joseph Gillespie to John M. Palmer, near Christmas 1863, John M. Palmer to Malinda

Palmer, March 14, 1864, and Malinda Palmer to John M. Palmer, all in *A Conscientious Turncoat*, pp. 130, 134, 137; "Dubois," in Mark E. Neely, Jr., *The Abraham Lincoln Encyclopedia* (New York: McGraw Hill, 1982), pp. 91–92.

28. *Journal*, April 28, 1864, p. 2, col. 2, May 3, 1864, p. 2, cols. 1 and 2 (Oglesby's letter), May 4, 1864, p. 2, col. 2, May 5, 1864, p. 4, col. 1, May 5, 1864, p. 2, col. 2, May 14, 1864, p. 2, col. 2, May 18, 1864, p. 2, col. 2, and May 19, 1864, p. 2, col. 2; *Chicago Tribune*, April 20, 1864, p. 2, col. 1.

29. *Journal*, July 17, 1866, p. 1, col. 4, May 18, 1864, p. 3, col. 4; *New York Times*, May 13, 1864, p. 4, col. 5; *Chicago Journal*, May 17, 1864, p. 1, col. 2, May 17, 1864, p. 2, col. 2.

30. *Journal*, May 24, 1864, p. 3, col. 3, May 26, 1864, p. 2, cols. 2–4, May 30, 1864, p. 2, col. 2; *Chicago Journal*, May 26, 1864, p. 1, col. 1; Alexander Davidson and Bernard Stuve, *A Complete History of Illinois from 1673 to 1873* (Springfield: Illinois Journal, 1874), pp. 907–8.

31. *Register*, June 7, 1864, p. 4, col. 1, June 9, 1864, p. 2, cols. 1, 2, June 15, 1864, p. 2, col. 2, July 17, 1864, p. 2, col. 1; *Journal*, May 28, 1864, p. 2, cols. 1–2, June 4, 1864, p. 2, col. 2, June 1, 1864, p. 4, col. 1.

32. Thomas L. Livermore, *Numbers and Losses in the Civil War in America: 1861–65* (1901, repr. Bloomington: Indiana University Press, 1957), pp. 110–16; *Register*, July 26, 1864, p. 1, col. 1; *Cairo Democrat*, July 14, 1864, in Arthur Charles Cole, *The Era of the Civil War: 1848–1870* (Springfield: Illinois Centennial Commission, 1919), pp. 313–14 (for secret societies, see page 310).

33. Oglesby's resignation on War Department form, May 30, 1864, Oglesby MSS; *Journal*, June 8, 1864, p. 3, cols. 3, 4, June 14, 1864, p. 2, col. 4, Aug. 13, 1864, p. 2, col. 2, Aug. 17, 1864, p. 2, col. 3, June 21, 1864, p. 3, col. 2. Oglesby was described as having a "splendid physique, and striking physiognomy," see "Healy's Oglesby," *Chicago Tribune*, July 14, 1864, p. 4, col. 5.

34. For Oglesby appointments, see *Journal*, July 4, 1864, p. 2, col. 1, Aug. 16, 1864, p. 2, col. 1, Aug. 31, 1864, p. 2, col. 1, Oct. 17, 1864, p. 2, col. 1; and Oglesby notes for 1864 campaign speeches, Aug. 25–Oct. 19, 1864, Oglesby MSS. Dean Mitchell Folkes, "Governor Richard J. Oglesby: First Term," master's thesis, Illinois State University, 1966, has compiled (p. 42) a list of thirty-nine campaign speeches delivered between August 9 and November 7, 1864. There may have been more impromptu or unscheduled speeches. Folkes's useful thesis also contains a compilation of the voting, by county, for president and governor in 1864 (pp. 50, 51) taken from the Ledger of Election Returns, ISA.

35. Davidson and Stuve, *A Complete History of Illinois*, p. 909; Suzanne Robbins, trans., "Political Rally at Galena in 1864," *JISHS* 45 (Spring 1952): 76–79; Elihu B. Washburne to RJO, Nov. 20, 1864, Oglesby MSS.

36. Moses, vol. 2, pp. 714–15; "His Style of Oratory," typed manuscript, John G. Oglesby Collection, ISHL.

37. "Reminiscences of Uncle Joe Cannon," *Saturday Evening Post*, July 13, 1918, p. 30; Charles H. Coleman and Paul H. Spence, "The Charleston Riot, March 28, 1864," *JISHS* 33 (March 1940): 56. I have been unable to confirm Oglesby's speaking date in Charleston. The comprehensive list of campaign speeches compiled from the Oglesby Papers and recorded in Folkes, "Governor Richard J. Oglesby: First Term," does not include Charleston.

38. Moses, vol. 2, pp. 706–8; Harris L. Dante, "Reconstruction Politics in Illinois, 1860–1872," Ph.D. diss., University of Chicago, 1950, p. 49; David E. Long, *The Jewel of Liberty:*

*Abraham Lincoln's Re-election and the End of Slavery* (Mechanicsburg: Stackpole Books, 1994), p. 105; *Official Records,* ser. 1, vol. 43, pt. 2, pp. 930–36; Lusk, pp. 163–66; James D. Horan, *Confederate Agent: A Discovery in History* (New York: Crown, 1954), pp. 134–38, 293, 298. See page 135 for Robinson's "weasel-worded" letter of assurance and Hines's note that states: "Verbal assurances from Mr. Robinson, fully committing himself to our movement had already been had. A large amount of money was furnished on these assurances."

39. *Journal,* Oct. 17, 1864, p. 2, col. 1 (appointments for Logan, Haynie, and Palmer), and Oct. 6, 1864, p. 2, col. 4 (Logan's endorsement of RJO); Mark A. Plummer, *Robert G. Ingersoll, Peoria's Pagan Politician,* Western Illinois Monograph Series no. 4 (Macomb, 1984), p. 21; Moses, vol. 2, p. 709.

40. RJO, Decatur, to Lincoln, Nov. 20, 1864, Oglesby MSS; see also Abraham Lincoln Papers, ser. 1, no. 38531, microfilm edition, reel 87, Library of Congress.

Lt. Richard James Oglesby during the Mexican War. (Illinois State Historical Library)

Maj. Gen. Richard J. Oglesby, in a Mathew Brady photograph. (Library of Congress)

Gov. Richard J. Oglesby during his first term (1865–69); the photograph is of a painting by George F. Wright, displayed at the Illinois State Capitol, Springfield. (Illinois Secretary of State)

Richard J. Oglesby, U.S. senator from 1873 to 1879. (Library of Congress)

Gov. Richard J. Oglesby during his second term (1885–89); the photograph is of a painting displayed at the Illinois State Capitol, Springfield. (Illinois Secretary of State)

Autographed photograph of Richard J. Oglesby on his sixty-eighth birthday, by Mosher Gallery, Chicago. (Illinois Secretary of State)

Anna Elizabeth White Oglesby (1835–68). (Illinois State Historical Library)

Emma Gillett Keays Oglesby (1845–1928). (Illinois State Historical Library)

Children of Richard and Emma Oglesby: Felicite, born in 1874; Richard James, born in 1875; John Gillett, born in 1878; and Jasper, born in 1882. (Illinois State Historical Library)

Gov. Richard J. Oglesby,
sculpture by Leonard
Crunelle, placed in Lincoln
Park, Chicago, in 1919.
(Author photograph)

Funeral of Governor
Oglesby, April 28, 1899.
(Illinois State Historical
Library)

## 6. Lincoln as an Icon

ONE EMINENT Lincoln biographer has designated Richard Oglesby as "ex officio a high priest of the Lincoln cult." He was one of many of Lincoln's associates who contributed to making him an icon. Oglesby, in turn, gained considerable prominence as an associate of the martyred president. Although much of his involvement was circumstantial, he participated in many events that contributed to the immortalization of Lincoln.[1]

Oglesby arrived in Washington on "Black Friday," April 14, 1865. In the late afternoon he called at the White House, where Lincoln read a humorous story to Oglesby and his party and he apparently turned down an invitation to accompany the Lincolns to Ford's Theatre. Later that night he joined the Lincoln deathbed vigil in William Petersen's house. He was the newly elected Illinois governor who accompanied the funeral train to Springfield and conducted difficult negotiations with Mary Todd Lincoln concerning the burial place. He served as president of the National Lincoln Monument Association throughout its thirty-year history, delivered the major address at the dedication of Lincoln's tomb in 1874, and counseled Lincoln associates who were writing biographies of the sixteenth president. Although Oglesby initially shared the view of Lincoln's law partner and aspiring biographer William Herndon that Lincoln should be remembered as a "human and hence as an imperfect—a very imperfect man," he eventually came to recognize that "no living man can add anything to his fame. It will be polished by the wear of time, to a luster which will eclipse the glory of all men, not born as he was, to the boon of immortality."[2]

The Illinois legislature adjourned on February 16, 1865, after having elected former governor Richard Yates to the U.S. Senate and rushing to become the first state to ratify the slavery-ending Thirteenth Amendment to the Constitution. Governor Oglesby was anxious to journey to Washington and beyond to seek a reduction in the large quota designated for Illinois in the recent draft and to observe the final battles of the war. On April 9, Secretary of War Edwin M. Stanton telegraphed: "This Department has received the official report of the surrender this day of General Lee and his army to Lieutenant General Grant." "A thousand thanks for your dispatch of last night," Oglesby answered. "I start for Washington tomorrow." He brought his adjutant general, Isham Nicholas Haynie, and Sheridan Wait, his canal commissioner. They left Illinois on April 11 and arrived in Washington on Good Friday, April 14, 1865. Haynie kept a diary.[3]

Oglesby's party checked in at Willard's Hotel and began renewing acquaintances from the army and Washington officialdom. Haynie met Ulysses S. Grant's chief of staff John Rawlins and General Grant "briefly" and called upon their wives, Mary Rawlins and Julia Dent Grant. Between four and five in the afternoon, the party met with Stanton. The governor and the secretary of war exchanged compliments on the success of the armies, and Stanton hailed Illinois for having never failed, even "in the darkest hours," to support the war effort.[4]

According to Haynie's diary entry for April 14, the Illinoisans walked to the White House a few minutes after five. The president was out, and they started to leave when Lincoln's "carriage with himself wife and Tad drove up—the President called us back—we went up with him to his reception room—and had a pleasant humorous time with him." Years later Oglesby, answering an inquiry by Haynie's son, recalled that his group had called at the White House near sunset. The president "had not returned from a drive with Mrs Lincoln," Oglesby remembered. They started toward the Willard Hotel when they "saw Mr. Lincoln standing in front of the White House waving his hat and calling 'come back boys'." Oglesby wrote that the president's "deportment was as comfortable and as affable as I ever saw it. We all at once felt at home." The group then followed the president to his room, where they congratulated him on the defeat of Lee's army and the prospects for peace. Oglesby then "proposed to return" to the hotel, but Lincoln said, "Do not go yet. I want to read you something funny."[5]

Haynie recorded that Lincoln "read four chapters of Petroleum V. Nasby's [a pseudonym for David Ross Locke] book and continued reading until he was called to dinner at about 6 PM and we left him." Oglesby recalled the humorist as John Pherris—John Phoenix, in another account—"or some other incorrigible writer." Although Lincoln often read passages from various vernacular humorists, Haynie's contemporary account is probably more reliable than Oglesby's equivocal testimony recorded thirty years later. Four weeks earlier, Lincoln had importuned Sen. Charles Sumner to listen to his rendition of some of Nasby's work. The admiring Lincoln had avowed, "For the genius to write these things I would gladly give up my office." On the afternoon of April 14, Oglesby recalled, Lincoln "opened the book and read rapidly—laughing heartily, commenting briefly and humorously" for half an hour before he received a call to dinner "and later another still, more imperative one." Oglesby insisted that they should go, but Lincoln "said wait for just this one and you may go—by the time he had finished the last brief tale of humor, a third summons came to dinner." The group rose and shook hands with the president. A "heavenly smile seemed to rest upon his beautiful face—we saw him no more," Oglesby concluded.[6]

The Lincolns' plans to see the play *Our American Cousin* at Ford's Theatre were in flux until that evening. The theater's management had combined two boxes and prepared for nine persons. Speaker Schuyler Colfax had been invited, uninvited (to make room for Grant's staff), and then reinvited by Mary Lincoln, but Colfax was leaving on a trip to the West. General and Mrs. Grant were invited but declined in the early afternoon of the performance. Maj. Henry R. Rathbone and Clara Harris were the first to accept. Robert Lincoln declined. After dinner, Lincoln told Noah Brooks, a newspaper correspondent and old friend, that he "had had a notion to send for him to go to the theatre," but Mary Lincoln had "already made up a party with other guests to take the place of General and Mrs. Grant." Several Decatur and Macon County historians assert that Oglesby was invited but declined, citing his three-day journey and an exhausting day in Washington. In 1898 he recalled for the benefit of students at the University of Chicago, "I did not go to the theatre with the president's party, as I had so often, but stayed in my room. Later, but still early in the evening, I heard that sound of premonition in the city streets that came before that louder noise of announcement that the president had been assassinated."[7]

The Lincolns, accompanied by Clara Harris with Major Rathbone, arrived at Ford's Theatre at about 8:30. The play was interrupted, the band played "Hail to the Chief," and the performance resumed. Major Rathbone seated himself on a sofa on the right front of the box. No one sat on the chair between the president and the door to the box. At approximately 10:15, John Wilkes Booth entered through the box's door and shot the president in the back of his head. Oglesby was later quoted as saying, "If I had been in the box I would have grabbed the assassin by the neck and choked him to death." Booth slashed Major Rathbone with a knife and made his escape by jumping from the president's box to the stage and onto a horse waiting in the alley. Lincoln was carried to the Petersen House across the street. The unconscious president was placed on a bed in a small back room that measured about seventeen by ten feet. Two larger parlor rooms fronted the "deathbed room."[8]

Haynie's April 14 diary entry succinctly reported: "At 11 PM Gov O & myself admitted to the room where the President lay dying—remained until 6 PM [AM] on 15th." Later, Oglesby was more detailed. On May 4, 1865, he recalled that he had rushed from the Willard, only about two blocks away, "within the first half hour after the fatal shot" and had remained "by the side of his precious remains" until "this day I have yielded him up to his quiet tomb." In 1895 he recalled that he and Haynie had hurried to the Petersen House but were refused entry even though Haynie explained that Oglesby was the governor of Illinois and a personal friend of the president. Oglesby met no "personal resistance" from the guard, and he entered and stayed all night. He recounted standing "by the side of the bed near Mrs. Lincoln who was kneeling by the side of her dying husband." Haynie must have followed almost immediately. A dispatch to the *Illinois State Journal* reported, "At midnight, the Cabinet, Messrs. [Senator] Sumner, [Illinois Congressman] Farnsworth, Judge [Attorney General] Bates, Gov Oglesby, [Quartermaster] Gen Meigs, Col [John] Hay, and a few personal friends, with Surgeon General Barnes and his immediate assistants, were around the bedside."[9]

As Haynie recorded the situation, "April 15th 1865 The President died at 7:22 AM to day. The excitement baffles description. The horrors of last night have no parallel in memory or history." He noted that the cabinet and others "all surrounded the dying chief" as the Secretary of War was "busy preparing dispatches—sending them off." He observed, "Surgeon Genl Barnes holding Presidents arm feeling his pulse." He placed Oglesby "at the head of the bed and myself near the door" as the "President lay with his feet to Westward head Eastward—insensible—in Comatose State—never spoke."

The Lincoln icon was enhanced by the numerous graphic paintings and engravings of the deathbed scene that were produced after the assassination. Those who visited the dying president were also immortalized. The number of Lincoln's associates who were to be pictured in the small room had grown from a dozen to forty-six by the time Alonzo Chappel painted *The Last Days of Lincoln.* Governor Oglesby was among those pictured in Alexander Hay Ritchie's *Death of President Lincoln,* which includes only twenty-six observers. He is pictured standing near the wall beyond the head of the bed. The Chappel painting, which was designed by F. B. Batchelder, included both Oglesby and Haynie (sometimes rendered as "Haynes") among the forty-six persons present. Batchelder carefully designed the painting by using Mathew

Brady photographs of the individuals and collecting detailed information about each subject. Governor Oglesby's secretary George Harlow replied to Batchelder's inquiry on November 7, 1867: "The governor is five feet and ten inches high . . . he was dressed in a black dress suit . . . hair slightly sprinkled with gray at the temples. His complexion is fresh and healthy." Harlow further asserted, "At the time of Mr. Lincolns death he stood at the side and foot of the bed and says the position you have placed him is as correct as you could have done it." Oglesby's full face is seen near the foot of the bed. The painting toured the country and was displayed in Springfield in January 1869, where it could be viewed for a 50 cent admission charge.[10]

A large number of Illinois politicians were in Washington when the assassination occurred. A few hours after Lincoln's death on Saturday, April 15, they began to organize for the purpose of returning Lincoln's body to Springfield for burial and met in Sen. Richard Yates's rooms at the National Hotel. The committee passed a resolution deeming it "proper, and just to the State of Illinois" that Lincoln's remains be "interred at the Capital of the State, so long his residence." Governor Oglesby was selected to head a committee to confer with the family on a burial place. His committee and an arrangements committee met at Oglesby's rooms in the Willard Hotel that same night. Only informal conferences were held on Easter Sunday, April 16. On April 18, Oglesby led a delegation to call upon the newly installed President Andrew Johnson at the Treasury Building. Mary Lincoln, who would seclude herself in the White House for more than a month, was not receiving visitors. Oglesby was aware, through Browning, who had conferred with Robert Todd Lincoln, that she preferred Chicago or the empty crypt in the Capitol that had been prepared for George Washington. Later in the day, Secretary of War Stanton invited Oglesby, Yates, Browning, and others to confer on the funeral. That night another meeting was held to complete arrangements for the funeral and for "the transfer of remains to Illinois." Mary Lincoln finally relented when her son Robert and David Davis, whom Robert had called to Washington to take charge of the martyred president's estate, were able to persuade her to allow a Springfield burial by promising to take their son Willie's body along. But the difficulties between Mary Lincoln and the Springfield boosters had only begun.[11]

Meanwhile, state and city officials in Springfield passed resolutions favoring a local burial. The resolutions were telegraphed to Oglesby in Washington, and he acknowledged receiving a copy of the "noble resolutions of a noble state, rendering just homage to the great qualities of its greatest citizen." Springfield boosters considered the new Oak Ridge Cemetery as Lincoln's burial place, but it was two miles from the heart of the city. City fathers quickly appropriated $20,000 for funeral expenses and appointed a committee to select a burial location. They chose a six-acre block (the location of the present capitol) owned by the Mather family, property that could be viewed from the major railroad line. The community donated $50,000 for the purchase of the land, and a Springfield mason began erecting an elaborate burial vault. But Mary Lincoln recalled that Lincoln had said he preferred a quiet place for his burial. On April 28 she had Secretary of War Stanton send a message to the committee proclaiming that "her final and positive determination is that the remains must be placed in Oakridge Cemetery—and no where else—see that this is done." The committee acquiesced on April 29. On the following day, another peremptory telegram arrived demanding that "arrangements for using the Mather vault must be changed." Yet another, dated May 1, reiterated that the remains of the president should be placed "in the vault of Oak Ridge Cemetery and nowhere else." The Oak Ridge Cemetery vault was readied, but work continued on the Mather block tomb as a "contingency."[12]

By virtue of being governor of Lincoln's home state and a personal friend of the slain president, Oglesby was accorded a high place of honor in all of the Lincoln obsequies. In Washington he headed the Illinois delegation to the April 19 funeral at the White House. He escorted the body on the fourteen-day railroad journey that retraced most of the route Lincoln had taken when he came to Washington in 1861. Massive services were held in the major cities of Baltimore, Harrisburg, Philadelphia, New York, Albany, Buffalo, Cleveland, Columbus, Indianapolis, and Chicago. Between stops, tens of thousands of citizens lined the railway, night and day, in tribute to the fabled rail-splitter. During the trip, Oglesby had telegraphed that the casket would be open at the Illinois capitol, and the burial would be on May 4. When the nine-car train reached the Springfield station at 9 A.M. on May 3, forty thousand citizens dressed in black were waiting. A reporter noted that "their tears literally fell like 'April rain'." The governor led the Illinois delegation in the procession from the train station to the capitol, preceded only by the military, the pallbearers, and four relatives and family friends and ahead of members of Congress, state governors, and legislators.[13]

Lincoln's casket was placed on a specially build catafalque for viewing in the Hall of Representatives, where he had made his "House Divided" speech in 1858. A banner quoted him: "Sooner than surrender these principles, I would be assassinated." Others read: "Washington the Father; Lincoln the Savior." The next day, the casket was loaded into an elegant hearse that had been quickly borrowed from St. Louis for the president's final processional. Gen. Joseph Hooker led the military contingent at the front of the procession, and seven other "divisions" followed. The governors were assigned to the fourth division, immediately behind the hearse and the family. Robert Lincoln was the only member of the immediate family present, because Mary Lincoln was still secluded in the White House. John Hanks of rail-splitting fame represented Lincoln's ailing step-mother. The rear of the procession included "citizens at large" and a group of "colored persons." After passing the governor's mansion, the procession seemed to be headed toward the Mather block, thus confusing many citizens, but soon turned toward Oak Ridge Cemetery. Amid all the confusion on a sweltering day, Lincoln was placed beside Willie in the Oak Ridge receiving vault. Bishop Matthew Simpson of Springfield gave a funeral oration. Dr. Phineas D. Gurley from Washington gave the benediction, which was followed by the singing of a funeral hymn he had written: "Rest, Noble Martyr! Rest in Peace."[14]

That evening Oglesby hosted the various delegations from other states at the governor's mansion. According to the *Illinois State Journal,* "He bade all welcome" but apologized for his inability to speak because of weariness. The *Journal* reported that he nonetheless addressed guests in "hearty tones of sincerity and eloquence. . . . he was worn out in the labor of love and affection that has devolved upon" him. He recounted that he had been in Washington when "this national calamity occurred" and had accompanied the body "all through our mourning journey of over fifteen hundred miles." Only today had he "yielded [Lincoln] up to his quiet tomb." He served notice that the martyred president was home to stay, because "Springfield claims him as her own, and will not give him up."[15]

The instrument for maintaining Springfield's claim to Lincoln's body was the National Lincoln Monument Association. A Lincoln Monument Association was formed in Springfield while Oglesby was en route on the funeral train. The absent governor was made president of the temporary association, and appeals for money to construct a tomb were circulated immediately. The National Lincoln Monument Association was formally chartered on May 11, 1865, with Oglesby as president, a position he would maintain until the tomb was turned over to the state in 1895. Fifteen charter members were given various fund-raising responsibilities to amass $250,000 to construct a tomb that would illustrate Lincoln's "virtue and renoun [*sic*]." Oglesby was charged with soliciting soldiers and sailors. Other members of the association as well as individuals who were not members were assigned to appeal to public schools, Sabbath schools, Union Leagues, and Masons, Odd Fellows, and other organizations. Among those who responded early in the campaign were members of Oglesby's old Eighth Illinois Regiment ($1,048.50) and the Seventy-third U.S. Colored Infantry (USCI), who gave $1,437. Lt. Col. Henry

Merriman of the African American regiment noted that he had limited contributions to $10, almost a month's pay, because money was so scarce among his troops. Soldiers and sailors contributed a total of $28,000, of which $8,000 came from African American troops.[16]

Less than a month after Lincoln's body had been placed in the public receiving vault at Oak Ridge, Mary Lincoln again clashed with the association in what became known as "the battle of the gravesite." Springfield boosters still preferred the Mather block for a tomb or a memorial site. As the *Illinois State Journal* reported on May 17, 1865, the association had decided, "in accordance with the almost unanimous desire of the friends of President Lincoln," to construct a tomb on the "commanding elevation" in the Mather block. On May 23 Mary Lincoln left the White House and moved to Chicago. She soon heard about the association's plans and dispatched a series of ultimatums to Governor Oglesby. On June 5 she gave the association ten days to send an official assurance that the monument would be erected in Oak Ridge Cemetery. If not, she would have her husband's "sacred remains deposited, in the vault, prepared for Washington, under the Dome of the National Capitol." Next she demanded that no one "save the bodies of the President, his wife, sons and son's families" should ever be placed in the tomb. She later gleaned from the newspapers that Oglesby and Ozias Hatch were coming to Chicago to try to persuade her to accept the Mather block. "My determination is unalterable" she wrote to Oglesby on June 10 and reiterated that June 15 was the final date to receive a formal promise that the tomb for "the immortal Savior and Martyr for Freedom" would be at Oak Ridge.[17]

By coincidence or by design, Lincoln's central Illinois cohorts assembled in Springfield in mid-June. Justice David Davis, the administrator of the Lincoln estate, came to preside over the U.S. Circuit Court, Robert Lincoln came to town, and Governor Oglesby returned from a brief sojourn. They likely conferred with association members on the delicate matter of the tomb's location. Faced with the June 15 deadline, the National Monument Association met on the evening of June 14 and reluctantly acceded to Mary Lincoln's terms. The vote was eight to seven, but the association had little choice. The central Illinois clique was also threatened by the possibility that the mercurial widow might authorize a move to Chicago. As one entrepreneur who was pushing a commercial fund-raising project warned, "Mrs. L is a vain woman and vanity will decide the matter tho she may think that there are other and higher motives." Springfield boosters, who represented a majority on the association, recognized the inadequacies of the governmental facilities in Springfield and feared that the capitol might follow the tomb to Chicago. That fear was not extinguished until construction of a new capitol (ironically, built on the

Mather block) began in 1868 and the Chicago fire of 1871. The official capitulation to Mary Lincoln was published on June 22, stating that the public should be apprised that "in accordance with the wishes of Mrs. Lincoln, the National Lincoln Monument Association have definitely decided to erect the National Monument . . . over his remains at Oak Ridge." The notice was signed by Oglesby as president and Clinton L. Conkling as secretary. Oglesby and the executive committee of the association moved quickly to select five acres of land on the hill immediately south of the tomb at the Oak Ridge Cemetery.[18]

Meanwhile, Oglesby helped build the Lincoln legend in his capacity as governor and as Lincoln's friend. On May 22, 1865, he issued a proclamation, following President Johnson's lead, that declared June 1 as a day of mourning for Lincoln. The following year Oglesby issued a proclamation "For a day of Fasting, Humiliation, and Prayer" on the anniversary of Lincoln's death. At the June 17 meeting of the U.S. District Court in Springfield, several speakers were called upon to honor their former colleague. Oglesby extemporaneously recalled his first meeting with Lincoln in 1840 but professed to "be too young to know much of his talents." He recalled, however, being attracted to him by his "mirthfulness." He also referred "feelingly" to his "last meeting with Lincoln and the tragical scene which soon after followed." He cautioned against the often-repeated assertion that Lincoln had died at the height of his fame. Had he lived to administer Reconstruction, Oglesby thought, "he would have exhibited greater qualities of head and heart than ever and would have shown that he was the safest and best man for the exigencies of the times." Oglesby, who had recently made a speech in which he, half-seriously, declared himself "in favor of moderation toward all those [southerners] we do not hang or otherwise punish," avowed that he, like most of the nation, would have been willing to abide by Lincoln's "views and conduct."[19]

Oglesby also contributed to the rail-splitter legend by supporting John Hanks, who took the Lincoln family cabin (from near Decatur) on tour a few weeks after the assassination. John and his cousin Dennis Hanks with the help James Shoaff, a Decatur newspaperman and Oglesby supporter, disassembled the cabin and reassembled it at the Chicago Northwest Sanitary Fair. Governor Oglesby wrote a letter, dated May 20, 1865, in which he certified that the cabin was the one built by Lincoln. The cabin was displayed from June 1 to June 24 in conjunction with the fair. For a 25 cent admission fee, John and Dennis Hanks would show visitors the cabin and answer questions. The governor visited the exhibit and was quoted as saying, "Well, John this is certainly the identical Lincoln cabin. I have been in it many years ago. My feelings are sad. I realize where I am." Hanks took the cabin on to the Boston Common, where it was exhibited from July 15 to September 9, 1865. The

Hankses sold souvenir "Lincoln rail" walking sticks and photographs of the cabin. The cabin was later shown by P. T. Barnum in New York. Another Oglesby letter, certifying the cabin's authenticity and dated April 6, 1867, was provided to John Hanks, who was planning to display the dwelling in France and elsewhere in Europe.[20]

Oglesby and others whom he described as "intimate friends of the late president" also supported the Hanks family by asking President Andrew Johnson to appoint Col. Augustus H. Chapman "to some lucrative position of responsibility." In one of the few letters written by Governor Oglesby to the new president, dated August 20, 1865, Oglesby noted that Chapman, Dennis Hanks's son-in-law, had afforded Lincoln's step-mother a home near Charleston, Illinois. He implied that Lincoln had intended to give him a position, but "the sudden death of the President disappointed the whole arrangement."[21]

The July 7, 1865, report of the treasurer of the National Lincoln Monument Association showed that only $31,145 of the proposed $250,000 had been contributed toward the construction of the tomb. Fund-raising was constricted by confusion with other Lincoln funds, including those for the relief of Mary Lincoln, and a lack of agents, as well as the perceived partisanship of the association, inertia, uncertainty about the design, and lack of governmental support. Mary Lincoln believed that Oglesby, Edward Baker, "the unprincipled man of [the] Springfield [Illinois State] J[ournal]," and others in the Springfield establishment meant to deflect private funds being collected for her as well as Lincoln's second-term salary, which she was demanding. She may have been correct concerning the private funds. Rhode Island governor James E. Smith wrote to Oglesby inquiring whether a fund initiated for her might be better sent to the tomb association, because published reports indicated that Lincoln's estate was valued at more than $100,000. Oglesby's carefully worded reply, dated July 29, 1865, declined to recommend "that you change the character of the fund in your hands raised for the benefit of Mrs. Lincoln and appropriate it to the National Lincoln Monument fund." One fund, he wrote, "is an honorable attempt to honor the living—the other the dead." Oglesby added: "At the same time expressing my views as a citizen I should suppose if you feel you have the right to do so, that Mrs. Lincoln could scarcely object to the change you are willing to make since it is intended for a purpose which must be very dear to her." Concerning the presidential salary, Mary Lincoln wrote to Cong. Elihu B. Washburne of Illinois on November 29, 1865, warning him that a coeditor of the *Illinois State Journal* and Governor Oglesby were on their way to Washington to sabotage the appropriation for her. But, she urged, "With your great energy and noble heart, all their malice can readily, be circumvented." Oglesby did travel to Washington, but his mission concerned efforts to secure the discharge of Illinois soldiers being held in the army and the settlement of certain claims against the federal government. Mary Lincoln was voted one year's salary of $25,000 at the December session of Congress.[22]

Oglesby seems to have been the leader of the faction on the association board that opposed the commercialization of the fund-raising campaign. When Jesse Fell, who had helped launch Lincoln's presidential campaign, wrote to suggest that solicitors should be engaged for a 10 or 15 percent commission, the letter was endorsed "not approved." When representatives of a publishing firm pushed a scheme to sell portraits of Lincoln and share the profits with the association in return for sponsorship and the solicitation of an endorsement by President Johnson, Oglesby balked. Although the association rejected an invitation from the Stephen A. Douglas Tomb Association to conduct a joint fund-raising drive, the Democratic *Springfield Register,* always a civic booster, stopped charging that the association was building a "partisan monument" while suggesting that the association membership should be broadened.[23]

During the last half of 1865, the association began to find its direction. Contributions continued at a modest rate. The Soldiers and Sailors Monument Association donated the $3,000 it had collected, and the association adopted a suggestion made by the *New York Times* that a contest be opened for the best design for the tomb. Oglesby, on behalf of the association, successfully petitioned the secretary of the interior to assign William Saunders, "Botanist and Superintendent of Propagating Gardens," to plat and lay out the grounds around the tomb. Saunders, who had designed the cemetery at Gettysburg, quickly complied. On October 3, 1865, by which time $53,000 had been received from individuals and groups, Oglesby issued an appeal to the governors of the various states. Missouri contributed $1,000; Nevada $500 in gold; and New York, after considerable lobbying by Oglesby and David Davis, promised $10,000. Governor Oglesby persuaded the Illinois legislature to make an initial contribution of $50,000. A temporary tomb was built at the Oak Ridge Cemetery to free the public receiving vault. Lincoln's and Willie's bodies were transferred to the new tomb, only a hundred yards up the hill and to the left, on December 21, 1865. Eddie Lincoln had been removed from another Springfield cemetery and deposited in the new temporary tomb a few days earlier. Robert Lincoln and all members of the association except Oglesby, who was out of town, witnessed the removal of his father and Willie. Mary Lincoln, escorted by Robert, made her first visit to the site of her husband's grave.[24]

Although Governor Oglesby was president of the Lincoln tomb association, he was also obliged to accommodate the backers of a proposed tomb in Chicago for Lincoln's old rival Stephen A. Douglas. In 1865 the Illinois legislature had purchased the land for the tomb from Adele Douglas for $25,000, and Oglesby had forwarded the exchange note to her, accompanied by a gracious letter calling her husband "a noble patriot and statesman." The Douglas tomb was promoted by the sculptor Leonard Volk, who was also a kinsman of Douglas. Volk and sixteen prominent citizens asked Governor Oglesby to speak at the cornerstone-laying ceremony on June 1, 1866. He initially demurred, stating candidly that he could not do justice to Douglas and that he had a previous engagement. They "unanimously" asked him to reconsider and to name a date. Oglesby replied, "Upon reflection I feel that I am not at liberty to decline this distinguished honor." June 13 was the date agreed upon, but the Douglas trustees changed the date to July 4, when Oglesby had another engagement. As he explained to a friendly trustee, "I declined as long as I gracefully could, then, after accepting, am virtually rejected by a change of time, arbitrarily and very suddenly made." Apparently the trustees, influenced by the *Chicago Times,* either came to believe that Oglesby was too outspoken in his criticism of Democrats or they may have anticipated that Andrew Johnson would speak at some future date. In August and September, Johnson conducted a "swing around the circle" whistle-stop tour in support of members of Congress friendly to his benign policy toward former Confederates. The ostensible purpose of the trip was to speak at Douglas's monument site in Chicago. Oglesby had already aligned with the "radical" Republicans who damned the president for vetoing the Freedman's Bureau and civil rights bills. Oglesby confided to his friend Leonard Swett, "It was very funny how they sneaked out of it after extracting a promise from me to try my hand on the little Giant." Oglesby concluded, "They were fearful I would make him a patriot."[25]

Oglesby presided over most of the weekly meetings of the National Lincoln Monument Association as fund-raising progressed. By January 1868 they had sufficient funds to advertise for designs for the monument, not to exceed $200,000. Thirty-seven designs were presented by thirty-one artists. Larkin G. Mead, with the support of the *New York Times,* had been lobbying since 1865. Leonard Volk, already involved with the Douglas tomb, submitted two designs. Vinnie Ream, commissioned to do the Lincoln sculpture for the Capitol in Washington, had the support of Sen. Lyman Trumbull. Cochrane and Piquenard, architects of the new Illinois capitol, also offered a design. In September the association's board held marathon meetings, trying to decide which design to accept. Mead, Volk, and other aspirants were in

Springfield lobbying for their designs. Mead's classical design was adopted on the fifth ballot by a vote of twelve to one, with two members (Oglesby and Phillips) recorded as "absent or not voting."[26]

Larkin Mead was awarded a contract worth about $70,000 to produce a Lincoln statue that would stand in front of an obelisk. A coat of arms was also part of the design, in addition to four statuary groups of Civil War soldiers and sailors at the corners of the monument. The award was the largest received by an American sculptor to that time. William D. Richardson was contracted to build the structure, less the statuary, for $136,000, with a completion date in 1870. In 1871 the board authorized Oglesby to consult with David Davis and Robert Todd Lincoln about setting a date for the removal of Lincoln's body to the new and incomplete monument. In September the body was moved from the temporary tomb to the central crypt, "quietly but reverently, and without any ceremonials whatever." Several old acquaintances viewed the body and certified that it was that of Lincoln. Thomas (Tad) Lincoln, who had died in July, joined Willie and Eddie at their father's side. The monument, which one art historian has labeled as "one of the earliest of the Civil War monuments to be commissioned, but one of the slowest to be completed," would not be dedicated until 1874. In March 1872 Oglesby visited Lincoln's secretary of state, William H. Seward, in New York to formally invite him to deliver the major address at a dedication, but Seward died a few months later.[27]

Mead's dilatory delivery of the Lincoln statue and coat of arms as well as sluggish fund-raising delayed the dedication of the tomb until October 15, 1874. In the meantime, Oglesby had finished a four-year term as governor in 1869 and been reelected in 1872. After serving a few days he was chosen for the U.S. Senate by the Illinois legislature. After Anna Oglesby died in May of 1868, he married Emma Gillett Keays in 1873. In and out of office, he continued to serve as president of the tomb association, a responsibility he often found frustrating because of the slow progress of construction. In calling a special meeting in 1871, he joked to another board member that he was anxious to raise the funds and complete the tomb sometime "before the day of final judgment." Oglesby and the association were determined to invite an important person who had been close to Lincoln to deliver the dedicatory address. Seward, Horace Greeley, Salmon Chase, and Charles Sumner had died. Oglesby thought he could enlist President Grant, but he was shy about making speeches. Gov. John A. Dix of New York declined, as did Gideon Welles, Lincoln's secretary of the navy. Oglesby traveled to Hot Springs, Arkansas, to solicit former governor O. P. Morton of Indiana, who declined for reasons of health. As an added incentive for Grant and Gen. William T. Sherman to attend, the association planed to have the ceremony while the veterans' organization, the Society of the Army of the Tennessee, was meeting in Springfield. To meet the deadline, the association turned to Oglesby to give the major address. The *Illinois State Journal* reported, "After much embarrassment and explanation of his great disinclination to undertake so delicate and responsible a service, Gov. Oglesby accepted the invitation." The editor was confident that the occasion would "call out the most brilliant resources of a man gifted by nature with unusual powers of eloquence." Oglesby was forced to prepare the oration quickly. He was aware that it could not be extemporaneous, as were most of his speeches. He later claimed that it was the only speech he ever wrote out. He limited its scope by handing over the task of describing the history of building the tomb to the vice president of the association, Jesse K. Dubois. That left Oglesby with the "life and public services of Mr. Lincoln" as his formidable task. The manuscript covered forty-five pages.[28]

The ceremony on October 15, 1874, began with a two-mile-long procession to the tomb. A crowd estimated at more than twenty thousand attended. On the speaker's stand were President Ulysses S. Grant and his wife Julia Dent Grant, Vice President Henry Wilson, and former Vice President Colfax. Generals William T. Sherman, Irvin McDowell, John Pope, and George Armstrong Custer were also present. David Davis and Robert Todd Lincoln, the only remaining child of the quartet of Lincoln boys, attended; Mary Lincoln, living in Chicago, did not. Former governor John M. Palmer, chair of the Committee on Arrangements, introduced a Bishop Wayman of the African M. E. Church, who opened the exercises with a prayer. That was followed by a choir that sang "With Malice toward None; with Charity for All." Dubois gave his history of the tomb, and Oglesby's extended oration followed. Afterward, tributes to Lincoln were made by Grant (who spoke only about four hundred words), Wilson, Colfax, Sherman, and others. Larkin Mead, the architect, was introduced; Normal University's president Richard Edwards read the poem "Lincoln's Monument"; and the Rev. Albert Hale pronounced the benediction.[29]

Oglesby apparently began the construction of his speech by composing a simple six-point outline that he labeled "Line of Argument." He proposed to open with the ending of the rebellion. Next came a section on the death of Lincoln and words about the monument to his memory. The third "line" concerning his birth, life, and education, followed by "his character and administration." The penultimate line was termed "his example and the lesson it teaches in behalf of free government and the humble in life." The final line was designated "conclusion."[30]

If there were memorable phrases in the speech they were masked by its length and by Oglesby's halting attempts to emulate Lincoln's Gettysburg Address style. He opened with "the tenth of a century is about taking its departure since the close of the great rebellion." Another awkward echo refuted the proposition "that the durable establishment of a democratic government was not possible in a country of great extent and with a numerous population." A few paragraphs later, he declared that the rebellion was crushed by "a heroic people, that good government might not perish from the earth." He also quoted extensively from Lincoln's farewell speech in Springfield, the two inaugural messages, the Conkling letter of 1863, and the Gettysburg Address. Oglesby's memorable phrases concerned slavery: "The curse of slavery had taken deep root in an unnatural soil," but Lincoln's election had broken "the charmed circle woven by the slave oligarchy around the temple of liberty." Curiously, he devoted more than fifteen hundred words to the Lincoln-Douglas debates. Lincoln was characterized as "calm, self-possessed, contemplative by nature, his mind capable of the deepest penetration, able to grasp any proposition and to analyze every element." Douglas, too, was admired. Neither did Oglesby forego the opportunity to connect himself to Lincoln and the rails. He mentioned his "long and somewhat intimate personal acquaintance" with Lincoln and pointed out that John Hanks, who had assisted Lincoln on a flatboat to New Orleans and in "splitting the rails and making the improvements upon the new home in Illinois," was in the audience. Oglesby closed by dedicating the "monument to the memory of the obscure boy, the honest man, the illustrious statesman, and great Liberator, and the martyr President . . . behold the image of the man."[31]

Oglesby seemed less suited to making formal speeches, either in the U.S. Senate or on such solemn occasions, than in making stump speeches, which often involved asides and interplay with the audience. Nevertheless, he received good reviews from friends and enemies alike. The *Chicago Daily Inter-Ocean* wrote that "no more just estimate has ever been formed of the life and character of Mr. Lincoln." The Democratic *Chicago Times,* Oglesby's worst enemy among newspapers, conceded that his "oration was much superior, in point of literary merit, to his ordinary efforts, if it does not rank as the best production of his life." That friendly attitude may have sprung from Oglesby's generous portrayal of Douglas. The *Chicago Journal* reminded readers of the rail-splitter connection between Oglesby and Lincoln, labeling Oglesby as "the orator of the rail," who, with the magical powers of "that piece of wood," had fueled an "enthusiasm which blazed into a national conflagration."[32]

Oglesby's guardianship of the tomb continued for twenty-one years after his dedicatory speech. The association dealt with an abortive attempt to kidnap Lincoln's body in 1876, the burial of Mary Lincoln in 1882, and the upkeep of the structure. It was not until 1886, during Oglesby's third non-consecutive term as governor, that the two remaining military statuary groups were installed as a result of a special $27,000 state appropriation. Governor Oglesby was also involved in furthering the Lincoln icon when the state accepted the Lincoln home from Robert Todd Lincoln in 1887. He became chair of the Lincoln Homestead Trustees, which administered the historic site. In 1895 Oglesby, as the surviving member of the National Lincoln Monument Association, deeded the tomb to the state.[33]

Governor Oglesby had unveiled the sculptured "image of the man" at the dedication, but who would craft Lincoln's biography? Could his Illinois clique preempt the print image as they had the shrine? And who knew Lincoln? David Davis, his closest political associate, confessed a week after Lincoln's death that he and Lincoln "had neither strong friendship nor enmities." Lincoln's law partner and self-proclaimed Boswell, William Herndon, called him the "most shut-mouthed" man who ever lived. Most of Lincoln's Illinois friends, including Oglesby, either lacked confidence in their literary skills or the tenacity to complete a biography, but they did influence other biographers and publishers. Among the few who did write, there was no agreement over whether Lincoln should be pictured as a God or as a flawed mortal. The dichotomy is illustrated by Oglesby's enthusiastic endorsement of the work of both Isaac N. Arnold of Chicago and Herndon. Arnold's *The History of Abraham Lincoln and the Overthrow of American Slavery* (1866) was adulatory, and Oglesby praised the "laborious and responsible work" and assured readers that Arnold was particularly qualified, as "an intimate" of Lincoln, to write a biography.[34]

The first public presentation of Herndon's views came in a series of lectures in Springfield during the winter of 1865–66. Oglesby headlined the lecture series by repeating his popular "Holy Land" discourse. He was unable to attend Herndon's lecture, but Herndon sent him a copy of a synopsis entitled "The Life and Character of Abraham Lincoln." Herndon saw it as his duty to tell the truth and not eulogize Lincoln, who was a "human and hence an imperfect—a very imperfect man." Oglesby praised Herndon's lecture as containing the most complete "descriptions and delineations of the great man" he had heard. "You went through the bark into the heart of this giant of the intellectual forest," Oglesby observed. The governor also volunteered his view of Lincoln's judgment. Lincoln, he thought, was a better judge of humanity "as a class" than of individuals: "I think Mr. Lincoln at all times possessed strong common sense but not upon all subjects. I mean to say he sometime seemed weak in his estimate of Men but he had an instinctive aversion to a mean man and despised a Knave, he pitied a fool and laughed heartily at an ass." In reply, Herndon declared that he had written the lectures because other biographers had created an unreal Lincoln, "a soft fool." Out of respect for "Truth, Justice and Affection," he had pictured a Lincoln that might "seem harsh." In subsequent lectures Herndon pictured a controversial non-Christian Lincoln whose only true love was Ann Rutledge and whose wife created a living hell for him.[35]

Herndon had ended his January 8, 1866, reply to Oglesby with a postscript: "I will publish sometime, if I don't get too lazy." Herndon was not lazy and continued to collect materials, but he seemed incapable of forging his own book-length biography of Lincoln. Near poverty in 1869, he sold the use of his materials to Ward Hill Lamon, Lincoln's unofficial bodyguard and marshal of the District of Columbia. Lamon then secretly contracted with Chauncey F. Black, son of Jeremiah S. Black, a cabinet member in the Democratic Buchanan administration, to ghostwrite a Lincoln biography. Black's manuscript was biased against Republicans and emphasized Lincoln's crudeness. Using Herndon's materials, he concluded that Lincoln and his mother were born out of wedlock, that Lincoln was a Deist and only loved Ann Rutledge, and that Mary Lincoln was a hellion. In Illinois, the protectors of the Lincoln icon could be damaged by such revelations. David Davis was eying the presidential race of 1872, and Oglesby was running for governor. Davis persuaded Lamon to revise the book, but even then Lincoln's illegitimacy was implied and he was described as having been an uncouth young man. The reading public was unwilling to accept an imperfect Lincoln. Sales were abysmal.[36]

Between 1886 and 1889, Herndon worked with a collaborator, Jesse Weik, and their union led to publication of *Herndon's Lincoln*. Before publishing the book, Herndon sought the opinion of many of Lincoln's contemporaries concerning illegitimacy in the Lincoln family. He interviewed Oglesby in the governor's office on September 6, 1887, and asked his opinion. Oglesby counseled silence on the issue. He argued that "the people's good sense had settled the matter long ago" and that they did not care who was illegitimate in the Lincoln family. "They go upon merit, the man and his own genius and character," he concluded. Herndon omitted many of his suspicions from the book.[37]

During the 1880s and 1890s there was renewed demand for the recollections of Lincoln's associates. Being one of the few survivors, Oglesby was frequently solicited by publishers. He steadfastly evaded their requests for Lincoln stories, however, by suggesting that most of the meaningful history had long since been disseminated. Yet he could not resist reminiscing to friends and admiring students. Many such accounts found their way into print, often after his death, thus ensuring his place in history as "Lincoln's rail-splitter." That image was also enhanced by the extensive campaign biography written in 1884 by Franc Wilkie and by a Bancroft Library oral history given in 1890. Oglesby was not the high priest of the Lincoln cult. He was, however, one of deacons who served and were served by the Lincoln icon.[38]

## Notes

1. David Donald, *Lincoln's Herndon* (New York: Alfred A. Knopf, 1948), p. 205.

2. Osborn H. Oldroyd, *The Lincoln Memorial: Album—Immortelles* (New York: G. W. Carleton, 1933), p. 227. Otto Kyle, *Abraham Lincoln in Decatur* (New York: Vantage Press, 1957), p. 124, asserts that Oglesby was invited to go to the theater with the Lincolns.

3. Moses, vol. 2, pp. 717, 721–22; Isham Nicholas Haynie, Diary, Haynie Collection, ISHL; telegrams in Governor's Correspondence, April 1865, ISA. W. H. Hanna of Bloomington, Col. James H. Bowen, aid de camp, and Col. D. B. James, aid de camp, joined the party along the way.

4. Entry for April 14, 1865, Haynie Diary.

5. RJO to Edwin Haynie, Dec. 26, 1895, Haynie Collection, ISHL.

6. Entry for April 14, 1865, Haynie Diary; RJO to Edwin Haynie, Dec. 26, 1895, Haynie Collection, ISHL. Another source of Oglesby's story is Katherine Helm, *The True Story of Mary, Wife of Lincoln* (New York: Harper and Brothers Publishers, 1928), pp. 255–56. The Helm account has Oglesby identifying the humorist as John Phoenix. "The Last Book Lincoln Read," *Lincoln Lore*, no. 1704 (Feb. 1980): 1–4, accepts Oglesby's story from Helm and assumes that Lincoln must have been reading John Phoenix [George Horatio Derby], *Phoenixiana; or, Sketches and Burlesques.* Sumner's doubtful statement is in the introduction to David Ross Locke, *The Struggles of Petroleum V. Nasby* (Toledo: Locke Publishing, 1980), p. 15.

7. Mary Lincoln to Schuyler Colfax, April 13 [14], 1865, in Justin G. Turner and Linda Levitt Turner, *Mary Todd Lincoln: Her Life and Letters* (New York: Alfred A. Knopf, 1972), pp. 220–21; Noah Brooks, *Washington in Lincoln's Time* (New York: G. P. Putnam's Sons, 1888), p. 257; W. Emerson Reck, *A. Lincoln: His Last Twenty-four Hours* (Jefferson, N.C.: McFarland, 1987), p. 56; Kyle, *Abraham Lincoln in Decatur*, p. 124; Richmond, p. 122. A clipping of April 24, 1898 in Scrapbook, 1890–1920, Oglesby MSS, has the university's president, William Rainey Harper, introducing Oglesby to speak on his connection with Lincoln.

8. Stanley W. McClure, *Ford's Theatre and the House Where Lincoln Died* (Washington, D.C.: U.S. Government Printing Office, rev. 1984), pp. 7–15; Dorothy Meserve Kunhardt and Philip B. Kunhardt, Jr., *Twenty Days: A Narrative in Text and Pictures of the Assassination of Abraham Lincoln and the Twenty Days and Nights That Followed* (New York: Castle Books, 1965), pp. 24, 26, 62; diagram of Petersen House prepared by Maj. A. F. Rockwell, in Reck, *Last Twenty-four Hours*, p. 152; author's diagram drawn March 29, 1996, at the Petersen House site.

9. *Journal*, May 5, 1865, p. 2, cols. 1, 2, April 15, 1865, p. 2, col. 1; RJO to Edwin Haynie, Aug. 19, 1895, Haynie Collection, ISHL.

10. Stefan Lorant, *Lincoln: A Picture Story of His Life* (New York: W. W. Norton, 1952), pp. 267–69; Harold Holzer, "Print of the Edition: Advertising the 'Death of Lincoln,'" *Lincoln Herald* 90 (Spring 1988): 34–35; Harold Holzer and Frank Williams, *Lincoln's Deathbed in Art and Memory: The "Rubber Room" Phenomenon* (Gettysburg: Thomas Publications, 1998), pp. 29–34; George Harlow to John P. Batchelder, Nov. 17, 1867, Letterpress Book, 1866–69, Oglesby MSS; *Journal,* Jan. 15, 1869, p. 3, col. 2.

11. *Journal,* April 17, 1865, p. 1, col. 6; entry for April 15, 1865, Haynie Diary; *Browning Diary,* vol. 2, pp. 20–23; Willard L. King, *Lincoln's Manager, David Davis* (Cambridge: Harvard University Press, 1960), p. 227.

12. *Journal,* April 18, 1865, p. 2, cols. 1, 3, April 21, 1865, p. 3, col. 4, April 24, 1865, p. 2, col. 3, April 25, 1865, p. 2, col. 1, April 26, 1865, p. 2, col. 1, May 1, 1865, p. 2, col. 1, May 4, 1865, p. 2, col. 1; Camilla A. Quinn, *Lincoln's Springfield in the Civil War,* Western Illinois Monograph Series no. 8 (Macomb, 1991), p. 88.

13. Quinn, *Lincoln's Springfield,* pp. 88–89; *Journal,* April 18, 1865, p. 3, col. 3, April 22, 1865, p. 2, col. 5, April 28, 1865, p. 2, col. 1, May 4, 1865, p. 2, col. 2.

14. Kunhardt, *Twenty Days,* pp. 255, 282–301; Quinn, *Lincoln's Springfield,* p. 91.

15. *Journal,* May 8, 1865, p. 2, cols. 1, 2.

16. *Journal,* April 25, 1865, p. 2, col. 1, May 13, 1865, p. 2, col. 2; Eighth Illinois Infantry contribution (May 30, 1865), Oglesby MSS; Seventy-third USCI, New Orleans, contribution (May 16–31, 1865), National Lincoln Monument Association Papers (NLMA), ISHL; John G. Nicolay and John Hay, *Abraham Lincoln: A History,* 10 vols. (New York: Century, 1890), vol. 10, pp. 3–4.

17. *Journal,* May 17, 1865, p. 2, col. 1; Turner and Turner, *Mary Todd Lincoln,* pp. 241–45.

18. *Journal,* June 14, 1865, p. 3, col. 3, June 15, 1865, p. 2, col. 3, June 16, 1865, p. 2, col. 1, June 23, 1865, p. 3, col. 3, June 26, 1865, p. 3, col. 3; H. H. Bryant to RJO, June 19, 1865, NLMA, ISHL ("Mrs. L. is a vain woman").

19. *Journal,* May 24, 1865, p. 2, col. 1, June 19, 1865, p. 3, cols. 3, 4, June 3, 1865, p. 2, col. 3, April 9, 1866, p. 1, col. 1.

20. Marilyn Gahm Ames, "Lincoln's Rail Splitter Cousin," M.A. thesis, Illinois State University, 1974, pp. 74–88. The cabin was apparently sold to an English syndicate and lost at sea. See also *New York Times,* July 21, 1865, p. 2, col. 3.

21. RJO to Andrew Johnson, Aug. 20, 1865, Oglesby Letterpress Book, ISA. Oglesby wrote three letters of recommendation to President Johnson (Nov. 23, Dec. 26, 1865, Jan. 4, 1866, Governor's Letterpress Book). The November 23 letter on behalf of Brevet Brig. Gen. S. Bronson was typical; Oglesby wrote that Bronson "wants a lucrative job in your administration." Oglesby did not write to the president after their positions on Reconstruction diverged.

22. RJO to Gov. James E. Smith, July 29, 1865, NLMA, ISHL; Mary Lincoln, Chicago, to Elihu B. Washburne, Nov. 29, 1865, in Turner and Turner, *Mary Todd Lincoln,* pp. 288–89; *Journal,* July 7, 1865, p. 3, col. 3, Nov. 29, 1865, p. 3, col. 3, Dec. 23, 1865, p. 3, col. 3.

23. Jesse Fell, Normal, to NLMA, ISHL, July 24, 1865; H. H. Bryant to NLMA, May 9, 10, 15, 16, 1865; RJO to Bryant, June 28, 1865, NLMA. The *Journal,* Nov. 20, 1865, p. 3, col. 2, praised the *Register* for supporting the building of the tomb.

24. "Resolution Accepting the Proposition of the Soldiers and Sailors Association," July 18, 1865, NLMA, ISHL; James Simonton, Editor, *New York Times,* to RJO, July 10, 1865,

NMLA; RJO to James Harlan, July 28, 1865, Oglesby Letterpress Book, Jan. 16–April 1865, ISA; *Journal*, Aug. 30, 1865, p. 3, col. 4, Oct. 14, 1865, p. 2, col. 3; RJO, New York, to David Davis, Feb. 20, 1866 (on New York's contribution), David Davis, Washington, to RJO, March 4, 1866, Davis to Thurlow Weed, March 5, 1866, Weed to Davis, March 6, 1866, Davis to RJO, March 12, 1866, and RJO, Springfield, to Andrew Shuman [editor of the *Chicago Journal* and Chicago postmaster], March 9, 1866, all in Oglesby MSS; Mary Fogleman, "The National Lincoln Monument Association," *Historic Illinois* 3 (Dec. 1980): 11.

25. RJO to Mrs. Adele Douglas, April 5, 1865, cited in Leonard W. Volk, *History of the Douglas Monument* (Chicago: Chicago Legal News, 1880), pp. 28–29; RJO to Volk, May 8, 15, 1866, Oglesby MSS; Volk Telegrams to RJO, May 19, 23, 25, 1866, Oglesby MSS; RJO to James H. Bowen, May 28, 1866, cited in Volk, *History*; RJO to Leonard Swett, June 11, 1866, and RJO to Iowa Governor Stone, Sept. 6, 1866, both in Oglesby MSS; see also Evelyn R. Moore, "Stephen Douglas Tomb, Illinois' First State Memorial," *Historic Illinois* 6 (Aug. 1983): 1–5.

26. William J. Hosking, "Lincoln's Tomb: Designs Submitted and Final Selection," *JISHS* 50 (1957): 51–61; Douglas G. Campbell, "In Memory of Virtue: A Study of Illinoisans' Designs for the Lincoln Tomb," *Lincoln Herald* 86 (1984): 32–40; James W. Simonton, *New York Times*, to RJO, July 10, 1865, NLMA, ISHL; Lyman Trumbull to RJO, Sept. 8, 1868, Oglesby MSS; *Journal*, June 5, 1868, p. 4, col. 2, Sept. 1, 1868, p. 4, col. l. A research paper by Thomas W. Benefiel, "The Construction, Design, and Financing of Lincoln's Tomb" (Illinois State University, April 1997) offers a useful summary. Descriptions of some of the models not chosen may be found in the *Journal*: April 21, 1868, p. 2, col. 3, Sept. 4, 1868, p. 4, col. 3, Sept. 5, 1868, p. 4, col. 2, Sept. 7, 1868, p. 4, col. 2, Sept. 8, 1868, p. 4, col. 2.

27. *Decatur Weekly Republican*, April 28, 1870, p. 4, col. 4, Sept. 21, 1871, p. 5, col. 4, March 14, 1872, p. 4, col. 1; Lorado Taft, *The History of American Sculpture* (New York: Macmillan, 1925), p. 238; Wayne Craven, *Sculpture in America* (New York: Thomas Y. Crowell, 1968), p. 323.

28. *Journal*, Sept. 10, 1874, p. 4, col. 3, Sept. 22, 1874, p. 1, col. 1, Sept. 25, 1874, p. 4, col. 1; RJO to O. M. Hatch, Aug. 19, 1871, Hatch Papers, ISHL; "Speeches," Oglesby MSS.

29. *Decatur Weekly Republican*, Oct. 22, 1874, p. 3, col. 4. Grant's speech is quoted in John Carroll Power, *Abraham Lincoln: His Life, Public Services, Death and Great Funeral Cortege* (Springfield: Edwin A. Wilson, 1875), pp. 334–35.

30. "Speeches," Oglesby MSS.

31. RJO speech quoted in Power, *Abraham Lincoln*, pp. 309–30.

32. *Chicago Daily Inter-Ocean*, cited in *Journal*, Oct. 19, 1874, p. 2, col. 3; *Chicago Times*, cited in *Journal*, Oct. 17, 1874, p. 1, col. 4; *Chicago Journal*, cited in *Journal*, Oct. 12, 1874, p. 1, col. 1.

33. *Lincoln Tomb State Historic Site*, Illinois Historic Preservation Agency pamphlet (n.d.); Wayne C. Temple, *By Square and Compasses: The Building of Lincoln's Home and Its Saga* (Bloomington: Ashlar Press, 1984), p. 105; James Hickey, "'Own the House till It Ruins Me': Robert Todd Lincoln and His Parents' Home in Springfield," *JISHS* 74 (Winter 1981): 279.

34. *Browning Diary*, vol. 2, p. 24; Richard N. Current, *The Lincoln Nobody Knows* (New York: Hill and Wang, 1963), p. 12; Benjamin P. Thomas, *Portrait for Posterity: Lincoln and*

*His Biographers* (New Brunswick: Rutgers University Press, 1947), pp. 91–93; RJO to Isaac N. Arnold, July 9, 1866, Oglesby MSS.

35. Mark A. Plummer, "The Herndon-Oglesby Exchange on the Character of Lincoln," *Lincoln Herald* 79 (Winter 1977): 169–73; Douglas L. Wilson and Rodney O. Davis, *Herndon's Informants: Letters, Interviews, and Statements about Abraham Lincoln* (Urbana: University of Illinois Press, 1997), pp. 152–53; Donald, *Lincoln's Herndon,* pp. 198–99.

36. Thomas, *Portrait for Posterity,* pp. 29–90; Donald, *Lincoln's Herndon,* pp. 250–84; King, *Lincoln's Manager,* pp. 275–76.

37. Wilson and Davis, *Herndon's Informants,* p. 639.

38. Allen Thorndike Rice, *North American Review,* to RJO, March 23, 1885. Rice asked Oglesby for a three-thousand-word essay on Lincoln. He urged, "Year by year those who know the most of him . . . are passing to the majority." Oglesby replied on March 30, "Most, perhaps, of what I could say, or what others will say, you will find to have already been stated in some form or other. In any event such an article should be carefully written, because it ought to contain the truth and the truth only." Both letters in Oglesby Correspondence, ISA. J. McDan Davis "Origin of the Rail-Splitter Legend," cited in Rufus Rockwell Wilson, *Lincoln among His Friends* (Caldwell: Caxton Printers, 1942), pp. 191–94, from *Century Magazine* 60 (June 1900); Adlai E. Stevenson, *Something of Men I Have Known* (Chicago: A. C. McClurg, 1909), p. 347. For University of Chicago appearance, see Scrapbook, 1890–1920, Oglesby MSS; see also Wilkie, p. 15, and Bancroft, pp. 11–34.

# 7. Governor, 1865–69

AFTER THE Union won the Civil War, Richard Oglesby thought it was his duty to follow the instructions Lincoln had given in the president's second inaugural address: "care for him who shall have borne the battle, and for his widow, and his orphan." The former major general responded by sending state agents south to aid wounded soldiers, expediting soldiers' discharges, and nurturing a facility for soldiers' orphans. Although he chose not to participate, his staff played a role in the establishment of the Grand Army of the Republic (G.A.R.), soon to be a powerful lobbying organization of veterans. During Reconstruction he seemed more intent on amplifying Lincoln's final inaugural admonition "with firmness in the right" than with eschewing malice toward the South. That position brought him into conflict with President Andrew Johnson. The new governor was also given the task of building state facilities, including the Illinois Industrial University, a new state capitol, and a penitentiary.[1]

With Oglesby leading the way, the Union (Republican) Party had been triumphant in the Illinois election of 1864. Reversing the losses of 1862, Republicans gained control of the Illinois General Assembly and its congressional delegation. Gov. Richard Yates was chosen by the legislature to replace a Democrat, William A. Richardson, as U.S. senator. Oglesby's inaugural was scheduled for January 10, 1865, but his young son Richard died of diphtheria on January 9, so ceremonies were postponed for a week. Oglesby was distraught by the death of his five-year-old namesake and by the illness and distress of his wife and daughter, whom Dr. Silas Trowbridge treated thirty-six times in less than six months.[2]

Steeled by the deaths he had seen in the war and the death of another daughter, Anna Elizabeth, two years earlier, the governor was able to compose an agenda for presentation in his inaugural address. The "military politician" demanded that "the rebellion and human slavery shall fall and perish together." Accordingly, Oglesby called for the abolition of the notorious "black laws" and support for the Thirteenth Amendment to the Constitution pending in Congress. In answer to the question, "What is to become of the negro after he is free?" he had a reply: "He can labor, he can learn, he can fight, improve, aspire." For those who had no higher motivation for emancipation, he would recommend it as "punishment to traitors for the crime of treason." The general assembly repealed the black laws, and Illinois became the first state to ratify the Thirteenth Amendment.[3]

The U.S. House and Senate had approved the Thirteenth Amendment by the necessary two-thirds vote on January 31 and February 1, 1865, and Sen. Lyman Trumbull immediately appealed to Oglesby, "Let Illinois be the first state [to ratify]." Oglesby, perhaps recalling that Lincoln's last message to Congress encouraged ratification "the sooner the better," forwarded the information to the general assembly, insisting, "It is just, it is humane" and should be ratified "now." He sent the message at noon, and by 4:30 P.M. the amendment had cleared both houses by a large majority and the governor had endorsed it. "All suppose you have signed the joint resolution by Congress," Oglesby telegraphed the president. "Great enthusiasm." Lincoln was so empathetic about the amendment that he did sign the resolution, although it was superfluous for him to do so. When serenaded at the White House that night, he boasted that Illinois had already ratified the amendment, which he regarded as "a King's cure for all the evils" of slavery.[4]

The Illinois constitution of 1848 allocated meager perquisites and powers to the governor. His salary was inadequate ($1,500 a year), he was ineligible for consecutive terms, and his veto could be overturned by a simple majority of the general assembly. The legislative branch was overwhelmed because of the lack of effective general incorporation laws. Thus the 1865 legislature passed more than 800 bills—including 155 related to town incorporation, 61 railroad charters, 84 insurance company charters, and 52 for schools—often without careful scrutiny. The governor tested his veto power by returning the Chicago Horse Railroad bill to the assembly. His objection was largely based on its lengthening the twenty-five-year monopoly by ninety-nine years. He had political friends on both sides of the question but had learned the futility of using his veto when the legislature overrode his objections within minutes after its presentation. In his 1867 message to the legislature, Oglesby recommended submitting to voters the question of convening a constitutional convention to redress the obvious weaknesses of the constitution of 1848. The legislators, who were constitutionally limited to a salary of only $2 a day, accepted his recommendation, and the constitution of 1870 was the eventual result.[5]

Moving quickly after taking office in January 1865, the new governor organized a staff, many of whom doubled as militia officers. Isham N. Haynie, an acquaintance of Oglesby's from the war, was appointed adjutant general. A former Democrat from southern Illinois, he had close ties to John A. Logan. John M. Snyder, formerly Governor Yates's private secretary, was carried over into the Oglesby administration. George H. Harlow, one of the founders of the Union League of America, organized in 1862 to counter secret organizations of Confederate sympathizers, was also appointed as a private secretary and doubled as assistant inspector general. John Wood, John Williams, William D. Crowell, James H. Bowen, and D. B. James were also appointed to the adjutant general's office. Oglesby's law partner Sheridan Wait was made canal commissioner, and Andrew Sherman, associated with the *Chicago Journal*, was appointed commissioner of the Joliet prison.[6]

Although Oglesby's constitutional powers in state government were limited, many important federal government functions were being expanded, and he was well-acquainted in Washington. He peppered officials with letters of introduction and recommendation for appointments for friends and political supporters. During his first nine weeks as governor, Oglesby addressed about a dozen requests to Lincoln, and many others were directed to cabinet members and members of Congress as well as to Ulysses S. Grant and military officials. Many military politicians came to recognize that political power was shifting to the national government. Draft quotas, reimbursement, and grants to the states were more significant than the routine acts of incorporation that were clogging the agenda of the state legislature.[7]

When Oglesby took office, he was immediately faced with the prospect of an additional draft quota of 35,541 men. Publicly he called for volunteer enlistments to avoid the stigma of the draft; privately, however, he sent Sheridan Wait to Washington armed with letters to Lincoln, Secretary of War Edwin M. Stanton, Cong. Elihu B. Washburne, Gen. John M. Palmer, and Provost Marshall James B. Fry, arguing that the quota was excessive. Apparently, Lincoln conceded to Palmer that he had made more demands on Illinois than on other states, but as a practical matter he "could get men more easily in Illinois . . . and neither you nor Dick can make any fuss about it." Oglesby, however, sent Adjutant General Haynie to see Lincoln and Fry in late February. The quotas were reduced slightly, and Illinois was given several deadline extensions. Oglesby had planned to travel to Washington himself to make his case to Lincoln and the War Department, but the trip was delayed and he did not arrive until the fateful Good Friday.[8]

The timely discharge of the Civil War soldiers and the welfare of veterans and their orphans dominated the remainder of Oglesby's first year as governor. He often spoke to regiments being discharged at nearby Camp Butler and enthusiastically traveled around the state to attend ceremonies honoring returned soldiers. He made a rousing speech at the Chicago Sanitary Fair, held for the benefit of the soldiers, and persuaded General Grant to greet soldiers and citizens in Springfield on September 12, 1865. There Grant made what the Springfield newspaper described facetiously as the longest speech of his life: a thank-you of forty-one words. Oglesby also convened the trustees of the new Soldiers' Orphans' Home to be built in Normal and personally donated $500 toward that cause, a gift, the *Illinois State Journal* commented, "perfectly characteristic of his excellency." He ordered military state agents to be sent into the South to aid soldiers who were still hospitalized, and in April he was appointed as one of the managers of the National Asylum for disabled volunteer soldiers in Columbus, Ohio, by resolution of Congress.[9]

Oglesby's break with Andrew Johnson came quickly. During the six-month period after the assassination, he wrote to the president no less than eighteen times for favors ranging from brevet promotions for his friends to indemnification to the state for wartime expenses. But it soon became apparent that although Oglesby believed that African Americans had earned citizenship and were the only reliably loyal persons in the South, Johnson believed that state governments there could only be reconstructed by whites, including some who were former Confederate officers. In his May 30, 1865, speech to the Chicago Sanitary Fair, Oglesby quoted Lincoln's "with malice toward none" phrase, but in the jocular manner that permeated his speeches he added that he was for moderation toward the South, "toward all those we do not hang or otherwise punish." With less humor he declared, "Liberty. . . . She is on a throne to-day more beautiful than ever before, for she takes to her bosom and covers with her shield two races of men." After Johnson vetoed the Freedmen's Bureau bill in early 1866, Oglesby warned a Springfield rally on February 26, 1866, that Johnson must not turn his back on freedmen. Johnson, he asserted, had "promised to be a Moses to the colored man, but God never made but one Moses and but one Judas Iscariot." Joseph Medill of the *Chicago Tribune* praised Oglesby's speech and arranged for its publication in the *Washington Chronicle;* there, it brought more letters of praise from various like-minded members of Congress and governors and from Chief Justice Salmon P. Chase.[10]

Oglesby's position was punctuated by his April 3, 1866, appearance at a lecture given by Frederick Douglass in the state capitol. He introduced Douglass by praising him "and his race" for their devotion to the country. He also agreed with Douglass's statements: "He had seen white and blue copperheads but never a black copperhead." Oglesby's decisive break with President Johnson came at a mass meeting in Jacksonville on April 21, a call for Congress to sustain its fight with the president over the civil rights bill. Johnson had vetoed the bill over the objection of both the Radical and Moderate Republicans in Congress. Oglesby admitted that he had supported Johnson for vice president but noted that Johnson had turned his back on those who favored freedom for blacks while accepting advice from Copperheads. His lenient policy toward former Confederates, Oglesby believed, would invalidate the purposes for which so many men had died in the Civil War.[11]

Simultaneously, the G.A.R. was established. Mary Dearing has argued that Dr. Benjamin F. Stephenson, ostensibly the group's founder, was only the obstetrician for the birth of the organization and that "the shrewd, friendly, and good-humored, the portly governor" "Uncle Dick" Oglesby was the unnamed father. Evidence for that viewpoint, however, is circumstantial. Several of Oglesby's staff members were involved in its organization; the first organizational meetings took place in Illinois governmental buildings; the first post was chartered in Decatur, Oglesby's hometown; and Oglesby favored veterans and had much to gain from the support of a strong veteran's organization.[12]

Other evidence suggests that the governor was more inclined to oppose Johnson within the traditional political apparatus. When a call for the first state G.A.R. convention was made, several Illinois generals who would become prominant politicians of the postwar era signed it. John A. Logan and John M. Palmer were listed among the sponsors of the organization that would, as stated in the announcement, aid in establishing and maintaining veterans' rights "morally, socially and politically." Oglesby did not sign the call, although John M. Snyder and Isham Haynie did. Neither did he attend the April 12 organizational meeting in Springfield. He did, however, send a letter asserting that every soldier was his friend "under all circumstances and every hazard." Unlike Missouri governor Thomas C. Fletcher, who heartily approved of the organization's objectives, Oglesby did not specifically endorse the meeting. Instead, he promptly left Springfield with his family for the Perry Springs resort in Pike County, Illinois. There he met Fletcher, who shared his anti-Johnson sentiments.[13]

Oglesby may have been reluctant to join the secret organization because he found the required oath repugnant. Left in his papers is a fragment that reads: "Are you willing to join a secret political association having for its object the promotion of soldiers rather than citizens to offices of trust and profit? Please answer on paper yes or no." In the same folder is a note, in Oglesby's handwriting, saying that Doctor Stephenson put "the within proposition" to him, and, Oglesby wrote, he "could not join and advised against such an organization." Oglesby considered the G.A.R. impracticable and thought it would not do "much if any good." It appears, however, that he used his influence to aid in the election of John M. Palmer as the first commander of the state organization. On July 3, 1866, Palmer had written to Oglesby that soldiers should have a permanent organization and that he would rather be its president than to have political office. Oglesby answered on July 20: "Not belonging to the organization I hardly knew how to present the case. I stated to Col Snyder what I thought about a permanent organization if they were determined to have any and suggested your name." He made the same suggestion to Logan and Haynie, and Palmer's election was "hasty and unanimous." Oglesby did not join the G.A.R. until January 22, 1884, during his third successful run for governor.[14]

When the first national G.A.R. encampment was held in Indianapolis on November 20, 1866, Maj. Gen. Stephen A. Hurlbut was elected commander-in-chief. Hurlbut, from northern Illinois, had been Oglesby's commander in Tennessee in 1863. John A. Logan succeeded Hurlbut in 1868. He moved the headquarters to Washington, where it became more of a tool for Logan and the Republican Party, perhaps earning Dearing's title as "The Grand Army of the Republican Party." Oglesby's short-term prognosis was probably correct. The G.A.R. was not preeminent in the 1866 election, and the three most prominent Illinois military politicians, Palmer, Logan, and Oglesby, were unable to unseat incumbent U.S. Senator Trumbull in the 1867 election in the Illinois legislature. Although each would later profit politically for having been soldiers, Logan's career seems to have been most directly influenced by the G.A.R.[15]

If Oglesby was reluctant to join a secret organization of soldiers, he was ardent in his public as well as private advocacy for soldiers. He chided his own "civilian" member of Congress, Henry P. H. Bromwell, for not stepping aside for Gen. Jesse H. Moore, asserting that the soldiers would not submit to "unjust discriminations and the people will generally go to their support." Oglesby was a featured speaker at soldiers' rallies across the Midwest during the summer of 1866. On one occasion, he joined John A. Logan and Gen. William T. Sherman for a Fourth of July "soldiers' picnic" in Salem that turned into an anti-Johnson mass meeting. Oglesby expressed dismay that President Johnson had consulted with "traitors" and never consulted "loyal men." He also denigrated Johnson's opposition to the Fourteenth Amendment and praised the African American soldier, who, "with the love of liberty swelling in his black breast came to our side . . . took up his musket and died" for the cause. Oglesby would "malign that race no longer nor hear them maligned."

They were citizens and should be protected, Johnson's policies for Reconstruction notwithstanding. Oglesby and Logan also spoke at a soldiers' mass meeting in St. Louis on August 10 and were joined by the governors of Wisconsin, Indiana, and Missouri. Together with the governor of Iowa, they seem to have considered extreme measures that might be necessary to preserve the fruits of the Union victory in the face of Johnson's malfeasance. Similar discussions may have taken place at the earlier Perry Springs resort meeting.[16]

Oglesby was reputed to be one of the best stump speakers in the West, and many opponents of Johnson's policies invited him to speak. Requests came from Ohio, Missouri, Minnesota, Wisconsin, and Indiana. By mid-August Johnson had escalated the battle for domination of the 1866 congressional elections by organizing a "National Union" convention in Philadelphia. A few Republicans and many Democrats joined. In spite of having a war-related recurring illness, Oglesby accepted invitations from Gov. Oliver P. Morton for a speaking tour in nearby Indiana. Between August 20 and September 3, he and Col. Robert G. Ingersoll spoke to large crowds in nine cities across Indiana. Morton sent word that he wanted more from the popular orators, but they needed to tend to Illinois.[17]

Oglesby felt especially challenged when President Johnson focused his "swing around the circle" whistle-stop campaign on behalf of sympathetic congressional candidates on Chicago. The announced purpose of Johnson's trip was to break ground for the monument to Stephen A. Douglas. Oglesby had previously been asked to perform that task, but the sponsors had reneged on the invitation, allowing the president to speak on September 6. The governor was dutifully invited to be in attendance at the occasion, but he declined. Oglesby explained to Gov. William M. Stone of Iowa that Johnson's pilgrimage to Douglas's tomb was an infringement upon the "supposed solemnity of the occasion" and that he would neither attend nor be present when Johnson visited Lincoln's tomb in Springfield. The *Illinois State Journal* was even more outraged. The editor noted that Johnson had turned the occasion into a partisan campaign for the benefit of rebels and traitors. When the Springfield city council passed a resolution to invite the president's party, including Adm. David G. Farragut and General Grant, to visit Springfield, both the Republican newpaper and the governor applauded the alderman who moved to strike Andrew Johnson's name from the invitation. "The capitol of Illinois loathes the driveling old embodiment of unscrupulous selfishness, who, by a strange accident (?) was made President," the *Journal* concluded.[18]

Oglesby had much to do with the Republican victory in 1866. He crisscrossed the state during September and October, making vehement speeches and indicting the Johnson administration. He charged that, given the chance, Johnson would declare himself a dictator. He also argued for African American suffrage in the South by declaring that no blacks were disloyal, whereas most whites were. President Johnson's stump speeches were also bombastic, but they were often characterized as being crude and "unpresidential." Heedless of northern opinion, the state governments of the South supporting Johnson passed restrictive black codes, elected former Confederate leaders to state and national legislative positions, and seemed to condone murderous race riots in Memphis and New Orleans. In Illinois, eleven of fourteen members of Congress elected were Republicans; John A. Logan was chosen as the at-large member by an overwhelming majority. Radical Republicans (defined as those who opposed Johnson's Reconstruction policies) experienced similar victory margins in other midwestern states, and the Republican Congress was empowered to seize complete control of the Reconstruction process.[19]

Oglesby, Logan, and Palmer each coveted the Senate seat held by Lyman Trumbull, and each hoped to replace him when the legislature met in January 1867. Oglesby, who had been allied with Trumbull in the 1860 election, politely refused to share Republican rallies with him during the canvass of 1866. The task of overthrowing him was made difficult because there was little disagreement concerning policy. Trumbull had pushed for the Thirteenth and Fourteenth Amendments and introduced the civil rights bill and the Freedmen's Bureau bill in early 1866. He had also joined the Radical Republicans soon after the president vetoed his bills. Many state legislators had profited from Trumbull's patronage during his twelve-year tenure. He campaigned vigorously and asserted that a vote against him would be considered a repudiation of his stance against Johnson. The senator's supporters had cleverly maneuvered Logan into accepting the at-large nomination, hoping that doing so might satisfy his ambitions. Trumbull's position was made stronger because the *Chicago Tribune*, the state's preeminent newspaper, continued to support the incumbent, as did many politicians who had not been soldiers, including Sen. Richard Yates and Cong. Elihu Washburne.[20]

"Oglesby's trying to make combinations to put him into the Senate . . . he is a lucky dog for the amount of talent he possesses, 'he may win,'" wrote Jesse K. Dubois, Oglesby's disgruntled rival for the Republican nomination in 1864. But luck eluded Oglesby and the soldier-politicians in the 1866 Senate race. Their tactic was to eliminate Trumbull by a secret vote in the Republican caucus on one question: "Should Trumbull succeed himself?" When the scheme failed after it was prematurely revealed in the *Illinois State Journal,* the three generals found it necessary to combine behind one man. Oglesby and Logan, both of whom had secure governmental positions, stood aside for John M. Palmer. Oglesby's list of legislators and their choices indicated that thirty-four preferred Trumbull and twenty-two backed Palmer. But after a test vote showed forty-eight for Trumbull and twenty-eight for Palmer, Palmer withdrew and Trumbull's reelection was assured. The three military politicians would have to wait to be seated in the U.S. Senate: Logan in 1871, Oglesby in 1873, and Palmer in 1891.[21]

The legislature reelected Senator Trumbull and approved the Fourteenth Amendment to the Constitution on a strict party-line vote. Governor Oglesby, in his mandatory message to the Twenty-fifth General Assembly, pronounced the state debt manageable and estimated that $800,000 would be received in taxes during the biennium. Legislators then began a scramble to dispense money for the construction of a new capitol, an industrial university, and a southern Illinois penitentiary. Northern Illinois interests charged that a down-state "industrial university—statehouse—penitentiary ring" was stealing prized institutions, while down-state interests charged that the northern part of the state was profiting by the "swindle" of the Illinois and Michigan canal expansion. But the state's economy and population were growing rapidly, and the demand for services, stifled by the war, could be met. All these projects and other lesser enterprises were authorized. Thousands of pages of private legislation, often packed into omnibus bills, were also passed without careful scrutiny.[22]

There was urgency about establishing an agricultural or industrial university. Congress had passed the Morrill land grant act in 1862, and Illinois had accepted 480,000 acres of land that could be sold, under the stipulation that an institution would be organized within five years. Several Illinois cities bid for the university. Jacksonville offered property, bonds, and cash totaling $491,000; Bloomington-Normal offered $470,000, including land adjacent to Illinois State Normal University, with the idea that the schools would be merged; Lincoln offered $385,000; and Champaign-Urbana's bid was valued at only $285,000. But Champaign County's state representative Clark R. Griggs, with the aid of a $20,500 contingency fund, lobbied around the state, lavishly entertained legislators and officials in Springfield, and offered mutual support to various communities for other projects. According to Griggs's memoirs, he recruited Governor Oglesby, Lt. Gov. William Bross, and Atty. Gen. Robert Ingersoll to Champaign-Urbana's cause. The difficulty of having submitted the fourth-best bid was overcome by reappraising their assets at $450,000 and arguing that the eastern part of the state should receive its share of largess. Governor Oglesby signed the bill creating Illinois Industrial University (later the University of Illinois) in February 1868.[23]

The state had outgrown its capital. Peoria, Chicago, and Decatur coveted the honor of being the new capital—and the structure that went with that honor. Springfield offered an attractive site, the large Mather block that had been purchased under the mistaken assumption that the Lincoln tomb would be there. Sangamon County also offered to purchase the old capitol as its courthouse. Decatur offered $1 million, perhaps unrealistically, and an appropriate site. Its citizens may have believed that the governor could help them obtain the prize. The enabling act, however, mandated that the legislators, not the governor, should appoint the statehouse commissioners. Some Decatur citizens and a few students of the constitution urged the governor to veto the bill on grounds that the 1848 constitution (Article 5, number 11) mandated that such appointments be made by the governor. Oglesby, however, understood the futility of a veto and tacitly accepted Springfield's claim. In return, he apparently extracted concessions that included limiting the construction contract to actual biennial appropriations, initially $450,000, rather than the entire $3 million. The law was challenged in court, but the capitol legislation was upheld.[24]

Southern Illinois shared in the legislature's bounty when a new penitentiary was established at Chester. The previous legislature had authorized a Soldiers' Orphans' Home, but its commissioners had not yet chosen a site. Jesse Fell of Normal and David Davis of Bloomington, close associates of Lincoln and Oglesby, organized a subscription campaign that yielded a bid of $40,370 in cash and land. Springfield's bid was apparently slightly higher, but the commissioners were attracted to the Normal site, where the orphans "might enjoy the moral influence" of Illinois State Normal University.[25]

After passing some 1,300 acts, which included ineffectual but portentous legislation such as an eight-hour day for workers and certain "Granger laws" designed to mitigate railroad and warehouse monopolies, the legislature reached its constitutional limitation of days in session and adjourned on February 28, 1867. Oglesby found it necessary to call two special sessions to correct mistakes in certain bills, to respond to a court interpretation concerning taxation on national banks, and to deal with changed circumstances in the prison system.[26]

Among the bills passed by the Twenty-fifth General Assembly was one reestablishing the position of attorney general. The governor was empowered to make the appointment. His friends Milton Hay and Lawrence Weldon were candidates, but he chose Col. Robert G. Ingersoll, the Peoria attorney who later gained notoriety for his classic bloody shirt speeches denouncing the Democrats as Copperheads and traitors, his "Plumed Knight" presidential nomination speech for James G. Blaine, and his controversial lectures on agnosticism. Oglesby and Ingersoll became personal friends as they campaigned against Johnson in Illinois and Indiana in 1866. Each spoke of the other as the best speaker in the country. Oglesby admired Ingersoll's intellect and seemed to enjoy his musings concerning biblical miracles, even his sarcastic comments on Oglesby's Holy Land speeches.[27]

Ingersoll was grateful for the appointment, as was his brother, Cong. Ebon Clark Ingersoll of Peoria. The position paid $3,500 a year (compared to the constitutionally mandated $1,500 for the governor), and Ingersoll could maintain his private practice. The governor needed Ingersoll's legal skills, especially in dealing with constitutional questions and the contracts being let for the use of prisoners. Ingersoll, however, was seldom in the capital. He compensated by sending a stream of scintillating letters to Oglesby. In one, written in 1867, he differentiated between Republicans and Democrats: "Times are getting hard—money getting scarce and consequently our [Republican] party getting a little *shaky.*" He continued, "When a man has his pocket full of money he feels like a gentleman, and when a man feels like a gentleman he votes our ticket." Ingersoll conceded, however, that "when his pocket is empty, and his shirt tail out he naturally slides over to the democracy [Democrats]."[28]

Oglesby's new attorney general assumed some of the burden in monitoring the Joliet prison, but dealing with pleas for pardons continued to dominate the governor's time. The constitution of 1848 gave him broad powers to grant reprieves, commutations, and pardons. It also required him to report on those cases at biennial sessions of the general assembly. Oglesby characterized the pardoning responsibility as a "very delicate power" that was difficult in execution. During the 1867 session, he asked legislators to provide some pardon application guidelines, but none was forthcoming. He reported that the prison population numbered 600 when he took office and had grown to 1,073 by the end of 1866. He pardoned 49 in 1865 and 191 in 1866, which, he asserted, was proportionally half as many pardons as his predecessors issued. A few death sentences were commuted, but some were not. Oglesby's notes suggest that he considered the massive file of requests for pardons very carefully, a practice he would revisit two decades later in the case of the "Haymarket Anarchists."[29]

Another time-consuming task that the legislature failed to alleviate concerned reimbursement to the state from the federal government for expenses related to the late war. Oglesby had commissioned Col. H. D. Cook as the Illinois military state agent in Washington at a monthly salary of $100. Three times during the 1867 session Oglesby asked the legislature to fund the continuation of the position, but it failed to do so. He reluctantly funded the state agent through his contingency account, which was limited. At the end of 1867,

Cook had recovered almost $100,000 in war claims, and the governor and other state officials were documenting $200,000 more for him to pursue.[30]

Life was sometimes good for the governor and his young wife in the mansion in Springfield. The memory of the death of the Oglesbys' namesakes, Dickie and Anna Elizabeth, was assuaged by the birth of Robert on October 8, 1865 and the renewal to health of two-year-old Olive. The Oglesbys could live very well despite the governor's minimal salary by using profits from his investments and his continuing partnership with Sheridan Wait as well as the allowances allocated for operating the mansion. Oglesby paid income tax for 1866 on $9,084, which ranked his income as Springfield's fourth largest but far behind that of banker Jacob Bunn, who reported $77,000. Oglesby's Decatur bank account at the end of 1867 showed a balance of $17,255.77, and he paid taxes on an income of $10,664.55. Soon after he became governor, he bought a new carriage and horses for about $1,000 and expensive silk gowns, a mink coat, and jewelry for Anna. He also commissioned a portrait "in pastille" of Anna. The governor personally kept meticulous expense records. Six young women with Irish names were employed in the mansion, for an average of $4 a week. A "Colored boy Joe" received $20 per month. During February 1867, Oglesby recorded about Joe: "He worked but little, but at my expense he was well cared for until he died . . . he was an excellent man. I thought very much of him and was greatly pained at his death." The governor apparently also paid for a runner and an attendant for Anna Oglesby from his own funds. His personal monthly mansion accounts and hotel bill statements almost always included generous amounts for his favorite beverages: bourbon, usually purchased by the barrel, and champagne.[31]

The biennial session of the legislature was also the social season in Springfield, and the first event was a grand ball to celebrate the opening of the luxurious new $297,000 Leland Hotel. The governor and other officials were listed as honorary managers of the event. The Oglesbys hosted three lavish parties in the mansion during the short season. The *Illinois State Journal* reported that "the warmhearted and noble and genial governor" and "his most estimable lady" entertained five hundred guests at a levee on January 22, 1867. Anna Oglesby was complimented on her "native grace and easy dignity," and there was dancing until midnight. The governor's carefully prepared tally put the cost at $1,200, including $304 for champagne and $50 for "Segars [*sic*] and Tobacco." A second reception, described as a "brilliant affair," was held about two weeks later. The *Journal* maintained that few "rulers" were blessed with "as large a circle of warm, personal friends as Governor Oglesby, and certainly none are more universally honored and respected." The grand finale, held on February 28, was a masquerade ball. Guests were costumed as "king to peasant and queen to flower-girl," and certain unidentified legislators became the "shrewd politician" and the "supercilious dandy."[32]

During the summer of 1867, the thirty-one-year-old Anna Oglesby became seriously ill. She had contracted what would eventually be diagnosed as pulmonary consumption (tuberculosis). The governor organized a party to journey to St. Paul, Minnesota, to escape the oppressive heat of central Illinois. On July 27 they boarded a Mississippi River steamer at Alton for passage to Lake Minnehaha. The party included Orin H. Miner, the state's auditor; state senator Joseph Delos Ward; and Isham N. Haynie. Missouri Governor Fletcher also joined the vacationing group. Ingersoll, left behind to work on prison contracts, wrote to rationalize that he was missing not only beautiful cool nights and moonlight excursions but also gnats, river flies, sand mud, poor hotels, tough steak, and hay tea. He hoped, however, that Anna Oglesby would return "in the bloom of health." The Oglesbys came back to Decatur on August 20, and newspapers reported that her health had improved. A few days later, however, Oglesby confided to a friend, "She is truly very ill and I fear will be for some time." The October 9, 1867, edition of the *Journal* reported that Anna Oglesby's health had gone from "quite delicate" to "exceedingly critical."[33]

As the 1868 quadrennial political season approached, the governor determined that he would not leave Anna. Political friends wrote him flattering letters urging a run for Congress. On February 8, 1868, he made it clear that he would not run, replying that he was "surrounded with serene sickness" and did "not at present feel that interest in political matters." He also declined invitations to speak to powerful veterans groups such as the Society of the Army of the Tennessee meeting in St. Louis and the Soldiers Convention in Chicago. Closer to home, he canceled a scheduled Holy Land speech and his attendance at the inauguration of the Illinois Industrial University.[34]

Oglesby's moratorium on politics did not extinguish his hostility toward Andrew Johnson, whom he considered a turncoat and usurper. When news came from Washington that the House of Representatives was considering the impeachment of the president, Oglesby swiftly addressed a telegram to Speaker Schuyler Colfax. Colfax gave it to John A. Logan, who neglected to use it in his speech embracing impeachment. The speaker then passed it to Cong. Ebon Clark Ingersoll, who read it on the floor of the House of Representatives. Oglesby asserted that the people of Illinois demanded impeachment of the traitor: "The peace of the country is not to be trifled with by this presumptuous demagogue." He ominously added, "Millions of loyal hearts are panting to stand by the Stars and Stripes." Albert Burr, a Democratic member of Congress from southern Illinois, rose to challenge Oglesby's telegram and accuse him of being an alcoholic. Ingersoll sprang to his feet to assert that the Illinois governor was "sober, patriotic, high-minded, and honorable." He also accused Burr of slandering a man "who today carries in his body minie balls fired from rebel muskets" and was notoriously "a man of sobriety." After the House voted overwhelmingly to impeach, Speaker Colfax wrote to Oglesby, congratulating him on his timely telegram and concluding, "Thank God, the hour of our deliverance draweth nigh."[35]

But deliverance from the man Oglesby labeled "this pest to the Republic" was postponed beyond May 1868, when the Senate failed to remove the president by one vote less than the required two-thirds majority. Oglesby and most state officials had signed a dispatch to the Illinois congressional delegation. They demanded a guilty vote against Johnson "in memory of our fallen soldiers" and for the "safety of the Republic." A critical not-guilty vote was cast by Lyman Trumbull. As Robert Ingersoll wrote to Oglesby, "Trumbull has gone to the [political] grave. We no longer deplore him." When Trumbull's term expired in 1873, Oglesby would take his place in the Senate.[36]

Oglesby's suspension of public activities constricted his influence in selecting a successor. He seemed comfortable with either John M. Palmer or John A. Logan, but both appeared determined not to run. Palmer, who had a large family, was concerned about the low salary, and Logan preferred to stay in Washington as an at-large member of Congress and commander of the G.A.R. until a Senate seat became available. Logan supported his business partner Isham Haynie, who was in poor health. Cong. Stephen A. Hurlbut, despite being court-martialed twice, was also mentioned. All were soldier-politicians from the Civil War. With the stronger politicians declining, Robert G. Ingersoll petitioned Governor Oglesby for his support. Oglesby warned that Palmer might accept a draft but agreed to privately recommend Ingersoll when his views were solicited. He did not attend the Republican nominating convention in Peoria on May 6, 1868. Despite Ingersoll's oratorical prowess, the majority of delegates—faced with his youth, lack of a political organization, and spotty war record (he had been captured by Confederate General Nathan Forrest) in addition to charges of intemperance, vulgarity, and irreligion—chose to draft Palmer, and he accepted. Taking a line from Charles Dickens's *David Copperfield*, Ingersoll wrote to Oglesby, "after all, 'Barkus is willing.'"[37]

The reluctance of the prominent soldier-politicians to accept the Republican nomination for governor may have been partially motivated by the rumors that Sen. Richard Yates might be forced to resign because of his addiction to alcohol. After it was reported that he had missed numerous Senate sessions during the impeachment trial, the *Chicago Journal* and *Tribune*

suggested that he resign. Oglesby's hometown paper seconded the recommendation, as did the Springfield Republican organ. Had Yates resigned,
Oglesby could have appointed a senator, pending the legislative session of
1869. There were unfounded rumors that the governor might resign and allow Lieutenant Governor Bross to appoint him to the Senate. Logan, Palmer, and Oglesby continued to covet the Senate seat, but Yates staved off demands for a resignation by issuing a mea culpa, dated April 21, 1868. He
frankly confessed to his weakness but promised to reform. He also condemned those who "ignobly" desired his ruin for the purpose of elevating
someone else to his place. "It is always manly and noble to reform," he concluded, and "generally good policy to speak ingenuously." Yates maintained
his office, if not his sobriety, until his term expired in 1871.[38]

Lincoln's "imperishable fame" affected Oglesby even during his period of
concern and bereavement for his wife. In Oglesby's message to the Illinois
General Assembly in 1867, he had written, "Our state was his loved home, and
here he sleeps in death." But Lincoln slept in a temporary vault at Oak Ridge
Cemetery, and Oglesby's efforts as president of the National Lincoln Monument Association continued. He had persuaded the legislature to contribute
$100,000 toward the building of the tomb, and his friend Missouri Gover-
nor Fletcher sent the first contribution made by another state. Oglesby issued a proclamation for "Fasting, Humiliation and Prayer," to be observed
on April 15, the third anniversary of Lincoln's death. He also characterized
Lincoln's death as a "profound and bitter sorrow" and a sacrifice to human
liberty. In one of his few public appearances during Anna Oglesby's illness,
the governor attended the day of fasting and prayer services held by various
Christian congregations in the state house. The *Illinois State Journal* remarked
that his comments were "eloquent and touching," and the *Alton Telegraph*
noted that Illinois Democrats had chosen the same day, April 15, for a state
nominating convention. The contrast was clear, the *Telegraph* asserted. The
loyal people of the state were engaged in fasting, humility, and prayer while
Democrats were celebrating "a political love-feast, as is befitting to the friends
of Jeff. Davis, J. Wilkes Booth & Co."[39]

On May 21, 1868, as Oglesby maintained a death watch for Anna, his forty-
three year-old friend Isham Haynie died of "congestion of liver." Haynie had
been with Oglesby in Washington at the time of Lincoln's assassination and
death. In addition to the diary Haynie kept of the Washington trip, his other
important contribution to history was to compile four volumes of the adjutant general's report on Illinois regiments that served in the Civil War. Oglesby called a meeting of veterans to make arrangements to attend the Haynie
funeral, and the *Illinois State Journal* described the mile-long procession to

Oak Ridge Cemetery as having been exceeded only by those of Gov. William H. Bissell and President Lincoln. The political mourning period for Haynie was very brief, however. On May 22, his business and political partner John A. Logan and a host of other important Republicans who were assembled at the Republican National Convention in Chicago flooded Oglesby with telegrams asking that Stephen Hurlbut be appointed adjutant general. After Haynie's funeral, Oglesby decreed that the position would not be filled, pending new legislation.[40]

On June 4, 1868, death came to Anna Elizabeth White Oglesby in the governor's mansion. She died of "that insidious disease, pulmonary consumption." Oglesby purchased a "full glass, full satin added metallic casket, silver mounted" from Thomas C. Smith Undertakers of Springfield. Funeral services were held at the Executive Mansion on June 6, with the Rev. L. B. Carpenter officiating. Most of the pallbearers were elected officials: Newton Bateman, Milton Hay, O. H. Miner, William Butler, George W. Smith, Jacob Bunn, James H. Beveridge, and John Williams. Oglesby arranged a special train to take the funeral party to Decatur later in the day. There he had hired eight carriages to take mourners to Greenwood Cemetery, where Anna was buried alongside Richard James, Jr. (Dickie) and Anna Elizabeth ("Little Sissie"). The simple burial service of the Methodist Church was read, a hymn was sung, and a short prayer was offered by Mr. Carpenter. The following spring, Oglesby had a marble gravestone installed for Anna.[41]

The governor returned to the lonely Executive Mansion and to the sad task of answering notes of condolence and collecting his late wife's effects. Expressions of sympathy came from political, military, and personal friends from across the country. Dan Elliot from New York, his "traveler friend in the Holy Land," sent condolences. To Mary Logan, wife of John A. Logan, he replied: "My dear Anna suffered long but suffers no more. She has left me with our sweet little children for a heavenly home. She died as only the happy can die." Oglesby regretted that Mary Logan had never seen Anna in good health and "in her real spirit." Oglesby, always the careful record-keeper, cataloged Anna's jewelry for deposit and placed her clothing, including silk dresses and a mink coat, in two trunks. A governess and Amanda Prather, Oglesby's sister, took charge of the children. Perhaps impressed with the impermanence of life, Oglesby also commissioned a $350 oil painting of the children from the same artist who had executed Anna Oglesby's portrait the previous year.[42]

Mary Logan had asked in her condolence message whether Oglesby could speak at a political rally on July 22. Still grieving on July 16, he replied, "I would like to go for the good of our cause and country, both need our attention, but I cannot." The governor needed time away from the memories of the

Executive Mansion. He virtually abandoned Springfield from July to November 1868, leaving his private secretary George H. Harlow to answer most correspondence and keep him informed by mail. Harlow noted in a July 1868 letter that it was one hundred degrees in Springfield and that business was very dull. He also urged Oglesby to stay away as long "as you can make it pleasant." The barrel of bourbon the governor purchased in Decatur perhaps helped him forget his sorrow. He split most of the time between his Decatur home and Hyde Park, near Chicago. Sheridan Wait had been purchasing town lots for development in the South Shore area, and Oglesby invested $10,000 in the enterprise.[43]

About two months after Anna's death, Oglesby began to accept invitations to speak on behalf of the Republican Party. He had been among the first to endorse Grant for president but attended neither the state convention nor the national convention in Chicago, where Grant was nominated. Oglesby was the major speaker, however, when Chicago Republicans staged their "ratification" of the Grant and Colfax ticket at a giant rally on August 12, 1868. He invoked the memory of "the immortal and sainted Lincoln," damned Democrats for prolonging the war and sabotaging Reconstruction, and praised Grant as "a cool-headed, clear minded, noble, honest, modest, moral man." An extensive summary of Oglesby's speech was published in the *New York Times,* as was a "bloody shirt" speech he gave to the "Boys in Blue" in Indianapolis on September 2. During September and October, he spoke almost every day or night in various locations, usually for three hours. The *Chicago Evening Post* characterized him as one of the most eloquent and powerful speakers in the West and observed that he drew immense crowds wherever he spoke and always stirred the crowd. It applauded his "great earnestness" and "profound conviction" while conceding that his "illustrations are sometimes more powerful than elegant." The *Chicago Journal* also placed him at the "very head and front of Western orators and statesmen." It was remarkable, the newspaper observed, that he had exerted such effort in the campaign even though he was not a candidate for any office. His bold "sledge-hammer" arguments, together with "stirring eloquence, indefatigable energy and pertinacity," impressed editors. The Republicans swept Illinois by large margins, and Ulysses S. Grant was elected president. Johnson's indulgent Reconstruction policy was discredited, and Oglesby could exult that the civil disorder that followed the rebellion was dying out.[44]

Oglesby's valedictory as governor came in his lengthy biennial message presented to the general assembly on January 4, 1869. He reviewed changes that had been made during his term. The state's debt was down and its revenues up, including those entreated from the federal government. Entities, including Normal University, the Industrial University, the Soldiers' and Sailors' Orphans' Home, prisons, the Illinois and Michigan canal, and a new capitol, were initiated or strengthened. Various newspapers praised his wisdom, discretion, and executive capacity. The *Peoria Transcript* allowed that he had less polish and experience than his predecessors but "a more straightforward, honest, and upright man than Oglesby never existed." The *Illinois State Journal* noted that he had the confidence of all classes of people and posited that he enjoyed the "respect and personal esteem of even his political opponents." His friend Robert Ingersoll wrote to congratulate him on retiring, "your great ability acknowledged by all and with your integrity unquestioned even by your bitterest foes."[45]

"Do you feel like an old man broken by the storms of state?" Ingersoll inquired a few days after Oglesby left office. Although Ingersoll was jesting, the forty-four-year-old former governor had experienced enough trauma in his lifetime to be a broken man. An orphan since he was eight, he had known combat in the Mexican War, deprivation during the California gold rush, and a critical wound in the Civil War. Gubernatorial honors brought him no respite from death. His son Dickie, the martyred president, his adjutant general, and his wife were all taken from him. He began his tenure as governor while the Civil War still raged, an advocate for Union soldiers. The postwar South and its northern sympathizers seemed to him to threaten the peace and the fruits of victory. He was among the radical Republicans who foiled President Johnson and the Democratic Party's plans for a forbearing peace that would have rebuffed freedmen. The ratification of the Thirteenth and Fourteenth Amendments to the U.S. Constitution, the impeachment of President Johnson, and Republican victories in the elections of 1866 and 1868 were triumphs in which Oglesby participated. The remarkable building program for state institutions was also a triumph.[46]

As Oglesby was preparing to leave Springfield, two exhibitions portended his future and reflected his past. One was the unveiling of the cornerstone for the new capitol. The governor's name was chiseled at the top of the list of state officials. The immense building would not be completed until Oglesby had been elected governor for the third time, twenty years later. The other was the Springfield showing of the traveling exhibit of Alonzo Chappel's painting *The Last Hours of Lincoln* (for ".50 cents at the Lathams Building, South Side Square"). Oglesby was one of the persons immortalized as being at the foot of the bed of the dying president. Lincoln's "imperishable fame" would continue to influence his political life.[47]

## Notes

1. *Collected Works,* vol. 8, p. 333.

2. *Journal of the Senate of the Twenty-fourth General Assembly of the State of Illinois* (Springfield: Baker and Phillips, Printers, 1865), pp. 90, 163; Receipt, Decatur, June 29, 1865, Oglesby MSS.

3. Arthur Charles Cole, *The Era of the Civil War* (Springfield: Illinois Centennial Commission, 1919), ch. 18, p. 387. Oglesby's inaugural address is in the *Illinois Senate Journal* (1865), pp. 15–62; see also Moses, vol. 2, pp. 720–21; and Church, p. 98.

4. "Annual Message to Congress," Dec. 6, 1864, *Collected Works,* vol. 8, p. 149; "Resolution Submitting the Thirteenth Amendment to the States," Feb. 1, 1865, *Collected Works,* vol. 8, pp. 253, 254n. Secretary of State Seward apparently sent notifications to the states on February 2, 1865. Oglesby certified the legislature's resolution of February 1 to Seward on February 7. Oglesby Letterpress Book, ISA; *Collected Works,* vol. 8, pp. 254–55; Harold Holzer, *Dear Mr. Lincoln: Letters to the President* (Reading: Addison-Wesley, 1993), p. 274.

5. Moses, vol. 2, pp. 1105–36, 787, 722; *Illinois Senate Journal* (1865), p. 415; *Journal of the House of Representatives of the Twenty-fifth General Assembly of the State of Illinois* (Springfield: Baker, Bailhache, 1867), p. 39.

6. Moses, vol. 2, p. 717. Nominations are in Oglesby Letterpress Book, ISA; see also *Journal,* Jan. 11, 1865, p. 3, col. 3. Harlow's career is described in *History of Tazewell County, Illinois* (Chicago: Chas. C. Chapman, 1879), pp. 707–9. Oglesby's speculator cohort, Dr. C. H. Ray, wrote to him on December 4, 1864, urging him to appoint Wait as commissioner of the Joliet penitentiary and require an annual $1,000 kickback. On the back of Ray's letter, the governor wrote, "ans Dec. 6, 1864, Said nothing improper or imprudent, said go and see Lincoln at once." Oglesby MSS.

7. For letters of recommendation, see Jan. 18, 20, 21, 31, 1865, Feb. 2, 17, 22, 23, 28, 1865, March 22, 23, 1865, Oglesby Letterpress Book, ISA; RJO to Abraham Lincoln, Feb. 24, 1865, Oglesby MSS.

8. RJO to James B. Fry, Jan. 24, 1865, and RJO to Abraham Lincoln, Jan. 25, 1865, both in Oglesby MSS; RJO to Edwin M. Stanton, Jan. 25, 1865, to Cong. Elihu B. Washburne, and to Gen. James B. Fry, Jan. 30, 1865, Governor's Correspondence, Jan. 1865, ISA; *Journal,* Feb. 7, 1865, p. 2, col. 1, and March 4, 1865, p. 3, col. 3; George Thomas Palmer, *A Conscientious Turncoat* (New Haven: Yale University Press, 1941), pp. 162–63.

9. *Journal,* July 12, 1865; All of the following appeared on p. 3, cols. 2, 3, or 4: July 14, 15, 21, 29, 1865, Aug. 5, 10, 17, 18, 26, 29, 30, 1865, Oct. 7, 16, 19, 1865, and Nov. 1, 1865. For the Grant appearance, see *Journal,* Sept. 12, 1865, p. 2, col. 2, p. 3, col. 4, and Sept. 13, 1865, p. 3, cols. 3–5. On the state agents, see *Journal,* July 15, 1865, p. 3, col. 3, and Aug. 18, 1865, p. 3, col. 3. For the Soldiers' Orphans' home, see *Journal,* Aug. 31, 1865, p. 3, col. 4 and Sept. 1, 1865, p. 3, col. 4. For RJO being named as an asylum manager, see *Journal,* April 28, 1866, p. 4, col. 1 and May 15, 1866, p. 4, col. 1. For an account of eight or ten disabled soldiers being sent to the Soldiers National Asylum in Columbus, Ohio, see *Journal,* Sept. 27, 1867, p. 4, col. 1. For Oglesby's Sanitary Fair speech, see *Chicago Tribune,* May 31, 1865. He also delivered the oration at the cornerstone-laying ceremony at Lincoln University in Logan County (*Journal,* Sept. 14, 1865, p. 3, col. 3).

10. RJO to Andrew Johnson in 1865: May 15 (three letters), May 16, June 15, 20, 27 (two

items), 28, July 17, 26, Aug. 21, 23, 25, 28, 31, Sept. 19 (two items), all in Oglesby Letterpress Book, ISA; *Journal*, June 3, 1865, p. 2, cols. 3, 4, Feb. 2, 1866, p. 2, cols. 2–5, April 23, 1866, p. 4, cols. 2, 3; Joseph Medill to RJO, March 6, 1866, and RJO to Salmon P. Chase, March 19, 1866, both in Oglesby MSS.

11. *Journal*, April 4, 1866, p. 4, col. 2, April 5, 1866, p. 4, col. 2; speech at Jacksonville, April 21, 1866, Oglesby MSS.

12. Mary R. Dearing, *Veterans in Politics: The Story of the G.A.R.* (Baton Rouge: Louisiana State University Press, 1952), pp. 81–82; Stuart McConnell, *Glorious Contentment: The Grand Army of the Republic, 1865–1900* (Chapel Hill: University of North Carolina Press, 1992), pp. 24–25. The April 6, 1866, charter for G.A.R. Post 1 in Decatur was signed by Benjamin F. Stephenson, commanding department, and Robert Woods, adjutant general, and contains the names of twelve charter members. Oglesby's name does not appear, but J. C. Pugh, his sometime rival, does. Photocopy from book A, page 5, Oglesby Mansion Collection, Decatur, Ill.

13. Robert B. Beath, *History of the Grand Army of the Republic* (New York: Bryan, Taylor, 1888), pp. 55–67. Governor and Mrs. Oglesby and Governor and Mrs. Fletcher headed a party of one hundred people involved in the festivities at the Perry Springs spa in Pike County, Illinois. The *Journal* (July 21, 1866, p. 4, col. 5) reported that "the party, feeling in high glee, made the woods ring with their songs and merry laughter." Oglesby also made his Holy Land speech at a local church.

14. Another undated fragment reads: "Are you willing to engage in a secret political order which has for its sole object the promotion of soldiers over citizens. If you join no one will know it unless you desire if you do not all we ask is your word of honor that you will never mention it." John M. Palmer, Washington, D.C., to RJO, July 3, 1866, and RJO to Palmer, July 20, 1866, Oglesby MSS. Oglesby's entry into the G.A.R. was reported in the *Journal* (Jan. 24, 1884, p. 4, col. 4).

15. RJO to Henry P. H. Bromwell, June 28, 1866, Oglesby MSS; *Journal*, Feb. 17, 1886, p. 4, cols. 3–6; Dearing, *Veterans in Politics*, p. 80.

16. James Pickett Jones, *"Black Jack": John A. Logan and Southern Illinois in the Civil War Era* (Carbondale: Southern Illinois University Press, 1995), p. 277; *Journal*, Aug. 10, 1866, p. 4, col. 1. Iowa governor William M. Stone wrote to RJO on August 9 that he was sorry he had received the notice of the "your state convention" [the St. Louis meeting] too late but that the governors should organize in opposition to Johnson. "*Look well to the front,*" he ominously concluded (Oglesby MSS).

17. Jones *"Black Jack,"* p. 277; *Journal*, Aug. 16, 1866, p. 1, col. 1, p. 4, col. 2, Sept. 1, 1866, p. 4, col. 1; July 28, 1866, in Letterpress Book, 1866–69, and W. R. Halloway to RJO, Sept. 11, 1866, both in Oglesby MSS.

18. RJO to Gov. Stone, Sept. 17, 1866, Oglesby MSS; *Journal*, Sept. 3, 1866, p. 1, col. 4, and Sept. 5, 1866, p. 4, col. 2, question mark in the original.

19. *Journal*, Sept. 4, 1866, p. 1, col. 1, and Oct. 22, 1866, p. 4, col. 2; James M. McPherson, *Ordeal by Fire: The Civil War and Reconstruction* (New York: McGraw-Hill, 1992), pp. 515–17; Lusk, p. 199.

20. Coles, *Era of the Civil War*, pp. 404–5; *Journal*, Nov. 1, 1866, p. 4, col. 1; Ralph J. Roske, *His Own Counsel: The Life and Times of Lyman Trumbull* (Reno: University of Nevada Press, 1979), pp. 135–36.

21. Jesse K. Dubois to Richard Yates, Jan. 14, 1866 [1867?], Yates Collection, ISHL; Oglesby's tally [1867], and RJO to John A. Logan, Nov. 7, 1866, both in Oglesby MSS; RJO to John M. Palmer, March 21, 1866, Palmer Papers, ISHL; Roske, *His Own Counsel,* pp. 134–36.

22. *Illinois House Journal* (1867), vol. 1, pp. 13–16; Cole, *Era of the Civil War,* pp. 405–7.

23. Moses, vol. 2, p. 768; Allan Nevins, *Illinois* (New York: Oxford University Press, 1917), pp. 32–40; Winton U. Solberg, *The University of Illinois, 1867–1894: An Intellectual and Cultural History* (Urbana: University of Illinois Press, 1968), pp. 74–79; Fred H. Turner, "Misconceptions Concerning the Early History of the University of Illinois," *Illinois State Historical Society Transactions for the Year 1932,* Illinois State Historical Library Publication no. 39 (Springfield, 1932), pp. 79–82.

24. RJO to J. Wilson, March 4, 1867, Oglesby MSS; Moses, vol. 2, pp. 768–69.

25. Moses, vol. 2, p. 769; *Journal,* May 3, 1867, p. 4, col. 2.

26. *Journal,* May 25, 1867, p. 1, col. 1, June 12, 1867, p. 1, col. 2, June 14, 1867, p. 1, col. 1, June 15, 1867, p. 1, col. 2, June 17, 1867, p. 1, col. 2, June 28, 1867, p. 1, col. 2; *Illinois Senate Journal* (1867), vol. 2, 2d sess. and 3d sess.

27. Mark A. Plummer, *Robert G. Ingersoll, Peoria's Pagan Politician,* Western Illinois Monograph Series no. 4 (Macomb, 1984), p. 36; Mark A. Plummer, "Robert G. Ingersoll on Leeks and Onions in the Holy Land," *Illinois Quarterly* 43 (Fall 1980): 5–10.

28. The twenty-seven letters are published in Mark A. Plummer, "'Goodbye Dear Governor. You Are My Best Friend': The Private Letters of Robert G. Ingersoll to Richard J. Oglesby, 1867–1877," *JISHS* 73 (Summer 1980): 79–116. Ingersoll's December 22, 1867, letter is on page 97.

29. Robert G. Ingersoll to RJO, Aug. 7, 1867, in Plummer, "'Goodbye Dear Governor,'" p. 95; *Illinois House Journal* (1867), vol. 1, pp. 30, 317–18; RJO to Col. William Rawley, Oct. 27, 1867, Oglesby MSS; *Journal,* May 1, 1868, p. 2, cols. 3–4.

30. *Journal,* Dec. 23, 1867, p. 4, col. 2; RJO to H. D. Cook, March 4, 15, 1867, Oglesby MSS. By the end of 1868, Cook had collected $253,655.58. *Journal,* Dec. 29, 1886, p. 3, col. 2.

31. *Peoria Daily Transcript,* April 20, 1868, p. 2, col. 2. The following are all in the Oglesby MSS: "Pay of Servants in Mansion; Expenses Not Chargeable to Table Account," July 10, 1866; Oglesby's bill at the Tremont House, Chicago, May 10, 1867, which included $10.20 for two and a quarter days' board and room and $6.75 for wine and ale; and a summary of business of Wait and Oglesby (Nov. 1, 1866–Oct. 31, 1867) showing $18,362.91 profit, half of it to Oglesby.

Much of Wait and Oglesby's profit came from a contract with the Illinois Central Railroad, personally solicited by the governor, to furnish railroad ties. See correspondence with John M. Douglas, president, Illinois Central Rail Road, Aug. 8, Oct. 25, Oct. 27, Nov. 14, and Nov. 26, 1865, Oglesby MSS. The following receipts are given for June 1865: carriage, $600; harness, $150; and approximately $250 for two horses, for a total of $1,000 (Oglesby MSS). A November 9, 1867, receipt for $75 for a portrait (plus $50 for the frame) was charged to the governor's mansion account (Oglesby MSS). The artist may have been German-born A[dalbert] Wunder from Hamilton, Ontario, known for his rapid portraits in crayon (H. W. French, *Art and Artists in Connecticut* [Boston: Lee and Shepard, Publishers, 1879], p. 136). Statement of income 1867 and Oglesby's account with Peddecord and Burrows, Decatur, in ledgerbook 2, Feb. 2, 1863–1867, both in Oglesby MSS. On April

13, 1868, Oglesby copied a letter dated April 13, 1865, from "Kate" [Luttwell?] to Anna in which Kate advises her to make a change (perhaps of a servant): "When a huzze will make mischief between man and wife what won't they do[?]" she wrote and offered to send a servant from Decatur (Oglesby MSS).

32. *Journal*, Jan. 1, 1867, p. 4, cols. 2–5, Jan. 9, 1867, p. 4, cols. 1–2, Jan. 23, 1867, p. 4, col. 4, Feb. 8, 1867, p. 4, col. 6, March 1, 1867, p. 4, col. 3; account for Jan. 22 ball, Oglesby MSS. In 1896 Emma Oglesby noted on the account statement that Jacob Bunn had paid the bill for the levee. Oglesby's illness, reported a few days after the January 22 levee, is something of a mystery. *Journal*, Jan. 29, 1867, p. 4, col. 6, Jan. 31, 1867, p. 4, col. 7.

33. *Journal*, July 24, 1867, p. 4, col. 1, July 26, 1867, p. 4, col. 1, July 29, 1867, p. 4, col. 1, Aug. 7, 1867, p. 4, col. 1, Aug. 21, 1867, p. 4, col. 1, Oct. 9, 1867, p. 1, col. 2; RJO to Governor Stone [?], Aug. 31, 1867, Letterpress Book, 1866–69, Oglesby MSS; Robert G. Ingersoll to RJO, Aug. 7, 1867, in Plummer, "'Goodbye Dear Governor,'" p. 95.

34. J. T. Hanna, Salina, Kan., to RJO, Jan. 8, 1868, and reply Jan. 25, 1868, Oglesby MSS; RJO to J. M. Beardsley, Rock Island, Ill., Feb. 8, 1868, Oglesby MSS; newspaper clipping, Feb. 1, 1868, Oglesby MSS; Herman Lieb to RJO, March 26, 1867, Oglesby MSS. Receipts (Oglesby MSS) show that Dr. T. S. Henning saw Anna Oglesby almost daily—thirty-seven times in January. See also the *Journal*, March 11, 1868, p. 4, col. 1, March 13, 1868, p. 4, col. 3, March 21, 1868, p. 1, col. 3, May 20, 1868, p. 1, col. 2, and June 12, 1868, p. 4, col. 1.

35. *Journal*, Feb. 24, 1868, p. 4, col. 4, March 1, 1868, p. 1, col. 2; *Peoria Daily Transcript*, Feb. 29, 1868, p. 2, cols. 2–5; Schuyler Colfax to RJO, March 2, 1868, Oglesby MSS. In response to Oglesby's "stand by the Stars and Stripes" statement, John S. Wilcox, Elgin, wrote to him on February 26, 1868: "If more blows are to be struck for Freedom, now is the time while our noble old army is yet in its vigor" (Oglesby MSS). The *Register* (March 2, 1868, p. 1, col. 2) suggested that Oglesby and the leading midwestern radical Republicans, including Yates, Morton of Indiana, and Chandler of Michigan, were either alcoholics or at least were "vicious and of bad moral characters."

36. *Journal*, Feb. 25, 1868, p. 4, col. 1, May 14, 1868, p. 4, col. 1; Robert G. Ingersoll to RJO, May 27, 1868, in Plummer, "'Goodbye Dear Governor,'" p. 101.

37. Plummer, *Robert G. Ingersoll*, pp. 37–45; *Journal*, Feb. 3, 1868, p. 2, col. 3, May 8, 1868, p. 1, cols. 2–4 and 3–4, May 12, 1868, p. 2, col. 3; Robert G. Ingersoll to RJO, April 1, 1868, in Plummer, "'Goodbye Dear Governor,'" p. 100.

38. *Journal*, April 4, 1868, p. 1, col. 2, April 8, 1868, p. 2, col. 3, April 27, 1868, p. 2, cols. 3–4 (Yates's statement); *Decatur Weekly Republican*, April 2, 1868, p. 2, col. 5. Elizabeth Cady Stanton praised Yates's confession before the Sons of Temperance at the Hall of Good Samaritan Division, in Washington, D.C., in late March of 1868. *Journal*, April 2, 1868, p. 2, col. 4.

39. *Illinois House Journal* (1867), vol. 1, pp. 13, 25; *Journal*, April 17, 1868, p. 2, col. 2; *Alton Telegraph*, as cited in the *Journal*, April 10, 1868, p. 2, col. 4.

40. Jack D. Welsh, *Medical Histories of Union Generals* (Kent: Kent State University Press, 1996), p. 163; Haynie Papers, ISHL; *Journal*, April 3, 1868, p. 4, col. 2, May 22, 1868, p. 4, col. 1, May 23, 1868, p. 4, col. 1, May 28, 1868, p. 4, col. 2. Oglesby received telegrams, dated May 22, 1868, from Chicago, sent by A. C. Babcock and other central committee members (editor of the *Chicago Journal* Charles Wilson, Jesse K. Dubois, John Logan, and George Bestor) and from Hurlbut himself, who wired: "I want the adjt Gens office for the pur-

pose of the Canvass" (Oglesby MSS). There is some confusion concerning the date of Haynie's death. Welsh gives it as May 22, 1868, as does an Oak Ridge Cemetery record, but the inscription on the tombstone in Oak Ridge Cemetery (lot 10) appears to be May 21. Both the *Journal* and the *Register* of May 22 state that Haynie died "at fifteen minutes before six o'clock yesterday afternoon." For Haynie's service as adjutant general, see Randy L. Nichols, "Role of the Adjutant General during the American Civil War," master's thesis, Illinois State University, 1989.

41. *Decatur Weekly Republican,* June 11, 1868, p. 2, col. 1; *Journal,* June 5, 1868, p. 4, col. 2, June 6, 1868, p. 4, col. 2, June 8, 1868, p. 4, col. 2. Oglesby carefully detailed all the expenses of the funeral, including $140 for a casket, $32.82 for crepe dresses for the children, $90 for a special train, and $32 for eight carriages. Fred Plummer was paid $5 for "digging grave and sodding over other." On May 22, 1869, Oglesby paid $143.25 to install the marble monument. The stone, valued at $300, was sent "compliments of the [Joliet Prison] Commissioners" (Oglesby MSS). On May 6, 1868, Joseph White, Anna's father, approached the governor to say that his son, being a drunkard and a gambler, had taken $18,000 from a business. White asked Oglesby for a $1,000 loan, which would stave off creditors (Oglesby Memorandum, $1,000 loan, May 6, 1868, Oglesby MSS).

42. Letters of condolence, June 1868, RJO to Mrs. S. Copes, Decatur, June 25, 1868, and memo on deposits of jewelry (totaling $575), June 8, 1868, Oglesby MSS; memorandum concerning Anna Oglesby's clothing (valued at $2,000), July 13, 1868, Oglesby MSS; receipt to A. Wunder for children's portrait, July 3, 1868, Oglesby MSS; RJO to Mrs. John A. Logan, July 16, 1868, Logan Collection, LC.

43. RJO to Mrs. John A. Logan, Springfield, July 16, 1868, Logan Collection, LC; *Journal,* Aug. 1, 1868, p. 4, col. 1; George H. Harlow to RJO, July 7, 1868, Oglesby Letterpress Book, ISA. On October 3, 1868, Oglesby paid Wait $91 for a barrel of bourbon; see also Chauncey T. Bowen to RJO, Hyde Park House, Aug. 14, 1868 (both in Oglesby MSS).

44. RJO to William Carry, Oct. 25, 1867, Oglesby MSS; *Decatur Republican,* Sept. 5, 1868, p. 1, col. 4; *Chicago Evening Post,* as quoted in *Journal,* Sept. 29, 1868, p. 2, col. 4, Jan 5, 1869, p. 2, col. 2; *New York Times,* Aug. 15, 1868, p. 1, cols. 1–4, Sept. 5, 1868, p. 1, cols. 6–7.

45. *Journal,* Jan. 5, 1869, p. 2, cols. 2–4, p. 3, cols. 2–4, Jan. 12, 1869, p. 2, col. 5; *Peoria Daily Transcript,* Jan. 18, 1869, p. 2, col. 3; Robert G. Ingersoll to RJO, Jan. 14, 1869, in Plummer, "'Goodbye Dear Governor,'" p. 104.

46. Robert G. Ingersoll to RJO, Jan. 14, 1869.

47. *Journal,* Nov. 8, 1867, p. 4, col. 1, Oct. 6, 1868, p. 4, cols. 1–8. Oglesby's immortality in stone at the capitol was undone when the cornerstone was found "unworthy to be retained or built upon." In 1870 the "stone was removed from the wall and buried in the ground in front of the corner" and replaced by a new stone, which contained no inscriptions (*Journal,* Nov. 23, 1870, p. 4, col. 2). The original stone is now displayed on the northeast corner of the state capitol (Wayne C. Temple, "Reminders of Lincoln in a Cornerstone," *Illinois Blue Book, 1967–1968* [Springfield: Illinois Secretary of State, 1968], pp. 29–39). Oglesby's statue, scheduled to be placed on one of the capitol's corbels in 1888, was also replaced. See Mark A. Plummer, "David Littler v. the State House Commissioners, 1885–88," in *Capitol Centennial Papers,* ed. Mark W. Sorensen (Springfield: Illinois State Archives, 1990), pp. 4–10.

# 8. The United States Senator

As RICHARD OGLESBY and Governor-elect John M. Palmer shared a carriage ride in the inaugural procession in January 1869, a *Chicago Post* correspondent noted how "grandly" Oglesby left office, "cheerful as though just elected." He "God-blessed" the "silver-haired, glad-hearted, honest-faced" Oglesby for his service. Half in jest, however, he referred to the retiring governor as "Richard, he that no revenue hath, and whom patronage will not follow." Oglesby aspired to occupy a seat in the U.S. Senate, but Richard Yates's term would not expire until 1871 and Lyman Trumbull's extended to 1873. Challenging his aspiration to capture and maintain a seat in the Senate over the next decade would be John A. Logan, an at-large member of Congress from Illinois and commander of the Grand Army of the Republic, whom patronage would follow.[1]

Over the next four years Oglesby would work to build his "revenue," care for his motherless children, revisit his past, and labor to capture a Senate seat. His transition to a non-officeholder was made more pleasant by the warm greeting he received when he returned home. Decatur citizens welcomed him with a "Grand Complimentary Banquet" and unremitting flattery. Briefly overcome by their cordiality, he regained his composure to joke that a little flattery was not an unpleasant thing: "I have managed to get along with my share of it very well." In a more serious vein, he said that he had known political responsibility "sufficient to warn me not to seek it." But seek it he would.[2]

A letter written on March 19, 1869, to Mrs. Mason Brayman, wife of a Springfield lawyer who served as a general with Oglesby in Tennessee, reveals much about Oglesby and his young children after Anna's death. Oglesby wrote that he had been at home with the children for weeks "with little dis-position to be anywhere else." He described Kate Luttwell as a devoted gov-erness for the children and noted that his sister, Amanda Prather, looked in on them every day. They often visited Anna's parents, but Oglesby preferred to have them home, fearing that going "from place to place constantly would soon destroy attachment to home" and distract them from their studies. Both children were recovering from the whooping cough. Olive, age six, had learned to read. Oglesby said that the children often sang the hymns they heard at their mother's funeral and had memorized the Lord's Prayer, the Ten Commandments, "and a large part of the Episcopal catechism." He quipped that the children's church theology was more advanced than his own.[3]

During his term as governor, he had relied on his business partner Sheri-dan Wait to manage his interests. Wait was also Oglesby's appointee as trustee for the Illinois and Michigan Canal and had established Chicago business connections with Chauncey Bowen and his brother James. Oglesby had ap-pointed James Bowen as a colonel in the state militia, and Bowen had been in the Illinois party that journeyed to Washington on the eve of Lincoln's death and had accompanied his body home. Oglesby joined the Bowens, Wait, and others as investors in the Stony Island Improvement Company, which speculated in land in the Hyde Park and Calumet areas.[4]

The former governor's property tax receipts show that he was taxed $657 in 1869 on property investments in the Woodlawn area near Chicago as well as others shared by the improvement company. In Decatur he paid $152 on town lots in Carvers and Western Additions, whose assessed valuation was about $12,000 (with an estimated market value of $36,000 to $48,000). He also owned land in Springfield and in Fayette County, Illinois. For 1869 Ogles-by paid income tax on $12,493, which included a profit of $7,077 on real es-tate sold. Over the next two years, he bought and sold numerous Decatur lots and invested more money in the Bowen brothers' enterprises.[5]

Oglesby's Lincoln connection continued after he left office, most visibly through the National Lincoln Monument Association. On May 13, 1869, he was reelected as its president, although the association might have logically chosen to elect John M. Palmer, the new governor. The former governor also symbolically honored Lincoln's Second Inaugural admonition to care for soldiers' orphans by making the dedication speech at the Illinois Soldiers' Orphans' home in Normal on June 17, 1869. A brief excursion to Kentucky to visit relatives provided opportunities to revisit scenes firmly fixed in his memory, extending even to the purchase of the family slave, "Uncle Tim," to provide him his freedom.[6]

Wait and Oglesby's Chicago business associate James H. Bowen, now president of the Fourth National Bank of Chicago, invited them to join a grand excursion to San Francisco to celebrate the opening of the first transcontinental railroad. Perhaps out of nostalgia for his Forty-niner days, the former governor accepted. The railroads provided sleeping coaches, and many cities along the route offered complimentary accommodations. The junket made extended stops in Omaha, Salt Lake City, Sacramento, and San Francisco during the six-week tour that began on July 5, 1869. The "Commercial Party" included nearly forty businessmen and officeholders, including Sen. Lyman Trumbull and Cong. Norman B. Judd. Joseph Medill, editor of the *Chicago Tribune,* was also included.[7]

Oglesby returned from his trip to find that the race for Yates's Senate seat, which would not be decided until the legislature met in January 1871, was already underway. The players were Yates, who wanted to be reelected, Gov. John M. Palmer, Cong. John A. Logan, and Oglesby. Yates's strategy was to pit the three ambitious Civil War generals against each other in the belief that each would prefer Yates to each other. The strategy failed, however, because Yates could not stay sober. Jesse H. Moore, the member of Congress from Oglesby's district, wrote to Oglesby on January 2, 1870, to describe the senator's pathetic escapades. Moore reported that Yates periodically "dried out" at the Washington home of his married girlfriend's father. Yates had arranged for the woman's husband to be given a position in New Orleans. Moore, a preacher and a Civil War veteran, concluded by saying that although Yates was his friend, "his case is hopeless." Many Illinois newspapers had reached the same conclusion. Governor Palmer tried to keep good relations with the other soldier-politicians because he would have two more years as governor and because Oglesby and Logan had stepped aside and supported him in the unsuccessful attempt to depose Trumbull in 1867. Still, he was willing to accept a draft, as he had done in the 1868 gubernatorial contest, should the others falter.[8]

John A. Logan was alarmed when he learned that Oglesby, Trumbull, and Judd had "shared" the Pacific Railroad excursion. Perhaps they were intriguing against him. He began to exercise his patronage power as an at-large member of Congress and to mobilize the Grand Army of the Republic to influence the legislators who would choose the next senator. His successful campaign for the annual observance of Decoration Day endeared him to many soldier-politicians and gave him added name recognition.[9]

On September 1, 1870, the Illinois State Republican Convention renominated Logan for the at-large congressional seat. Both he and Oglesby, competitors but old friends, stayed at the same Springfield hotel and attended the convention. Logan's nomination mandated an acceptance speech, which was noisily applauded. He also frequently attended Republican county conventions, where legislators were being nominated. "Logan is on the move, Lookout," Palmer warned Oglesby on September 8. Oglesby's friend on the Supreme Court, David Davis, wrote on September 13 that Logan was canvassing the state and insisted that he meet the challenge. Oglesby soon made himself available to the Republican State Central Committee and began a speaking tour on September 29. Anxious to use both Logan and Oglesby and evade conflict, the committee arranged schedules that avoided duplication. In November, Logan defeated his Democratic opponent by a twenty-four-thousand plurality and then sought assurances from Ulysses S. Grant that he would not oppose his elevation to the Senate. Grant sent word that it would be improper for the executive branch to intercede and that he had never expressed any wish for Logan's defeat.[10]

After the general election, the campaign for the Senate seat shifted to influencing the newly elected members of the legislature. Both Logan and Oglesby wrote dozens of private letters to legislators and their friends who could influence the law-makers. To one legislator who was leaning toward Logan, Oglesby asked rhetorically if it would be wise to take General Logan from "his present high position," with the resultant expense of calling a statewide special election to fill the vacated congressional seat. Also, was it fair to "lift him over the heads of all hard working" original members of the "great and noble" Republican Party? Logan, a Democrat when the war began, had delayed joining the Republican Party until after the Civil War. Oglesby also pleaded with the legislators who favored Logan to withhold judgment until the January caucus, which would decide the question. Oglesby heard from supporters that Logan was telling the doubtful legislators that Logan's lead was insurmountable and they should jump on his bandwagon. Jesse H. Moore alleged that Logan was charging that "you get *tite* [sic] and may do as Yates has done."[11]

The responses received from the legislators ranged from equivocal support ("unless something happens"), to unpledged, to admiration for Oglesby while supporting Logan. Virtually all of the responses to Oglesby's pleadings included expressions of friendship and respect, but many were labeled "confidential." Oglesby was liked, but Logan was feared. The ever-cynical Robert Ingersoll may have been preparing Oglesby for defeat when he wrote "[you are] too good a man, too sincere a gentleman to go the Senate. The People want some wire working cunning cuss. They delight in mediocrity. They like to see men like themselves in power."[12]

Oglesby took rooms at the Leland Hotel in Springfield on January 2, 1871, in preparation for the senatorial election. John and Mary Logan occupied a second-floor suite, and Mary presided over well-stocked "levees" in the first-floor parlor, aided by a beautiful niece, Kate Logan. Mary Logan's reception rooms were very popular with legislators and reporters looking for a social setting and anxious to hear the latest gossip concerning the selection of a senator. She would not initiate political discussions, but when the subject was introduced she would tersely state her husband's case. In one newspaper's account, she was credited with possessing "wide experience of the social world, a good fund of information, abundant wit, and a ready tongue freighted with complaisance and suavity." She was "never aggressive or intrusive," but "fearless and confident" in exercising her "woman's right of speech" with "persuasive tact." Joseph Medill later confessed to Oglesby that he did not have "moral courage enough" to face Mary Logan and tell her that he was working against John.[13]

Nor was Oglesby himself a match for Mary Logan in a bantering contest. The *Chicago Evening Post* reported a hall conversation between them in which Mary reprimanded Oglesby for forgetting his old-school politeness in not calling on her. Oglesby chivalrously replied that he was afraid to subject himself to her blandishments for fear he might leave a Logan man. In the same vein, he suggested that she leave town and give him, a poor bachelor, a fair chance in the contest. She retorted that it was only right that he should suffer "the disabilities of bachelorhood."[14]

Logan's entourage included about twenty federal officeholders who were beholden to him. Oglesby's supporters mused that it was the first time he had to fight the United States government. Logan's followers claimed ninety votes in the caucus, an absolute majority; Oglesby claimed fifty-six. If both were correct, some of the 130 Republican legislators were "double pledged." Oglesby believed many were pledged to Logan on the first ballot only, in accordance with instructions received from their district conventions. He thought he could maximize the possibility of going to a second ballot by encouraging those who favored Governor Palmer and Gustave Koerner, who controlled the "German vote," to persevere through the first ballot. Oglesby's supporters also demanded voting by secret ballot, thinking that some legislators feared Logan.[15]

Oglesby's campaign failed miserably. When the Republican caucus met on January 13, a motion to vote by ballot was defeated by a vote of 78 to 39, and a voice vote was mandated. That test vote made it clear that Logan had an absolute majority. Fearful of being caught on the losing side, several of Oglesby's supporters and most of Palmer's men recorded votes for Logan. The result was Logan, 98; Oglesby, 23; Koerner, 8; and Palmer, 1. A few days later, the legislators officially elected Logan to the Senate by a vote of 131 to 89 over the Democratic candidate Thomas J. Turner. In a post-mortem, the *Decatur Republican* wrote that Logan's winning cards were "Federal patronage, perfect organization, incessant labor, and democratic abuse" against Oglesby's "dignified tactics." Joseph Medill, in a private letter to Oglesby, was less sympathetic: "Logan has worked while you must have slept on your dignity." Oglesby may have recalled Mary Logan's words from their hotel conversation: "Now General, you see, you can be Senator next time—or what do you say to Congressman-at-large?"[16]

Humiliated and dispirited, Oglesby gave an emphatic veto to calls that he replace Logan for the at-large seat in a special election. He would not accept the consolation prize and be beholden to Logan and his minions, although some of his friends suggested that he could use the position as a ladder to the next Senate seat. Others cautioned that Logan and the party would use him as ballast to win the election for themselves and then throw him overboard. With the special election scheduled for November 1871, Oglesby was aware that the term would only run for a year and that the at-large position would be superseded when the new congressional apportionment became operative in 1872. On his forty-seventh birthday, he wrote an open letter to the *Chicago Evening Journal,* which was urging his candidacy, to state that he would not, under any circumstances, be an at-large candidate for Congress. He alluded to his ten years of continuous service in government and to his contentment to remain with "his family in the affairs of private life." Perhaps he was burned out with public service and disgusted by it when he wrote, "I seek not again to offer my services to the public." In his final paragraph, however, he promised to stand ready to assist the "best party on earth" in "sustaining a just appreciation of public virtue" while rebuking "the spirit of personal ambition."[17]

His refusal did not stop the clamor for Oglesby's candidacy. In neighboring Missouri, Carl Schurz and Gratz Brown had successfully bolted from the Republican Party in 1870 and been elected senator and governor. The "Liberal Republicans" demanded the withdrawal of federal troops from the South, amnesty for southern leaders, civil service reform, and the curbing of monopolies. The movement seemed to be spreading to Illinois and beyond. Grant and the regular Republican Party might be in jeopardy. The Illinois at-large election, scheduled for November 1871, might be taken as a straw in the wind for the 1872 presidential election.[18]

On August 17, an article in Oglesby's hometown newspaper indicated that President Grant wanted him to run, but Oglesby continued to refuse. The notion of drafting him held until the Republican nominating convention on September 20. Oglesby received a large block of votes on the informal ballot

but then dispatched Jesse H. Moore to the floor to ask the delegates to accept his refusal. Moore explained that Oglesby's letter of refusal should be
believed because he was "incapable of any duplicity." The party then nominated Gen. John L. Beveridge. If the convention could not have Oglesby as
a candidate, at least they could have one of his Grand Old Party speeches.
The *Illinois State Journal* headed its summary of the speech, "A NOBLE VIN-
DICATION OF THE REPUBLICAN PARTY." Other newspapers marveled at the
great power of his speeches. The editors reported that Oglesby's history of
the party "awakened shouts of responsive enthusiasm, such as no other man
in Illinois can arouse." It was the *Journal*'s opinion that the state needed such
men, "and by and by they will call the Governor again to a place of position
and power."[19]

During 1872, many of Oglesby's erstwhile political friends bolted the Republican Party and joined the Liberal Republican movement while Oglesby
remained loyal to the party he had so long acclaimed. The dissidents each objected to some policy or practice of President Grant and wagered their political futures on defeating him for reelection. Thus were most of Oglesby's potential Republican rivals for Trumbull's Senate seat removed. Governor Palmer
had taken exception to Grant's dispatching federal troops to Chicago after the
great fire of October 1871. Palmer argued that maintaining order in Chicago
was a state and not a national responsibility. Ingersoll wrote to Oglesby that
Palmer had "committed political harri Karri. . . . Killed, with a dose of States
rights." Senator Trumbull objected to the massive spoils system being administered by Grant and the party faithful. Trumbull and Palmer, together with
Supreme Court Justice David Davis, joined the race for the Liberal Republican Party's presidential nomination. All failed, in part because they split the
Illinois delegates into three factions. Horace Greeley, the mercurial publisher
of the *New York Tribune,* was selected. The Democrats swallowed hard and also
nominated Greeley in a separate convention. Failing presidential nomination,
Trumbull hoped to be reelected to the Senate with the support of the Illinois
Liberal Republican and Democratic parties. Palmer, eligible for reelection as
governor under the new state constitution of 1870, seemed willing to accept
the Republican nomination but would not support Grant.[20]

Oglesby's aspiration to win Trumbull's Senate seat at the January 1873
meeting of the state legislature was widely assumed. The party became
alarmed, however, that it might lose the fall 1872 elections for lack of a popular gubernatorial candidate. As early as February 2, 1872, an important political operative wrote to Oglesby, "It begins to look as though you will be
constrained to lead on the State ticket." His usual answer to such statements
was, "I have no plan about Governor or U. S. Senator."[21]

Shelby M. Cullom, a powerful legislator and future Illinois governor and senator, forced the issue by soliciting a petition of Illinois legislators to draft Oglesby for governor. Twenty-two general assembly members asked him to become a candidate. In his memoirs, Cullom recalled having sent an agent to Decatur to wait for a favorable reply and then taking it to Chicago for publication. Oglesby's written reply, dated April 9, stated that he had no wish or expectation to be a candidate for governor. If, he allowed, the party should "with unanimity, require my services, I would not feel at liberty to decline." He then launched into a lengthy defense of the Republican Party as the "guardian angel over the Republic" and chastised those who "wish to tamper with this grand political organization" because of "personal disappointment, defeated hopes, or some such imaginary grievance." The letter was widely published and praised in Illinois Republican newspapers.[22]

The *New York Times* published Oglesby's letter in full, but its correspondent wrote a condescending sketch of him that was similar to British ambassador Lord Lyons's characterization of Lincoln in 1860. The reporter wrote that Oglesby had been engaged as a hostler and in other rough businesses as a young man but had somehow been admitted to the bar. "Being a man of decided natural talents, he has worked his way pretty well up," the eastern writer conceded, "but unfortunately has not worked out the roughness nor some of the objectionable habits of his early days."[23]

The Republican state nominating convention was held in Springfield on May 22, 1872. With the defection of Palmer, Trumbull, Gustave Koerner, and other "trouble makers," the event turned into a love feast. Oglesby was nominated for governor without a dissenting vote. Republicans who liked Oglesby but feared Logan in the 1871 senatorial race could now please them both. Word filtered down that Grant and General Logan wanted Oglesby to lead the state party in the 1872 elections, with the understanding that he could then accept the Senate seat. As the *Chicago Tribune* put it, Oglesby was running for governor "with a senatorial attachment." Gen. John Beveridge, the former Cook County sheriff who had accepted the at-large berth in Congress after Oglesby refused it, was named as the party's candidate for lieutenant-governor with the implicit prospect that he would move up to governor.[24]

After the delegates nominated Oglesby, they called on him for a speech that the *Illinois State Journal* characterized as touching the audience's heart. It was "one of the most wonderful torrents of invective, wit, sarcasm, satire and pungent eloquence that has been delivered in many a day." According to the *New York Times,* Oglesby defended the Grant administration and the Republican Party on civil service reform by saying that "Grant wants it but the Liberals can't agree on what they want except to be in power." On the question of amnesty for southerners, he quipped that all but a hundred or so had been pardoned and that the rest could be pardoned after amnesty was granted to the Liberal revolters. Oglesby's friend Gustave Koerner, who as his opponent in the gubernatorial race received many of the former governor's barbs, later wrote that Oglesby was perfectly honest in private affairs, but "as for political morality, he had as little of it as most politicians."[25]

Oglesby's national fame as a speaker grew when he was called to speak at the Republican National Convention in Philadelphia. Noting with pride that African American delegates had been included for the first time and praising the speech of abolitionist Gerrit Smith, "that great agitator," Oglesby launched into a "eulogy" of Grant, whom he characterized as "purer, greater and nobler still than even we have ever thought him." "Illinois gave the immortal Lincoln," he thundered, and was now giving the country Grant "without a lingering shadow of suspicion of doubt" about his "high patriotism, good sense and purity." Shelby Cullom recalled the speech as electrifying the audience, and the *New York Times* featured it on page one, column one. The *Chicago Tribune,* which had joined the Liberal Republican movement, lampooned Oglesby for having "delivered his oration over the body of the martyred Lincoln" and in concert with other speakers lifting Grant above George Washington to a position "first in war, first in peace, and first in the hearts of his Postmasters."[26]

Oglesby returned to Illinois to begin his usual energetic campaign. The *New York Times* reported his speech in Decatur on June 18, when he argued that if Grant, a man "without guile," were "defeated and dishonored," then "American history will weep for a thousand years over the mistake." He arranged to speak in Indiana in exchange for speeches from Indiana senator Oliver Morton in Illinois. He also assaulted the Liberal Republican Party at its birthplace in St. Louis, where he attacked its chief perpetrators, Missouri governor Gratz Brown and Sen. Carl Schurz.[27]

Opponents charged that Oglesby was "playing possum" by running for governor when his goal was the Senate. He responded by saying, "If I am not running for governor, I am the worst deceived man in this state." He declared that he had not spoken a word "to any human about the Senate," although he allowed that some had spoken to him about the future possibility. He dismissed the complaint by vowing to make the election of the national and state ticket his "whole business." Few could doubt his determination to lead the state ticket. His lengthy speeches were enthusiastically received from Rockford in the north to Shawneetown in the south and from Champaign in the east to Rock Island and Quincy on the Mississippi River. Few towns or whistle stops escaped his attention. His October 21 speech in Decatur, where he shared the platform with Indiana Senator Morton, was billed as his eighty-eighth of the campaign. Oglesby made Grant's reelection the focus of his vigorous campaign, and it succeeded. Grant gained a fifty-six-thousand plurality over Greeley in Illinois, and Oglesby defeated Koerner by forty thousand votes. The Republicans won both branches of the general assembly, assuring the election of a Republican senator. Nationwide, Grant polled a larger majority than he had in 1868 in both the electoral college and the popular vote.[28]

There was a broad consensus within the Republican Party that Oglesby had rallied the masses and had earned his long-sought seat in the U.S. Senate. Trumbull, the incumbent, would be the candidate of the Liberal Republican and Democratic legislators, but they could be overwhelmed by the Republican majority. There was a minor scare when Elihu Washburne, minister to France, returned home in November. Both the Democratic *Chicago Times* and the Liberal Republican *Tribune* pointed out the possibility that Washburne might be chosen for the Senate seat. Logan and many other party leaders rallied to protect Oglesby's hard-earned prize. One wrote to reiterate the general understanding that it was Oglesby's for the taking. "No lazy plenipotentiary should be allowed to come home and gather your laurels," he protested. Soon, assurances came from Washburne's intimates that Grant's wartime political guardian would not contest Oglesby's selection. The matter seemed settled when Oglesby attended a banquet for Minister Washburne at the Tremont House in Chicago. Washburne toasted Oglesby and said he had no designs on the Senate seat. "Uproarious applause" followed Oglesby's compliments to Washburne and the quip that his joy at seeing Washburne was only equaled by his knowledge that he was going to leave very soon.[29]

Oglesby had been nominated for governor unanimously, and the Republican senatorial caucus of January 9, 1873, also slated him by affirmation. After his humiliating defeat in 1871, he felt vindicated, although some awkward procedural problems were created by his candidacy for governor "with a senatorial attachment." After the caucus, his selection to the Senate was certain but not yet official. Lieutenant Governor–elect Beveridge had a similar problem. He answered a letter from Oglesby by saying, "I too feel the inconvenience of holding, as it were, one office, as a step to another." Oglesby met the issue head-on in his acceptance speech to the caucus and outlined the steps he intended to take to complete the transition: It would be necessary to follow form, including giving an inaugural speech as governor, and he would not resign to take the Senate seat until confirmed by the legislature.[30]

As planned, he was sworn as governor and made his inaugural address on January 13. The *Journal* labeled his message "an admirable and thoughtfully prepared document." Beveridge was duly sworn as lieutenant governor. A week later, the general assembly chose Oglesby as U.S. senator by a vote of 117 to 78 over the eighteen-year incumbent Lyman Trumbull. The opposition cried foul and quoted a clause in the new state constitution that said that state officials would be ineligible for other offices. The complaint was summarily dismissed as the "the last faint squeak of the dying Siamese twins of Liberalism and Democracy in Illinois." Oglesby resigned as governor at noon on January 23, 1873. Beveridge, who had resigned his at-large seat in Congress on January 4, became governor.[31]

In February 1873, Oglesby left for Washington to attend the special session of the Forty-third Congress. President and Mrs. Grant invited him to dinner on February 25. Logan was invited to join the party later in the evening, and he accompanied Oglesby to the swearing in ceremony for new senators on March 4. The *Illinois State Journal* remarked that the two men, who had stood side by side in combat, were friends who had attained equal honors and had "absolutely nothing to divide them." The junior senator from Illinois was assigned to the back row in the chamber and appointed to three committees: Public Lands, Indian Affairs, and Pensions. The special session lasted only twenty-two days.[32]

The forty-nine-year-old senator had been a widower for five years, and there were rumors that he might marry again. The *Decatur Magnet* of January 8, 1871, had commented about Oglesby's rumored matrimonial intention and reported that he "denies the soft impeachment in vigorous English—'It's a d——d lie!'" On January 3, 1873, however, the *Peoria Transcript* reported that Oglesby had "in contemplation" leading to the altar "a beautiful and accomplished lady of a neighboring city." The "beautiful and accomplished lady" was a twenty-eight-year-old widow, Emma Gillett Keays, daughter of cattle baron John Gillett of Elkhart, twenty miles north of Springfield. According to oral tradition, the couple met when Oglesby was speaking in Lincoln. He had seen the beautiful Emma Gillett Keays on the porch of Mrs. Robert Latham's house and, he recalled, had "acute fear that she was married." Hiram Keays, he learned, had died nearly five years earlier after being injured by a team of horses. The courtship was facilitated by Emma's occasional visits to the family of her relatives, Mr. and Mrs. V. H. Parke, who lived on the 300 block on William Street in Decatur, a block from the Oglesby home, and by Oglesby's frequent forty-mile carriage rides to court the handsome Emma. She attended the Rurode-Peddecord wedding in Decatur on October 1 and made a favorable impression "by her appearance of quiet dignity and lady like bearing." The "bachelor reporter" of the *Illinois State Journal* revealed her name on October 25. The wedding was set for November 18, 1873.[33]

Nearly three hundred family and personal friends of the couple were invited to the wedding ceremony, which took place in the mansion of the bride's parents on Elkhart Hill. Special railroad cars brought guests from Decatur, Springfield, and Chicago, and carriages took them to the home. Emma's six sisters and four other friends were bridesmaids; the senator was accompanied only by Sheridan Wait. At noon, the Springfield Silver Cornet Band played the wedding march, and then the Rev. F. M. Gregg, rector of St. Paul's Episcopal Church in Springfield and also the bride's pastor, led the couple through their vows. Emma wore "white corded silk, en train, with point lace and silk puffings, and the regulation orange flower wreath with point lace veil." A reporter from the *St. Louis Democrat* described her as "one of the most lovely women in Illinois." A wedding breakfast (luncheon) was then served, after which "the Senator led off a cotillion in an elegant manner." Dancing continued for most of the afternoon.[34]

The couple honeymooned in New York City at the Fifth Avenue Hotel. Carriages, "extra" dinners, and champagne were among the special charges on the hotel bill. The newlyweds then traveled to Washington in time for the December 1, 1873, session of Congress. The Oglesbys resided at 1336 I Street NW. They returned to Decatur for the Christmas break and were greeted with a lavish introductory party given by Mr. and Mrs. Lowber Burrows of Oglesby's banking firm of Peddecord and Burrows. Guests were introduced to the bride, and Professor Goodman's "fine orchestra" played for dancing until midnight, when a supper was served. The dancing continued until 2 A.M.[35]

Senator Oglesby and the new Mrs. Oglesby returned to Washington with their family to complete the first session of the Forty-third Congress. Robert, Olive, and Emma's young son Hiram Keays were enrolled in school in Washington and were attended by a nurse in residence. Emma recalled being thrilled to meet Gen. William T. Sherman, James G. Blaine, Roscoe Conklin, and David Davis and being invited to Nellie Grant's White House wedding. The Oglesbys lived rather extravagantly. By the senator's accounting, expenses from December 1873 to June 1874 totaled more than $6,000. Oglesby, whose salary was $5,000 a year, spent $800 on a shopping spree for his wife and young relatives, "Misses Gillett and Peddecord," in New York City in March; $288.50 for livery service; $250 cash for Emma; and $100 for opera, theater, "Segars," and confections.[36]

The timing of Oglesby's six-year term in the Senate was inauspicious. His arrival in Washington coincided with the Panic of 1873, which marked the beginning of a six-year economic depression. He was also greeted with exposés regarding the corruption of the Grant administration and the Republican Party. Soon Illinois farmers were complaining of being overcharged by railroad monopolies, underpaid for their products by eastern commission merchants, and being forced to repay loans in deflated dollars. Oglesby's maiden speech on the floor of the Senate, delivered on January 20, 1874, called for railroad-rate regulation similar to that being demanded by the so-called Grangers in Illinois. The speech was uncharacteristically terse. Both he and Logan yielded to the demands of the "Greenbackers," who favored legislation to increase the amount of money in circulation by issuing more paper money. Grant, however, vetoed the "inflation bill" although it had widespread support in farm states. Oglesby also introduced a bill to cheapen the cost of railroad transportation by building an additional line from the Atlantic Coast to the Pacific, a "Fortieth Parallel Railway" that would pass through the heart of Illinois. In addition, he pushed for more lenient bankruptcy bills to protect the mortgaged farmers. As a member of the Committee on Indian Affairs, Oglesby presented a memorial asking that a commission, to include women, visit reservations and devise means for improving the living conditions of Native Americans. The bill he introduced to enable Native Americans to become citizens was unsuccessful, although it anticipated the Dawes Act of 1887 by thirteen years.[37]

The Oglesbys arrived at home in Decatur in June 1874 and were soon made welcome by a serenade by Professor Goodman and the Decatur Cornet Band. Oglesby's oratory was in demand in the 1874 off-year elections, but he declined most invitations until after mid-October because of the birth of Emma Louise ("Felicite") Oglesby on August 27 and because he had suddenly been thrust into making the dedication speech at Lincoln's tomb on October 15, 1874. Three weeks later, in the context of a continuing depression and charges of graft, both the Republican Party of Illinois and the national party took a drubbing in the election. The new U.S. House of Representatives had a majority of Democrats for the first time since the Civil War, and Illinois elected only seven Republicans to Congress out of nineteen seats.[38]

Richard James Oglesby was born thirteen months after his sister Felicite. With five children under the age of thirteen and the prospect of more, the Oglesbys decided to build a house. Although the depression had reduced the senator's fortune, Emma's father John Gillett offered $10,000, and she wanted a new home. Oglesby may have anticipated that need when on August 20, 1873, a few weeks before his wedding, he bought two more lots (5 and 6 in block 5 of Decatur's Western Addition) adjacent to his house on lots 1 to 4 for $1,000. In 1874 he had the land surveyed by the city engineer. In 1868–69 he had hired a Chicago architect, William Le Baron Jenney, to draw plans for a mansion, and during May and June of 1869 Jenney sent fifteen letters negotiating various aspects of the design. Oglesby apparently thought the designs too expensive, however, and Jenney offered less expensive alternatives. Finally, on December 27, 1869, the former governor wrote that he was "out of the notion of building next year, but when I do build will give full notice to complete details or to modify the plans." He did agree to pay 3 percent rather than the usual 3.5 percent, which Jenney claimed, of the estimated cost of $15,000 for Jenney's preliminary plans.[39]

Construction of the new house began on July 10, 1875. DeWitt C. Shockley, who had built the wigwam for the Decatur Republican convention at which Oglesby had introduced the rail-splitter theme in 1860, was the contractor. He may have used certain of Jenney's plans, but there is no evidence that Oglesby or Shockley corresponded further with Jenney. The Oglesbys decided to use their old seven-room house as a kitchen and servant quarters for the new mansion. Thus, Jenney's plans, which had a first-floor kitchen and space for servants on the third floor, would have required substantial modification. Stockley apparently contracted to build the Italianate-style house for a base price of $10,000, and M. Troutman, a bricklayer, ordered 102,000 bricks for the construction. As the house took form, the *Decatur Daily Republican* reported on January 8, 1876, that the imposing mansion grounds covered half a block, fronted both William and Edward Streets, and had a spacious porch across its entire eastern front. The incomplete interior promised to be both attractive and convenient.[40]

The spacious house featured high ceilings, seven fireplaces with mantels of walnut, two large areas floored with strips of maple and walnut, and a library with an intricately beautiful parquet floor and an unusual ceiling of walnut and plaster. Its exterior featured "three vertical, two story projections" and "bay windows of contrasting design" with diamond-shaped panes. Curious citizens were able to peruse the completed mansion on various occasions that included a "parlor concert for the benefit of the Illinois Industrial School for Girls" in November 1878.[41]

With the senator spending more than half his time in Washington and in campaigning in Illinois and elsewhere, Emma was left to supervise a staff that included a male and a female servant, a nurse, and a governess. The senator paid a pew tax at Decatur's St. John's Episcopal Church for his family. Although he did not become a communicant in the Episcopal Church, Oglesby maintained a close friendship with Bishop George F. Seymour of Springfield. The bishop, who would bury Oglesby in 1899, was the Oglesbys' occasional house guest. In January 1876, the Oglesbys' son Richard James was baptized in the Decatur church by the Rev. F. M. Gregg, the Springfield clergyman who had married his parents. In the presence of a large congregation, young Richard was baptized with water that his father had collected from the

Jordan River in 1857. The first Oglesby to be born in the new house was John Gillett on March 19, 1878. Emma's father's namesake, he was destined to be the only politician among the children and was elected lieutenant governor of Illinois in 1908 and 1916. Toward the end of Oglesby's term, Emma had six children in her care. One more, Jasper Ernest, born February 10, 1882, would be added before the Oglesbys sold the Decatur house.[42]

The senator showed his appreciation for Emma by writing to her mother on the couple's fourth anniversary and thanking her for "the precious gift of your lovely daughter," whom he described as the best wife in the world. He apologized because "the hand of fate, politics and adversity" had kept him away from Emma and the family too often. When reunited, however, "all the sad hours of separation disappear, and we live in each others presence and the delightful love of our darling children as though no past had been and no unpleasant future could come."[43]

The vagaries of the "money question" engulfed Oglesby and the Congress following the Panic of 1873. The focus was on greenbacks and on the monetization of silver. In general, Illinois and the "debtor" states preferred some inflation over deflation, and both Illinois senators tried to please their constituents. But the issue was difficult to explain. Years later, Adlai E. Stevenson, a Democrat but a friend of Oglesby's, recalled the senator's campaign device for dismissing complicated questions by quipping, "These Democrats undertake to discuss the financial questions. They oughtn't to do that. They can't possibly understand it. The Lord's truth is, fellow citizens, *it is about all we Republicans can do to understand that question.*"[44]

Oglesby tried hard to explain the issue to voters, even though he pronounced it "devilish hard" to interest them in the details. He campaigned for Connecticut and Ohio Republicans in their 1875 off-year elections and at the Opera House in Cincinnati opened with his usual speech, described as "discursive, historical; [and it] dealt considerably in reminiscences and splendid record of the Republican party." Then Oglesby attacked the greenback question. He argued that greenbacks had been necessary to sustain the war and pay soldiers "who stood side by side with the great giant of America—the immortal and sainted Lincoln." He chided Ohio's Democrats for being inconsistent in displaying "malice" against the wartime greenback while smothering postwar greenbacks "in kisses." Considering his success without formal education, it is interesting that Oglesby's final plea in Cincinnati was not about greenbacks but rather about public education. He argued that Democrats were for "slavery and ignorance." His parting words were, "Whatever else shall fail, be sure that school keeps."[45]

Oglesby and Logan voted for the inflation bill, which was vetoed, and the modified resumption of specie payment bill in 1874. Both senators favored remonetization of silver. Both would later speculate in silver mines in Colorado. In 1876 Oglesby characterized himself as a "Republican greenbacker." He and Logan were sufficiently popular in Illinois that various newspapers recommended each for the vice-presidential nomination, but they were on slippery ground. Neither man pleased orthodox Republicans by favoring the inflation bill; nor did they please Greenbackers who opposed the deflationary resumption of specie payment.[46]

The two senators from Illinois shared more than similar positions on the money question. Although both were war heroes and masters of waving the bloody shirt, financial panic tended to diminish the efficacy of continuing to blame Democrats for the war. Some other adhesive was necessary to hold the new Republican Party together. The best cement was patronage. As Logan wrote to his wife, "The people are wont to follow where power and patronage is." The senior senator from Illinois seemed to be more successful in filling patronage positions in the federal government than was Oglesby. A survey of appointments, dated January 28, 1876, in the Department of the Interior, for example, shows that Logan's recommended candidates were appointed thirteen times, whereas Oglesby had only one in addition to two made jointly with Logan. Shelby Cullom remembered Logan as being more anxious to do favors than Oglesby. He recalled the case of a Springfield banker, Jacob Bunn, who asked Oglesby to introduce him to the commissioner of internal revenue so he could negotiate a settlement. Oglesby, who had a long friendship with Bunn, nevertheless quizzed him extensively. Bunn said it was easier to convince the commissioner of the legality of his position than it was Oglesby. He made the same request of Logan, who complied immediately.[47]

Logan's name was often associated with the scandals of the Grant era. Although charges were never proven and Logan does not seem to have profited financially, his name was associated with the "Salary Grab" because he voted to raise senators' pay retroactively; the Credit Mobilier because he accepted but later returned railroad stock given to him; and the "Whiskey Ring" because his political supporters were involved. As a late-comer to the Senate, Oglesby escaped all such charges and was anxious to preserve his unsullied reputation. The votes of the two senators in the Belknap impeachment case illustrate their differing positions. In the spring of 1876, Secretary of War William W. Belknap was accused of graft in selling traderships on army posts in the West. When exposed, he quickly persuaded Grant to accept his resignation just as Congress was moving to impeach. In the trial, Logan voted not guilty, based on Belknap's resignation, and Oglesby voted guilty.[48]

The Illinois delegation to the Republican National Convention in 1876 leaned toward James G. Blaine, but Rutherford B. Hayes was nominated to oppose the Democratic candidate, Samuel J. Tilden, for president. Logan's reelection to the Senate would be determined by the makeup of the Illinois General Assembly. Both he and Oglesby campaigned vigorously for the Republican candidates. After the November elections, both the presidential election and the senatorial election were in dispute, and the spotlight fell on Supreme Court Associate Justice David Davis of Bloomington. The disputed presidential election of 1876–77 was decided by a fifteen-member electoral commission on which Justice Davis was expected to be the "neutral" swing vote. Simultaneously, however, neither party was able to muster a majority in the Illinois state legislature. The balance of power in the senatorial election was held by about a dozen Illinois Greenbackers and other independents. Logan was the Republican candidate, and former governor John M. Palmer—who had left the Republican Party—represented the Democrats. Neither was acceptable to the Greenbackers. The Democrats, fearing "some trick" that would elect Logan, joined the Greenbackers in electing Davis on the fortieth ballot. A Republican prophetically remarked that they had "lost a United States Senator and saved a President." Davis accepted the Senate seat and refused the commission appointment. He was replaced by Justice Joseph Bradley, who ruled in favor of Hayes for president.[49]

Oglesby, now the senior senator from Illinois, was probably more comfortable with his old ally David Davis than he had been with Logan. He may have been forewarned, however, when one of Logan's lieutenants told the *Chicago Tribune* immediately after Logan's defeat that although Logan was disappointed, "he is plucky and looking forward most hopefully to the future." Oglesby had good reason to wonder if Logan would attempt to grab his seat in 1879. He may have been trying to stifle that fear by taking a leading role in encouraging President Hayes to appoint Logan to his cabinet as secretary of war. Hayes, however, appointed George McCray of Iowa. After Logan failed to receive a cabinet post, his wife Mary personally asked Hayes for the collectorship of the port of Chicago for her husband. Hayes instead offered the Brazilian ministry, which Logan refused. Oglesby wanted Sheridan Wait, who was in financial difficulty, to have the lucrative Chicago post, but Hayes finally appointed his own faithful supporter, William Henry Smith.[50]

Both Davis and Oglesby found it difficult to deal with Hayes on matters of patronage. Oglesby discovered that he had to deal with more demands and fewer available positions. Because certain positions were consolidated in the name of reform, he often had to choose between close political friends. He was also unable to gain enough appointments to meet the wishes of Gov. Shelby Cullom and many of the legislators—not a good omen for his reelection in 1879. He wrote to Davis that "office hunting has little abatement." Davis replied that Hayes's civil service reform was a mere pretense: "Civil Service reform is an easier thing after one's personal friends are provided for." Oglesby was also disappointed when his former attorney general, Robert G. Ingersoll, was not appointed to a diplomatic post in Berlin. Newspapers joked that the atheist Ingersoll was not qualified because he could not, in good conscience, say "*Mein Gott.*"[51]

The depression deepened during Oglesby's last two years in the Senate. "Times are terrible in Illinois," one of his correspondents summarized on February 9, 1878. He observed bankruptcies as everyday occurrences, "corn rotting in the fields, hogs dying with Cholera, cattle ruinously low, real estate without any market value, and a cloud of almost utter despair brooding over the people." Oglesby's father-in-law John Dean Gillett wrote that he had not seen such a gloomy outlook for successful enterprise of any kind in forty years. Wait wrote that Congress had allowed financial conspirators to squeeze the capital, but it was not a good thing to "continue a system which tends to make paupers of the great body of the people." Oglesby came to accept the charge, heard most frequently west of the Appalachians, that Wall Street capitalists, who favored gold and "hard money," were taking advantage of western debtors who had borrowed money when it was cheap. At various Greenback or Free Silver mass meetings and in newspaper interviews, Oglesby declared in favor of remonetization of silver and the reissue of greenbacks. If fifty million silver dollars were coined, would that not give "employment to a million idle men"? he asked rhetorically. He could not resist adding a patriotic spin. He promised to vote to increase the greenbacks to $400 million "as it was in the war, and keep it as one of the results of the war, as we do emancipation (Great Applause)." His Senate actions were consistent with his public speeches, and his votes were carefully noted in the press.[52]

The Illinois State Republican Convention was held on June 26, 1878. Delegates heard from the state's leading politicians, including the aspirants for the U.S. Senate seat held by Oglesby. Oglesby brought the Decatur Cornet Band and the Decatur Grant Glee Club to Chicago. Logan, Oglesby, Governor Beveridge, and Cong. Stephen A. Hurlbut made speeches. The official convention was silent on its choice for the Senate, and the race was on. The contest was to be a virtual copy of the 1870–71 contest. Beginning in August, Oglesby and Logan criss-crossed the state, speaking every day of the week except Sunday. The central committee again booked their speaking engagements to avoid conflicts. Ostensibly, Logan and Oglesby were campaigning for the state Republican ticket, but it was an off-year election; only the state treasurer and the superintendent of schools were on the ballot. The Senate aspirants were appealing for votes from prospective members of the general assembly. On the stump and at soldiers' reunions, each praised the other's bravery and war record, and both spoke in Chicago on November 1 at the end of the campaign. Both houses returned Republican majorities for the first time in six years.[53]

As in 1870, the next stage of the campaign concentrated on Oglesby and Logan and their close political friends, who tried to influence elected legislators by writing letters, planting newspaper articles, and obtaining endorsements in advance of the January 1879 senatorial election. "To be candid," Oglesby wrote to a supporter who criticized him for not being more aggressive, "I have no organization for the contest for I did not feel I had a right in a campaign to work for myself." His faith was that his "honest effort to secure our cause" during his first term would be rewarded by legislators representing the people of Illinois. Oglesby's more partisan friends accused Logan of having selfishly allowed the election of the independent Davis to the Senate seat in the protracted 1877 contest by refusing to withdraw in favor of some Republican who could have obtained a few independent votes. Another supporter suggested a newspaper article that would call for the election of Oglesby as a good but "not noisy" senator, "strong with the people . . . not of the lobby but esteemed by his fellow senators, no rings, a man who never needed the pencil of [political cartoonist Thomas] Nast, to keep him in line." The *Chicago Tribune* came out in support of "Honest Dick Oglesby," praising him as a founding Republican. In contrast with Logan, a latecomer to the party, Oglesby was "a man without deceit or fraud; who has been a Senator without reproach, careful, attentive, and industrious, ever mindful of the public interest; pure in his personal conduct and character."[54]

Logan forces countered that the *Illinois State Journal* in Springfield, the *Chicago Daily Inter-Ocean,* and seventy-five other newspapers favored the gallant Logan. His supporters argued that Oglesby was congenial but old and lacking in verve, "a mere cipher." One wrote to Mary Logan from Chicago, "No one of Senator Oglesby's friends can point to a measure presented or speech made by him which has in any manner distinguished him or his state." Logan and his followers saw no reason to apologize for using what Oglesby called "all sorts of plans, promises and threats" combined with "coaxing and courting."[55]

The final stage of the campaign took place after the legislature had assembled in Springfield in January 1879. Mary Logan set up her husband's headquarters; Oglesby came alone. One legislator later confessed to Oglesby that he had changed his vote after "Mrs. Logan took me into her room and cried and said darling had so many votes to spare and she felt badly to have me against him, begged and cried so I could not refuse her." Based on letters from legislators who professed great admiration but hedged on endorsing him, Oglesby again overestimated his strength. Supporting Oglesby, the *Tribune*, of January 15, claimed that Logan had only thirty-five votes, but when the Republican caucus voted two days later he had eighty. Oglesby polled only twenty-six, and Logan's election was assured.[56]

Oglesby's hurt was expressed in his hometown newspaper, which characterized his defeat as "putting an indignity upon a faithful and patriotic servant." He felt betrayed by Logan, who he believed had promised to stand aside, and professed friends who had deserted him. When called upon to speak during the celebration after the caucus, Oglesby uncharacteristically declined. His efficacy as a senator had been limited by his own insecurities and by circumstances. In writing his biography for the *Congressional Directory* in 1873, he had observed that he had received "less than a common school education." Perhaps recognizing that his stump-speech style was inappropriate to the dignified Senate, he seldom spoke. He never gained seniority sufficient to move out of the back rows in the chamber and never served on powerful committees. Although he had a reputation for congeniality and honesty, Oglesby's term coincided with the grim results of the Panic of 1873 and the scandals of the Grant era. Logan shared those difficulties, which contributed to his defeat in 1877, but was more able and willing to manipulate the patronage system and the Grand Army of the Republic to secure reelection. As one of Oglesby's supporters wrote, "John Logan is relentless as fate."[57]

The Panic of 1873 threatened Oglesby financially as well as politically. He had invested heavily in town lots and other properties in the Woodlawn, Hyde Park, and Calumet areas south of Chicago since the late 1860s. In 1871 he started to buy town lots in the Forest Park area of St. Louis, Missouri. The investments, sometimes purchased with loans, involved tens of thousands of dollars. Sheridan Wait joined Chauncey and James Bowen in various enterprises in the Chicago and St. Louis areas, and Oglesby usually shared in Wait's investments. As money grew scarce and lot sales virtually ceased, it became increasingly difficult to make loan payments and cover taxes. Wait and company were sometimes forced to allow parcels of the property to be foreclosed or sold at tax sales. By 1877 he was desperate. Failing appointment as collector at the port of Chicago, he and Oglesby persuaded the reluctant John D. Gillett to invest in their St. Louis property and managed to forestall foreclosure of some that Wait deemed "as valuable as [Chicago's] Michigan Avenue land." The reprieve was short-lived, however. Wait, near bankruptcy by 1879, decided to go to the newly discovered Colorado silver mines in an effort to renew his fortune. A month later, on July 24, Oglesby received a mournful telegram that announced Major Wait's death "of congestion of the lungs" and inquiring where his body should be sent.[58]

Oglesby buried his faithful business partner in the Oglesby family plot in Decatur's Greenwood Cemetery. Honor-bound to assume Wait's obligations and troubled about his own financial situation, Oglesby was ready to bury political ambition. A few weeks before Wait's death, he had written, "I see my family on the verge of want and I am troubled." Many of Oglesby's supporters were writing to urge him to run for governor in 1880 with the prospect of taking Davis's Senate seat in the 1882–83 election. Still smarting from his defeat, Oglesby replied that the party "has retired me most conspicuously and I am content to let it have its way." "The truth is," he added, "I am too poor to be in politics." He was still in demand, however, as a speaker in the campaign to nominate various Republican candidates for president. Jesse Fell and Leonard Swett, old friends from the Lincoln campaigns, tried to interest him in a Blaine and Oglesby ticket. The former senator replied that the idea of nominating him as vice president was news and assured them that the "march of circumstances would dissipate" such a ticket. Washburne wrote on April 8 to ask Oglesby to come to Chicago to a big Grant meeting: "You must come and make us a talk—an old fashioned ringing speech . . . as you can make and wake up the 'boys'." Oglesby asked to be excused. Joseph G. Cannon, a member of Congress destined to be the powerful speaker of the House, sent Oglesby $500 for expenses to make a canvas of Illinois for Grant. On April 27, 1880, he returned the check, saying that he was making arrangements to go to Colorado "very soon."[59]

Oglesby had made his first fortune in the gold rush of 1849–50; perhaps he could revisit good fortune in the silver mines of Colorado three decades later. He decided to go to Leadville and apparently left Decatur in May, not returning until fall. He would try to salvage some of Wait's investments and initiate new ones. The former senator lived in a crude log cabin owned by a state senator from Chicago, grew a "beard, like Santa Claus," and paid $4,500 for a one-fourth share in a mine called the Sangamon. He returned to Illinois to find that both Grant and Blaine had been pushed aside in favor of a dark-horse candidate for the presidency. James A. Garfield and Chester A. Arthur led the Republican ticket, and the rising Shelby Cullom was nominated for governor. Arthur, soon to be president after Garfield's assassination, wrote to ask Oglesby to make speeches in New York, but Oglesby was determined to stay out of politics and make money.[60]

Meanwhile, Grant had been persuaded to participate in a reunion of the veterans of his first command, the Twenty-First Illinois Infantry Regiment, to be held in Decatur on October 6 and 7, 1880. Oglesby met Grant's entourage at the Bement rail junction and escorted the exhausted former president in a "splendid carriage" from the depot to his new home. "The general was greeted with the wildest enthusiasm," the *Decatur Daily Republican* reported, "and was followed to Gen. Oglesby's home by crowding and cheering masses of humanity, on foot and in vehicles of various kinds." A crowd of some eight thousand flooded the grounds at Oglesby's house. Oglesby and Grant appeared on the east veranda, and Grant briefly thanked them. Oglesby good-naturedly explained that his overnight guest was weary from traveling all day and had not eaten. He asked the crowd to "be kind enough to let him retire and get a little chicken." People dispersed knowing that Grant was to meet the regiment at the "Tabernacle" that night and would be at the fairgrounds the next day.[61]

The diary that Oglesby kept from April to July 1881 provides a glimpse into his family life. Although he later reported that he had lost $100,000 during the depression, the economy was gradually improving by 1881, and his family was uneasy but comfortable. Oglesby sold a few lots, and Emma Oglesby had some money of her own. She was able to enroll her son Hiram Keays in school in Quincy, Massachusetts, in January 1881. Oglesby's seventeen-year-old daughter Olive was in a private school in Knoxville, Illinois, and fifteen-year-old Robert was in school in Racine, Wisconsin. Only the young children of both parents—Felicite, Richard, and John—were at home. The family was involved with the Episcopal Church, and all attended church on Palm Sunday in Decatur and on Easter in Springfield, where Oglesby was delighted to hear his friend Bishop Seymour. They opened their house for a St. John's Church benefit, for which Oglesby had a stage built in the library. He pronounced the party a "great success, eating, drinking, playing, raised $75.00." They also hosted "Art classes" for one hundred people. On patriotic occasions Oglesby could expect to be called upon the make the major address. On Decoration Day, May 31, for example, he spoke before two thousand citizens. As he tersely reported to his diary, "spoke one hour and sweat profusely."[62]

Oglesby often used the diary to reflect upon the past. On May 19, during a visit with Emma's parents at Elkhart, he noted that he had first visited her there eight years earlier. He asserted, "We have enjoyed a delightful anniversary of love and courtship." He used the June 19 entry to recount his and Emma's family tree "for the benefit" of the children. Oglesby also related that he had begun a successful diet. He recalled weighing between 230 to 240 pounds for most of his adult life. By May 27, 1881, however, he weighed 211. He would be almost skinny by the time his next portrait was painted as governor.[63]

Oglesby's May 8 entry is informative and poetic. "This is one of the loveliest mornings this world affords," he wrote before praising the beauty of his apple tree, Siberian crab apples, and a wild crab apple tree in full bloom. He reveled in Dick and John's delight in gathering flowers, picking "Dandy Lions," and being trundled about in a wheelbarrow by their doting father. The children, he said, were "full of life and joy at the growth and warmth of nature and the never ceasing Song of birds. . . . It [was] one of the most delicious mornings of life . . . a day on which to be resigned and perfectly happy," and "one of those sweet living mornings which whisper to the conscience a gentle and serene foretaste of Heaven." The grass, the flowers, the sun, the sky, and the air were "all in perfect accord." He concluded, "It is one of those mornings which make man wish to live forever."[64]

Home was pleasant, but Oglesby's interest in the Colorado mines remained unabated. Olive and Robert, home from school, were boarded out to Aunt Ophelia Peddecord and Emily Luttrell. Little Dickie was to stay with Mattie Richards, the children's former governess near Chicago. Oglesby cashed a check for $200 to enable Emma to take Felicite and John to New Haven, Connecticut, to spend the summer with her relatives and her son Hiram. On July 6, 1881, he accompanied them on the train to Toledo, Ohio, and then doubled back for Leadville.[65]

In Leadville, Oglesby purchased shares ranging from one-twentieth to one-fourth of the ownership in various mines, including the Sangamon, Three Brothers, and Alpine. He purchased an interest in mines labeled "MP" and "KP" in a twelve-thousand-foot mountain named for Oglesby in the Mesquite district in nearby Park County. Fellow investors wanted to incorporate under the name Oglesby Consolidated Silver Mining Company, but Oglesby demurred, and the Link Silver Mining Company was registered with him as president. Favorable assays were frequently reported but usually required further investments. John Gillett, who was loaning money to Oglesby's associates, informed his son-in-law on September 8, 1881, that he wanted to invest in mines no more. He reported that crop prices were good, and he only wanted to buy farmland. He estimated that only one in five hundred mines made money and hoped that Oglesby's would be the one, "as you appear to be willing to risk your all for the chance hit or miss." But Oglesby had no large "chance hits" in 1881. As he wrote to another investor who owed him money, "I suppose you are poor but you cannot be so badly off as I am."[66]

On September 8, 1881, Gillett reported to Oglesby that Emma had come back from New England and the children had whooping cough. On September 30, he wrote suggestively, "Emma and children in Decatur getting along." Oglesby soon came home to rejoin his pregnant wife and children. Jasper Ernest was born February 10, 1882. On March 30, 1882, the Oglesbys sold their Decatur house to James E. Bering for $16,500. Oglesby offered to return the

$10,000 that Emma's father had contributed toward building it, but Gillett asked that the funds be given to Emma. Accordingly, Oglesby wrote two $5,000 checks, dated July 28, 1882, to his wife. Emma may have wanted to move closer to her parents and sisters in the Elkhart Hill area because her husband seemed always to be prospecting or politicking. Or perhaps they needed money. Oglesby had lost three senatorial elections while winning one, although he had won two gubernatorial elections. Perhaps he would try again. Whether because of financial reasons, Emma's demands, Richard's political acumen, or coincidence, in 1882 the Oglesbys moved into a house furnished by Emma's family in Lincoln, Illinois, a few miles from Gillett's Elkhart Hill farm.[67]

## Notes

1. *Decatur Weekly Republican*, Jan. 28, 1869, p. 1, col. 5, reprinting "A Beautiful Tribute" from the *Chicago Post*.

2. *Decatur Weekly Republican*, Jan. 28, 1868, p. 2, cols. 1–3.

3. RJO, Decatur, to Mrs. [Mason] Brayman, Washington, March 19, 1869, Bailhache-Brayman Papers, ISHL. Oglesby's 1869 list of expenses show he paid $100 in wages to a maid named Maud, $30 to part-time servants, and $325 in donations. Oglesby MSS.

4. The *Chicago Tribune* apparently made an attack on Wait as trustee for "gross malfeasance" in not accounting for money and script and for granting a lease to Norton and Company of Lockport. *Decatur Weekly Republican*, Feb. 4, 1869, p. 6, col. 1.

5. Memo on expense funds drawn, 1869, memo on income tax paid, Feb. 15, 1870, and tax receipts, 1869, 1871, all in Oglesby MSS.

6. *Journal*, May 14, 1869, p. 3, col. 2, June 15, 1869, p. 3, col. 2; *Collected Works*, vol. 8, p. 333. The *Journal* (June 1, 1870, p. 1, col. 2), citing the *Peoria Transcript*, ran the heading "A Colored Revenue Appointee." The appointee was W. L. Barnes of Peoria, who may have been the first federal appointee of his race in Illinois. Oglesby wrote him "a warm and eulogistic letter recommending him for his fidelity and honesty," and he was appointed to the office of revenue storekeeper upon the nomination of Cong. Ebon C. Ingersoll. Barnes had once been General Oglesby's "manservant" before joining the Mississippi River gunboat fleet.

7. Printed schedule, "Chicago and San Francisco Trip," July 5, 1869, and J. H. Bowen to Sheridan Wait, June 10, 1869, both in Oglesby MSS. According to a September 15, 1869, bill, the Bowen brothers charged $505.83 to Oglesby's account for trip expenses. Oglesby MSS.

8. Richard Yates to William Jayne, quoted in George Thomas Palmer, *A Conscientious Turncoat: The Story of John M. Palmer, 1817–1900* (New Haven: Yale University Press, 1941), pp. 226–27; Jesse H. Moore to RJO, Jan. 2, 1870, Oglesby MSS.

9. John M. Palmer to RJO, Sept. 21, 1869, Oglesby MSS; James P. Jones, *John A. Logan: Stalwart Republican from Illinois* (Tallahassee: University Presses of Florida, 1982), p. 44.

10. John M. Palmer to RJO, Sept. 8, 1870, and David Davis to RJO, Sept. 13, 1870, Oglesby MSS; Jones, *John A. Logan*, pp. 46–48; *Journal*, Sept. 1, 1870, p. 4, col. 1, Sept. 24, 1879, p.

2, col. 1; Giles A. Smith, Washington, D.C., to John A. Logan, Dec. 21, 1870, John A. Logan Papers, LC.

11. RJO to Sen. Jason W. Strevell, Pontiac, Dec. 10, 1870, John M. Palmer to RJO, Dec. 6, 1870, and Jesse W. Moore to RJO, Dec. 24, 1870, all in Oglesby MSS. Palmer also mentioned a correspondent's concern about "the temperance question" and Oglesby (Dec. 6, 1870).

12. Letters to RJO from Robert Clow (Dec. 22, 1870), Willard C. Flagg (Dec. 21, 1870), J. W. Strevell (Dec. 2, 1870), and D. H. Whiting (Dec. 16, 1870), all in Oglesby MSS; Robert G. Ingersoll to RJO, Sept. 25, 1870, in Mark A. Plummer, "'Goodbye Dear Governor. You Are My Best Friend': The Private Letters of Robert G. Ingersoll to Richrd J. Oglesby, 1867–1877," *JISHS* 73 (Summer 1980): 106.

13. *Journal,* Jan. 2, 1871, p. 2, col. 2; clipping from *Chicago Tribune* dispatch, Jan. 3, 1868, John A. Logan Papers, LC, cited in Jones, *John A. Logan,* p. 53.

14. Clipping from *Chicago Evening Post* dispatch, Jan. 6, 1871, Scrapbook, John A. Logan Papers, LC.

15. Clipping from *Chicago Evening Post* dispatch, Jan. 6, 1871, and *Chicago Tribune* dispatch, Jan. 3, 1871, Scrapbook, John A. Logan Papers, LC; Jones, *John A. Logan,* p. 53; Thomas J. McCormack, ed., *Memoirs of Gustave Koerner, 1809–1896,* 2 vols. (Cedar Rapids: Torch Press, 1909), vol. 2, pp. 519–23.

16. Jones, *John A. Logan,* p. 53; *Decatur Weekly Republican,* Jan. 19, 1871, p. 4, col. 1; *Journal,* Jan. 14, 1871, p. 2, col. 2; Joseph Medill to RJO, Jan. 11, 1871, Oglesby MSS; *Chicago Evening Post* dispatch, Jan. 6, 1871, John A. Logan Papers, LC.

17. Robert G. Ingersoll to RJO, July 11, 1871, in Plummer, "'Goodbye Dear Governor,'" p. 108; Henry R. Sanderson, Galesburg, to RJO, July 21, 1871, Oglesby MSS; letter to *Chicago Evening Journal,* as quoted in the *Journal,* July 29, 1871, p. 2, col. 3. As Oglesby approached his forty-seventh birthday, he commissioned a painting of himself by a Mr. [Charles] Moeller, who had painted the portraits of several prominent citizens of Decatur (*Decatur Weekly Republican,* Nov. 10, 1870, p. 1, col. 2). Oglesby's Aunt Judy had gone to live with the Edmiston McClellan family after her husband Richard's death. On December 30, 1870, Oglesby paid McClellan $25 for a portrait, possibly of Aunt Judy. Oglesby MSS.

18. Mark M. Krug, *Lyman Trumbull, Conservative Radical* (New York: A. S. Barnes, 1965), p. 303.

19. *Decatur Weekly Republican,* Aug. 17, 1871, p. 1, col. 3. Grant and Oglesby met in Lafayette, Indiana, in May 1871. Sheridan Wait to RJO, May 15, 1871, Oglesby MSS; *Journal,* Sept. 21, 1871, p. 2, col. 2, Sept. 26, 1871, p. 2, col. 3, Sept. 27, 1871, p. 2, col. 3 (quoting the *Bloomington Pantagraph*), and Sept. 29, 1871, p. 2, col. 3.

20. Krug, *Lyman Trumbull,* p. 295; Plummer, "'Goodbye Dear Governor,'" p. 104.

21. Buford Wilson to RJO, Feb. 2, 1872, and RJO to L. M. Havenstick[?], April 1, 1872, Oglesby MSS.

22. Shelby M. Cullom, *Fifty Years of Public Service* (Chicago: A. C. McClurg, 1911), p. 194; *New York Times,* April 14, 1872, p. 1, col. 6, copied the letter from the *Chicago Evening Journal.*

23. *New York Times,* April 18, 1872, p. 8, col. 5.

24. *Journal,* May 23, 1872, p. 4, col. 2; Robert G. Ingersoll to RJO, March 23, 1872, in Plummer, "'Goodbye Dear Governor,'" p. 111.

25. *Journal,* May 23, 1872, p. 4, col. 2, May 24, 1872, p. 1, col. 1 and p. 4, col. 1; *New York Times,* May 23, 1872, p. 1, col. 3 and May 27, 1872, p. 1, cols. 4–6; Koerner, *Memoirs,* vol. 2, p. 578.

26. *Journal,* June 6, 1872, p. 1, col. 1; *New York Times,* June 6, 1872, p. 1, cols. 1–2; Cullom, *Fifty Years,* p. 175; *Chicago Tribune,* June 6, 1872, p. 1, col. 1.

27. *New York Times,* June 30, 1872, p. 4, col. 7; *Decatur Weekly Republican,* July 11, 1872, p. 4, col. 2; *Peoria Daily Transcript,* June 29, 1872, pp. 3–4, col. 4.

28. *Decatur Weekly Republican,* June 6, 1872, p. 4., col. 4, Oct. 24, 1872, p. 1, col. 4; *Journal,* June 3, 1872, p. 2, col. 2. For Oglesby's itinerary, see *Journal,* July 25, Aug. 17, Sept. 7, 25, and Oct. 1, 14, 15, 1872 (all p. 2, cols. 2–4); Church, p. 117.

29. Letters to RJO from A. T. Fort (Nov. 9, 1872), J. T. Harper (Nov. 11, 1872), J. B. Brown (Nov. 15, 1872), and James S. Taggart[?] (Nov. 12, 1872), all in Oglesby MSS; *Decatur Weekly Republican,* Nov. 28, 1872, p. 4, col. 3.

30. *Decatur Weekly Republican,* Jan. 16, 1873, p. 4, col. 1; *Journal,* Jan. 10, 1873, p. 4, col. 2, Jan. 13, 1873, p. 4, col. 3; John L. Beveridge to RJO, Dec. 5, 1872, Oglesby MSS.

31. *Journal,* Jan. 14, 1873, p. 1, col. 1, p. 4, col. 2, p. 2, col. 2, Jan. 21, 1873, p. 1, col. 1, Jan. 22, 1873, p. 2, col. 1, Jan. 23, 1873, p. 1, col. 1, Jan. 24, 1873, p. 2, col. 2, Jan 25, 1873, p. 2, col. 2; Lusk, p. 241.

32. President U. S. Grant to John A. Logan, Feb. 24, 1873, John A. Logan Papers, LC; *Journal,* Feb. 12, 1873, p. 2, col. 2, March 12, 1873, p. 1, col. 1.

33. *Bloomington Daily Pantagraph,* Jan. 10, 1871, p. 2, quoting the *Decatur Magnet,* Jan. 8, 1871; *Peoria Transcript,* Jan. 3, 1873, p. 1, col. 1; author's interviews with James T. Hickey, March 3, 1977, and with Roy Schilling, Oct. 1, 1996; "Biographical Sketch of Emma Gillett," four-page typescript, Oglesby MSS.

34. *Journal,* Nov. 19, 1873, p. 4, col. 2; *St. Louis Democrat,* quoted in *Decatur Weekly Republican,* Nov. 27, 1873, p. 2, col. 4; *Decatur Weekly Republican,* Nov. 20, 1873, p. 2, col. 1.

35. Hotel receipts, Nov. 28, 1873, Oglesby MSS; *Decatur Weekly Republican,* Jan. 8, 1874, p. 1, col. 5.

36. "Biographical Sketch of Emma Gillett," Oglesby MSS; clipping from the *Washington National Republican,* May 22, 1874, John A. Logan Papers, LC (guest list for Nellie Grant's wedding); "Recapitulation of Items of Expense Session of Congress, Dec. 1873 to June 23, 1874," Oglesby MSS.

37. Jones, *John A. Logan,* p. 75; *Journal,* Jan. 22, 1874, p. 2, col. 2, Jan. 28, 1874, p. 2, col. 4, April 9, 1874, p. 1, col. 2, May 1, 1874, p. 1, col. 3, May 2, 1874, p. 2, col. 1, May 9, 1874, p. 1, col. 3, Feb. 4, 1874, p. 1, col. 3, Feb. 5, 1874, p. 1, col. 2; *Peoria Daily Transcript,* Jan. 30, 1874, p. 1, col. 2. On May 1, 1874, Joseph Medill wrote to Oglesby from Florence, Italy—fourteen pages of arguments against the "greenback evils" (Oglesby MSS).

38. *Decatur Weekly Republican,* July 2, 1874, p. 1, col. 1; Lusk, pp. 243–44.

39. Felicite (Aug. 27, 1874–July 1954) and Richard James (Sept. 26, 1875–Nov. 8, 1913), from Banton, p. 91; Thomas Inscha and Wife to RJO, Aug. 20, 1873, warranty deed filed Sept. 8, 1873 (Deed Books 49, p. 261, and 55, p. 66, Macon County Courthouse, Decatur). On March 30, 1882, the Oglesbys sold the house to James E. Bering for $16,500 and purchased, for $2,500, lots 4 and 5 in block 3 of the Western Addition (Deed Book 92, pp. 391, 390, Macon County Courthouse, Decatur). See also certificate of survey of block 5, July 10, 1874, and William Le Baron Jenney to RJO, May 7–Dec. 28, 1869, Oglesby MSS. When Oglesby decided not to build a new home, in 1869, he added a stable that cost $1,641.30.

He also spent $1,558.83 repairing and refurnishing the old house. Mark A. Plummer, "Richard J. Oglesby and His Decatur House," *Historic Illinois* 2 (Oct. 1979): 13.

40. *Decatur Daily Republican,* June 9, 1875, p. 3, col. 2. Drawings labeled "Plans 1 and 2" remain in the Oglesby MSS; each includes a kitchen and two or three servants' rooms. The stairwell is perpendicular to, rather then facing, the entrance.

41. Evelyn Moore, "Decatur Preserves Oglesby Mansion," *Historic Illinois* 2 (Oct. 1979): 14; *Journal,* Nov. 26, 1878, p. 1, col. 1. One hundred years after the Oglesbys moved into the house in 1876, the Macon County Conservation District purchased the mansion at the urging of the Governor Oglesby Mansion, Inc., which had been chartered on March 13, 1969. The group supports and displays the house. Banton, pp. 92–94.

42. Oglesby's estimate of expenses for 1875 (Oglesby MSS) was $8,000. Annual salaries included: Peter, $240; Mary, $200; a "nurse girl," $100; and a governess for six months, $180. Other estimated expenses included: donations, $500; church, $150; "to cloth family decently," $800; and "Wine, Liquors & Segars," $200. The records of St. John's Episcopal Church in Decatur were examined for me by George B. De Frees, the parish secretary (letter dated Aug. 10, 1977). Young Richard's baptism was reported in the *Journal* (Jan. 2, 1876, p. 1, col. 2) and the *Peoria Weekly Transcript* (Jan. 6, 1876, p. 2, col. 1). Bishop Seymour stayed at Oglesby's house on July 30 and 31, 1878 (*Journal,* Aug. 2, 1878, p. 4, col. 4).

43. RJO, Washington, D.C., to Mrs. John Gillett, Nov. 18, 1877, typescript in possession of Carolyn Ogen, Champaign, Ill.

44. Adlai E. Stevenson, *Something of Men I Have Known* (Chicago: A. C. McClurg, 1909), p. 346, emphasis in the original.

45. *Journal,* Sept. 9, 1875, p. 3, col. 2, Sept. 20, 1875, p. 2, col. 1, March 29, 1875, p. 1, col. 1.

46. Jones, *John A. Logan,* pp. 75–81.

47. Ibid., p. 81; Cullom, *Fifty Years,* p. 183; Jacob Bunn to RJO, Feb. 4, 1876, and G. B. Bostwick to RJO, Aug. 24, 1878, both in Oglesby MSS. Bunn's bank suspended payments in 1878. The banker and his children eventually returned the depositors' money, with interest. See "For the Honor of the Family," in James Krohe, Jr., *A Springfield Reader: Historical Views of the Illinois Capital, 1818–1876* (Springfield: Sangamon County Historical Society, 1976), pp. 223–28.

48. Jones, *John A. Logan,* pp. 89–90. On August 3, 1876, C. L. Merriam of Locust Grove, Dakota Territory, wrote to Oglesby: "Your summing up, in the disgusting Belknap case, will find a response of approval everywhere—the more so because of the contrast of an honest plain spoken man, one who bases his actions upon common sense" (Oglesby MSS).

49. Willard L. King, *Lincoln's Manager, David Davis* (Cambridge: Harvard University Press, 1960), pp. 290–96; *Journal,* Jan. 26, 1877, p. 1, col. 4.

50. The *Chicago Tribune* article is quoted in Jones, *John A. Logan,* p. 98, see also pp. 98–103.

51. RJO to David Davis, May 12, 1877, David Davis Collection, ISHL; David Davis to RJO, Sept. 10, 1877, Oglesby MSS; Mark A. Plummer, *Robert G. Ingersoll: Peoria's Pagan Politician,* Western Illinois Monograph Series no. 4 (Macomb, 1984), p. 82; *New York Times,* Nov. 12, 1877, p. 1, col. 3. The most earthy criticisms of Hayes came from James E. Hill of Lincoln, Illinois. Hill, with his brother-in-law Oglesby as sponsor, was being rebuffed by Hayes in his quest for appointment as U.S. marshal for southern Illinois. Hill called Hayes a "Dungaree," which, he recalled, Lincoln had defined "as half shitass and half fool." James E. Hill to RJO Nov. 17, 1877, Oglesby MSS.

52. James A. Connolly, U.S. attorney, Southern District of Illinois, Springfield, to RJO, Feb. 9, 1878, J. D. Gillett, Elkhart City to RJO, Jan. 4, 1878, and Sheridan Wait to RJO, March 5, 1878, all in Oglesby MSS; *Journal,* Jan. 25, 1878, p. 1, col. 1, Jan. 3, 1878, p. 2, col. 2.

53. *Journal,* June 27, 1878, p. 4, cols. 2–5, Aug. 17, 1878, p. 2, cols. 3, 4, Aug. 26, 1878, p. 1, col. 1, Sept. 5, 1878, p. 1, col. 1, Sept. 30, 1878, p. 2, col. 4, Oct. 2, 1878, p. 2, col. 5, Oct. 10, 1878, p. 2, col. 5, Oct. 24, 1878, p. 2, col. 1, Oct. 29, 1878, p. 2, col. 1, Nov. 4, 1878, p. 3, col. 4, Nov. 11, 1878, p. 2, col. 3.

54. RJO to W. H. Robinson, Dec. 10, 1878, George Harlow, secretary of state, Springfield, to RJO, Washington, D.C., Dec. 8, 1878, William C. Kueffner, Bellville, to RJO, Nov. 9, 1878, and Gen. John Rinaker, Carlinville, to RJO, Dec. 10, 1878, all in Oglesby MSS; *Chicago Tribune,* Dec. 11, 1878, p. 2, col. 1.

55. *Journal,* Jan. 14, 1879, p. 2, col. 3; Jones, *John A. Logan,* p. 109; W. H. Mason, Atlanta, Ill., handwritten copy of a letter to the *Chicago Tribune,* Dec. 25, 1878, Oglesby MSS; F. W. Palmer to Mrs. John A. Logan, March 20, 1878, Logan MSS, LC; RJO to W. Y. Crosthwait, Dec. 29, 1878, Oglesby MSS.

56. William Henry Smith, cited in Jones, *John A. Logan,* pp. 110–11; William H. Thompson, Chicago, to RJO, April 17, 1884, Oglesby MSS. Oglesby exchanged dozens of letters with legislators, see correspondence, Nov. 17, 1878–Jan. 1, 1879, Oglesby MSS. A telegram from Cong. Green Berry Raum, Washington, D.C., to Logan, Jan. 11, 1879, reads: "I have just seen the President he reiterates the wish to see you reelected and says he will do anything to aid you. He says if J. R. Jones counsels a bolt to defeat you that he will remove him" (John A. Logan Papers, LC). Hayes's diary says nothing about this meeting, and his faithful confident in Chicago, William Henry Smith, advised Hayes to distrust Logan (Jones, *John A. Logan,* pp. 111–12). It may be that Hayes was concerned about the rumored "bolt" in which Democrats might join a few disgruntled Oglesby supporters, but, given Oglesby's party loyalty, that was not likely to happen.

57. Decatur newspaper quoted in the *Journal,* Jan. 20, 1879, p. 2, cols. 2, 3; RJO, Willard's Hotel, to Ben: Perley Poore, March 4, 1873, Sprague Collection, Chicago Historical Society; J. Stillwell to RJO, July 22, 1879, Oglesby MSS.

58. Sheridan Wait, Chicago, to RJO, March 10, July 14, 1877. Lots 26–28 and 52 of Lindell's Second Addition in St. Louis were assessed at $117,000 in 1875; $1,937.79 was due in property taxes in October 1876. The mortgage was $57,400 in 1877. See "Statement of Conditions St. Louis Real Estate," Sept. 8, 1876, Sheridan Wait to RJO, June 22, 1877, M. F. Kanan, Leadville, Colo., telegram to RJO, July 24, 1879, all in Oglesby MSS.

59. RJO to Sheridan Wait, June 22, 1879, RJO to C. G. Bradshaw, Bloomington, Ill., Feb. 25, 1880, Elihu B. Washburne, Chicago, to RJO, April 8, 1880, Joseph D. Cannon to RJO, April 24, 1880, RJO reply, April 27, 1880, and RJO to Charles E. Fuller, Sept. 25, 1879, all in Oglesby MSS.

60. Account book, 1880–83, Oglesby MSS; Church, pp. 135–48; Chester A. Arthur to RJO, Sept. 10, 1880, and RJO reply, Sept. 17, 1880, Oglesby MSS.

61. *Decatur Daily Republican,* Oct. 7, 1880, p. 3, cols. 2, 3; Richmond, pp. 399–400.

62. Oglesby's seventeen-thousand-word diary (April-July 1881) is in General Orders Book 10, Oglesby MSS. See also Bancroft, p. 48.

63. RJO Diary, April-July 1881.

64. Entry for May 8, 1881, RJO Diary.

65. Entries for July 5, 6, 1881, RJO Diary.

66. Account Book, 1880–83, map of Oglesby Mountain, Sept. 24, 1881, S. J. Hanna, to RJO, Oct. 18, 1881, R. E. Goodall to RJO, Nov. 14, 1881, John D. Gillett to RJO, Sept. 8, 30, 1881, and RJO to J. D. Ward, Dec. 26, 1881, all in Oglesby MSS.

67. Gillett to RJO, Sept. 8, 30, 1881, Oglesby MSS; Richard J. and Emma G. Oglesby to James E. Bering, lots 1–6 in block 5 of the Western Addition, March 30, 1882 (Deed Book 92, p. 391, Macon County Courthouse, Decatur); two checks for $5,000 each from Oglesby to Emma, Oglesby MSS. On the back of one check, Emma Oglesby wrote, "In 1875 my father gave me $10,000 to rebuild Mr. Oglesby's old house in Decatur. In 1882 Richard sold the house and offered the money to him, but Father asked him to give it to me and these were the cheques."

## 9. The Governor and the Haymarket Anarchists

RICHARD OGLESBY's new address in Lincoln, Illinois, renewed his association with Abraham Lincoln's "imperishable fame." Veneration for Lincoln renewed during the 1880s, and the nation's leading periodical and book publishers demanded his letters as well as anecdotes and biographies about him. Newspapers frequently published stories about Lincoln, confirmed or spurious. In Springfield, the curators of the Lincoln tomb and home vied for artifacts as the number of visitors grew exponentially. Oglesby seldom made a public address without invoking Lincoln's name, and his 1884 campaign biography would recall the many connections between the Great Emancipator and Oglesby "the abolitionist." Civil War soldiers' reunions were commonplace during the 1880s, and veterans were reinvigorated politically. Oglesby's move to the town of Lincoln coincided with his renewed interest in running for senator or governor. When former Vice-President Schuyler Colfax wrote in 1884 to suggest that Oglesby, as a soldier and a westerner, might be a good dark horse candidate for president, he replied that he had "not so much as a silent wish to ride that animal." He preferred to stay in Illinois, where, he said, "I can discharge the not very perplexing duties [as governor] with reasonable equanimity." But his duties would be perplexing, and it would be difficult to maintain "reasonable equanimity" because his term as governor would be marked with great labor upheaval. Oglesby was destined to gain international prominence as the governor who was "the court of last resort" in the case of the "Haymarket anarchists" convicted and sentenced to hang for conspiracy in the fatal bombing at Haymarket Square in Chicago on May 4, 1886.[1]

Early in 1882, Oglesby's old political and veteran friends began to encourage his candidacy for David Davis's Senate seat, which would expire in January 1883. Davis had been elected by Independents and Democrats and had no standing with a Republican majority. A typical message came from a politically connected veteran who wrote, "YOUR old soldiers are praying for your success." But his trip to the Colorado mines, the move to Lincoln, and his concerns about his family and new son kept delaying his active candidacy. In January 1882 his characteristic answer was that he ought not "at present" become a candidate and that he was occupied with home affairs. By May he was saying that he might announce if he "felt overwhelming support." In June he still counseled that it was "unsure and premature" to announce but that he "would feel gratified to be chosen."[2]

Oglesby was ill in July 1882, but he traveled to Leadville in August and returned in September. His Colorado mining venture and the Chicago and St. Louis property investments looked better, and his bank balance was in the thousands rather than the usual hundreds. Perhaps he could afford to be in politics again. He was not as active in the 1882 off-year state elections as usual, however. Still smarting over his embarrassing displacement by John A. Logan in 1879, he preferred to have legislators seek him and thus be vindicated. Republicans won a small majority in the Illinois legislature, but Oglesby seems not to have corresponded with them as fervently as in previous attempts at the Senate.[3]

The Republican caucus to select a senator met on January 11, 1883. Shelby Cullom, in his sixth year as governor, was the front-runner. The other candidates were Oglesby, Green Berry Raum, the former member of Congress and friend of John Logan, and Gen. Thomas J. Henderson. Logan, still offended by Oglesby's public criticism after the 1879 election, had a working relationship with Cullom, but Logan's friendship with Raum likely prevented him from interceding in the contest. "Black Jack" Logan's supporters often supported "Old Dick" Oglesby once Logan was well placed. The first ballot showed forty-four for Cullom, thirty-nine for Oglesby, twenty-two for Raum, and nine for Henderson. On the second ballot, Oglesby received forty votes of the fifty-four needed for selection, but Cullom's vote count increased steadily until he received sixty-three on the fifth ballot. The Democrats supported Gen. John M. Palmer in the legislative vote, but Cullom was elected by the majority party. Lt. Gov. John M. Hamilton moved up to be governor for the two years remaining in the term.[4]

If Oglesby had been skittish about putting himself forward in the senatorial contest, he felt less compunction about standing for the 1884 governor's race. He could appeal directly to voters and not be stifled by the "wire-pulling" machine. It required little encouragement and flattery to summon the old war horse. George Harlow, his former private secretary and more recently Illinois secretary of state, maintained that being elected governor was a higher honor than to be elected U.S. senator. And if it was a honor, Harlow warranted, to be elected once in 1864 and again in 1872, then it would be sublime to win "the three fold honor." For Harlow, the incumbent "kid," John M. Hamilton, was but an "accidental" governor serving out Cullom's term. The ultimate appeal was that the Republican Party could not win without Oglesby. The state constitution of 1870 had enhanced the governor's salary and perquisites, strengthened his veto power by requiring a two-thirds override, and eliminated term limits.[5]

In mid–1883, Oglesby set the tone for his campaign. After meeting with supporters in Springfield, his advocates announced that Oglesby would be a candidate if given "anything like" a cordial invitation. They asserted that "no manipulation of the party machine [could] overcome the popular sentiment" in his favor. They maintained that he was not opposed to the "Logan element," but "if he could not be the candidate of the whole Republican party he would not be a candidate at all."[6]

In the autumn and winter of 1883 and 1884 Oglesby accepted dozens of invitations to speak at Grand Army of the Republic events, at old soldiers' reunions, and at county fairs. Although the gatherings were advertised as nonpolitical, the majority of veterans were demanding a return to political dominance. As one wrote, "We don't purpose the 'kids' shall run the Republican Party." The swell of support from the Grand Army of the Republic may have contributed to Oglesby's belated decision to join that organization, and he was mustered into Decatur's Dunham Post 141, the reorganized Post 1, on January 22, 1884. Oglesby's late enlistment was not unique; the Illinois G.A.R. commander reported that dozens of new posts had been commissioned in 1883 and 1884. A February 28, 1884, dispatch named recent posts, beginning with Number 393 at Arcola. Two weeks later in Nashville, veterans forming a new post ignored G.A.R. rules against politicization and named their group "Dick Oglesby Post, 419." When asked if politics was being discussed at G.A.R. rallies, Oglesby replied, "No, I seldom hear any politics. I go around a little to these Grand Army Posts and see the boys; but they don't talk politics there."[7]

On January 21, 1884, a supporter queried Oglesby, "How does the political dog wag?" He asked if Sen. John Logan were friendly to Governor Hamilton's candidacy and then correctly answered his own question: "I give Logan credit for too much sagacity and shrewdness to do such a stupid thing." Logan wanted to be on the national ticket, and he needed Oglesby's popularity to carry Illinois. He would have no objection to Oglesby's nomination for governor, provided Oglesby did not aspire to turn the tables on him and take back his Senate seat in 1885. Without dealing with Logan directly, Oglesby let it be known that he only wanted to be governor, and Logan's friends should not "feel uneasy." When Hamilton rushed off to Washington to try to enlist the aid of Senators Logan and Cullom, he came back empty-handed. By making the unsuccessful appeal to Logan, Hamilton also cost himself the support of the anti-Logan minority, especially in Chicago.[8]

The same supporter who inquired how the political dog wagged suggested that Oglesby choose a man to challenge the pro-Hamilton Grand Army of the Republic state commander at the Decatur encampment in early 1884. Oglesby refused, to the frustration of his friend, who scolded him by writing that if Oglesby had one-tenth of Cullom's "cheek and demagoguery," coupled with his personal popularity and magnetism, he "would not be in private life, not by a damn sight, but your notions and principles are too firmly fixed to be now changed." Oglesby did not need to change his "notions and principles" because the commander was removed without his intervention. When another supporter referred to the coup as the first victory of Oglesby's campaign for governor, he replied with thanks but insisted that he did not know that partisan candidates were at the encampment.[9]

Oglesby thought it would be unseemly to begin campaigning in advance of the nominating convention, but he could gain more name recognition by reviving his highly popular Holy Land speeches. He spoke in dozens of communities and often donated his proceeds to charity. One humorous invitation came from friends in Dixon, Illinois, who asked that he give his speech at the local Opera House. They referred to alleged complaints that Oglesby sometimes was "liable to *swear*" and conceded that a man could swear at a Democrat and still be a Christian. They hoped, however, that if no Democrats were present he "could squeeze through without swearing."[10]

Oglesby's "non-political" campaign received another boost when the state's preeminent newspaper offered to do an in-depth biographical sketch. The managing editor of the *Chicago Tribune* wrote to him on February 4, 1884, to ask permission to send Franc B. Wilkie, "a polished writer, and a man of sound judgment and good discretion," to Lincoln to prepare the essay. R. W. Patterson, the managing editor, suggested that the article "would make absolutely no allusion" to the "present political situation." Oglesby quickly telegraphed his agreement, and Wilkie caught the train to Lincoln. After three days of interviewing Oglesby, he produced a ten-thousand-word article that was both friendly and factual. Although the story was ostensibly nonpartisan, the *Tribune*'s headings were politically useful. The largest type labeled the piece "'Uncle Dick' at Home." Subheadings read: "A Visit to the Hon. R. J. Oglesby at His Home in Lincoln—A Pen Picture," "A Marvelously Varied

Career—Carpenter and Lawyer, and a Soldier in Two Wars," and "Not a Good Politician, but a Plain, Honest Man Who 'Keeps Close to the People.'" The article also gave extensive coverage to the "Uncle Tim" story about how the Kentucky-born Oglesby became an abolitionist.[11]

Wilkie's feature, especially the Uncle Tim and Lincoln stories, was widely excerpted or summarized in other newspapers. The *Tribune* had printed a large number of extra copies that could be obtained at its office and correctly claimed that the article was "the first full and accurate biographical sketch of ex-Gov. Oglesby that has ever been printed." Oglesby was allowed to make a few minor corrections before the story was published in pamphlet form and deleted references to working in a livery stable and being a bartender during his early days in Decatur. Published as a twenty-one-page pamphlet, it was entitled *A Sketch of Richard J. Oglesby.*[12]

Oglesby's first political appearance came at the Chicago meeting of the State Central Committee of the Republican Party, held on February 12, 1884. Both Hamilton and Oglesby made brief statements. The *Illinois State Journal,* which supported Hamilton, characterized his speech as being "in excellent taste and spirit." But recognizing that the tide might be turning, it described Oglesby's remarks as showing "his old fire" and arousing great enthusiasm. Oglesby defused Logan's fear that he might not support sending a delegation to the national convention pledged to Logan as a favorite son for president. He called for unity behind the Republican candidates, national and state, and noted, "There is an indication that Illinois may furnish the country with another President [Logan]—we will go into this election determined to support our candidates as a unit and we shall come out victorious." Illinois, Oglesby concluded, was alive and strong and "still carries in her breast the sainted, holy emotions planted there by the immortal Lincoln."[13]

Private Hamilton, who had only served a hundred-day enlistment in the Civil War, was no match for Major General Oglesby, who still carried a minié ball in his breast. Results from county conventions showed a drift and then an avalanche of delegates committing to him, as were most of the state's Republican newspapers. On March 22, the *Carbondale Free Press,* in John Logan's sphere, announced for Oglesby. Two days later, he and Hamilton tested each other's strength in Springfield at the Sangamon County convention. Oglesby won, and Hamilton "discreetly and properly, made no effort to obstruct" the verdict. The rout was complete. On March 26 Hamilton issued an open letter withdrawing his candidacy.[14]

Hamilton struck his flag on the day that Illinois regimental battle flags were dedicated in a new memorial hall in the capitol. The festivities included parades, campfires, and dinners of hardtack and coffee for the two thousand veterans who attended. Oglesby was in a mood to forgive vanquished political opponents and even to good-naturedly forgive the South. He followed Gen. William Tecumseh Sherman to the platform and gave a benediction to the war: "Farewell old civil war, good bye old sour apple tree, all are past, it is all crumbling to dust, the fertile fields of the South will bloom and grow, and at last I hope they will look with affection on the old flag that protects them now, and gives them liberty."[15]

Memories as well as events conspired to reelect Oglesby as governor. The *Chicago Daily Inter-Ocean* published a lengthy poem entitled "At Corinth," which recalled his heroic wound:

> Hear the end—O the picture that memory brings!
> "Uncle Dick" reached his left, where stout Chetlain stood firm.
> Straight he bade him advance, then—but scarce did he turn
> To ride on to the next regiment of his men—
> Tis a deed that will glow 'neath the historian's pen
> When the one vengeful ball of the thousands that sped
> With their whistling so deadly past Oglesby's head
> Found its home in his form. That was all; then his frame
> Reeled to dust from his horse, and the light of his name
> Seemed put out. We fought on. To the sheltering rear
> Tender hands bore our chieftain, with heart-stilling fear. . . .
> With your heart all aglow and cheek ready to burn
> To give praise to the man who knew nothing of fear
> Riding coolly through terrors that daunt ye to hear
> To give praise to the name that stirs blood to the quick
> He's our leader again, is our old "Uncle Dick."[16]

Hamilton's retreat came so quickly that some of Oglesby's old soldier proponents were almost disappointed. H. A. Parker of Chicago wrote, "I half regret the unexpected surrender. Having enlisted for the war one dislikes to march home again without the smell of powder." At the state nomination convention, held in Peoria on April 16, General Oglesby was nominated by acclamation, and delegates stood and "cheered vociferously." The entire state ticket was composed of former Union army officers, including Oglesby, who carried a lead souvenir in his breast, and State Auditor Charles Swigert, who had lost an arm in the war. Oglesby had won the nomination without negotiating any political alliances, and he felt vindicated. One supporter noted that his unanimous selection had given him carte blanche: "You are not beholden to some miserable loud mouthed office seekers."[17]

From May to mid-August, the Republican nominee enjoyed brief respites from politics in favor of social, business, and family affairs. On May Day, the Oglesbys visited friends in Decatur as Richard attended to business affairs. His residential lots in Decatur, Woodlawn, and St. Louis were selling again. The next night Oglesby gave his Holy Land speech in Bloomington and was the house guest of his former Senate colleague David Davis. On May 6 at the Gillett home, the Oglesbys were special guests at the wedding of Emma's sister Grace to the Hon. D. T. Littler and were ushered into the hall through separate doors, simultaneously with the groom and the Rev. F. M. Gregg. Felicite was a flower girl. Emma and Richard Oglesby then embarked on a two-week trip to Kentucky to visit his sister. In June, McKendree College in Lebanon granted Oglesby an honorary doctor of laws degree, and on June 5 he attended the Republican National Convention in Chicago, where Senator Cullom nominated Logan for president. But Logan received only the votes of the Illinois delegates as well as a smattering from other midwestern states. When James G. Blaine neared a majority, Logan threw his votes to the front-runner, and Blaine was nominated for president. Logan was rewarded with the vice-presidential nomination. Not feeling well and anticipating an arduous campaign, Richard took Emma on a three-week vacation at Deal Beach, New Jersey, beginning in late July.[18]

The Democrats nominated Carter H. Harrison, mayor of Chicago, to oppose Oglesby. The national ticket featured Grover Cleveland and Thomas A. Hendricks against Blaine and Logan. Logan, Oglesby, Governor Hamilton, Joseph Medill, Charles B. Farwell, and other leading Republicans opened the campaign with a giant rally in Chicago's Lake Park on August 23. Logan and Oglesby next took the campaign to Rockford and other northern Illinois cities. Logan, in a "kindly letter," suggested that Oglesby "husband" his strength by making one-hour speeches rather than speaking for his typical two hours. He noted that Oglesby appeared exhausted after his Rockford speech, and, "If you wear yourself out, they will say CH [Carter Harrison] has sat you down." But, he added, "Your own health is the point."[19]

Oglesby may have shortened his speeches, but the travel connected with the campaign was excruciating. He spoke five or six days each week. During one forty-eight-hour period, he spoke in Quincy, took the night train to Chicago, and then doubled back to Belleville the next day, traveling five hundred miles and making four speeches. Some Democratic newspapers conceded that he was honest compared to other Republicans and also strong with the "soldier element." Gen. John F. Farnsworth, recently a Democratic member of Congress, noted that Oglesby was very popular and could not "be beaten before the people." Republican newspapers referred to him as a gallant, incorruptible man of the people. Oglesby reveled in his popularity as opposed to the "wire pullers" who maneuvered to become U.S. senators. On September 1 he wrote to a supporter that he only wanted to be governor, not senator, and he wanted to serve out a full term—"nothing else." He gave the friend permission to repeat the message to anyone. That self-denying statement might separate him from professional politicians who had so often disappointed him in Senate races, but it would constrict his future political opportunities.[20]

When asked what majority he expected to gain for governor, Oglesby offhandedly replied that he had a thirty-one-thousand plurality in 1864—forty-one thousand in 1872. His goal was fifty-one thousand in the 1884 election. E. C. Lewis, a perceptive supporter, explained why Oglesby's majority might be fewer than Blaine's and Logan's. Explaining Mayor Harrison's "machine" control over Chicago, he noted, "He has more power to deliver a large number of votes in exchange for personal help than any one else in the campaign." Many Irish Democrats, Lewis noted, would vote for Blaine in favor of a higher tariff, and many Germans would vote for Harrison for "saloon reasons." The "drys," however, would "fire into the brush" and waste their votes on the Prohibitionist third party.[21]

Lewis's forecast, made six months before the election, was remarkably accurate. In Illinois, Blaine's and Logan's electors exceeded Cleveland and Hendricks by 25,118 votes, while Oglesby defeated Mayor Harrison by only 14,599. Almost half of Oglesby's deficiency came from Cook County. All Republican candidates statewide were elected with pluralities similar to his, but Illinois elected ten members of Congress from each party. The Thirty-fourth General Assembly, which congregated on January 7, 1885, was composed of twenty-six Republican state senators, twenty-four Democrats, and one Greenbacker. The Illinois House of Representatives included seventy-six Republicans, seventy-six Democrats, and an independent, Elijah M. Haines. The Republicans lost the presidency for the first time since the war.[22]

Republicans quickly organized the senate, but the house was unable to elect a speaker until Haines was chosen on January 29. Pending organization of the house, Oglesby's inaugural and Logan's reelection to the Senate were delayed. Oglesby was duly sworn on January 30. Neither party, meeting in joint session, could elect a senator, however, and thus the U.S. Senate was organized with only one senator from Illinois. The crisis continued through eighteen weeks, 120 ballots, and the deaths of three assemblymen. Logan publicly displayed no interest in the special election being held in the Thirty-fourth Representative District to replace a deceased Democratic member. The Democrats, thus thinking their candidate would win easily, conducted no campaign, and Logan's agents swarmed into the district on the afternoon of the special election, quietly mobilizing Republican voters. The still hunt was successful, and Logan was reelected to the Senate on May 19.[23]

Oglesby and his administration were in limbo during the organizational fight in the house, and he characterized the failure to swear him in as governor on the timetable mandated by the constitution as "semi-revolutionary." Portending the major problem that would confront his administration was news of a revolutionary event in London: The Houses of Parliament and the Tower of London had been dynamited by fanatics. At a dinner he gave on January 24, Oglesby told friends that he hoped nothing of that sort would happen in Illinois during his term.[24]

Oglesby's uncertain status did not deter office-seekers. One supplicant quoted a delegate to the Chicago convention of 1880 as saying: "Mr. President what are we here for if it isn't for the offices." Oglesby, having decided to keep competent civil servants chosen by his Republican predecessors, had but few positions to give, however. Nevertheless, his old friends who shared the experience of hard times from the depression were quick to apply. A. L. Chetlain, who had stood by Oglesby as the governor was shot at Corinth, bemoaned that his investments "proved useless." He needed a job "that you could give a fellow that would have a little money in it that could be looked after without taking up all my time." William Aldrich, a former member of Congress, wrote that he was "in straightened [sic] circumstances—worse off than I want to tell you in a public way." Horace Chapin of the *Illinois State Journal* sent a list that included a brother who would "be faithful and loyal." He recommended the retention of another, a man who had lost both legs. An applicant for canal commissioner wrote, "I have met with reverses during the last few months and am devilish poor." A supporter from Chicago asserted that Oglesby would receive no application from a person "in such sore need as myself." As "an old soldier in such straits," he wrote, "I am without business and not worth a dollar." "Saddest of all," his only son had returned home to die of consumption, leaving him to support his son's wife and child.[25]

Oglesby's reply to "an old soldier" was typical of his other responses. The governor opened by assuring him that he had read every line of his letter and knew about his services for the Union, but "the trouble is, it is not in my power to grant the request you make." The state had but few places, and he "found every office filled by a Republican so that there are necessarily but few vacancies." He concluded, "I do not aid your wishes," not because "I do not wish to but because I am unable to." Some found it hard to accept the fact that he would not remove former Governor Hamilton's appointees. Nelson Rogers of Elgin, for example, wrote that after looking after Oglesby's political fortunes for twenty years he did not expect to be cast "off for a Hamilton boomer" who held the "Chief clerkship of the State Grain inspection." Oglesby answered that he was replying in the spirit of friendship, although he found "that portions of your letter exhibit a little ill nature. The truth is, I find it impossible to accommodate the large number of worthy and deserving personal and political friends whom I would cheerfully gratify if it were in my power."[26]

The paucity of patronage slots also put Oglesby and the Republican Party in jeopardy of losing support from African Americans, who thought they had been taken for granted. James H. Magee of Metropolis, an African American member of the State Republican Central Committee, noted that "most colored people are natural born Republicans" and would like a few state or federal appointments. During the 1884 campaign, Oglesby's opponent Carter Harrison had given Chicago city jobs to four minority men who then campaigned for him. Magee countered with a circular asking, "Can we be bought for a few well timed positions before the election: Which is better, sweet Liberty to six millions of colored people, or a few positions. . . . Colored men, we are not for sale." He was eventually appointed to the well-paid position as third inspector in the chief grain inspector's office, although he continued to write complaining letters to Oglesby.[27]

African Americans in Illinois had other complaints about Oglesby and the Republicans, but in the face of continuing depredations in the South could not bring themselves to become Democrats. Oglesby was among the last of the white politicians to surrender the bloody shirt, although some African Americans, including the Rev. C. S. Smith of Bloomington, were not ready to haul down that flag. Speaking at the 1884 Illinois State Republican Convention, Smith listed the atrocities being committed in the South and proclaimed: "I will wave the bloody shirt until they take it out of my hand and wash it in the waters of sincere repentance and bring forth good works."[28]

Complaints about segregation in Illinois also became more numerous. One citizen protested to Oglesby because there were no "colored children" in the Soldiers' Orphans' home in Normal. A southern Illinois correspondent complained because children who lived "150 yards from a half empty school" were required to travel two and a half miles over a "no good road" to attend a "colored" school. He pleaded, "Mr. Oglesby Dear Friend for the sake of the poor Negro race, for Heavens sake and for the sake of our noble school law, please meddle in this case." Oglesby did not meddle, and a critic gleefully noted that the governor had sent his children to private schools to avoid having them mix with black children. The Oglesby children's schooling was motivated by their parents' ability to hire tutors and afford boarding schools rather than by issues of race, but repeating the charge was useful to those who criticized Oglesby for insisting that public schools were essential for democracy. African Americans were pleased when the 1885 legislature approved, and Oglesby signed, "An act to protect all citizens in their civil and legal rights and fixing a penalty for violation of the same." The bill declared that all persons were entitled to "equal privileges of inns, restaurants, eating houses, barbershops, public conveyances on land or water, theaters and all other places of public accommodation and amusement."[29]

In spite of the excitement about organizing the general assembly and the standoff concerning the election of Logan, the legislature managed to pass required appropriation bills, including $531,712 for completion of the statehouse. Reflecting the concern of the Civil War veterans, a soldiers' and sailors' home in Quincy was authorized. A joint resolution led to the passage of a constitutional amendment to prohibit prisoners from being contracted to private persons or corporations. At the end of the session on June 26, Oglesby, seated in his chair behind the speaker to signify that he had no more messages for the general assembly, was unexpectedly called upon to speak. He good-naturedly pronounced the final verdict on the body as having been a respectable and honorable general assembly. He also said that he was certain that constituents would welcome them home "and be glad that our session is ended (Laughter and applause)."[30]

With the legislature out of town, the sixty-year-old governor may have thought he could perform his anticipated "not very perplexing duties" with ease. But he would be faced with a mountain of routine duties and extraordinary labor problems. When an Indianapolis newspaper editor asked him to comment on the "cause of the depression and remedy," Oglesby declined, citing public duties that were "so varied, complicated and exacting" as to require all his time. Then there were other expectations to be met: "to visit fairs, societies, reunions, agricultural fairs etc." A study of Oglesby's three-volume letterpress book covering 1885 suggests that he either dictated or wrote fifteen hundred letters. Most may be characterized as thoughtful and courteous. Perhaps the most perplexing routine problems concerned petitions for clemency for prisoners. He sometimes commuted death sentences, usually on the recommendation of the judges or the prosecution. The volume of paperwork was enormous, and he apparently read material carefully and often made further inquiries before acting. On December 22, 1885, he added a postscript to a letter to a Chicago friend: "I am head over ears in trouble with the pardon business. There is no let up any time especially about Christmas time there is a great pressure."[31]

The beautiful and vivacious Emma Oglesby took over most of the social duties and perquisites connected with the Governor's Mansion. A charming woman, her father's fortune was measured at more than $2 million. The state's first lady, a graduate of the Monticello Seminary at Alton, was very comfortable presiding over Springfield's social life. The Oglesbys enjoyed good conversation, and they hosted dozens of official and private dinners. Emma Oglesby inaugurated a plan for holding a reception each Wednesday afternoon. The governor's daughter Olive and Emma's sisters or nieces from Lincoln, Elkhart, Springfield, or Decatur were often invited to assist. On February 15, 1885, she sponsored a "Dickens' Disciples" costume party for the benefit of St. Paul's Episcopal choir and appeared as Lady Dedlock from *Bleak House,* dressed in a costume described as "light blue brocade trimmed with feathers, ornaments, and diamonds." A reporter remarked that had Charles Dickens been present for the event he would have found material for another novel. Late in the evening, the younger set danced "the light fantastic" as "the elder portion" engaged in "promenading and social conversation." The Oglesbys led by dancing an old-fashioned Virginia reel, and the governor "went through the reel as buoyantly as the youngest."[32]

Olive and Robert Oglesby had lived in the Governor's Mansion two decades earlier. Olive now served as hostess with Emma in the mansion and would be married there in 1888. In 1885 Robert was studying in a Decatur law office, but he was a frequent guest at the mansion and would eventually replace H. J. Caldwell as the governor's private secretary. Hiram Keays, Emma's son, was attending Harvard University and would graduate in June 1887. The Oglesbys tried to protect their younger children, Felicite, Richard, John, and Jasper, from publicity, but five-year-old Jasper was mentioned in the newspapers on May 22, 1887, when he rode his mare out of the mansion grounds before being retrieved, in good health, by the frightened servants. On a visit to his grandfather in Elkhart the next month, eleven-year-old Richard James broke his arm when he was thrown from a horse. The governor and his wife spent many weekends in Lincoln and Elkhart. On one occasion, they attended opening night at the Opera Festival in Chicago, where the production was Meyerbeer's *L'Africaine.* Emma and Olive Oglesby and Emma's mother also made frequent shopping trips to Chicago. When Ulysses S. Grant died in late July 1885, the governor led a party of Illinois politicians to the New York funeral; Emma's mother and Richard's son and daughter also attended.[33]

Major General Oglesby, Retired, had not expected to command troops again, but he was called upon to muster the Illinois National Guard even before the senatorial race was resolved and the legislature adjourned in 1885. The sheriffs of Cook and Will Counties asked Oglesby to call out the militia to curb the violence of the striking quarrymen in the Lemont and Joliet areas. Because Illinois statutes were vague and funding was uncertain, however, he was reluctant to send troops. He dispatched Adj. Gen. Joseph W. Vance to the scene but did not send the militia until Vance agreed that the sheriffs needed reinforcements. The striking quarrymen, shouting "no men shall work," marched on the work sites, and seventy were arrested by the militia under the sheriff's direction. They were released the next day, however. More serious trouble occurred on May 4, when the National Guard fired into the on-rushing, stone-throwing crowd. Two workers were killed and eleven wounded, most of them by bayonets and rifle butts. On May 7, General Vance reported to Oglesby by telegram: "Parsons, Chicago communist is here, and in conversation inciting workmen and it's understood is to make speech this afternoon." Vance suggested that the sheriff should arrest him, but a few hours later he reported, "The meeting this P.M. failed when Parsons found he could not organize a commune. He made no speech." The disturbances soon ceased and troops were withdrawn on May 13, but Albert R. Parsons would be heard from again.[34]

The next call for the National Guard came from the East St. Louis area in April 1886, where railroad switchmen were striking and disabling trains. The railroad companies and the St. Clair County sheriff asked for intervention against the "mob." Oglesby initially refused, arguing that the sheriff had posse power sufficient to keep order, and "it is not such a precise riot, mob or unlawful assembly as contemplated by the statute for the use of the militia." The governor made a personal inspection trip to East St. Louis and spoke to many of the workers, including members of the Knights of Labor. Later, a posse paid by the railroad companies fired into a group of threatening demonstrators and killed and wounded several workers. His opposition to paid posses and the inability of the sheriff to keep order influenced Oglesby's decision to dispatch seventeen companies of the National Guard, which kept order until the threat of violence had diminished.[35]

Ironically, the Chicago Haymarket affair of May 4, 1886, which would later make Oglesby's name known worldwide, did not involve the governor and the militia. His opponent in the gubernatorial race, Carter Harrison, had alerted hundreds of Chicago police about the labor strife centered at the McCormick Harvesting Machine Company. Trouble was anticipated on May Day, focus of a national campaign to win the eight-hour day for workers. The day passed peacefully, although it was filled with tensions that had fed the bitter struggle on May 3 between strikers and strikebreakers near the McCormick Works. After the police killed several demonstrating workers and wounded others, the anarchist newspaper *Arbeiter-Zeitung* demanded: "Blood! Lead and Powder as a cure for the workmen!" The paper's staff produced a circular headed "Revenge! Workingmen to Arms!!!" A mass meeting was called for the evening of May 4. Anarchist speakers protested near Haymarket Square, but the mayor left thinking there would be no trouble. Later, Inspector John Bonfield led 125 members of the police force down a narrow alley to break up the demonstration. When someone threw a bomb into police ranks, Mathias Degan was killed. Six others on the force were mortally wounded, and scores more were injured. The police then shot into the crowd, contending that they were returning fire, and wounded or killed many workers.[36]

Chicago police immediately launched a roundup of the city's labor radicals. Lt. Gov. J. C. Smith from Chicago, a Civil War brevet general, kept Oglesby informed. On May 5, he reported that the police were arresting the leaders of the commune and "bringing in the red flags." The mayor had issued a proclamation prohibiting "meetings or processions." Smith advised that if the governor sent troops, he should send a whole brigade, "as it will not do to temporize with this commune element." Oglesby answered on May 7 that the details of "the vicious and riotous disturbance by the anarchists" had been received in Springfield. He was pleased that the Chicago police seemed to have the situation under control and that they were not calling for the militia. "It is not good policy to drift too readily to rely upon the militia," he advised.[37]

Two weeks later, Oglesby, meeting with the Republican State Central Committee in Chicago, told party faithful that they needed the laborers: "If we show a sincere regard for labor, and the laboring men of the land, we will be victorious in 1888." On Memorial Day, the governor was again in Chicago to join the columns marching to Rosehill Cemetery to decorate soldiers' graves under the auspices of the Grand Army of the Republic. Seven hundred police officers headed the procession, and dispatches noted that they "were wildly cheered."[38]

Meanwhile, dozens of suspects were rounded up, and thirty-one were formally indicted in the Haymarket bombing. Eight were brought to trial on June 21, 1886. Most of those charged were connected with anarchist newspapers such as the *Alarm*, which had advocated violence, especially the use of dynamite, as the great equalizer against capitalists. On August 20 the jury—despite lacking evidence directly linking the accused to the Haymarket bomb—found August Spies, Michael Schwab, Samuel Fielden, Albert R. Parsons, Adolph Fischer, George Engel, and Louis Lingg guilty of murder and fixed the penalty at death. Oscar W. Neebe was to serve fifteen years in the penitentiary. "The verdict is unquestionably the voice of justice and the solemn verdict of the world's best civilization" the *Inter-Ocean* observed. "Law is not throttled. Justice is not dead." The *New York Times* noted that "the execution of the death penalty upon the socialist malefactors in Chicago will be in its effect the execution of the death penalty upon the socialist propaganda in this country." The executions, however, were postponed because the case was appealed to the Illinois Supreme Court.[39]

In the off-year elections of 1886, Oglesby spent more time making speeches at soldiers' reunions than making traditional political speeches. He characterized the political atmosphere as "a very dull year in politics." The Republican Party regained a majority of the congressional seats and claimed control of both houses of the legislature.[40]

A few days after the November 2 election, Oglesby was again called upon to provide National Guard troops. Cook County Sheriff Seth Hanchett sent a telegram asking for help in putting down a disturbance at the stockyards. Oglesby, concerned that the sheriff might accept company-paid Pinkerton detectives as deputies, decided to oblige him. He lectured Hanchett, however, "I do not like the use of Pinkerton Detective Agency in connection with the preservation of the peace and the enforcement of the law in this state." He reasoned that corporation-hired deputies would lack "the prudence, forbearance, and good sense" of regularly chosen deputies. Hanchett argued that he could not otherwise find enough men to swear in who were not in sympathy with the workers. Oglesby sent the troops, and order was restored.[41]

John Logan died the day after Christmas 1886, and Oglesby led a group of mourners to Washington, D.C., for the funeral of his old senatorial antagonist. During his absence from Springfield, telegrams and letters poured in from supporters urging him to work to be elected as Logan's successor. Oglesby was mindful of his 1884 election statements that he was only running for governor and intended to serve the full term. His concept of honor, combined with distaste for groveling to legislators, made him unwilling to accept anything short of a draft. Given the political ambitions of other aspirants and the desire of Chicago to have a senator, Oglesby soon disclaimed any interest in the seat. On January 4, 1887, he wrote, "I do not desire under any circumstances to become a candidate for U. S. Senator." As he advised a supporter on January 10, "I propose to remain in the office to which I was elected by the people with the understanding (upon my part at any rate) that I would serve my time out." Had Oglesby realized how difficult it would be to rule on pardoning the Haymarket anarchists, he might have decided that Senate duty would be less perplexing than continuing as governor. The legislature selected Charles B. Farwell, a former member of Congress from Chicago, to complete Logan's term.[42]

Oglesby began his January 6, 1887, message to the new Thirty-fifth Illinois General Assembly with a discourse on labor problems that confronted the state. "The public peace," he noted, had frequently been interrupted since the last legislature met. There had been unfettered discussion by "the public press, the stump orator, and political parties, as to the condition of laboring men." It was Oglesby's opinion that strikes were "not unlawful. Indeed, it is but a natural emotion to sympathize with the earnest efforts of laboring men to better their conditions." In the United States, he argued, "the public ear is open to the persuasions of reason" but "instinctively closed against force." Although Oglesby supported the right of workers to remonstrate against "the aggressions of capital upon labor," he and most other Americans believed that labor would forfeit much good will when it "[put] on the appearance of open resistance to law, or [set] itself up to say who shall and who shall not work."[43]

The governor followed with a brief report concerning those occasions when he had called the National Guard for active duty. He also asked for the legislature's guidance as to when troops should be dispatched. The constitution simply stipulated that a governor "shall take care that the laws be faithfully executed," and the "military shall be in strict subordination to the civil power." What Oglesby wanted to know so as to limit the "perplexity in endeavoring to execute the law" concerned whether he had the duty, independent of calls from sheriffs or mayors, to mobilize the National Guard, as many corporations had demanded during strikes. The governor had been limiting himself to occasions when local authorities could not maintain peace, but he wanted that interpretation to be written into law. That would protect him from representatives of "incorporated wealth" who "impatiently demand the use of the militia in all cases of threatened or real violence." He added, "Incorporated wealth can command a part of the press of our country to malign, misrepresent and aim to intimidate" officials, a matter that should be "constantly watched by the ardent friends of constitutional liberty." He also asked for a contingency fund for the National Guard. The legislators introduced 1,285 bills, 165 of which became law. They did not, however, pass a law to guide the governor on whether to call out the National Guard, although the legislature did pass laws to compensate guardsmen for their service in 1886 and establish a contingency fund for 1887–88.[44]

Neither Oglesby's social nor political life was curtailed while the Haymarket anarchists case was being appealed. The Oglesbys sponsored the usual dinners and receptions for members of the legislature and frequently entertained family and friends. They seemed more inclined, however, to retreat on weekends to their newly acquired retirement property in Elkhart. The only reported violence occurred when the couple once shared a carriage ride with their two young daughters and the horses bolted. The governor "nearly cut his hands" in pulling the reins to stop the "mettlesome steeds." A few days earlier, while riding a train with Auditor Swigert, the governor had felt the hand of a pickpocket and "let loose his good right fist, and nearly knocked the fellow down." Swigert grabbed the thief's coat with his only hand, but the thief escaped by slipping out of the coat.[45]

Nor was the ghost of Lincoln exorcised from Illinois and its governor by anarchists' threats. Oglesby spoke at the New York City Lincoln Day dinner and also attended memorials for Lincoln associates David Davis, Jesse Fell, and Elihu B. Washburne. The public was reminded of the Lincoln-Oglesby connection when a wedge, which Lincoln may have used to split rails in New Salem, was added to the collection at Lincoln's tomb. On the anniversary of Lincoln's death, the body was literally dug up and reburied in a vault in the presence of Oglesby and others. Under Oglesby's leadership, the Lincoln house became a museum. In Chicago's Lincoln Park, Augustus Saint-Gaudens's "standing Lincoln" was unveiled. The National Guard named its Springfield camp for Lincoln, and Oglesby often reviewed the troops there.[46]

Throughout the appeals process on behalf of the Haymarket anarchists, Oglesby maintained a "circumspect reticence" in public as well as private correspondence. He was, however, following Chicago newspaper accounts, reading letters and petitions, and conversing with Illinois Attorney General George Hunt. Hunt informed him when he joined Cook County State's Attorney Julius S. Grinnell (who had prosecuted the original case) in opposing the appeal before the Illinois Supreme Court. Oglesby have noted that the defendants had been represented in the original trial by an able team of defense lawyers headed by Capt. William P. Black and had been tried by one of Chicago's most respected judges, Joseph E. Gary. Leonard Swett, Oglesby's old political and personal acquaintance, had joined the defense team before the Illinois Supreme Court.[47]

The state supreme court, in a unanimous 267–page opinion dated September 14, 1887, rejected the appeal. There had been, the high court ruled, no prejudicial error committed in the trial. The defendants were "dominating members" of the International Arbeiter Association, and the Haymarket riot had occurred as a planned incident in the general activities of that association. It also found that each defendant had carried out assigned parts in the conspiracy and the death of Patrolman Degan was a direct consequence of their concurrent acts. The court ruled that the instructions to the jury that allowed them to vote guilty even if persons unknown threw the bomb were in accordance with the law on conspiracy to murder.[48]

On October 21, 1887, the U.S. Supreme Court began hearing arguments on a "writ of error" in the anarchists' case. The defense added three prominent attorneys who had national reputations: John Randolph Tucker, Roger A. Pryor, and Gen. Benjamin F. Butler. State's Attorney Grinnell and Attorney General Hunt appeared for the state of Illinois. On November 2, Chief Justice Morrison R. Waite read "a long and carefully prepared opinion" that ruled that due process had not been denied. The Court's unanimous opinion was that the jurors had been selected in accordance with Illinois law, and it refused to accept jurisdiction.[49]

Defense Attorney Black was not surprised by the Supreme Court's decision and had made plans to appeal to Governor Oglesby in advance of the scheduled execution date. He was aware that certain procedures were required in making application for a pardon. The pertinent law, passed in 1879, read, in part, that applications "shall be made by petition in writing to the governor, signed by the party under conviction, or other persons in his behalf." The petition was to "contain a brief history of the case and the reasons why such pardon should be granted; and shall be accompanied by a statement in writing, made by the judge and prosecuting attorney of the court in which the conviction was had."[50]

Captain Black rushed to Chicago to press the defendants to sign a petition for commutation of their executions. On November 3, he obtained the acquiescence of Samuel Fielden and Michael Schwab to a contrite statement, but Spies was "obdurate." Later in the day, however, a group of friends and relatives persuaded him to participate. "I believe I am making a mistake," he protested but signed the letter after adding a final paragraph to the appeal. The complete letter was published in Chicago on November 5 but did not reach Oglesby until November 9, when the defense attorneys handed it to him.[51]

Contemporary as well as later historical accounts fail to mention Spies's addition to the letter. The original three-page letter, dated "Nov. 3. 87," was probably written for the prisoners by Henry DeMarest Lloyd and William M. Salter. The document's handwriting changes after what was apparently intended to be a dramatic final sentence: "We may have erred at times in our judgment—Yes, we may have 'loved mankind, not wisely, but too well.'" The words "Very Respectfully" are lined out, and words in Spies's handwriting have been added: "If in the excitement of propagating our views we were led into expressions which caused workingmen to think that aggressive force was a proper instrument of reform, we regret it." Spies continued, "We deplore the loss of life at the Haymarket, at McCormick's, at East St. Louis and the Chicago Stockyards, Very respectfully." The first signature is that of A. Spies, followed by those of Michael Schwab and Samuel Fielden.[52]

Meanwhile, the other four defendants seemed bent on martyrdom. Each wrote to Oglesby, refusing commutation and demanding "Liberty or death."

"I am innocent," Albert Parsons wrote, "and I say to you that under no circumstances will I accept commutation to imprisonment. In the name of the American people I demand my right—my lawful, constitutional, natural, inalienable right to liberty." Adolph Fischer also declared innocence and emphasized his refusal to ask for mercy. He stated that he could no more be properly charged with the murder of a policeman than every abolitionist could have been "responsible for the deeds of John Brown." Nor would he offer excuses for being an anarchist. "Society may hang a number [of anarchists] but their blood will work miracles in bringing about the downfall of modern corrupt society," he wrote.[53]

George Engel likewise wrote to protest his innocence and insist that "powers may *murder* me, but they cannot *legally punish* me. I protest against commutation of my sentence and demand either liberty or death. I renounce any kind of mercy." Louis Lingg, too, demanded "Liberty or death" and charged that "a mere mitigation of the verdict [hanging] would be cowardice, and proof that the ruling classes, which you represent, are themselves abashed at the monstrosity of my condemnation."[54]

On Sunday, November 6, four days after Lingg had written the "open letter" to Oglesby, several bombs were found in Lingg's jail cell. According to the *Illinois State Journal*, the governor was handed a dispatch that reported the incident. "He read and reread the dispatch and a cloud of gloom vexation and anxiety swept over his face as the full import of the information dawned upon him. I can say nothing, said he to the JOURNAL representative." The *Journal* also reported that Oglesby's life had been threatened "in behalf of the condemned anarchists" but that "the governor has been very anxious to keep this from the knowledge of his family and the general public." On November 7 the governor continued to minimize threats by stating that the "reports greatly exaggerate the number of threatening letters." The *Journal*'s reporter, who evidently read much into Oglesby's expressions, wrote that "it was evident from his face that he was not at all alarmed."[55]

Meanwhile, Oglesby's mail was overwhelming. During the four days before his November 10 decision, he received 1,556 letters and scores of telegrams from all over the world. The Western Union reported sending a record 87,808 words out of Springfield on November 10 alone. The file of "Anarchist Case" letters at the Illinois State Archives includes three boxes labeled "Letters for Clemency" and two marked "Letters against Clemency." Twelve boxes contain petitions signed by thousands of persons. Most of the petitions, including one from the Knights of Labor containing thirty-one thousand signatures, were for clemency for some or all of the defendants. Oglesby later carefully preserved the documents by dispatching them to the secretary of state's office with a cover letter labeling the material "an important historical and judicial fact in connection with a great historical event in our state."[56]

Oglesby's close friends all agreed that the anarchists were guilty and advised everything from hanging them all to commuting all their sentences to life imprisonment. Herman Raster, editor of the German-language *Illinois Staats-Zeitung*, was perhaps concerned that other Germans needed to separate themselves from the anarchists and wrote: "Let the law take its course; if otherwise this accursed pestilence of anarchism will always be with us as a disorganizing element of all our political and social fabric." Lt. Gov. J. C. Smith, writing from Chicago, struck a similar note, arguing that the petitions for pardon were from Socialists or persons who were frightened. "I think I know the public pulse and it is that the law take its course," he concluded. Some politicians warned that commutation for any of the convicted would cost the party thousands of votes. The vast majority of Illinois newspapers and those outside the state favored execution. The *St. Louis Globe-Democrat* was typical. It argued, "The thing for Gov. Oglesby to do is to do nothing. Let him stand still and see the fulfillment of the law."[57]

Joseph Medill of the *Chicago Tribune*, however, thought it would be better to commute the sentences "so no martyrs will be made." Medill also sent a letter of introduction for Henry D. Lloyd, a "son-in-law of Lt. Governor Bross [under Oglesby from 1865 to 1869] who bears a petition for commutation." Oglesby's old friend and former attorney general Robert G. Ingersoll sent a carefully written, seven-page plea for commutation. "Ideas" he argued, "cannot be put to death."[58]

Because the governor steadfastly refused to comment on the case, reporters went to great lengths to divine his intention. His sister, who lived near Louisville, Kentucky, was quoted as saying that he had "fully resolved not to interfere with the sentence of the courts." From Lincoln, Oglesby's hometown, came word that either the entire group of seven or all of them except Schwab and Fielden would hang. Emma Oglesby's weekend shopping trip to Chicago on November 4 and 5 caused a stir on the false assumption that it was somehow connected with the anarchist case. Milton Hay, Oglesby's "personal and political" friend and "near neighbor" of many years, visited the governor on November 5, which led to speculation about the advice given or the governor's expressed opinions. Hay insisted that he had urged no particular viewpoint and that although the governor listened to the suggestions of others, "a more independent man in following the convictions of his own judgment when fully made up, I never knew."[59]

On November 5, Captain Black wrote to request a pardon hearing on November 9 in Springfield. Oglesby set the open hearing at 9 A.M. in the executive rooms of the capitol but noted that he "would greatly prefer to meet you Tuesday morning the 8th inst." He may have wished to have three days rather than two between the hearing and the scheduled execution on November 11, but the logistics of transporting some fifty petitioners from New York and Chicago may have necessitated the delay. In addition, on Tuesday, Black was still trying unsuccessfully to persuade Parsons, Engel, Fischer, and Lingg to sign a petition to the governor. Lingg not only refused to sign a petition for himself but was also quoted as saying that he "would not lift one of my fingers to save" those who had petitioned for clemency. As the delegation readied itself for the train trip, Black expressed confidence that at least Schwab and Fielden would be spared. "Of course there is no hope for Lingg. He has signed his own doom," he concluded.[60]

When the hearing took place in the capitol on November 9, Oglesby and Attorney General Hunt were seated at a table. Black delivered "a most elaborate and careful argument" for the condemned men. Gen. M. M. Trumbull appealed to Oglesby, a fellow soldier, in the name of fairness and mercy, and Cora L. V. Richmond, a "Spiritualist," invoked the humanity of Abraham Lincoln. Speaker of the House Elijah M. Haines spoke against capital punishment. Labor leaders presented petitions with thousands of signatures, and Samuel Gompers of the American Federation of Labor, "in the name of mercy, in the name of humanity," called upon the governor to spare the men and argued that anarchy would be given impetus if they were executed. During the morning and afternoon, the governor spent more than six hours listening to the public and private pleas on behalf of the convicted men. Oglesby also met with the tearful relatives of the condemned men, but the most important and dramatic events occurred when certain letters from the anarchists were presented to the governor in private meetings.[61]

Labor leader Joseph R. Buchanan asked Oglesby for a private audience because he was carrying a letter from August Spies, which, if read at the public hearing, he explained, might "create a disturbance." After Spies had reluctantly joined Fielden and Schwab in signing an appeal, he had come under criticism from fellow radicals and was accused of cowardice. He meant to undo that impression. Buchanan read the letter before the governor and "five of the most radical Chicago Germans present." Spies wrote that "if a sacrifice of life must be, will not my life suffice? . . . I offer to you that you may satisfy a semi-barbaric mob, and save the lives of my comrades." Buchanan recorded later that after Oglesby had heard the letter his face took on "a look of deep sorrow, and his eyes were filled with tears." Oglesby, however, later noted on the back of the Spies's letter, "My opinion at the time was that it was intended for publication at some time by friends of the anarchists. It was of course not expected to have any impression upon my mind in deciding the cases." Oglesby added, "The suggestions are too absurd for serious consideration by one upon whom would fall the duty of deciding the cases in the light alone of the exercise of clemency."[62]

Buchanan's unhappy duties were not yet complete. Immediately before entering the private meeting, Captain Black had asked him to read another letter, this one from A. R. Parsons, the former editor of the *Alarm*. Parsons, defiant to the end, cynically wrote that in the name of "law and order" the executions should be postponed until his wife and "two little children" could be brought to justice. Because they had been present when Officer Degan was murdered, they were equally guilty of conspiracy, Parsons reasoned. Buchanan remembered that the governor had cried, "My God, this is terrible!" and that "every person in the room felt with him and for him." Oglesby later noted on the back of Parsons's letter that there was "neither law or decency" in the proposition.[63]

Engel, Lingg, Fischer, and Parsons seemed determined to embrace martyrdom by refusing commutation. Spies joined them by separating himself from the contrition of Fielden and Schwab. Fielden's case was further enhanced when he wrote an individual letter to Oglesby admitting that he had become "intoxicated with applause" while advocating violence but professing that "I no longer believe it proper that any class of society should attempt to right its wrongs by violence." Fielden's fellow stonecutters wrote that his "natural gift of rude eloquence" had allowed him to be used by the anarchists. More important, Judge Joseph Gary testified that Fielden was a "misguided enthusiast" who, "in his own private life," was an "honest, industrious, and peaceable laboring man." Judge Gary's conclusion that "action" by the governor "favorable to him is justified" was endorsed by the prosecutor, Julius Grinnell, and his special assistant, George C. Ingham. The prosecution made similar statements on behalf of Schwab, whom Grinnell characterized as a "pliant, weak tool of a stronger will and more designing person." Only Fielden and Schwab, among the seven, were characterized by Grinnell as "respectful and decorous" during the trial, and only Fielden and Schwab had "made application" to the governor as a part of the pardon procedure.[64]

On November 10, the day after the hearing, Oglesby made his decision and wrote his explanation. The governor reasoned that the "petitions" of Parsons, Fischer, Engel, and Lingg demanding "Liberty or Death" and "protesting in the strongest language against mercy or commutation" excluded "executive intervention" under the "constitutional power to grant reprieves, commutations and pardons" unless he was convinced of "their entire innocence." Because he saw no reason to "impeach the verdict of the jury or the judgment of the trial court, or of the Supreme Court," their sentence would stand. Oglesby next mentioned Fielden's, Schwab's, and Spies's petitions for executive clemency and the separate and supplementary petitions for commutation of the sentences of Fielden and Schwab. "A most careful consideration of the whole subject leads me to the conclusion that the sentence of the law as to Samuel Fielden and Michael Schwab, may be modified . . . [to life imprisonment] in the interest of humanity and without doing violence to public justice." He concluded, "While I would gladly have come to a different conclusion in regard to the sentences of defendants, August Spies, Adolph Fisher [*sic*] George Engel, Albert R. Parsons, and Louis Lingg, I regret to say that under the solemn sense of obligations of my office, I have been unable to do so."[65]

In advance of the announcement of his decision on Thursday at 7 P.M., Oglesby wired Cook County Sheriff C. R. Matson the substance of his decision and notified the sheriff that his secretary (his son Robert) would bring the commutations of Fielden and Schwab on the night train to Chicago and "the sentence of the others remains as fixed by the court." A public announcement was made on schedule. It shared the morning headlines on Friday, November 11, execution day, with the story of Louis Lingg, who had used a smuggled-in dynamite cap to kill himself.[66]

Robert Oglesby met the sheriff in the early morning as planned, and he kept his father informed by telegraph. At 8:20 A.M. he wired, "Commutation papers delivered. Sentence to be executed against remaining four about eleven A.M." At 1:15 P.M., he telegraphed, "Condemned men hung at 3 minutes before 12, crowds dispersing and people becoming quiet."[67]

Most Illinois newspapers and politicians commended Oglesby's decision. Some took exception to his commutation of Fielden and Schwab, but Judge Gary's and State's Attorney Grinnell's recommendation for clemency made it acceptable. As Judge Gresham was quoted, "I don't see how he could well have done otherwise." It was "both merciful and courageous," according to J. Otis Humphrey. Even Joe Buchanan, the labor leader who had worked so desperately to save the lives of the defendants, found it difficult to fault Oglesby's role. Three days after the execution, he wrote in his newspaper, the *Chicago Enquirer,* that any one of twelve jurymen, a criminal judge, seven state supreme court judges, and eight Supreme Court justices could have halted the hangings. Instead, "The whole huge mistake was shifted to the shoulders of an old man two hundred miles from the scene, whose function is executive rather than judicial, and who had a right to trust in the ability of the courts."[68]

Oglesby's mail included many threats that he characterized as "vile, silly, and malignant," but the majority congratulated him on saving the country. Lew Wallace, his fellow Civil War general turned famous author, wrote, "It was nobly done! Thank you." The letter he may have appreciated most came from his former fellow U.S. senator from California, Newton Booth. Booth had also served as a governor and "had to determine the fate of twenty-five men under sentence of death" during his term. "During the season of your great trial," he wrote, "my heart has constantly gone out to you in loving sympathy." Booth told Oglesby that he had assured questioning friends that Oglesby "will do right and he knows what is right better than you or I." He continued, "You have done the right thing in the right way. I think it fortunate that you could commute the sentences of the two who seemed the least guilty and most penitent. It will show the world that these men have not been pursued in any spirit of vengeance."[69]

When he had responded to the news that Great Britain's House of Parliament and the Tower of London had been dynamited by fanatics in 1885, Oglesby quipped, "Having faced the bullets, shot and shell of two wars, he preferred to be excused now from facing dynamite." But as the court of last resort in the case of the Haymarket anarchists, he could not be excused. "Seldom, if ever," the *Journal* noted, "has a weightier burden rested upon the shoulders of any man. He has brought to the consideration of the subject a conscientious regard for his official duty, tempered by a most profound sympathy" for those affected. For Oglesby and his generation, the anarchists' alleged use of dynamite to overthrow the sacred Republic seemed tantamount to war. Parsons, who acted upon the axiom that "a pound of the good stuff beats a bushel of ballots all hollow," was beyond the pale. Nor did the convicted anarchists' refusal to accept commutation allow the governor much leeway according to the laws of the time. Oglesby, the old soldier, believed that he had "done his duty" and helped save his country from rebellion yet a second time. But doing his duty was exhausting. His future political ambitions were limited by the burdens of office and by his age. The weekend following his fateful decision, he took his family to his father-in-laws's home on Elkhart Hill. The *Journal* reckoned, "There is nothing Gov. Oglesby so much enjoys or rests him half so much as to get out in the county and roam about in the fields and look at the cattle and horses and see the great stacks of grain after the harvest." Retirement to Elkhart Hill looked better every day. But first he would have to serve out his lame-duck year as governor.[70]

## Notes

1. Schuyler Colfax to RJO, May 21, 1884, and RJO to Colfax, May 28, 1884, both in Oglesby MSS.

2. W. H. Christian, telegram, to RJO, Jan. 10, 1882, RJO to Col. H. C. Babcock, Jan. 21, 1882, RJO to Phil Dallas, editor, *Warsaw Bulletin,* May 10, 1882, and RJO to Col. G. M. Mitchell, Charleston, June 7, 1882, all in Oglesby MSS.

3. T. S. Wood, Denver, to RJO, Sept. 13, 1882, Frank Obeyer, St. Louis, to RJO, July 21, 1882, and Oglesby passbook, all in Oglesby MSS.

4. Moses, vol. 2, pp. 875–82.

5. George H. Harlow to RJO, Sept. 27, 1883, Oglesby MSS.

6. A. L. Chetlain, Chicago, to RJO, June 18, 1883 (includes newspaper clippings), Oglesby MSS.

7. S. W. Mann, Joliet, Sept. 12, 1883, Oglesby MSS; *Journal*, Jan. 24, 1884, p. 4, col. 4, Feb. 28, 1884, p. 7, col. 5 and p. 8, col. 3, March 10, 1884, p. 8, cols. 2–3.

8. H. McIntosh, Joliet, Jan. 21, 1884, to RJO, H[enry] D[odge] Dement to RJO, Feb. 4, 1884, and Gen. H. Hilliand, Chicago, to RJO, Feb. 5, 1884 (Oglesby note on back of letter), all in Oglesby MSS; *Journal*, April 8, 1884, p. 4, col. 4.

9. H. McIntosh to RJO, Jan. 26, 1882, and Woodbury M. Taylor to RJO, Feb. 1, 1884 (Oglesby note on back of letter), both in Oglesby MSS.

10. Letters to RJO from: Jesse Fell (March 14, 1884), W. M. Smith, Lexington (March 18, 1884), and Henry T. Noble and Others, Dixon, Ill. (Feb. 7, 1884), all in Oglesby MSS.

11. R. W. Patterson, managing editor, *Chicago Tribune*, to RJO, "Private," Feb. 4, 1884, Oglesby MSS. Patterson wrote: "I suppose you are aware that you have many warm friends in *The Tribune* and I am one of them." See also *Tribune*, Feb. 16, 1884, p. 16, cols. 1–7.

12. Oglesby made the deletions on a copy of a *Tribune* article, "Uncle Dick at Home," Scrapbook, 1884, Oglesby MSS. The pamphlet was published as Franc B. Wilkie, *A Sketch of Richard J. Oglesby* (Chicago: The Tribune[?], 1884).

13. *Journal*, Feb. 13, 1884, p. 4, col. 4; Scrapbook, 1884, p. 3 (*Tribune*, Feb. 14, 1884), Oglesby MSS.

14. *Journal*, Feb. 11, 1884, p. 2, col. 1 (from the *Chicago Journal*); *Journal*, March 24, 1884, p. 4, col. 4 (from the *Carbondale Free Press*); *Journal*, March 25, 1884, p. 1, col. 4, March 27, 1884, p. 4, col. 3.

15. *Journal*, March 27, 1884, p. 1, col. 5 and p. 2, cols. 1–6.

16. "Fidicen," "At Corinth the Veteran's Tale," *Chicago Daily Inter-Ocean*, April 17, 1884, p. 4, cols. 5–6; Gen. Augustus Louis Chetlain, Chicago, to RJO, April 17, 1884, Oglesby MSS.

17. H. A. Parker to RJO, March 27[?], 1884, and George Eisenmeyer, Mascoutah, to RJO, March 28, 1884, both in Oglesby MSS; *Journal*, April 17, 1884, p. 1, cols. 5–6. Swigert is identified as "a one-armed soldier" from Kankakee (Moses, vol. 2, p. 864).

18. *Journal*, May 2, 1884, p. 4, col. 3, May 5, 1884, p. 4, col. 1 and p. 5, col. 3, May 7, 1884, p. 7, col. 4, July 29, 1884, p. 4, col. 1, S. M. Dineen, McKendree College, to RJO, June 16, 1884, Henry T. Chase, telegram, to RJO, July 17, 1884, RJO to William Mason, Chicago, July 25, 1884, and RJO to Peddecord and Burrows, May 10, 1884 (giving Beards Station, Oldham County, Kentucky, as their postal address), all in Oglesby MSS. See also James Pickett Jones, *John A. Logan: Stalwart Republican from Illinois* (Tallahassee: University Presses of Florida, 1982), pp. 171–85.

19. *Journal*, Aug. 25, 1884, p. 1, cols. 5–6, Aug. 27, 1884, p. 4, col. 1; John A. Logan to RJO, Aug. 29, 1884, Oglesby MSS.

20. Lusk, p. 470; *Journal*, April 22, 1884, p. 4, col. 4, Aug. 30, 1884, p. 4, col. 3 (Oglesby spoke for forty minutes at a Decatur rally), Sept. 6, 1884, p. 1, col. 5 ("nothing else"), Sept. 15, 1884, p. 1, col. 6, Sept. 26, 1884, p. 4, col. 1, Oct. 3, 1884, p. 7, col. 5, Oct. 9, 1884, p. 4, col. 5.

21. *Journal,* April 28, 1884, p. 4, col. 3; E. C. Lewis, Deer Park, Ill., to RJO, Aug. 21, 1884, Oglesby MSS.

22. Lusk, pp. 470–78; Moses, vol. 2, pp. 896–99; Howard W. Allen and Vincent A. Lacey, eds., *Illinois Elections, 1818–1990* (Carbondale: Southern Illinois University Press, 1992), pp. 204–7; Church, p. 155.

23. Church, pp. 155–58; Moses, vol. 2, pp. 902–7.

24. *Journal,* Jan. 21, 1885, p. 2, col. 1, Jan. 26, 1885, p. 4, col. 1 and p. 7, col. 4.

25. Letters to RJO in Incoming Correspondence, ISA: Judge Franklin Blades, Bloomington (1880 convention statement by Hamilton of Texas), Jan. 2, 1885; A. L. Chetlain, Chicago, Jan. 3, 1885; William Aldrich, Chicago, Jan. 8, 1885; Horace Chapin, treasurer, *Illinois State Journal,* Springfield, Jan. 5, 1885; W. L. Hopkins, Morris, Jan. 30, 1885; and Lyman Guinnip, Chicago, March 26, 1885.

26. RJO to Col. Lyman Guinnip, Chicago, March 28, 1885, Oglesby Letterpress Book, ISA; Nelson Rogers to RJO, and RJO to Nelson Rogers, Elgin, June 16, 1885, Incoming Correspondence, ISA.

27. Roger D. Bridges, "Equality Deferred: Civil Rights for Illinois Blacks, 1865–1885," *JISHS* 74 (Summer 1981): 101; "To the Colored Voters of Illinois," poster, ISA; J. H. Magee, Chicago, to RJO, June 4, 1885, and RJO to Magee, Nov. 4, 1885, both in Incoming Correspondence, ISA.

28. Clipping from *Chicago Tribune*[?], Scrapbook, 1884, p. 63, Oglesby MSS. Smith also caught the attention of the *Journal* (Oct. 16, 1885, p. 4, col. 2) at the Colored Convention held in Springfield. Apparently, Oglesby was not invited. *Cleveland Gazette,* Dec. 5, 1885, p. 1, col. 5 (transcripts furnished by Roger Bridges).

29. *Journal,* Oct. 17, 1885, p. 4, cols. 4–5; J. L. Patton, Murphysboro, to RJO, Sept. 27, 1886, Incoming Correspondence, ISA; *Cleveland Gazette,* Oct. 31, 1885, p. 1, col. 4. For the civil rights bill, see *Journal of the House of Representatives of the Thirty-fourth General Assembly* (Springfield: Springfield Journal Co., 1885), p. 447.

30. Moses, vol. 2, p. 908; *Journal,* June 27, 1885, p. 2, cols. 1–3.

31. RJO to Oliver T. Norton, Indianapolis, Sept. 2, 1985, and RJO to Hon. William J. Campbell, Chicago, Dec. 22, 1885 (postscript), Oglesby Letterpress Book, ISA; *Journal,* July 11, 1885, p. 2, col. 1 (the story of a pardon made on recommendation of a judge and others).

32. *Journal,* Jan. 16, 1885, p. 4, col. 1, Feb. 10, 1885, p. 8, col. 4 (Emma's receptions), Feb. 17, 1885, p. 8, col. 2 (Dickens' Disciples), June 12, 1888, p. 4, col. 1 (on Emma Oglesby's education). John. D. Gillett's wealth is reported in the *Lincoln Daily Journal,* May 8, 1885 (clipping in Oglesby MSS). For dinners, see the *Journal:* Feb. 4, 1885, p. 18, col. 2, March 20, 1885, p. 8, col. 1, April 24, 1885, p. 8, col. 1, and June 17, 1885, p. 8, col. 3.

33. For social events, see the *Journal:* Feb. 2, 24, 1885, March 30, 1885, May 4, 6, 26, 1885, June 3, 24, 1885, July 6, 1885, Aug. 22, 1885, and Sept. 18, 1885 (all p. 8). Jasper's and Richard's mishaps are in the *Journal,* May 22, 1887, p. 4, col. 2 and June 20, 1887, p. 4, col. 3; for an account of the Grant funeral party, see the *Journal,* Aug. 6, 1885, p. 8, col. 2.

34. Moses, vol. 2, pp. 910–11; telegrams to RJO from: J. W. Vance, May 2, 1885, Seth F. Hanchett, sheriff, Cook County, May 3, 1885, Vance, Lemont, Ill., May 4, 7, 1885 (received at 2:20 and 6:30 P.M.), all in Oglesby MSS; *Journal,* May 5, 1885, p. 4, cols. 5–6.

35. *Journal,* March 31, 1886, p. 1, cols. 1–2, April 1, 1886, p. 8, col. 3, April 2, 1886, p. 1, cols.

1–3 and p. 4, col. 6, April 6, 1886, p. 4, col. 3 and p. 8, col. 1, April 8, 1886, p. 1, col. 4, April 10, 1886, p. 1, cols. 1, 3, 4, April 11, 1886, p. 4, col. 1, April 14, 1886, p. 2, cols. 1–2, April 18, 1886, p. 2, cols. 1–2 and p. 4, col. 1, April 23, 1886, p. 4, col. 1, May 12, 1886, p. 2, col. 1; George M. Bogue, Chicago, to RJO, March 31, 1886, 1886 East St. Louis Strike Folder, Incoming Correspondence, ISA; RJO to Bogue, April 7, 1886, Oglesby Letterpress Book, ISA. Gustave Koerner wrote to Oglesby on April 28, 1886, demanding troops (1886 East St. Louis Strike Folder). Oglesby replied on May 5 (Oglesby Letterpress Book, ISA). Koerner later criticized his former opponent and friend for "being a politician, a standing candidate for United States Senator" who "was averse to extreme measures." Thomas J. McCormack, ed., *Memoirs of Gustave Koerner, 1809–1896*, 2 vols. (Cedar Rapids: Torch Press, 1909), vol. 2, p. 744; Moses, vol. 2, p. 911.

36. Ernest Ludlow Bogart and Charles Manfred Thompson, *The Industrial State, 1870–1893* (Springfield: Illinois Centennial Commission, 1920), pp. 168–70; John H. Keiser, *Building for the Centuries: Illinois, 1865 to 1898* (Urbana: University of Illinois Press, 1977), p. 238; Paul Avrich, *The Haymarket Tragedy* (Princeton: Princeton University Press, 1984), p. 190. The identity of the person who threw the bomb may never be known. Bogart and Thompson (*The Industrial State*, p. 172n26) quote a statement made by Wallace Rice, dated June 25, 1919, to the effect that Lingg made the bomb, and it was thrown by Rudolph Schnaubelt. Clarence Darrow and George Schilling concurred. Avrich, after the publication of *The Haymarket Tragedy*, came to suspect that the bomber was George Meng. *Chicago Tribune*, Nov. 14, 1985, sec. 2, p. 3; Paul Avrich, "The Bomb-Thrower: A New Candidate," in *Haymarket Scrapbook*, ed. David Roediger and Franklin Rosemont (Chicago: Charles H. Kerr, 1986), pp. 71–73.

37. J. C. Smith, Chicago, to RJO, May 5, 1886, Incoming Correspondence, ISA; RJO to Smith, May 7, 1886, Oglesby Letterpress Book, ISA.

38. *Journal*, May 21, 1886, p. 1, col. 1, May 30, 1886, p. 1, col. 2.

39. Francis X. Busch, "The Haymarket Riot and the Trial of the Anarchists," *JISHS* 48 (Autumn 1955): 247–70; the *Daily Inter-Ocean* and the *New York Times* are quoted in the *Journal*, Aug. 21, 1886, p. 1, cols. 1, 3. On the use of dynamite, see Avrich, *The Haymarket Tragedy*, pp. 160–77.

40. RJO to O. P. Davis, Monticello, Oct. 13, 1886, Oglesby Letterpress Book, ISA; Lusk, pp. 543–47.

41. RJO to Seth F. Hanchett, Nov. 6, 1886, Oglesby Letterpress Book, ISA; *Journal*, Nov. 8, 1886, p. 2, col. 1.

42. *Journal*, Dec. 29, 1886, p. 4, col. 3, Dec. 30, 1886, p. 2, col. 2 and p. 4, col. 2, Jan. 4, 1887, p. 2, col. 3, Jan. 14, 1887, p. 2, col. 2; RJO to Gen. W. C. Kueffner, Belleville, Jan. 4, 1887, and RJO to Nelson Rogers, Elgin, Jan. 10, 1887, both in Oglesby Letterpress Book, ISA.

43. *Journal of the House of Representatives of the Thirty-fifth General Assembly of the State of Illinois* (Springfield: Baker, Bailhache, 1887), pp. 20–21. The *Journal* newspaper reported (Jan. 7, 1887, p. 1, cols. 1–4) that the reading of the governor's message was dispensed with, and five thousand copies were ordered printed.

44. *Illinois House Journal* (1887), pp. 22–28; Moses, vol. 2, pp. 918–19; *Journal*, June 16, 1887, p. 2, col. 3.

45. *Journal*, Jan. 26, 1887, p. 4, col. 3, Jan. 28, 1887, p. 4, col. 3, Feb. 3, 1887, p. 4, col. 1, Feb. 17, 1887, p. 4, col. 1, Feb. 23, 1887, p. 4, col. 3, March 1, 1887, p. 1, col. 6, March 2, 1887, p. 4,

col. 2, March 3, 1887, p. 4, col. 3, March 13, 1887, p. 4, col. 4, March 16, 1887, p. 4, col. 3, April 6, 1887, p. 4, col. 3, April 28, 1887, p. 4, col. 2, July 9, 1887, p. 4, col. 5, Aug. 29, 1887, p. 4, col. 3, Sept. 6, 1887, p. 4, col. 3 ("mettlesome steeds"), Sept. 2, 1887, p. 4, col. 2 (pickpocket).

46. *Journal*, Feb. 13, 1887, p. 1, col. 3, Feb. 16, 1887, p. 4, col. 2, Feb. 27, 1887, p. 2, col. 2, April 15, 1887, p. 1, cols. 4–5, April 16, 1887, p. 1, col. 4, July 15, 1887, p. 4, col. 1, July 28, 1887, p. 4, col. 1, Aug. 23, 1887, p. 4, col. 1, Sept. 2, 1887, p. 1, col. 8, Oct. 24, 1887, p. 1, col. 5.

47. *Journal*, Sept. 23, 1887, p. 4, col. 2; Busch, "The Haymarket Riot," pp. 247–70; Avrich, *The Haymarket Tragedy*, pp. 297–312. Much of what follows in this chapter is taken from Mark A. Plummer, "Governor Richard J. Oglesby and the Haymarket Anarchists," in *Selected Papers in Illinois History 1981*, ed. Bruce D. Cody (Springfield: ISHS, 1982), pp. 50–59.

48. The court's decision is paraphrased from Busch, "The Haymarket Riot," pp. 263–65.

49. *Journal*, Oct. 22, 1887, p. 1., col. 4, Oct. 24, 1887, p. 1, col. 6, Oct. 28, 1887, p. 1, cols. 4–6, Oct. 29, 1887, p. 1, cols. 4–5, Nov. 3, 1887, p. 1, col. 4; Busch, "The Haymarket Riot," p. 267; Avrich, *The Haymarket Tragedy*, pp. 334–35.

50. Quoted in the *Journal*, Oct. 28, 1887, p. 1, col. 7.

51. *Journal*, Nov. 4, 1887, p. 1, col. 6; Joseph R. Buchanan, "The Story of a Labor Agitator: The Last Appeal," *The Outlook* [New York], Jan. 9, 1904, p. 118; A. Spies, Michael Schwab, and Samuel Fielden, Chicago, to RJO, Springfield, Nov. 3, 1887, Index Division, Executive Section, Clemency Files, Haymarket Papers (RS 103.96), ISA.

52. A. Spies to RJO, Nov. 3, 1887, Haymarket Papers, ISA. The word *aggressive* was inserted before *force* in Spies's addition. Avrich notes that Spies's objections were incorporated into the letter without observing that Spies had written the additional lines himself (*The Haymarket Tragedy*, pp. 355–567).

53. A. R. Parsons, prison cell 29, Cook County Jail, Chicago, to RJO, Haymarket Papers, ISA. The original is dated October 13, 1887; on its back, Oglesby noted that it was received on November 2, 1887. The letter was published in the *Journal* (Oct. 17, 1887, p. 2, col. 4). Adolph Fischer, Cook County Jail, Chicago, to RJO, Nov. 2, 1887, Haymarket Papers, ISA. On the back of it, Oglesby wrote, "Adolph Fischer Recd Nov 7, 1887." According to Busch, most of the defendants were connected with anarchist publications similar to the *Alarm* ("The Haymarket Riot," p. 248). Spies was managing editor of the *Arbeiter-Zeitung;* Schwab, its coeditor and editorial writer; Fischer, a contributor and stockholder; Parsons was editor-in-chief of the *Alarm;* Fielden was a stockholder in the company that controlled it and a frequent contributor to its columns; Engel was the moving spirit of the *Anarchist;* and Lingg was a bomb-maker (p. 252).

54. George Engel, Cook County Jail, to RJO, Nov. 7, 1887, and Louis Lingg "An Open Letter" to RJO, both in Haymarket Papers, ISA. The Lingg letter was registered in Chicago on November 2, 1887, and received in Springfield on November 3.

55. *Journal*, Nov. 7, 1887, p. 4, col. 1, Nov. 7, 1887, p. 4, cols. 2–3, Nov. 8, 1887, p. 4, col. 1.

56. *Journal*, Nov. 10, 1887, p. 4, col. 3, Nov. 12, 1887, p. 4, col. 3. On January 30, 1888, Oglesby transferred a trunk, a box, and several bundles of material along with the letters of the defendants (entry for Jan. 30, 1888, Oglesby Letterpress Book, ISA). Most of the documents are now in the Illinois State Archives, although Oglesby took some of the letters with him when he left office. They may be found in the Oglesby MSS, ISHL.

57. Herman Raster, Chicago, to RJO, Nov. 7, 1887, J. C. Smith to RJO, Nov. 7, 1887, and George White, Newman, Ill., to RJO, Oct. 27, 1887, all in Oglesby MSS. The *St. Louis Globe-Democrat* is quoted in the *Journal* (Nov. 10, 1887, p. 2, col. 1). See Henry David (*The History of the Haymarket Affair: A Study in American Social-Revolutionary and Labor Movements* [New York: Farrar and Rinehart, 1936], pp. 386–88) concerning the opinions of the press.

58. Joseph Medill, Chicago, to RJO, Nov. 4, 8, 1887, Oglesby MSS; Robert G. Ingersoll, New York, to RJO, Nov. 5, 1887, Ingersoll Collection, Manuscript Division, LC.

59. *Journal*, Nov. 7, 1887, p. 2, cols. 2–3, Nov. 8, 1887, p. 4, cols. 1–2; David, *The History of the Haymarket Affair*, p. 432, citing the *Chicago Herald*, Nov. 8, 1887. After Oglesby's decision was announced, the *Journal* (Nov. 12, 1887, p. 4, col. 2) noted that Hay and Attorney General Hunt's advice, together with Judge Gary's and State's Attorney Grinnell's statements, had been critical in sparing the lives of Fielden and Schwab. Years later Oglesby recalled, "It was work of labor to find sufficient ground in my own mind to release Fielden and Schwab from the sentence of death pronounced against them." *Chicago Journal*, July 5, 1893, in Scrapbook, 1890–1920, Oglesby MSS.

60. RJO to W. P. Black, Chicago, Nov. 6, 1887, Oglesby Letterpress Book, ISA; *Journal*, Nov. 9, 1887, p. 1, col. 7.

61. Samuel Gompers, New York, to RJO, Nov. 7, 1887, Haymarket Papers, ISA; *Journal*, Nov. 10, 1887, p. 1, col. 7 and p. 2, col. 2; David, *The History of the Haymarket Affair*, pp. 440–43.

62. Buchanan, "The Story of a Labor Agitator," pp. 119–21; August Spies, Chicago, to RJO, Nov. 6, 1887, Oglesby MSS. The Oglesby note began: "Handed to me by Mr. Buchanan Nov. 9, 1887 private at present, it bares [*sic*] date Nov. 6th 1887. I did not read it at the moment it was delivered as Mr. Buchanan said to me I could read it at my leisure. I of course read it before the case was decided on Nov 10 1887."

63. Buchanan, "The Story of a Labor Agitator," p. 121; A. R. Parsons, dungeon no. 7, Cook County Jail, Chicago, to RJO, Nov. 8, 1887 (original letter in the Oglesby MSS). The Parsons letter began: "Capt W. P. Black. You go to Governor Oglesby tommorrow [*sic*] and have inquired if I have any message for you to convey to him. I have. Please Read him this communication and leave it with him."

64. "Petition of Samuel Fielden for Clemency Presented by Edward Johnson and John Rawle," Haymarket Papers, ISA; see also David, *The History of the Haymarket Affair*, pp. 443–46.

65. Oglesby's decision is in "Executive Office, State of Illinois, November 10, 1887." The typed copy, signed by Oglesby, is in an envelope marked "Decision in the 'Anarchist Cases'"; it is also copied in the Oglesby Letterpress Book (Nov. 10, 1887, pp. 250–52). Both the original and the copy are in the Illinois State Archives, and two handwritten drafts are in Oglesby MSS. The *Journal* (Nov. 11, 1887, p. 4, col. 1) described "decision day" at the Governor's Mansion: "Attorney Gen. Hunt was in conference with the governor most of the day. . . . [The governor's] face was a study, but he looked determined. His eyes gave evidence of loss of sleep, but he had the brave, stern and fearless appearance that won victory and glory for Illinois during the war of the rebellion. He was equal to the emergency."

66. RJO to Sheriff C. R. Matson, Chicago, Nov. 10, 1887, Oglesby MSS. Robert Oglesby

made the public announcement in Springfield and boarded the 9 P.M. train for Chicago. *Journal,* Nov. 11, 1887, p. 1, col. 3 and p. 4, col. 2.

67. Robert Oglesby to RJO, Nov. 11, 1887, telegrams, 8:20 A.M. and 1:15 P.M. Robert Oglesby also sent wires at 9:25 A.M. and at 11:14 A.M. The 11:14 A.M. telegram apparently acknowledged the governor's final word: No additional reprieves would be granted. During the night, Captain Black and Joseph Buchanan had returned to Springfield to request a reprieve on the basis of a report that the bomb-thrower had been found in New York. Buchanan, "The Story of a Labor Agitator," pp. 122–24.

68. *Journal,* Nov. 12, 1887, p. 2, col. 1, Nov. 11, 1887, p. 4, col. 2, reprinted in Buchanan, "The Story of a Labor Agitator," p. 124.

69. Lew Wallace, Crawfordsville, Indiana, to RJO, Nov. 22, 1887, and Newton Booth, Sacramento, to RJO, Nov. 13, 1887, all in Oglesby MSS.

70. *Journal,* Jan. 26, 1885, p. 7, col. 4, Nov. 11, 1887, p. 2, col. 2, Nov. 14, 1887, p. 4, col. 2 (Elkhart weekend); RJO to Joseph Medill, Nov. 21, 1887, Oglesby Letterpress Book, p. 879, ISA. Oglesby, apparently responding to Medill's "All's well that ends well" summation of the case (presumably meaning that the anarchists had been stifled without incident), noted: "P S True Enough. 'All is well that ends well.' My present belief is not only that it is ended, but that it is substantially ended forever in the U.S." The famous "dynamite" letter was published in the *Alarm* and was cited in the trial (Avrich, *The Haymarket Tragedy,* p. 170).

# 10. Draped in Lincoln's Flag

As RICHARD OGLESBY served out his final term as governor, he must have thought about his place in history. Would he be remembered as the orphan boy who worked his way up to being the only Illinois governor to be elected to three nonconsecutive terms? Would he be remembered as the Civil War general who was "shot through" at the battle of Corinth and who later championed the cause of veterans? What would history think of his role in the Haymarket anarchists' case? Would his luster be magnified or obscured by his proximity to Lincoln? Would he be immortalized in bronze or stone as an important leader in the history of Illinois?

The life-or-death burden of ruling on the sentences of the Haymarket anarchists was paralleled by a court case of "botherment and bemusement" that prevented Oglesby's fame from being celebrated in statuary in the new statehouse. *Littler v. the State House Commissioners* began in the circuit court of Sangamon County on October 2, 1885, and was decided in the Illinois Supreme Court on March 28, 1888. The case was popularly known as the "Big Eight Controversy," or "corbels case," because it involved a decision by the newly appointed statehouse commissioners to place eight ten-foot statues of Illinois politicians on corbels high in the dome of the unfinished capitol. The case might also have been called *Littler v. Oglesby* because Rep. David T. Littler detested his new brother-in-law, Gov. Richard J. Oglesby, whose likeness was among those proposed to stand on the corbels. Littler was determined to deny Oglesby that honor.[1]

The commissioners, whom the governor had appointed, reasoned that Oglesby was among those entitled to the honor because he had been governor when construction of the statehouse had begun in 1868 and would be governor upon its completion two decades later. His place in the short history of Illinois was assured by having been elected as governor in 1864, 1872, and 1884, serving as a U.S. senator from 1873 to 1877, and being wounded during the Civil War, when he held the rank of major general. He was also closely associated with the "imperishable fame" of Lincoln. The statues of the "Honored Eight" were to include four statesmen who were living and four who had died. The latter included Ninian Edwards, territorial governor and the third governor of Illinois; Shadrach Bond, the state's first governor; Sidney Breese, a former state supreme court justice; and former president Ulysses S. Grant. Living dignitaries selected for honor were former U.S. senator Lyman Trumbull, Sen. John A. Logan, Cong. William Morrison, and Gov. Oglesby. When approached informally by representatives of the commission about being included, Oglesby modestly objected but did not refuse.[2]

On May 6, 1884, David Littler had married Emma Oglesby's sister Grace in an elaborate ceremony in the Gillett house in Elkhart. Littler may have resented that the Oglesbys were ushered into the wedding ceremony simultaneously with the rector and himself. According to accounts published later in the *Chicago Tribune,* Oglesby regaled several guests during the reception by stating that the joke was now "on himself [Oglesby] in that he now had Littler for a brother-in-law, whereas he had always reviled Milt Hay for having such 'a derned fool' for a brother-in-law. Littler by an earlier marriage having held that relationship to Hay." Littler had angered Oglesby when he accepted a federal appointment made by President Andrew Johnson in 1866, as Oglesby and the Radical Republicans were boycotting Johnson's appearances in the "Swing around the Circle" campaign. In April 1884, his brother-in-law's gubernatorial candidacy had thwarted Littler in his ambition to be the Republican Party's nominee for state treasurer. Littler's opponents argued that it would be excessive to have two high state officers from the same area and the same family.[3]

On October 2, 1885, less than a week after the Big Eight choices were made public, Littler filed for a peremptory injunction restraining the statehouse commissioners from using appropriated funds for making the eight bronze figures. He contended that the commission's action was illegal and unwarranted and that unless restrained "they will execute the necessary vouchers . . . and the present governor will probably approve the same." A week later, Judge James A. Creighton of the circuit court heard Littler's motion. Although it was directed at the commissioners for having allegedly exceeded their authority by wasting thousands of dollars on the Big Eight and failing to follow proper bidding procedures, Littler's real target was Oglesby. "I connect him by my pleadings with a direct personal interest in robbing the treasury, in order to magnify himself in history," Littler pleaded in his oral argument. On October 14, Judge Creighton granted a temporary injunction restraining statehouse commissioners from purchasing the statues pending a full hearing on the matter.[4]

Attorneys L. F. Hamilton and James W. Patton, arguing for the commissioners, maintained that Littler had no right to bring the suit and that he was motivated by "unfriendly feelings toward Governor Oglesby." Patton argued that some bidders had testified that they had sufficient information available to bid and that it was the intention of the original commissioners to have the statues placed upon corbels in the statehouse rotunda. On April 19, 1886, Judge Creighton ruled against Littler but allowed the restraining order to remain pending an appeal to the appellate court. A $15,000 bond was required of Littler.[5]

Although the commissioners were the respondents in the case, Littler candidly admitted to the press: "Dick Oglesby is the man I'm after. He can stop the commissioners any day, but he don't want to stop it, and so I'm going to get his scalp; you see if I don't." Nor did Littler disguise his target when he presented oral arguments against the motion to dissolve the writ of injunction in the Sangamon County circuit court on March 12, 1886. Near the end of his argument, he asserted that the problem was that "the governor wanted to go down to posterity as a ten foot bronze statue." Alluding to a purported Oglesby speech in which he had criticized "brawling politicians," Littler charged that if all the "brawling politician" were melted out of Oglesby the residue would be so small that Littler himself would be willing to bear the expense of erecting a statue. He accused Oglesby of having fed from the public trough for thirty years and receiving "something like $100,000 for a very poor service rendered."[6]

The appellate court would not reach a decision on Littler's appeal of the dissolution of the injunction until December. Meanwhile, armed with the friendship of Senators Shelby Cullom and John Logan and holding the position of Illinois National Republican committeeman, Littler had a forum to continue his attacks on his brother-in-law. As the final speaker at the May 20, 1886, Republican State Central Committee meeting in Chicago, he charged that Oglesby had been "cowardly" in dealing with rioters in recent labor strikes. He also attacked civil service reform and Republicans who accepted appointments from the Cleveland administration, a statement he may have regretted later when Cleveland appointed him to the Pacific Railroad Commission. The *Chicago Tribune* reported that Oglesby sat through the tirade, "chewed tobacco, and said not a word." After the meeting, he was quoted as saying that Littler's speech was in bad taste and cowardly because it came when he could not reply. "He [Littler] married into that [Gillett] family and has been acting the fool ever since," he concluded.[7]

On Christmas Eve 1886, the majority on the appellate court ruled that the statehouse commissioners had acted legally in the "case of the bronze statesmen." The court believed that advertising for making the statues had been sufficient and that legislative authority to finish the structure was inclusive enough to justify the commissioners' action. The *Journal* surmised, "The Commissioners may proceed to embalm Gen. Logan, Gov. Oglesby, Lyman Trumbull and Col. W. R. Morrison in bronze under the existing contract."[8]

Sometime between March 16 and August 17, 1887, however, the image of former governor Edward Coles (1822–26) was substituted for Oglesby's. The commissioners' official minutes as well as extant Oglesby letters and letterpress books are silent on the change. Oglesby, burdened by such pressing matters as widespread strikes and the knowledge that the case of the Haymarket anarchists would soon land on his desk, apparently asked that his name be removed from the list of those to be honored.[9]

Although Littler was delighted to have dethroned his new brother-in-law, he decided to continue his appeal to the Illinois Supreme Court because the commissioners had filed for damages and costs resulting from the injunction. The court ruled on March 28, 1888, in favor of Littler on the technicality that the original bidding for the statues had been based upon insufficient advertisement. The commissioners were assessed court costs. Thus, as the *Illinois State Register* put it, "DAVE LITTLER is on top, at last, in the corbels case. That is, as far as the courts are concerned. But the 'Big Eight' occupy the corbels all the same." As he prepared to leave office, Oglesby's name, chiseled on the capitol's cornerstone during his first term in 1868, had been buried, and a blank, more plumb, cornerstone had been substituted. The original cornerstone was unearthed during reconstruction in 1944 and subsequently displayed adjacent to the "working" cornerstone on the northeastern corner of the capitol. His ten-foot likeness, however, was never to be hoisted to the corbels in the capitol dome. Oglesby's immortality in bronze was thus delayed by Littler's action until 1919, when a state commission dedicated Leonard Crunelle's massive statue of the three-time governor at the highest point in Chicago's Lincoln Park.[10]

During Oglesby's final year as governor, various newspapers suggested that he should either continue on or make himself available as a presidential or vice-presidential candidate. The *St. Louis Globe-Democrat* described him as capable, honest, worthy, and electable. But Phocion Howard of the *Chicago Daily Inter-Ocean* quoted Oglesby as saying that he was tired of politics and wanted a rest. When pressed, he replied, "In the name of God, won't you newspaper men give me a rest? The people of Illinois have honored me far beyond my deserts, I ask nothing more at their hands . . . I am a candidate no more for anything." The state convention took him at his word and nominated Joseph W. ("Private Joe") Fifer of Bloomington for governor. The minions of U.S. senators Charles Farwell and Shelby M. Cullom, together with the enmity of Littler, may account for the convention's neglect in calling for the usual address by the sitting governor. Nor was he chosen as a delegate to the national convention in Chicago.[11]

Oglesby's enthusiasm for participating in the 1888 political campaign was further dampened by the illness of his father-in-law, John D. Gillett, who had also become his friend and occasional business partner. In July 1888 the governor requested and received the use of a special railroad car from the Illinois Central Railroad to take Gillett to Mackinac, Michigan, where it was hoped he could avoid the heat and recover from "Brights disease of the kidneys." Oglesby and several Gillett family members accompanied him, and the governor stayed on for a few days before returning to Springfield, where he reported that Gillett was doing better and would stay at Mackinac indefinitely.[12]

The sixty-nine-year-old patriarch died on August 25, 1888, at Mackinac, however. The cattleman had amassed a fortune estimated at $2 million, of which $1,200,000 was in land. In his will, he made lifetime provisions for his wife and gave his only son, John, two parts of his fortune; each of the seven daughters was to receive one part. John Parke Gillett, and sons-in-law Oglesby and David Littler were to be the executors. Gillett's will and subsequent wills made by family members would keep Logan and Sangamon County lawyers employed for generations as heirs fought over their inheritances. In Gillett's memory, the widow and some of the children had a private Episcopal chapel built in the Elkhart Cemetery.[13]

Otherwise, the governor's final year in office fit the assumption he had made in 1884: His duties were "not very perplexing." He attended fairs, made his Holy Land speech occasionally, attended Grand Army of the Republic encampments, issued proclamations against the introduction of cattle infected with Texas fever, hosted Chauncey Depew's Lincoln tribute delivered in Chicago, and made "felicitous" speeches to visiting lodges and other organizations. Following legislation passed by the general assembly, he instituted Arbor Day on April 13. The governor and other state officials planted numerous trees on the capitol's grounds, including a sturdy hard maple to the right of the main entrance at Capital Avenue in memory of Lincoln. A Stephen A. Douglas memorial tree was planted nearby. Then came a row of trees honoring Ulysses S. Grant, John A. Logan, William H. Bissell, Richard Yates, Shelby M. Cullom, and Oglesby himself. Littler made no public objection.[14]

On the death of Gillett, Oglesby asked the Republican Party to postpone his appointments to speak in the election campaign. On August 30, 1888, he wrote to the party secretary, "My wife and the entire family are overwhelmed with grief at the loss of their father. I could not under such circumstances think of making political speeches anywhere." Oglesby joined the campaign about a month later and embarked on a schedule that followed his long-established custom of speaking six days a week in various towns and cities in defense of his beloved party. He often spoke for two hours in support of Fifer, the Republican candidate who was running against Oglesby's old friend and adversary former governor John M. Palmer (1869–73). Oglesby became more personally involved when Democrats claimed that he had spent more for expenses at the Governor's Mansion than had Palmer. Republicans retaliated by showing that aggregate appropriations and tax rates were higher in Palmer's administration. Fifer was elected by a 12,500–vote plurality. Both houses of the general assembly elected a majority of Republicans, virtually assuring Cullom's reelection.[15]

The Springfield social event of Oglesby's final year as governor was the December 27 marriage of his daughter Olive. The "charming and petite brunette" had met her groom at an Omaha wedding in which Chester A. Snider, a successful businessman from Hannibal, Missouri, had served as best man. As presented in the *Journal,* "It was a case of mutual love at first sight with [Snider] and Miss Oglesby and as their acquaintance grew their affection increased." The Episcopalian ceremony was conducted by the governor's friend, the Rev. George F. Seymour, bishop of the Springfield Diocese, who was assisted by the Rev. Frances W. Taylor, rector of St. Paul's parish. A reception was held at the Governor's Mansion. Among the ushers were her brother Robert and Hiram Keays; fourteen-year-old Felicite Oglesby was a "fairy bridesmaid." The Oglesbys had eight hundred invitations printed. Most of their guests were from Springfield, Chicago, Decatur, and Lincoln; Governor-elect Fifer was also in attendance. Among those sending regrets were Julia Dent Grant and Robert Todd Lincoln and his wife Mary. The governor, always a careful bookkeeper, calculated wedding costs at $1,541.88, plus $500 given to Olive as she and her new husband embarked on their wedding trip to the East Coast. They would then winter in California before settling in Missouri.[16]

On January 14, 1889, the gubernatorial transition ensued smoothly as Oglesby passed the torch to Fifer. The two friends exchanged compliments. The new governor, in his inaugural message, was effusive in his praise of his patriotic predecessor, whose "heroic breast stood a bulwark between the great republic and her enemies." Governor Fifer alluded to Oglesby's service as a state and as a national senator who had also been paid the rare compliment of being elected governor on three occasions. "He proved himself well able by wise statesmanship to preserve in council what his intrepid valor helped to win in the field," he continued. On the afternoon of Fifer's inauguration, Oglesby and some of his family embarked on a three-week vacation to Texas and the "solid South."[17]

"In building up his noble fame he has neglected to accumulate a fortune," a correspondent had written near the end of Oglesby's term. During his final term he had sold most of his property, much of it encumbered by loans and delinquent taxes, in Hyde Park, Decatur, and in the Forest Park area in St. Louis. He had also relinquished his Colorado mining holdings. The balance in his primary checking account on August 13, 1889, was $9,529.96, but he had other modest assets and retained a smattering of city lots. He also supervised several working farms in the Elkhart area and had secured the "Thompson farm" on the northwest slope of Elkhart hill below the Gillett mansion. Emma had some property and inherited much more after her father died. The Oglesbys were able to build a substantial house on the Thompson farm, also known as "the old Latham place."[18]

Perhaps inspired by tales of Oglesby's grand tour in 1856 and 1857, Richard's eldest son Robert and Hiram Keays began a tour of Europe. Most of the Gillett daughters soon followed suit, using their newly inherited money. Emma Oglesby, eldest of the "Gillett girls," also wanted to make a grand tour. Equipped with a letter of introduction from Secretary of State James G. Blaine, which Oglesby had solicited, and a $5,000 letter of credit, she began a seven-month tour of Europe in January 1890. She took fifteen-year-old Felicite to Paris, where she enrolled her in school before continuing on to Rome, Florence, Barcelona, Tangier, Lake Como, Geneva, Vienna, the Hague, Ghent, and London. Richard, fourteen, and John, twelve, were sent to the Adams Academy in Quincy, Massachusetts. The former governor was left with seven-year-old Jasper; a governess, Mattie Richards; an Irish maid, Maggie; a "colored" servant, "Col. B. Walkup"; and a farmhand named Seabott. He would maintain the house, supervise their farms and other properties, and await a potential recall to public service.[19]

Oglesby's 1889–91 diary, an extensive Bancroft oral history that was transcribed on July 17 and 18, 1890, and a rich cache of personal papers now available at the Illinois State Historical Library provide an opportunity to survey the life of a successful politician who had married into an aspiring aristocratic family. Oglesby's daily life, family affairs, the children's education, religion, and the political culture of his era may thus be more thoroughly explored.[20]

Oglesby enjoyed being a country gentleman and presiding over several

farms near his home on Elkhart Hill. Although living in the country afforded considerable privacy, he had easy access to Springfield and Chicago. The
Chicago and Alton Railway was only a few hundred yards from his home, and
there were several daily passenger trains. Freight trains, too, often accepted
the former governor as a passenger. It required only about forty minutes to
traverse the twenty miles and reach Springfield, where he could transfer to
other lines that connected to Decatur and other destinations. It was a five-
hour trip to Chicago by train. From Chicago, he could board a Pullman car
and comfortably reach the East Coast. From his house to the county seat at
Lincoln it was a two-hour carriage ride in his "Victoria" or a thirty-minute
train ride. It was a quarter-mile walk to the "village" of Elkhart. "Grandma"
Gillett's mansion was a walk or horse ride of less than a mile up the hill.[21]

The gentleman farmer always recorded the weather in his diary. He
thought most farmers paid too little attention to recording the weather from
year to year, even though their prosperity depended upon it. Pleasant weather
brought him "much joy, comfort, and repose." Buoyed by good weather, he
wrote, "I am very happy and love life free from politics and public life."
Oglesby, sixty-six, was very active in his supervision of the family farms and
occasionally would even join the field hands in work. At harvest, crews of
eighteen or more men required supervision and feeding. Oglesby was also a
careful student of the market, always concerned about the timing of his grain
sales. Still, there was occasion to read the classics, including Homer and
Shakespeare, although he did not neglect the *Congressional Record*. He also
enjoyed receiving visitors, especially old friends and those who would engage
in dialogue with him. "I find no companions more interesting than a good
book though I admit to being fond of good company," he observed in the
diary.[22]

Emma was more acquisitive than the governor. Although she left for Europe with a $5,000 letter of credit, she returned with nine trunks, nine par-
cels, and an overdrawn account. Soon she was insisting that they build a larger
house a few hundred yards up the slope of Elkhart Hill. She estimated the
cost at $10,000, but Oglesby thought it would be no less than $20,000. A
Springfield architect was engaged, but no contracts were let until after their
existing house burned to the ground on March 2, 1891. Oglesby estimated the
loss at $25,000, all uninsured. Many items from the first floor, including
portraits, books, and the piano, were saved, but Oglesby's mementos and
trophies, including a $2,200 gold sword presented to him in commemora-
tion of the Battle of Corinth, either melted or burned. Some villagers suspected that Emma Oglesby had won the argument for a new house when they
heard that the architect was on the train to Elkhart when the fire began. A

Springfield architect, however, had been employed months before the fire. Emma Oglesby's skin and hair were "deeply scorched" during the evacuation of the house, and she lost all her jewelry and her "fine Parisian gowns." Oglesby escaped with a burn on "his magnificent forehead and a big hole burned through his hat brim." The governor concluded that the fire had started in Colonel Walkup's upstairs room, where some additional hired hands were staying. The Oglesbys found temporary quarters nearby and began building a thirty-two-room mansion, "Oglehurst."[23]

Oglesby was philosophical about Emma's apparent dominance in the family. A few days after she returned from Europe, he recorded in his diary: "Jap [Jasper] and I cannot have our way so completely as recently but we yield this much of sovereignty for the exchange of love and affection and a happier home." Although Emma had more assets than Richard, he seemed anxious to give her any money that had come from her father. When they sold the Decatur house, he put the $10,000 his father-in-law had given him to build it into Emma's account, and when bank credits for her European trip were exhausted Oglesby deposited an additional $2,000, most of which came from half of his $3,000 fee for co-administrating the Gillett estate. He confided to his diary: "I expected to use the whole amount in the education of our children but this disposition is I feel a very good one as it will free her mind from anxiety about interest." On November 18, 1890, the seventeenth anniversary of their marriage, he reported to his diary that he and Emma had renewed their "vows of love fresh and strong and pure as then and none was ever more so." On the same day, Oglesby took his wife and her sister to Mt. Pulaski, where they voted for commissioners for a new drainage district, Emma and Amy's first vote ever. Oglesby was also proud that Emma had been named as one of the lady managers of the World Columbian Expedition in Chicago. He was bemused at being idle at the Palmer House Hotel while the lady managers completed their eight-day meeting. On the last day he noted, "The day was a rather dull one to me. My wife has been very happy and that makes me happy." He paid the hotel bill, "like a good husband." In turn, she surprised him with a new suit, "which fit pretty well" and which he managed to wear all day while "feeling tolerably comfortable."[24]

The couple may have disagreed over the education of the children. Emma Oglesby had attended a "finishing school," whereas her husband recalled going to school only three months, where teacher Lemuel Allen taught him "all the grammar, arithmetic, and physical science I've ever learned or half learned." Philosophically and politically, the former governor preferred public schools. Their youngest son, Jasper, briefly attended the "Village Common School," which Oglesby described as "the one I like best for a good, practical education for the beginning of life." The Oglesbys experimented with having the children tutored by Father Dunn, the local Catholic priest, and later by the newly appointed Reverend Babin, the Episcopal priest who was also assigned to the Gillett chapel. But Jasper and John were "troublesome boys to manage," an attribute, Oglesby joked, that "came from the Gillett side," where they always wanted to have their own way. On February 8, 1891, he recorded: "Jasper ran off only once today." Oglesby liked having his "darling eight year old baby boy" around, but Jap was later dispatched to a boarding school in Pekin, Illinois, with brother John. They later attended St. Mark's preparatory school in Southborough, Massachusetts. John, who matriculated to Harvard University, was destined to become Oglesby's political heir. He was twice elected lieutenant governor of Illinois (in 1908 and 1916). The two oldest children of both Richard and Emma Oglesby were sent to Chicago, where Felicite, who was sixteen in 1891, attended the Loring School and Richard later enrolled at the University School.[25]

Oglesby's religious beliefs are difficult to discern. Like Lincoln, he was nondenominational, although he paid pew rent for his family and acknowledged the existence of a fate controlled by God. Oglesby recalled that his family in Kentucky had not been religious. He was familiar, however, with the doctrines of the Christian Church (Disciples of Christ) because it was the church of his surrogate mother, Aunt Judy, in Decatur and of his lawyer, Edward Blinn of Lincoln, later in life. His tour of the Holy Land had been partially motivated by a search for religion, but he observed more fraud than faith. Although he found the agnostic views of Robert G. Ingersoll stimulating, Oglesby continued making his Holy Land speeches, which reinforced some Christian belief in the Bible. Anna, his first wife, had been a Methodist, and they were married by the Methodist pastor. Emma was a communicant in the Episcopal Church, and they had been married by a member of the Episcopal clergy. Oglesby made contributions to Methodist, Episcopal, Baptist, and Christian churches, but there is no available record in Decatur, Springfield, or Lincoln that confirms his church membership. He did have a long-term friendship, however, with Bishop George Seymour.[26]

In the Bancroft oral history dictated on July 17, 1890, Oglesby stated: "I don't belong to any church, I couldn't tell you what my ideas are about a future state, I don't know; as to my believing in the Bible, we won't debate those questions . . . they are too complicated for biography." A week later, on his sixty-seventh birthday, he lamented that he was "unprepared for a doom I do not comprehend, for a destiny no man has yet discovered." The encounter with the biographers and his birthday, together with the return of his wife and family, may have set him to thinking more about religion. According to his diary, he attended various churches for the next four Sundays, although he had attended none during the first seven months of the year. He visited the Christian Church on August 24 and reported hearing "a good Camelite [Thomas and Alexander Campbell were the church founders] sermon, the doctrine of the church of my youth." The next day, he invited Father Dunn of the Elkhart Catholic Church, "a clever, intelligent Irish priest of good character and morals in addition to his highly religious convictions," to dinner. For the next two Sundays the Oglesbys attended services, presumedly at the Episcopal Church. On the following Sunday they went to the Catholic Church to hear Father Dunn, whom they engaged to teach some of the children for an unspecified period. After Thanksgiving dinner, with Father Dunn as guest, Oglesby reported, "We gradually drifted into and upon religious subjects. Father Dunn gave us most arresting account of the Truth and Dogma and history of the Catholic Church for he is an intense as well as an intelligent Catholic." But Oglesby's political senatorial candidacy soon distracted him from his religious quest, and the rector of the new chapel built in memory of John D. Gillett replaced the priest as the children's mentor.[27]

Sen. Shelby M. Cullom, a frequent critic of Oglesby, recalled in his memoirs that the governor had "a perfect horror of death, which became an obsession with him" late in life. He asserted that Oglesby joined a church and constantly talked to friends about the mystery of death. No record of his church membership is available, but other sources confirm that he frequently introduced the topic of religion into conversations. He and Blinn often speculated about life after death. Typical of Oglesby's manner of joking about serious subjects, they made a pact that the first to go would attempt to inform the other what he found. In one of the final letters he wrote before his death in 1899, Oglesby professed not to understand why, "when the Lord has such a good set of fellows," they are not allowed to "live as long as they may care to." Although he was feeling "of little account," Oglesby was "in no hurry to die." Recognizing death's inevitability, however, he offered: "There is not in death very much to be afraid of. It winds a fellow up; that is about all there is to it." Bishop Seymour's participation in Oglesby's funeral, described as the "regular funeral service of the Episcopal church," together with a letter of sympathy by a former Elkhart rector who assumed that last rites had been administered, suggest that the clergy was satisfied that their friend would join in the "re-union of souls" in the next life.[28]

By admission to his close friends, his diary, and by his carefully filed receipts, Oglesby saw bourbon as the elixir of life—if not the next life. On April 9, 1890, a cold, windy day when the temperature dropped to 45 degrees following an 84-degree day, he confided to his diary that the event of the day was when a friend brought a bottle of Old Taylor Kentucky sour mash whiskey. The bourbon, he wrote, "produced the desirable, mean temperature and restored the usual equilibrium so necessary to one of my age, originally born in Kentucky, where such medicine was the universal remedy for any well regulated household." Oglesby frequently ordered bourbon by the barrel and champagne by the case in order to entertain guests and satisfy his own thirst. His hotel bills habitually included charges for drink. After the Oglesby residence burned, he confided to close friends that one of the greatest losses had been a customized valise that Robert Ingersoll had given him. It featured a special opening from which a bottle of whisky could be extracted without notice.[29]

If Oglesby entertained doubts about religion, he professed none about his other "church," the Republican Party and saw himself as a "very sure and reliable Republican." "I believe intensely in Republicanism and shall until I cease to believe in anything," he wrote in his diary. When the political season came again in the form of the off-year elections of 1890, Oglesby was a much-sought-after campaigner. He felt obliged to campaign, because he had "received liberally from Illinois political honors and promotion." He was also aware that a U.S. Senate seat would be available, although he denied being a candidate. When the *Chicago Daily Inter-Ocean* sent a reporter named Busby to do an "Uncle Dick" story similar to the one that had helped elect him governor in 1884, Oglesby declined to talk about his candidacy, although he did assert, "I do not desire to hold that great office again." Busby nonetheless wrote a front-page story in which he labeled Oglesby as the "Cincinnatus of Illinois" and invoked the Lincoln connection by headlining Lincoln's admonition: "Dick, keep close to the people, they are always right." Soon Oglesby was again criss-crossing the state to make "soldier and political" speeches five days a week. His first was in Du Quoin on September 25, and his last in Chicago on November 1. Although his efforts were highly praised, it was not enough to offset the nation's displeasure with the McKinley Tariff. Illinois Republicans were able to elect only six of twenty candidates to Congress. A similar nationwide trend delivered the U.S. House of Representatives to the Democrats.[30]

Oglesby and incumbent senator Charles Farwell were surprised when the Republican caucus of the new legislature chose Oglesby as their senatorial candidate. Farwell, the *New York Herald* wrote, had expected to be renominated with no fight and was "thunderstruck" when Oglesby, "who didn't come near Springfield" and did not seem interested, was nominated. Politicians in the caucus may have thought the more independent Oglesby would have a better chance of capturing swing votes in the legislative election for

U.S. senator. On January 15, 1891, he was notified via a new device, the telephone, and telegrams and letters of congratulation also poured in to Elkhart. His pride for having won without soliciting Republican legislators was typified by an old textbook adage he copied into his diary:

> Honors unsought unfairly won
> Are honors soon to be undone;
> But honors unsought fairly won
> Freely honor the honored one.[31]

Oglesby attributed his victory to the "great good common people, God bless them," but he also feared that it was an empty honor because the Republican legislators had only one hundred votes and victory required three more. Yet only 101 legislators backed John M. Palmer, the Democratic candidate. The balance was held by three members of the Farmers' Alliance. Some political friends suggested that Oglesby bargain with Farmers' Alliance members or use dubious devices to capture the seat. But the other U.S. senator, Shelby M. Cullom, better understood Oglesby when he telegraphed: "You must be elected if there is any honest means of securing the result. I know you could not be induced to resort to any other." The marathon contest would last for weeks and require 154 ballots, more even than John Logan's famous still hunt in the 1885 election. One correspondent suggested that Oglesby have followers wait until the legislators grew tired and called for adjournment. Then, he recommended, Oglesby should check train schedules and send false dispatches to some opponents so they would be late for the resumed session. But there would be no still hunt for Oglesby, who was content to let the election process sort out the victor. He wanted the honor to come to him "fairly won." The Republicans were finally beaten when two of the three Farmers' Alliance members (both former Democrats) joined the Democrats in electing Palmer. Stories were later repeated by Palmer's biographer grandson that the two were compensated by means of a fixed poker game for one and a new church for the other, who was a pastor.[32]

Oglesby's defeat was almost simultaneous with the burning of Oglehurst, and he received many letters of sympathy on both accounts. He rationalized that he did not want to be a candidate for the Senate anyway, and plans for a new house were already under way when the old house burned. But with no salary and annual expenses he estimated at $7,000 even as "plain livers," his bank account could soon be exhausted, although Emma's income on property he managed could be used. A friend, Judge Loomis of Carlinville, suggested that he write about "his life, struggles for education, trip to Asia etc." and predicted that he could sell a million copies and make enough money to build the new house. Loomis knew that Oglesby doubted his literary ability but suggested that he "have some literary cuss smooth it over a little." Oglesby replied that he did not care to go into "the bookmaking business, it is not my fort [*sic*]." He did allow another friend, Judge Lawrence Weldon, to write a lengthy piece on him for the Century Publishing Company. When editors ruled that the seven-thousand-word sketch was too long, Oglesby modestly suggested that Weldon could easily reduce it by omitting excess complimentary words.[33]

Oglesby's reputation as the Cincinnatus of Illinois, who, like George Washington, had voluntarily retired, grew as he aged. The *Chicago Tribune* wrote: "The grand old man at Elkhart is as popular to-day as he ever was, and no one has greater power in Illinois." The *Tribune* added: "Republicans everywhere, and especially G.A.R. men, would throw up their hats for him at a movement's notice." David Littler, Oglesby's antagonist and brother-in-law, tried to use Oglesby's popularity to unseat Governor Fifer in the 1892 race for the Republican nomination. Littler, S. H. "Sam" Jones, and Senator Cullom, the leaders of the Springfield "ring," proposed that Oglesby be announced for governor in opposition to Fifer. Oglesby, who was Fifer's friend, quickly recognized that their real purpose was to depose the sitting governor in favor of John Tanner, another member of the Springfield ring, and summarily dismissed the presumption. In response to Judge N. G. Veasey's letter insisting that he run for governor, Oglesby replied, "Only those who do not favor him [Fifer] talk of me—that is all there is of it." With Oglesby's support, Fifer was renominated. Oglesby's Grand Old Man status was recognized when he was sent to Minneapolis as a delegate to the Republican National Convention. Before the convention, Robert Todd Lincoln, U.S. minister to Great Britain, asked him "as an old friend" to withdraw Lincoln's nomination for president, should it be made, "quietly if possible, but at all events peremptorily and decisively." Benjamin Harrison was renominated, however, and there was no groundswell for Abraham Lincoln's son. Oglesby accepted requests from the Illinois Republican Central Committee to speak three to five times a week during the fall campaign, but it was a disastrous year for the Republicans. Fifer lost to Democrat John Peter Altgeld, and Grover Cleveland defeated Harrison.[34]

Oglesby's reputation as an impromptu speaker was enhanced by his classic tribute to corn, delivered at the Fellowship Club in Chicago in 1894. According to an account given by a club member, each speaker was to propose a toast on "What I Know about Farming." Oglesby, "seemingly waiting for an inspiration," spotted the harvest decorations in the room and focused upon the corn. "The corn, the corn, the corn" he began and then wandered into introductory remarks about his life and rebirth. He also paid tribute to a man sitting next to him who was the son of an old friend. Next, he launched into a flowery essay on corn as "Monarch." The dissertation, complete with lapses of grammar, reflected his recent readings and was laced with strange adjectives and allusions:

*The corn, the corn, the corn,* that in its first beginning and its growth has furnished aptest illustration of the tragic announcement of the chiefest hope of man. If he die he shall surely live again. Planted in the friendly but somber bosom of the mother earth it dies. Yea, it dies the second death, surrendering up each trace of form and earthly shape until the outward tide is stopped by the re-acting vital germ while breaking all the bonds and cerements of its sad decline, comes bounding, laughing into life and light the fittest of all the symbols that make certain promise of the fate of man. And so it died and then it lived again. And so my people died. By some unknown, uncertain and unfriendly fate, I found myself making my first journey into life from conditions as lowly as those surrounding that awakening, dying living infant germ. It was in those days when I, a simple boy, had wandered from Indiana to Springfield, that I there met the father of this good man [Joseph Jefferson] whose kind and gentle words to me were as water to a thirsty soul, as the shadow of a rock to a weary man. I loved his father then, I love the son now. Two full generations have been taught by his gentleness and smiles, and tears have quickly answered to the command of his artistic mind. Long may he live to make us laugh and cry and cry and laugh enough by turns as he may choose to move us.

But now again my mind turns to the glorious corn, see it! Look on its ripening waving field. See how it wears a crown, prouder than Monarch ever wore, sometimes jauntily and sometimes after the storm the dignified survivors of the tempest seem to view a field of slaughter and to pity a fallen foe. And see the pendant caskets of the corn field filled with the wine of life and see the silken fringes that set a form for fashion and for art. And now the evening comes and something of a time to rest and listen. The scudding clouds conceal the half and then reveal the whole of the moonlit beauty of the night, and then the gentle winds make heavenly harmonies of a *thousand thousand* harps that hang upon the borders and the edges and the middle of the field of ripening corn until my very heart seems to beat responsive to the rising and the falling of the long melodious refrain. The melancholy clouds sometimes make shadows on the field and hide its aureate wealth and now they move and slowly into sight there comes the golden glow of promise for an industrious land. Glorious corn, that more than all the sisters of the field wears tropic garments. Nor on the shore of Nilus or of Ind does nature dress her forms more splendidly. My God, to live again that time when for me half the world was good and the other half unknown! And now again, the corn, that in its kernel holds the strength that shall (in the body of the man refreshed) subdue the forest and compel response from every stubborn field, or, shining in the eye of beauty make blossoms of her cheeks and jewels of her lips and thus make for man the greatest inspiration to well doing, the hope of companionship of that sacred, warm and well embodied soul, a woman.

Aye, the corn, the Royal corn, within whose yellow heart there is of health and strength for all the nations. The corn triumphant, that with the aid of man hath made victorious procession across the tufted plain and laid foundation for the social excellence that is and is to be. This glorious plant transmuted by the alchemy of God sustains the warrior in battle, the poet in song and strengthens everywhere the thousand arms that work the purposes of life. Oh that I had the voice of song or skill to translate into tones the harmonies, the symphonies and oratorios that roll across my soul, when standing sometimes by day and sometimes by night upon the borders of this verdant sea, I note a world of promise, and then before one-half the year is gone I view its full fruition and see its heap-ed [*sic*] gold await the need for man. Majestic, fruitful, wondrous plant. Thou greatest among the manifestations of the wisdom and love of God, that may be seen in all the fields or upon the hillsides or in the valleys.[35]

The essay on corn was widely praised and referred to for years to come. Although the speech was impromptu, Oglesby had been thinking about the topic and forming sentences on it for several years. A *Chicago Tribune* correspondent, writing in 1924, recalled one occasion when Oglesby found Illinois soldiers drinking corn whiskey. They should not disgrace their corn-producing state by drinking whiskey, he told them, and then poured the bottle's contents on the ground. "The corn," he said, "the corn, the royal corn, within whose golden heart there is of health and strength for all the nations." He could wax eloquent about all growing crops, however. When an *Inter-Ocean* reporter visited him in 1890, Oglesby's first statements concerned the beauty of his wheat ("a waving field of gold") and the mustard plants ("a sea of bright yellow") surrounding the house. He even spoke in praise of weeds: "The creator was all wise and I have never found fault with him for creating weeds. I have loved them ever since I came to Illinois as a boy."[36]

In 1895 Oglesby was stricken by influenza ("la grippe"), which weakened him considerably, and treated by physicians in Chicago and Boston. On July 21 he wrote to Felicite, asking her to hurry home. "I am still only tolerably well; am not yet strong, am indeed still quite weak, and sometimes almost feeble," he continued. An October 6 letter was more preemptive: "I want you to come home. It is very lonely here without you." On January 20, 1896, he responded to an invitation to be present for the Lincoln Day dinner in Chicago, at which William McKinley would speak, by noting that he would come if well enough.[37]

Fragile health, however, was not sufficient to keep the old war horse out of the memorable campaign of 1896, both on state and national levels. He favored William McKinley for president, but Shelby Cullom wanted the Republican nomination. Cullom was supported by Oglesby's nemesis David Littler, who expected to be nominated as delegate-at-large to the national convention. The Logan County delegation to the state convention was considered critical to obtaining a "favorite son" nomination for Cullom. McKinley forces made an all-out effort to gain the endorsement of Illinois Republicans, and they succeeded with Oglesby's help. A *Washington Post* dispatch from Springfield noted that Logan County was the home of former governor Oglesby, "who has never been friendly to Cullom." Littler and Cullom, in Washington when the county convention took place, were shocked when they heard they had failed to elect friendly delegates. A friend reported to Oglesby that he had seen the men in Washington and that they looked like they "had lost their last friend." Littler said that he could "have beaten hell out of Oglesby" had he been home. "Yes," Cullom replied, "but he has beaten Hell out of me." Oglesby was made delegate-at-large to the Republican National Convention in St. Louis, where McKinley was nominated on the first ballot.[38]

Oglesby considered John R. Tanner, the Republican candidate for governor, to be a "ring leader." He had often opposed Tanner, but the threat of Democratic governor John P. Altgeld being reelected troubled him more than supporting Tanner. Altgeld had released the surviving Haymarket anarchists and declared that all those convicted had been innocent. Oglesby and most Republicans believed that Altgeld was a dangerous revolutionary. Tanner repeatedly appealed to him, the man "nearer the hearts of the Republicans than any other living person," to help in the campaign. In order to oppose Altgeld and William Jennings Bryan, the Democratic presidential candidate, Oglesby was finally persuaded to join a flying squadron composed of Republican governors. Their whistle-stop campaign contributed to an Illinois plurality of 142,607 for McKinley—123,392 for Tanner.[39]

In 1898 Oglesby was invited to attend a Washington's Birthday banquet at the Union League in Chicago, where he shared the platform with former president Harrison. Although Oglesby had protested that he knew little about Lincoln that was not already known, he was filling in for Senator Palmer, who had been scheduled to speak about *his* personal recollections of the president. Oglesby used the occasion to decry the jingoism that seemed to be leading the country into war with Spain over Cuba, an island he considered not significant enough to justify a war.[40]

President William Rainey Harper of the University of Chicago, who was in attendance at the banquet, persuaded Oglesby to stay over and speak to his students about Lincoln. The ex-governor, whose formal education was limited to a few months, was flattered to be called upon to speak to university students. Harper aided Oglesby in ascending the platform at the university, and a newspaper described the former governor as "beat and feeble" but noted that he quickly "straightened" and warmed to his topic. Gone was Oglesby's reluctance to claim a special relationship with the martyred president. He described how he had followed Lincoln since he first heard him speak and shook hands with him at a "Log cabin and hard cider mass meeting in 1840" when he was fifteen. He also recalled how he had introduced the rail-splitter image into the campaign of 1860, how Lincoln had praised his Holy Land speech, and how he had often dined with the president and attended plays with him in Washington. He recalled rushing to Lincoln's deathbed and seeing, "if any man can see, his departure to another world."[41]

Oglesby continued to be concerned about "departure to another world" during the last year of his life. Influenza had weakened him, and he suffered from vertigo. In October 1898 he had fallen while visiting in Chicago. Given his weakened condition and reduced girth, his usual ration of whiskey may have affected his balance. He also had reason to be depressed about his financial status. The aftermath of the financial panic of 1893 had diminished his bank account. In late 1898 he was forced to sign a promissory note in order to pay an insurance premium, and the bank account was overdrawn at the time of his death. In one of his final letters, he complained to a friend that he used to be "pretty well off" but was now poor. "The world does not care much for old people and especially if they be also poor," he lamented.[42]

At about noon on April 24, 1899, Governor Oglesby was found unconscious on the floor in the "toilet room" by his son John. He had apparently fallen and hit his head on the sharp edge of a piece of the furniture. His face was bloodied, and there was a slight discoloration on the right temple. Dr. C. B. Taylor, the family physician, was summoned, but he arrived only a few moments before Governor Oglesby died at 1 P.M. "Death resulted from concussion of the brain" the *Tribune* reported.[43]

Only Emma Oglesby and sons John and Richard were at home. Robert and Olive, the children of his first marriage, were called from Joplin and Kansas City, Missouri. Jasper returned from prep school, but Felicite was in Paris. Hiram Keays returned to Oglehurst, but ill-health prevented Emma's only brother, John P. Gillett, from traveling from his Indiana home. Tributes poured in from prominent politicians. President McKinley and Vice President Garret A. Hobart wired condolences. Robert Lincoln sent "heartfelt sympathy" and announced that he would attend the funeral. Illinois Governor Tanner ordered flags to be flown at half-staff. Republican and Democratic newspapers praised the life of "Uncle Dick" with feature stories, biographies, editorials, testimonials, and reminiscences from prominent acquaintances. The opposition newspaper, the *Illinois State Register,* editorialized that he was respected even by political foes. "He had that genial, clever, courteous, jovial way about him that made him a favorite in every circle," the editor noted.[44]

The funeral was set for April 28, although entombment would await the return of Felicite from Paris. The ceremonies took on the character of a military funeral as the Grand Army of the Republic, led by Decatur Post 141 (the reconstituted Post 1); various companies of the National Guard, including two companies recalled from Pana, where a labor strike had become violent; and numerous military and town bands joined the march. Special trains came from both directions, and four thousand people poured into Elkhart for the funeral.[45]

A procession formed near the railroad station and marched up the hill to Oglehurst. There Bishop Seymour gave the funeral address inside the large hall as throngs of people on the grounds strained to hear the services, which followed "Episcopal ritual." The bishop honored his old friend as a politician who "was clean and upright" and loved by the common people. Following the service, a procession of military and veterans' organizations accompanied the body to the nearby St. John the Baptist Chapel in Elkhart Cemetery. The pallbearers were eight black servants, employees of the Oglesbys and Gilletts who were chosen because the former governor had once expressed a wish that he should "be carried to his grave by his friends, the colored people." The body, guarded by state militia, lay in state in "a magnificent rosewood and metallic coffin," awaiting the return of Felicite from Europe.[46]

In honor of Oglesby's relationship to Lincoln, Governor Tanner had ordered that the flag that had draped Lincoln's coffin should be retrieved from the state museum for use at Oglesby's funeral. The flag, hitherto undisturbed, was apparently carried in the funeral procession to the chapel. On May 8, shortly after the return of Felicite, an Episcopal committal service was conducted at the chapel by Frederick W. Taylor. Oglesby's casket, "draped in the flag that was used on the casket of President Lincoln," was carried to the newly built vault of concrete across the cemetery from the chapel. In life as in death, Oglesby had been symbolically draped in Lincoln's flag. He might have preferred to be remembered for his own life-long achievements, but Lincoln and his legacy created an irresistible pull. Oglesby was indelibly linked to the realm of Lincoln.[47]

Former governor Joseph W. Fifer maintained that Oglesby stood higher in the estimation of the people of Illinois than any other political figure except Lincoln himself.[48] The tribute by "Private Joe" may have been exaggerated, but Oglesby was one of the most appealing and skillful stump speakers in the Midwest. He enjoyed a reputation as a man of the people and not a part of any political ring. His three nonconsecutive elections as governor, each in a time of crisis, reflect his strength with rank-and-file voters. He often lost in races for the U.S. Senate, where legislators rather than the voters chose the senators. But he never lost a race for governor, where the popular vote was supreme. Oglesby had devised a popular image for Lincoln—the railsplitter. By associating himself with the martyred president, and his admonition to stay close to the people, Oglesby contributed to his own popular image.

## Notes

1. The *Journal* (Sept. 7, 1887, p. 4, col. 2) used the word "botheration" to describe the corbels case. The rival *Illinois State Register* seemed only "bemused" by the struggle between Republican brothers-in-law. For a more complete discussion of the case, see Mark A. Plummer, "David Littler v. the State House Commissioners, 1885–88," in *Capitol Centennial Papers,* ed. Mark Sorensen (Springfield: ISA, 1990), pp. 4–10. Some of the material that appears here was included in that publication. For more about the capitol and its architect, see Wayne C. Temple, "Alfred Henry Piquenard: Architect of Illinois' Sixth Capitol," also in *Capitol Centennial Papers,* ed. Sorensen, pp. 11–41.

2. Transcript filed as *David T. Littler v. William Jayne et al.,* Circuit Court of Sangamon County, Springfield, case 330 ½, ISA; "Minutes of Meetings of Commissioners to Superintend Completion of the State House," March 13, 1885 to July 11, 1888, ISA. My thanks to Wayne Temple, Mark Sorensen, Karl Moore, and Roy Turnbaugh for their help in finding these sources. The *Journal* (Sept. 26, 1885, p. 4, col. 4) listed the names under the heading "The Honored Eight."

3. *Journal,* May 7, 1884, p. 7, col. 4; *Chicago Tribune,* May 21, 1887, found in Scrapbook, 1894, Oglesby MSS; Moses, vol. 2, p. 895.

4. *Journal,* Oct. 3, 1885, p. 4, col. 4, Oct. 10, 1885, p. 4, col. 4, Oct. 15, 1885, p. 4, col. 1.

5. *Register,* Feb. 24, 1886, p. 2, col. 3, quoting *Chicago News; Journal,* March 13, 1886, p. 8, col. 2, and p. 3, col. 6.

6. *Journal,* March 13, 1886, p. 8, col. 2, April 20, 1886, p. 3, col. 6.

7. *Journal,* May 21, 1886, p. 1, col. 1; *Chicago Tribune,* May 21, 1886, p. 1, col. 7; *Register,* May 23, 1886, p. 2, col. 2.

8. *Journal,* Dec. 25, 1886, p. 2, col. 1, Jan. 2, 1887, p. 2, col. 3.

9. *Journal,* Sept. 8, 1887, p. 4, col. 2.

10. *Register,* March 29, 1888, p. 2, col. 1. The Supreme Court decision was reported in the *Journal* (March 29, 1888, p. 2, cols. 3, 4) and in the *Northeastern Reporter* 16 (1888): 374–78. See Mark A. Plummer, *Robert G. Ingersoll: Peoria's Pagan Politician,* Western Illinois Monograph Series no. 4 (Macomb, 1984), p. 38, for the intriguing story of the rumors that circulated asserting that the cornerstone had been stricken of its engraving because Robert G. Ingersoll, an atheist, was included. "Dedication of Monument," *JISHS* 12 (1919–20): 596–97. The statue of Oglesby cost $50,000. Gov. Frank O. Lowden made a short speech

at the dedication on November 21, 1919, in the presence of Oglesby's widow Emma; his two sons, Lt. Gov. John G. Oglesby and Richard Junior; and Felicite Oglesby. Springfield banker John Bunn called Oglesby "the strongest character I ever knew, next to Lincoln." *Chicago Daily News,* Nov. 21, 1919, in clipping from Scrapbook, 1890–1920, Oglesby MSS. See also "'Uncle Dick' Lives Again," *Chicago Tribune,* Nov. 22, 1919, p. 5, cols. 2–3; and "Oglesby's Statue Bit of History," *Chicago Herald Examiner,* Sept. 7, 1930, Scrapbook, 1890–1920, Oglesby MSS.

11. The *Journal* quoted other newspapers: Jan. 5, 1888, p. 2, col. 3 (*Globe-Democrat*); March 3, 1888, p. 2, col. 3 (*Chicago Daily Inter-Ocean*); March 3, p. 2, col. 3 (*Chicago Evening Journal*); and March 16, p. 2, col. 3 (*Carlinville Democrat*); Lusk, p. 560.

12. RJO to S. Fish, president, Illinois Central Railroad, New York, July 10, 1888, Oglesby MSS; *Journal,* July 16, 1888, p. 4, col. 4, July 23, 1888, p. 4, col. 3, July 28, 1888, p. 4, col. 4, Aug. 27, 1888, p. 4, col. 2. When telegraphed that Gillett was seriously ill in Elkhart, the governor summoned a switch engine that had a caboose and made the nineteen-mile run to Elkhart in twenty-two minutes (*Journal,* April 2, 1888, p. 2, col. 4).

13. *Journal,* Aug. 27, 1888, p. 4, col. 2; William Maxwell, *Ancestors* (New York: Alfred A. Knopf, 1971), pp. 158–61.

14. *Journal,* Feb. 16, 1888, p. 2, col. 3, Feb. 23, 1888, p. 1, col. 4, Feb. 29, 1888, p. 2, col. 5, March 14, 1888, p. 2, col. 1, March 19, 1888, p. 4, col. 3, April 14, 1888, p. 1, col. 4, April 25, 1888, p. 4, col. 2.

15. RJO to Daniel Shepard, secretary, Republican State Central Committee, Aug. 30, 1888, Letterpress Book, ISA; *Journal,* Sept. 25, 1888, p. 4, col. 2, Sept. 26, 1888, p. 1, col. 7, Oct. 10, 1888, p. 4, col. 3, Oct. 10, 1888, p. 2, col. 3, Oct. 16, 1888, p. 2, col. 2, Nov. 3, 1888, p. 4, col. 2; Church, pp. 164–66.

16. "Linked for Life: The Governor's Daughter Marries a Worthy Gentleman," *Journal,* Dec. 28, 1888, p. 1, col. 9; wedding costs (in RJO's handwriting), Nov. 26, 1888, Oglesby MSS.

17. *Journal,* Jan. 11, 1889, p. 1, col. 5, Jan. 12, 1889, p. 4, col. 3, Jan. 15, 1889, p. 1, cols. 5, 6, Jan 15, 1889, p. 2, col. 3. The *Journal* (Jan. 15, p. 1, col. 6) used the term *solid South.*

18. *Journal,* Dec. 10, 1888, p. 2, col. 2. The following are all in Oglesby MSS: RJO passbook, Peddecord and Burrows, Decatur; John P. Gillett to RJO, Aug. 31, Sept. 11, 1888; RJO to S. A. Foley, Sept. 11, 1888; Foley to RJO, Sept. 15, 1888; Edward D. Blinn, Lincoln, to RJO, Sept. 15, 1888; Henry T. Chace, Chicago, to RJO (on Woodland and stockyards property) May 19, 1885, Feb. 19, 25, March 15, April 5, 1886, Feb. 25, 1887, Feb. 16, 27, 1888, and March 6, 1890; Heath and Co., St. Louis real estate agents, to RJO, March 19, 1885, Sept. 23, 1886, and Aug. 18, 1888; L. Burrows, Decatur, to RJO, May 18, 1886, Sept. 6, 1888, and March 11, 1889; Nathan Garland, county treasurer, Fayette County, to RJO, May 13, 1885; and J. H. Abel, Assuption, Ill., to RJO, June 27, 1892 (Oglesby sold 320 acres at Ramsey for $1920). According to 1889 tax returns, Emma Oglesby owned 1,118 acres of land on four farms near Elkhart; the Kickapoo farm (on which she paid $165.59 in tax); personal property (mostly cattle, horses, and hogs) taxed at a $2,525; and the Boyd block (on which she paid $473.49 taxes) in Lincoln (tax receipts, Feb. 27, 1890). On May 29, 1892, Oglesby explained to C. P. Link, son of the founder of the Link Silver Mining Company of which Oglesby was once president, "Far as I knew every one lost in the enterprise." Oglesby withdrew about $7,500 from his Peddecord, Burrows and Company account on November 10 and 13, 1888, to build the house in Elkhart (Oglesby MSS).

19. Entries for Jan. 1, 9, 14, 17, 19, 1890, Oglesby Diary, Dec. 31, 1889–March 2, 1891, Oglesby MSS (transcribed from the original by Joanne Forrest, Oglesby Mansion, Decatur, Ill.); James G. Blaine, secretary of state, Washington, to RJO, Fifth Avenue Hotel, New York City, Jan. 11, 1890. Blaine said, "In reply to your communication of the 8th instant, I take pleasure in herewith endorsing a letter of introduction to our Diplomatic and Consular Officers in favor of Mrs. Oglesby." A special passport was enclosed.

20. Entries for Dec. 31, 1889–March 2, 1891, Oglesby Diary, Oglesby MSS; see also Bancroft.

21. Entries for Aug. 8 and Sept. 10, 1890, Oglesby Diary, Dec. 31, 1889–March 2, 1891, Oglesby MSS. The fare from Chicago to New York City was $22 plus $10 for a Pullman berth.

22. Entries for Dec. 31, 1889, Feb. 14, 1890, April 2, April 20, June 20, and Sept. 22, 1890, Oglesby Diary, Dec. 31, 1889–March 2, 1891, Oglesby MSS.

23. Entries for Jan. 9, Aug. 10, 29, 1890, and March 2, 1891, Oglesby Diary, Dec. 31, 1889–March 2, 1891, Oglesby MSS (on the fire and its origin); Bullard and Bullard Architects, Springfield, Ill., to RJO, Jan. 16, 1890, Oglesby MSS. The *Worcester Daily Spy,* April 5, 1891, as transcribed, noted that Emma Oglesby's "remarkable beauty" was not seriously marred. It also noted that J. B. Babin, the Episcopal rector and tutor who lived in the house, "saved his clothing but lost his sermons" (Oglesby MSS). The $2,200 presentation sword was said to be the most expensive cast by the Ames Sword Company of Chicopee, Massachusetts. Designed by John Quincy Adams Ward, it was presented to Oglesby in 1863 by "The Officers and Soldiers of 2nd Brigade, 2nd Division, 13th Army Corps., Army of the Tennessee (in appreciation) . . . of his gallant Conduct at the Battle of Corinth, October 3–4, 1862." Lewis I. Sharp, *John Quincy Adams Ward: Dean of American Sculpture with a Catalogue Raisonné* (Newark: University of Delaware Press, 1985), pp. 158–59.

24. Entries for Aug. 14, 1890, and Nov. 14, 18, 19, 25, 26, 1890, Oglesby Diary, Dec. 31, 1889–March 2, 1891, Oglesby MSS.

25. Entries for March 15, 19, 1890, and Sept. 15, 1890, Feb. 8, 1891, Oglesby Diary, Dec. 31, 1889–March 2, 1891, Oglesby MSS. Receipts in Oglesby MSS: Feb. 17, 1891, Loring School, 2535 Prairie Ave., Chicago; April 24, 26, 1893, University School, Dearborn Ave. and Elm St., Chicago; Sept. 17, 1892, Mr. Blatchford's School [Cathedral School], Pekin; Oct. 9, 1894, William G. Thayer, St. Mark's School; Sept. 20, 1895, April 7, 1896, Southborough; and June 30, 1897, Harvard University. John and a friend were accused of starting a fire at the Cathedral School in Pekin, but S. Arthur Johnson, a teacher, wrote on April 29, 1893, to say that he thought John did not do it. John wrote to his father, about April 29, 1893, to explain: "Dr. Bailey the coroner of Tazewell Co. the man who helped us out of our troubles before is interested in the case. . . . Our part is being taken care of" (Oglesby MSS).

26. David Herbert Donald, *Lincoln* (New York: Simon and Schuster, 1995), p. 114; Wayne C. Temple, *Abraham Lincoln: From Skeptic to Prophet* (Mahomet, Ill.: Mayhaven Publishing, 1995), p. 51; entries for Jan. 1, May 11, 1857, Oglesby Diary; Mark A. Plummer, "Robert G. Ingersoll on Leeks and Onions in the Holy Land," *Illinois Quarterly* 43 (Fall, 1980): 5–9. George B. DeFrees, parish secretary of St. John's Episcopal Church, Decatur, informed me on August 10, 1977, that all members of the Oglesby household are listed under "families" in the church's register (p. 26), but only Emma and Olive were listed as communicants in 1874 (p. 242). Gary Zwicky, Eastern Illinois University, also examined the Decatur vestry

records and found that Emma and some of the children were communicants, although Oglesby was not listed. Private telephone conversation, Jan. 28, 1987; Robert D. Edwards, Trinity Episcopal Church, Lincoln, Oct. 13, 1997; telephone conversation, Springfield Episcopal Diocese office, Dec. 29, 1998. The Oglesby MSS contains the following checks: $25 to Decatur Methodist Church, June 9, 1854; $25 to "Miller settlement" Christian Church, Jan. 1, 1856; $250 to Decatur Baptist Church, Nov. 27, 1875; $50 to St. John's Church, Decatur, for "Pew and Preaching for 1874," Nov. 21, 1874; and $100 for a new Decatur Episcopal church, July 19, 1889. See also *Decatur Republican,* Jan. 8, 1876, p. 2, col. 1.

27. Bancroft, p. 43; entries for July 25, 1890, Aug. 24, 25, 31, 1890, Sept. 7, 11, 15, 1890, Nov. 27, 1890, and Feb. 26, 1891, Oglesby Diary, Dec. 31, 1889–March 2, 1891, Oglesby MSS.

28. Shelby M. Cullom, *Fifty Years of Public Service* (Chicago: A. C. McClurg, 1911), p. 202; Maxwell, *Ancestors,* p. 226; RJO to William H. Piatt, Monticello, Ill., March 21, 1899, and "Illinois Pays Her Last Sad Tribute" (clipping, April 28, 1899), both in "Political Men and Women 1896," in J. T. Pitner Scrapbook, ISHL. H. W. Cunningham (Calvary Church rectory, Wilmington, Del., April 27, 1899) wrote to Emma Oglesby that he could imagine "him borne by loving hands to the dear little chapel under the trees now preaching the coming of a new life and I hear the last rites performed there and at the grave and I, your unworthy minister for four years, mindful of so many things left unknown, and words left unsaid would speak to you, all words of comfort and sympathy."

29. Entry for April 19, 1890, Oglesby Diary, Dec. 31, 1889–March 2, 1891, Oglesby MSS. The following are also in the Oglesby MSS: bills for one keg, fifteen gallons, of rye whiskey ($64.75) and ten gallons of Black Rose ($25), Chicago, Aug. 18, 1892, and from the California Wine Co. for six cases, May 3, 1892; check stubs for payments to John P. Gillett for two cases of claret wine ($15, Aug. 6, 1892); for wines and whiskey ($92.75, Aug. 18, 1892); and for two cases of Joel B. Frazier old sour mash bourbon whiskey ($24, Dec. 13, 1894). The valise story is included in "Anecdotes of Gov. Oglesby," *Chicago Tribune,* April 25, 1899, p. 1, col. 3, p. 2, col. 1.

30. Oglesby Diary, Sept. 24, 1889–Nov. 7, 1890, Oglesby MSS; Church, pp. 168–69; "Dick, Keep Close to the People, They Are Always Right," *Chicago Daily Inter-Ocean,* June 18, 1890, p. 1, col. 7, p. 2, cols. 1–3. The article included engravings showing Oglesby from the shoulders, the (old) farmhouse, the veranda, the library, the porch with rocking chairs, and a "favorite Meeting Place" (also on the porch).

31. Clipping from the *New York Herald,* Jan. 16, 1891, twenty-two telegrams sent to RJO at Elkhart on Jan. 16, 1891, and entry for Jan. 16, 1891, Oglesby Diary, Dec. 31, 1889–March 2, 1891, all in Oglesby MSS.

32. Entries for Jan. 15–21, 1891, and June 18, 1890, Oglesby Diary, Dec. 31, 1889–March 2, 1891, Oglesby MSS; Church, p. 170; S. M. Cullom, Washington, D.C., to RJO, Feb. 18, 1891, and Charles Deane, Washington, Iowa, to RJO, Jan. 24, 1891, both in Oglesby MSS; George T. Palmer, *A Conscientious Turncoat: The Story of John M. Palmer, 1817–1900* (New Haven: Yale University Press, 1941), p. 264.

33. Entries for Feb. 27, March 2, 1891, Oglesby Diary, Telegrams, March 2, 3, 1891, T. L. [?] Loomis, Carlinville, to RJO, March 10, 1891, and Lawrence Weldon to R. M. Powers, Century Publishing, Dec. 8, 1891, all in Oglesby MSS. The heavily edited sketch of Oglesby became a part of John M. Palmer, *The Bench and the Bar of Illinois* (Chicago: Lewis Publishing, 1899); Weldon's original in Oglesby MSS.

34. *Chicago Tribune*, April 8, 1892, Scrapbook, 1890–1920, Oglesby MSS; N. G. Veasey to RJO, April 21, 1892, Robert Todd Lincoln, London, to RJO, May 25, 1892, and J. H. Clark, chairman, Illinois Republican State Central Committee, Chicago, to RJO, Sept. 19, 1892, all in Oglesby MSS; Church, pp. 170–73.

35. *Impromptu Speech of Ex-Gov. Richard Oglesby, Made at the Fellowship Club at Chicago, September 19th, 1894, on the Occasion of the Harvest Home Festival, Written from Memory, November 5th, 1898, by Volney W. Foster, a Member of the Club*, printed circular, Oglesby MSS. It seems doubtful that Foster could have remembered each word. Oglesby may have provided him with a copy of his remarks, or perhaps someone took notes.

36. Clipping from the *Chicago Tribune*, July 25, 1924, Scrapbook, 1890–1920, Oglesby MSS; *Chicago Daily Inter-Ocean*, June 21, 1890, p. 2, col. 1.

37. Receipts from Dr. William T. Belfield, Clark and Washington Streets, Chicago, June 5, 1895, and Dr. Charles P. Briggs, 125 Marlborough St., Boston, April 1, 1896, both in Oglesby MSS; RJO to E. C. Dewitt, Marquette Club, Chicago, Jan. 20, 1896, Oglesby MSS; RJO to Felicite, July 31, Oct. 6, 1895, courtesy of Carolyn Ogen, Champaign, Ill.; see also Jack D. Welsh, *Medical Histories of Union Generals* (Kent: Kent State University Press, 1996), pp. 242, 406.

38. Church, pp. 178–79; *Washington Post* clipping attached to C. H. Grosvenor, Washington, D.C., to RJO, March 16, 1896, Oglesby MSS; see also M. F. Kanan, Decatur, to RJO, March 27, 1896, George B. Tuiff[?], Springfield, to RJO, April 27, 1896, George E. Adams, Chicago, to RJO, June 1, 1896, and list of delegates, June 1896, all in Oglesby MSS. McKinley's victory in Illinois owed much to the efforts campaign manager Marcus Alonzo Hanna and Charles Gates Dawes of Chicago. See D. Aaron Chandler, "McKinley in 1896: The Run for the Presidency in Illinois," *Journal of Illinois History* 1 (Winter 1998): 113–130.

39. John R. Tanner to RJO, Aug. 26, Sept. 7, 16, 1896, Oglesby MSS; Cullom, *Fifty Years of Public Service*, pp. 109–202; Church, p. 182. During portions of Oglesby's 1865 and 1885 terms as governor, he was apparently friendly enough with David Littler that he would retreat from the capitol and visit Littler's nearby mansion, where a bottle of whiskey was always available in the pantry. By Littler's reminiscences, made public at the time of Oglesby's death, Oglesby ended his estrangement with his brother-in-law by appearing unannounced at Littler's home. "Is the whisky bottle in the same old place, Dave?" Oglesby asked. "It is, and there's whiskey in it," Littler replied, "and that was how the family feud ended forever." "Anecdotes of Gov. Oglesby."

40. *Chicago Tribune*, Feb. 23, 1898, p. 1, col. 7; *Exercises in Commemoration of the Birthday of Washington* (Chicago: Union League Club, 1898).

41. Unidentified clipping, [Feb. 24, 189?], Oglesby Scrapbook, 1890–1920, Oglesby MSS; *Chicago Tribune*, Feb. 24, 1898, p. 12, col. 2.

42. Welsh, *Medical Histories of Union Generals*, p. 243; passbook account with Peddecord and Borrows, Oglesby MSS; Loren Jenkins, agent, Glen Falls Insurance Co., Lincoln, Ill., to RJO, April 7, 1898 (with Oglesby's notation as having endorsed the promissory note on April 13), Oglesby MSS; RJO to William H. Piatt, March 21, 1899, Oglesby Mansion, Decatur, Ill. On April 25, 1899, the *Chicago Tribune* asserted that, aside from his residence and a small farm nearby, "it is understood that he leaves little or no property." Emma Oglesby was left with a forty-one-room mansion. She also had property of her own and soon came into control of much more when her brother John Parke Gillett died and willed

his wealth to her son Hiram Keays. "Elkhart Hill Has Mystique of Fame and Fortune," *Bloomington Pantagraph*, June 26, 1988, sec. C; Andy Lindstrom, "Who's King of the Hill Now?" *Springfield Journal-Register*, May 21, 1977, 12a–15a.

43. *Chicago Tribune*, April 25, 1899, p. 1, col. 7; *Journal*, April 25, 1899, p. 1, cols. 1–2; Welsh, *Medical Histories of Union Generals*, pp. 242–43. An oral tradition attributed to Oglesby's son John suggests that Oglesby had been imbibing before the fall.

44. *Journal*, April 25, 1899, p. 1, cols. 2–3; *Chicago Tribune*, April 25, 1899, p. 2, cols. 1–3, p. 6, col. 2; *Register*, April 25, 1899, p. 2, col. 1.

45. *Journal*, April 28, 1899, p. 1, col. 7; *Chicago Tribune*, April 29, 1899, p. 4, col. 3.

46. *Bloomington Pantagraph*, April 29, 1899, p. 2, cols. 1–2. The "colored" pallbearers were listed by the *Pantagraph:* Henry Fant, James Neatly, Colonel Walkap, Samuel Bonapart, George Brush, John Cecel, Laban Allison and Thornton Gious[?].

47. *Bloomington Pantagraph*, April 28, 1899, p. 2, col. 1, May 9, 1899, p. 1, col. 1. Both the *Pantagraph* (May 9, 1899, p. 1, col. 1) and the *Illinois State Journal* (May 9, 1899, p. 1, col. 5) reported that Emma and Felicite Oglesby were going to discuss the possibility of removing the body to Chicago with leading citizens of that city. Nothing came of the inquiries, however.

48. *Bloomington Pantagraph*, April 25, 1899, p. 7, col. 3.

# Index

MARK A. PLUMMER is professor of history, emeritus, at Illinois State University, where he was several times the chair of the Department of History. He has been a Fulbright Professor of History at National Taiwan University and the president of the Illinois State Historical Society.

Typeset in 10.5/13 Adobe Minion
with Minion display
Composed by Jim Proefrock
at the University of Illinois Press
Manufactured by Thomson-Shore, Inc.

University of Illinois Press
1325 South Oak Street
Champaign, IL 61820-6903
www.press.uillinois.edu